CANADA AMONG NATIONS 2000

CANADA AMONG NATIONS 2000

Vanishing Borders

Edited by
Maureen Appel Molot
and Fen Osler Hampson

OXFORD
UNIVERSITY PRESS

OXFORD
UNIVERSITY PRESS

70 Wynford Drive, Don Mills, Ontario M3C 1J9
www.oupcan.com

Oxford University Press is a department of the University of Oxford.
It furthers the University's objective of excellence in research, scholarship,
and education by publishing worldwide in

Oxford New York

Athens Auckland Bangkok Bogotá Buenos Aires Calcutta
Cape Town Chennai Dar es Salaam Delhi Florence Hong Kong Istanbul
Karachi Kuala Lumpur Madrid Melbourne Mexico City Mumbai
Nairobi Paris São Paulo Singapore Taipei Tokyo Toronto Warsaw

with associated companies in Berlin Ibadan

Oxford is a trade mark of Oxford University Press
in the UK and in certain other countries

Published in Canada
by Oxford University Press

Copyright © Oxford University Press Canada 2000

The moral rights of the authors have been asserted

Database right Oxford University Press (maker)

First published 2000

Canadian Cataloguing in Publication Data
The National Library of Canada has catalogued this publication as follows:
Canada among nations

Annual.
1984–
Produced by the Norman Paterson School of International Affairs at Carleton University.
Each vol. Has also a distinctive title.
Published: Ottawa : Carleton University Press, 1993?–1997; Toronto : Oxford University Press, 1998– .
ISSN 0832-0683
ISBN 0-19-541540-X (2000)

1. Canada—Foreign relations—1945– —Periodicals. 2. Canada—Politics and
government—1984– —Periodicals. 3. Canada—Politics and government—1980–1984 Periodicals.
I. Norman Paterson School of International Affairs.

FC242.C345   327.71   C86–031285–2
F1029.C3

1 2 3 4 - 03 02 01 00

This book is printed on permanent (acid-free) paper ∞.
Printed in Canada

CONTENTS

Contributors   vii

Abbreviations   ix

Preface   xi

Chapter 1   Does the 49th Parallel Matter Any More?   1
Fen Osler Hampson and Maureen Appel Molot

Part One: The Bilateral Relationship

Chapter 2   Waiting at the Perimeter: Making US Policy
in Canada   27
Andrew F. Cooper

Chapter 3   How Canada Policy Is Made in the
United States   47
Christopher Sands

Chapter 4   US National Missile Defense, Canada, and
the Future of NORAD   73
Joseph T. Jockel

Chapter 5   The Role of Dispute Settlement in Managing
Canada-US Trade and Investment Relations   93
Michael Hart

Chapter 6   Catching Up Is Hard to Do: Thinking About
the Canada-US Productivity Gap   117
Daniel Schwanen

Chapter 7   A Comparison of Canadian and US Labour
Market Performance in the 1990s   145
Andrew Sharpe

Chapter 8   Friendly, Familiar, Foreign, and Near   165
Robert Bothwell

Chapter 9   Economic Integration and Harmonization
with the United States: A Working-Class Perspective   181
Nancy Riche and Robert Baldwin

Chapter 10   Canada, the United States, and the World:
Making the Most of Global Opportunities   199
Thomas d'Aquino

Part Two: Multilateral and Regional Relationships

Chapter 11   Real Borders in a Not So Borderless World   207
Steven Lee

Chapter 12   Too Close to the Americans, Too Far from
the Americas: A Liberal Policy Towards the Hemisphere   223
Brian J.R. Stevenson

Chapter 13   Our Dictatorship: Canada's Trilateral
Relations with Castro's Cuba   247
Yvon Grenier

Chapter 14   Canada's Participation in the NATO-led
Intervention in Kosovo   275
Hevina S. Dashwood

Chapter 15   Canada at the UN: A Human Security Council?   303
Paul Knox

Chapter 16   The WTO in the Aftermyth of the Battles
in Seattle   321
John M. Curtis and Robert Wolfe

CONTRIBUTORS

Thomas d'Aquino is President and Chief Executive Officer of the Business Council on National Issues, Ottawa.

Robert Baldwin is National Director, Social and Economic Policy, Canadian Labour Congress.

Robert Bothwell is Director of the International Relations Program at the University of Toronto.

Andrew F. Cooper is a professor of Political Science at the University of Waterloo.

John M. Curtis is Senior Policy Adviser and Co-ordinator, Trade and Economic Analysis, Department of Foreign Affairs and International Trade.

Hevina S. Dashwood is an assistant professor of Political Science at the University of Windsor.

Yvon Grenier is an associate professor of Political Science at St Francis Xavier University.

Fen Osler Hampson is a professor in The Norman Paterson School of International Affairs, Carleton University.

Michael Hart is a professor in The Norman Paterson School of International Affairs, Carleton University.

Joseph J. Jockel is a professor of Canadian Studies at St Lawrence University, Canton, New York.

Paul Knox reports on international affairs for the *Globe and Mail*. He has covered the United Nations since 1995 and was a staff correspondent in Latin America from 1985 to 1991.

Steven Lee is Executive Director of the Canadian Centre for Foreign Policy Development.

Maureen Appel Molot is a professor and Director of The Norman Paterson School of International Affairs, Carleton University.

Nancy Riche is Secretary-Treasurer of the Canadian Labour Congress.

Christopher Sands is a fellow and Director of the Canada Project at the Center for Strategic and International Studies in Washington, DC. He was Fulbright Visiting Fellow at The Norman Paterson School of International Affairs at Carleton University during the 1999-2000 academic year.

Daniel Schwanen is Director of Research, C.D. Howe Institute, Toronto.

Andrew Sharpe is Executive Director, Centre for the Study of Living Standards, Ottawa.

Brian J.R. Stevenson is Associate Vice-President (International) and associate professor in the Faculty of Business, University of Alberta, and a former Senior Policy Adviser to International Trade Minister Art Eggleton and then to Foreign Affairs Minister Lloyd Axworthy.

Robert Wolfe is a professor in the School of Policy Studies at Queen's University.

ABBREVIATIONS

ABM	anti-ballistic missile
ADM	Assistant Deputy Minister
APEC	Asia-Pacific Economic Co-operation
ASEAN	Association of Southeast Asian Nations
BCNI	Business Council on National Issues
CAP	Common Agricultural Policy (EU)
CAPA	Canada-Caribbean-Central America Policy Alternatives
CARICOM	Caribbean Commonwealth Market
CCA	Canadian Council for the Americas
CCIC	Canadian Council for International Co-operation
CCIP	Cuba-Canada Interagency Project
CIDA	Canadian International Development Agency
CLC	Canadian Labour Congress
CPI	consumer price index
DFAIT	Department of Foreign Affairs and International Trade
DSU	Dispute Settlement Understanding
EC	Extraordinary Challenge
EDC	Export Development Corporation
EI	Employment Insurance
EU	European Union
FDI	foreign direct investment
FIRA	Foreign Investment Review Agency
FRY	Former Republic of Yugoslavia
FTA	Canada-US Free Trade Agreement
FTAA	Free Trade Area of the Americas
GATS	General Agreement on Trade in Services
GATT	General Agreement on Tariffs and Trade
GBI	ground-based interceptors
GDP	gross domestic product
ICC	International Criminal Court
ICSID	International Centre for the Settlement of Investment Disputes
ICTY	International Criminal Tribunal for the former Yugoslavia
IDRC	International Development Research Centre
IFOR	Implementation Force
IJC	International Joint Commission
ILO	International Labour Organization
IOS	International Organization for Standardization
ITARs	International Traffic in Arms Regulations

ITWAA	integrated tactical warning/attack assessment
JMC	Joint Ministerial Committee (Canada-Mexico)
KDOM	Kosovo Diplomatic Observers Mission
KFOR	Kosovo Force
KLA	Kosovo Liberation Army
KVM	Kosovo Verification Mission
MAI	Multilateral Agreement on Investment
MERCOSUR	Mercado Común del Sur
NAFTA	North American Free Trade Agreement
NAIRU	non-accelerating inflation rate of unemployment
NATO	North Atlantic Treaty Organization
NEP	National Energy Program
NGO	non-governmental organization
NMD	National Missile Defense
NORAD	North American Aerospace Defense Command
OAS	Organization of American States
OECD	Organization for Economic Co-operation and Development
OSCE	Organization for Security and Co-operation in Europe
PCO	Privy Council Office
PMO	Prime Minister's Office
R&D	research and development
RUF	Revolutionary United Front (Sierra Leone)
SACEUR	Supreme Allied Commander Europe
SDI	Strategic Defense Initiative
SEA	Single European Act
SFOR	Stabilization Force
START	Strategic Arms Reduction Talks
TMD	Theatre Missile Defense
TRIPs	trade-related intellectual property rights
UI	Unemployment Insurance
UNITA	União Nacional para a Independencia Total de Angola
UNOSOM 1	United Nations Operation in Somalia
UNPROFOR	United Nations Protection Force
UNSC	United Nations Security Council
UNSCOM	United Nations Special Commission
USTR	United States Trade Representative
WEF	World Economic Forum
WEU	Western European Union
WTO	World Trade Organization

Preface

Vanishing Borders is the sixteenth in the annual *Canada Among Nations* series published each year by The Norman Paterson School of International Affairs. This edition is the first to focus so much of its content on Canada's relationship with one country. The decision to concentrate heavily on the bilateral relationship attests to the overwhelming importance of the United States for Canada and the editors' belief that the relationship warranted the kind of wide-ranging attention in a single volume that it rarely receives. The volume argues that Canada-US trade relations are much less contentious than bilateral security issues, where a host of new problems are generating frictions over the management of the border. Some of these concerns are spilling over into Canada's broader multilateral relations within the hemisphere and globally.

The editors gratefully acknowledge the financial assistance of the Canadian Centre for Foreign Policy Development, the Security and Defence Forum program of the Department of National Defence, and the Office of the Dean of the Faculty of Public Affairs and Management at Carleton University. Their contributions supported a workshop in December 1999 at which the authors presented their papers and discussed the policy issues around the bilateral relationship, as well as other key aspects of Canada's international relations over the last year that are reflected in this volume.

We also appreciate the continued support of The Norman Paterson School of International Affairs for this annual undertaking. Brenda Sutherland once again supervised the editing of the manuscript and the inputting of the original text; her expertise with the process is such that she now suggests substantive changes to the editors. Janet Doherty organized yet another authors' workshop and managed the financial side of the project. Susan Johnston and Audrey Lapierre undertook some of the editing and proofreading, provided research assistance to the editors, and prepared the list of abbreviations. We are grateful as well to Phyllis Wilson and her staff at Oxford University Press for their editorial support and involvement in the production process.

It is always a pleasure to participate in the conception of each new *Canada Among Nations* volume and see it through to completion. We enjoyed working with all of the contributors to *Vanishing Borders* and appreciate their co-operation, which allowed us to meet our deadlines. We hope that this volume stimulates debate on Canada's most important relationship and that Americans who read it develop a new sense of understanding about the concerns and perspectives of those who live north of the 49th parallel. The border may be less significant for some kinds of transactions; it is being transformed, but not vanishing.

Fen Osler Hampson
Maureen Appel Molot

March 2000

1

Does the 49th Parallel Matter Any More?

FEN OSLER HAMPSON AND MAUREEN APPEL MOLOT

On a crisp October morning in the fall of 1999 the sky was blue and cloudless; a major street in Canada's capital had been closed to traffic and chairs placed on the road to seat over a thousand guests. Music by John Philip Sousa boomed over loudspeakers and was audible throughout much of Ottawa's central core. Hoards of people taking their seats impatiently waited for the event to begin. The occasion was the dedication of the new US embassy in Ottawa by President Bill Clinton. The photo of President Clinton and Prime Minister Jean Chrétien on the front cover of this book was taken that October morning. Both leaders addressed the assembled guests. Both spoke of the importance of the event, not just the completion of a building long under construction, but as testimony to the long history of friendship between the two countries. This was the only time a US President had ever opened a US embassy in a foreign capital.

Symbolism and pageantry were heavy. From this embassy dedication, President Clinton went to the Forum of Federations Conference in Mont-Tremblant, Quebec, where he delivered an off-the-cuff speech on the value of federalism as a system of government and the tough criteria that had to be met should a regional group or unit seek independence. The speech was a tour de force, which demonstrated the President's knowledge of federalism as well as his concern for Canada. Also on the President's agenda during his Canadian visit were discussions on a range of cross-border issues, including the very sensitive issue of the export of military technology.

Can the activity-packed visit and the hundreds of preparatory phone calls and trips made by officials prior to it be seen as a metaphor for the Canada-US relationship? Is the photo an exaggeration of harmony or its appropriate capture? How, in fact, do we assess the complexities of the bilateral relationship as we enter a new century? The title, *Vanishing Borders*, is meant to capture not only the growing depth of the relationship since implementation of Canada-US Free Trade Agreement (FTA) in 1989, but also the larger impact of globalization, which, in commercial and financial terms, has further reduced the significance of borders. Electronic commerce and telecommunications render the conduct of much commerce borderless. The volume of bilateral trade is such that exporters and importers are pressing governments to create new modalities to facilitate the movement of goods in both directions across the border. Can we anticipate, as Hufbauer and Schott (1998: 63) suggest, an era in 25 years when the Canada-US border will be no more intrusive than that between Germany and the Netherlands? At the same time, there are more nefarious items crossing the border—drugs, guns, and illegal migrants—with the result that there is pressure to tighten border controls. Borders may be vanishing in some respects, but in others they are being erected.

The authors in this volume analyse various aspects of the multifaceted Canada-US relationship, suggesting areas where the relationship is functioning smoothly and others where there is potential, if not actual, friction. If a common theme runs through the volume, it is the importance of careful management of all aspects of the bilateral relationship and the need for clearer understanding on the part of Canadians of changes occurring in the US polity that shape attitudes and policies towards Canada. However, as Steven Lee reminds us in Chapter 11, the concept of borders is much broader than the one that separates Canada and the United States. Canada also has a northern border. Moreover, there are other kinds of boundaries—for example, the divide between the rich and the poor and the changing relationship between citizens and their governments.

A UNIQUE RELATIONSHIP

How do we begin to analyse a relationship as complex as that between Canada and the United States? There are no obvious models or appropriate cases on which to base a comparison. The example sometimes used, that of the European Union (EU), conjures up the wrong images. There are 15 EU members, not two, and its major members are more comparable in size than the dramatic asymmetry in population and gross domestic product (GDP) that characterizes the Canada-US case. Most important, the members of the EU agreed in the Treaty of Rome to the eventual establishment of an economic union, in other words, to the pooling of their individual national sovereignties for the creation of a new, larger entity. There are common EU policies across a range of areas, a number of supranational institutions that make and implement these policies, since January 1999 a common currency and a European central bank, and, as of the beginning of March 2000, a new institutional arm to handle defence issues.[1]

In contrast, no agreements between Canada and the United States set out any long-term vision of the relationship. Rather, a host of bilateral agreements are designed to structure and manage various aspects of the ties between the two countries. Among the most significant are the Canada-US FTA and the North American Free Trade Agreement (NAFTA), the North American Aerospace Defense Command (NORAD), and the International Joint Commission (IJC). Any institutions created by these agreements are issue-specific; the most important economic agreements, the FTA and its successor, NAFTA, do not establish any permanent overarching supranational institutions, nor do they anticipate how the economic linkage might deepen. The very contemplation of closer links to the US, particularly if these are more structured or formalized, strikes fear in the hearts of many Canadians. As Robert Bothwell reminds us in Chapter 8 in his historical review of Canada-US relations, 'Canada exists, where the United States is concerned, in a state of sovereign ambiguity.'

Although more issue-specific than the comprehensive Treaty of Rome, the various Canada-US agreements have constructed a signif-

icant bilateral regime, particularly in the realm of trade and investment, with its own principles, norms, and rules, as well as some institutions. This regime has promoted stability in the relationship by
lowering transaction costs and reducing uncertainty.[2] This bilateral
regime is embedded in a range of larger, multilateral regimes, the
most critical of which are the General Agreement on Tariffs and
Trade (GATT) and its successor, the World Trade Organization (WTO),
the North Atlantic Treaty Organization (NATO), and the United Nations.
Although the principles and rules of these specific regimes vary, in
particular with respect to whether decisions are binding on members,
they establish the overall context within which the Canada-US relationship is conducted. Perhaps most obviously, the two free trade
agreements required approval from the GATT under Article XXIV,
which permits GATT signatories to negotiate regional preferential trading arrangements. Stable international regimes with predictable, if not
enforceable, rules are of particular importance to small states because
they constrain the proclivity on the part of larger ones, most notably
the global hegemon, the United States, to take unilateral actions,
which have the potential to side-swipe smaller actors.

The management of these multilateral and bilateral regimes is
almost always problematic and the outcomes of consultations and
meetings often uncertain, as John Curtis and Robert Wolfe, in Chapter
16, explore in their analysis of the November 1999 WTO ministerial
in Seattle. On an increasingly broad range of issues transnational
actors and domestic interests are now playing a role in setting the
agenda. This mobilization of actors is facilitated by modern technology, especially by the Internet.

For most of its tenure, arguably as a means of distinguishing itself
from its Tory predecessor, the Chrétien government has studiously
eschewed any activities that might be interpreted as bringing Canada
closer to the United States. Nonetheless, at its annual two-day retreat
in June 1999, the Liberal cabinet spent some time focusing on
Canada-US relations (*London Free Press*, 1999). Such attention at a
cabinet retreat hardly signals a more subtle and sophisticated way of
managing the bilateral linkage or even agreement on the way to handle some of the more contentious Canada-US issues. Subsequent to
the cabinet session Prime Minister Chrétien made clear that his government wanted to find ways to dilute the influence of the US on
Canada rather than to promote further integration. That some aspects
of the management of the relationship are getting attention, however

brief, at the highest levels of the Canadian government is modestly reassuring.

As the essays in this volume demonstrate, there is no shortage of issues and disputes on the bilateral agenda. They include the pressures generated by the intensity of trade relationships, problems arising from renewed US interest in the strategic defence of North America and the need to renew the NORAD agreement, and a growing number of border security and immigration irritants. Also of concern to analysts are differences between the two countries on foreign policy and security issues—Cuba, landmines, and Foreign Minister Lloyd Axworthy's attention to human security as a focal point of Canadian foreign policy.

In an analysis of the outcomes of a number of Canada-US disputes, Keohane and Nye (1977) argued more than 20 years ago that despite the imbalance in power, smaller actors frequently win. One of reasons they suggested is that the relationship is more important to the smaller partner, which therefore concentrates more attention and resources on it. The larger state has to manage far more relationships and, in the case of the United States, has to do so in a political system that disperses power and decision-making capacity. Also important from the perspective of the smaller state, according to Keohane and Nye, was the lack of issue linkage. In other words, conflicts in one area of the relationship, for example over trade, did not affect the tenor and outcomes in another, such as defence. Historically, issues tended to be managed separately with little direct spillover from one area to another.

Given the complexity of the relationship and the number of issues continuously on the table, it is virtually impossible in a large polity for there to be the level of policy co-ordination necessary for issue linkage to occur. Facilitating this lack of issue linkage, particularly on highly contentious issues, was the fact that, as Christopher Sands notes in Chapter 3, major US policy-makers, in both Congress and the administration, were likely to have some familiarity with Canada and, as a result, sensitivity to Canadian concerns. Power in the United States has shifted over the last 20 years, however, both generationally and regionally: politicians who knew Canada as a result of connections during World War II and immediately after have passed from the scene, and political power in the US has moved from the Northeast, where individuals had some proximity to Canada, to the South, which is more distant from this country both geographically and philosophically. This, as well as the difficulty of separating issues in the now-globalized environment—defence is linked to economic well-being and border concerns to trade—now means that there is greater potential for issue linkage across Canada-US relations. Some of the analysis below will illustrate this.

The present chapter now turns to a consideration of specific components of the bilateral relationship—economic, border security, defence, foreign policy, and policy-making. Each section ends with a question for readers to consider.

ECONOMIC ISSUES

Since the days of World War II, the US has been Canada's most important trading partner. The trading relationship has become much more intense, both in value of goods traded, and as a percentage of Canada's overall exports, since the signing of the FTA and then NAFTA. More than Cdn$1.5 billion of goods crosses the Canada-US border daily. Table 1.1 provides data on Canada-US merchandise trade over the last decade and illustrates the very considerable increase in Canadian exports to the US as a percentage of total exports. In 1999, 86 per cent of all Canadian goods exports went to the United States.

Canada is also the most important export destination for American goods (and has been since 1946). US exports to Canada accounted for 23 per cent of total US exports in 1998. In that year the US sold more than twice as much to Canada as it did to Japan; put in a slightly different way, Canada's market of 30 million people purchases more from the US than does the European Union's 300 million plus consumers. As a small open economy, Canada is much more highly trade dependent than is the United States. In 1999, 43 per cent of Canada's GDP was trade-related; in the United States, the relevant figure is 11 per cent. The most important categories of goods exchanged between the two countries are automotive products (30 per cent of Canadian exports to the US and 27 per cent of US exports to Canada), machinery and equipment (22 per cent and 33 per cent, respectively), and industrial goods (17 per cent and 21 per cent). Approximately 26 per cent of what Canada sells to the US can be considered primary products; for the US the comparable figure is 8 per cent. Other than in automobiles and parts and petroleum, trade between the two countries has grown more quickly in those sectors liberalized by the Canada-US FTA than in those not liberalized

Table 1.1

Canada-United States Trade:
Merchandise Trade Exports and Imports, 1989–1999

	1989	1990	1991	1992	1993	1994	1995	1996	1997	1998	1999
Canada Exports: total*	146,963	152,056	147,669	163,464	190,213	228,167	265,334	279,892	301,381	322,262	360,600
Canada Exports: to US	108,024	111,565	108,616	123,377	149,100	181,049	205,691	222,342	242,482	269,497	309,663
Canada Exports: to US (%)	74%	73%	74%	75%	78%	79%	78%	79%	80%	84%	86%
Canada Imports: total*	139,217	141,000	140,658	154,430	177,123	207,873	229,937	237,917	277,708	303,400	326,662
Canada Imports: from US	97,298	97,512	97,578	110,379	130,244	155,661	172,517	180,217	211,425	233,635	249,173
Canada Imports: from US (%)	70%	69%	69%	71%	74%	75%	75%	76%	76%	77%	76%

*Millions of Canadian dollars.
Source: Statistics Canada, Canadian international merchandise trade, December 1999 (released March 2000) ISSN: 1198–7391.

(Schwanen, 1997: 6). These trade data illustrate what economists predict will occur following the implementation of a free trade agreement, namely, increases in intra-firm and intra-industry trade[3] as corporations rationalize production across a larger economic space. While the automotive industry in North America most graphically demonstrates both forms of trade growth, the same trend can be seen in other sectors as well, for example, in chemicals and pharmaceuticals, industrial machinery, food products, and telecommunications equipment.

In any trading relationship as intense as the Canada-US one, there are bound to be disputes. Some of the more recent disputes, such as those over softwood lumber and durum wheat exports, have been very contentious because complainants have not been prepared to accept the decisions of bilateral panels. As Michael Hart notes in Chapter 5, most bilateral trade disputes have been resolved through the dispute settlement mechanisms established by either the Canada-US FTA and NAFTA or the GATT and the WTO. In Hart's view the use of regime dispute settlement provisions suggests confidence in the institutions and the general willingness of the two governments to live with the outcomes of the dispute settlement process. Institutions do not necessarily reduce disputes, but they do ensure a predictable basis for their management.

Foreign direct investment is at least as important as trade in linking the Canadian and US economies. The United States has long been the largest foreign investor in Canada. More than two-thirds of all foreign direct investment (FDI) in Canada comes from the US. At the end of 1998, the total stock of US investment in Canada was over $147 billion (Cdn). Almost half of US FDI in Canada is in manufacturing; finance (other than banking), insurance, and real estate account for 21 per cent; and the petroleum industry for 12 per cent. Eleven per cent of total US FDI is in Canada, a sum exceeded only by US FDI in the United Kingdom. The US is, and has long been, the major destination for Canadian FDI. Canada is the fifth largest source of foreign capital in the United States. Manufacturing industries account for 35 per cent of Canadian FDI in the US, insurance has attracted 11 per cent, banking 3 per cent, and other finance 10 per cent (Embassy of Canada, 1999: 2). As with trade, investment flows in both directions have increased significantly since the implementation of the FTA and NAFTA. Although the Canadian economy is approximately one-fourteenth the size of that of the United States, our FDI in that economy is several orders of magnitude larger than relative economic size might dictate (Rugman et al., 1997: 207). In keeping with the realities of a small open economy, Canadian firms have to be competitive in the major global economy to be successful. Cross-border investments, both greenfield and takeovers and mergers, proceed apace. A few examples during 1999 include: Nortel's investments in the US continued to grow, with many of its head office functions located in that country; JDS Fitel merged with Uniphase to create a cross-border giant in fibre optics; and Weyerhauser, the large US pulp and paper multinational, purchased Macmillan-Bloedel.

When there is competition for investment and workers, as there is in what is becoming an increasingly continental market in many key economic sectors, there are likely to be comparisons made between the constituents of that market. When one party is as dependent for its economic well-being on the other as Canada is on the United States, it is perhaps not surprising that in some arenas the US has become a standard of comparison. US recovery from the recession of the early 1990s was much more rapid and robust than that of Canada, unemployment in the US through the 1990s was (and remains) dramatically lower than that in Canada, and Canadian living standards have fallen substantially behind those in the United States. In 1999 the *World Competitiveness Yearbook* ranked Canada tenth overall in global competitiveness, just ahead of Ireland and Australia and behind not only the United States, which was first, but also a number of European economies as well as Hong Kong and Singapore (Little, 1999).

Four chapters in this volume address various aspects of this continuing and, to some, quite contentious comparison. Andrew Sharpe, in Chapter 7, compares Canadian and US labour market performance over the last decade, illustrating the differences in employment patterns between the two countries as well as lower overall worker productivity in Canada. More Canadians than Americans are self-employed, for example, a function of the lagging Canadian economy. Sharpe attributes this poor economic performance to restrictive macroeconomic policies. Nancy Riche and Robert Baldwin of the Canadian Labour Congress also address issues of employment in Chapter 9, and suggest that free trade and the concomitant pressure from the business community have contributed to the deterioration of the social and economic situation of Canadian workers. In their view, Canadian government policy has been insufficiently sensitive to the conditions of labour and overly attentive to considerations of Canadian export competitiveness and attractiveness to foreign direct investment. The experience of Canadian workers since the implementation of the Canada-US Free Trade Agreement explains their opposition to further trade liberalization (as in Seattle in November 1999) and investment agreements.

Daniel Schwanen picks up the theme of productivity in Chapter 6, arguing that comparisons of Canadian and US productivity indicators are somewhat more complicated than the simplistic picture presented by the media. Presenting a business perspective on the relationship and picking up on this theme of productivity, Thomas d'Aquino of the Business Council on National Issues identifies in Chapter 10 some of the areas in which Canadians should seek to reduce barriers to the flow of goods, services, and people across the Canada-US border. He argues that prior to doing so, however, the country has to become more competitive by reducing personal and corporate tax rates and removing a range of restrictive regulations. While, in his view, integration generates pressures for policy convergence in some areas, Canada must retain its distinctive social policies.

These four contributions do not share the same assessment of the accelerating bilateral economic integration and its policy implications. There are some obvious differences between the two countries that raise important questions about the pressures for, and limits to, policy harmonization and convergence. Canada has to be more competitive, yet must retain its distinctive set of social policies. Are both possible? If so, how? When policy harmonization is considered, an immediate question is whose standards will prevail? As the smaller trading partner, will we be expected to adopt the standards or regulations of the larger? Are there useful lessons from the experience of the EU with respect to either policy harmonization or the mutual recognition of standards, which are alternatives to facilitate the movement of goods and services across borders? This is the first of the policy challenges thrown out to readers of this volume.

MANAGING THE BORDER

In an article written more than a decade ago, the distinguished Columbia University economist Jagdish Bhagwati captured the contrary pressures on borders generated by economic activity, on the one hand, and the reluctance of states to surrender control over their borders, on the other. Immigration controls, he commented, are 'the most compelling exception to liberalism in the world economy' (1984: 680). The heated debates in the EU over the Schengen Agreement, the accord under which all signatories agreed to accept the border controls and therefore assessments made on those crossing borders by immigration authorities of other EU members, testify to the reluctance of states to give up one of the major exercises of sovereignty. These contrary pressures are evident in the management of the Canada-US border.

For Canada, the motor in its relationship with the United States is economic. One of the priorities of Canadian business, to which the government is sensitive, is the demand to ensure that the huge volumes of trade between the two countries cross the border with minimum impediment. Members of the business community want to reduce transaction costs and, therefore, to simplify border procedures. To this end, Canadian and American officials have been working on a range of border management questions. During President Clinton's visit to Ottawa in October 1999, he and Prime Minister Chrétien issued a joint statement on border co-operation and congratulated officials from both countries for 'the excellent progress' they had made in making the border 'a model of co-operation and efficiency'. Among the 'guiding principles' for Canada-US border co-operation is to streamline, harmonize, and collaborate on border policies and management. Moreover, many Canadians and Americans are taking advantage of Article 16 of NAFTA and its appendices that facilitate the cross-border exchange of business people on a temporary and reciprocal basis. This is not the free movement of labour provided for in the EU, but it does allow some categories of professionals from both countries to work in the other temporarily.[4]

For the US, although trade is important, so, too, are border security considerations that loom large in US domestic politics. The US has for some time had concerns about Canadian capacity to handle some of the newer cross-border issues—drug smuggling, money laundering, and other international criminal activity, as well as the smuggling of people. The second and third 'guiding principles' in the two leaders' pronouncement on the border addressed security matters: the two countries would expand their co-operation not only with respect to customs but also in terms of immigration and law enforcement, and they would collaborate on common threats emanating from outside both countries (US Embassy, 1999). US concerns about the security of its borders are not new. Congressional fears about illegal immigration, a problem arguably more significant on the southern border of the US than on its northern one, has, among other policies, resulted in the inclusion of Section 110 in the Illegal Immigration Reform and Immigrant Responsibility Act of 1996. This provision requires all 'aliens' to register upon entry into and exit from the US. The implementation of this provision, postponed at least until 2001, would cause havoc with cross-border trade.

US immigration authorities' apprehension in December 1999 of Ahmed Ressam, an Algerian who had been living in Montreal under a suspended deportation order, after the discovery of a car trunk full of explosive materials, raised newly heightened concern about the porousness of the Canadian border. Earlier in 1999 there were concerns about Chinese migrants coming to Canada with the intent to then illegally cross the border into the United States. In January 2000, the Subcommittee on Immigration and Claims of the US House of Representatives Committee on the Judiciary held hearings on terrorism; a frequent theme in the testimony was the danger posed to the US by terrorists coming into the United States from Canada (http://www.house.gov/judiciary). Although it may be easier and more politically feasible in an American election year to criticize Canadian immigration and controls on the Canada-US border than to address some of these concerns on the Mexico-US border,[5] the Ressam incident highlighted a critical question of border management. Is it sufficient to institute restrictive measures or are new ways of thinking required? It may not be only the Canada-US border that needs attention, but, rather, all borders of both countries, including their coasts.

Earlier this year, Canadian bureaucrats floated a proposal for a perimeter security system for North America that would result in the elimination of the Canada-US border and the construction of a new, and presumably integrated, perimeter defence mechanism with the attendant harmonization of policies with respect to entry and the sharing of intelligence information (Duffy, 2000). This is not to say that bilateral co-operation among law enforcement agencies and immigration authorities does not exist; it does and works well. But existing institutions cannot manage the complex new issues and formulate imaginative and appropriate solutions. We are talking about co-operation on a higher level, if not a move in the direction of joint policy formulation. This would move the two countries some distance along the road to an EU-style arrangement of perimeter controls like that established by the Schengen Agreement. How would our understanding of the symbolism, if not the reality, of the border change if Canada and the US were to establish an integrated perimeter security arrangement?

SECURITY AND DEFENCE

One obvious component of security is the border. The link between the border, on the one hand, and the security and defence relationship, on the other, is new threats spawned by the end of the Cold War. These threats are different and much more difficult to handle; they are no longer between countries and alliances but are within countries. As Hevina Dashwood points out in Chapter 14 in regard to Kosovo, these intense intra-country disputes frequently draw in members of the international community who feel compelled to intervene to stop the conflict and protect human life. But as Dashwood's discussion of these debates in the Canadian context also reveals, military interventions involving the use of force are raising increasingly important questions of political accountability, particularly regarding the role of Parliament in the deployment of Canadian Forces overseas in so-called 'peacekeeping' and 'peace enforcement' missions. At the international level, the absence of UN authorization of the NATO bombing of Kosovo was extremely problematic and sat uneasily with critics of Canadian foreign policy and even the government itself. Canada's dispatch of troops to East Timor to assist in the UN peacekeeping mission is another example of the international community stepping in to prevent continued conflict and to provide humanitarian assistance, although it did not raise the same kinds of political concerns as Kosovo.

In addition to the range of intra-state conflicts, there are those of terrorism, crime, and drug trafficking. Because at this point we have no modalities for handling them, differences over the management of these issues have the potential to spill over into other aspects of the bilateral relationship, such as the implications for trade of enhanced border security.

Tensions in the Canada-US security relationship are not new. The two states have not always seen global and continental issues in the same way. Historically, there were differences over issues that were products of the Cold War—over NATO, NORAD, Vietnam, and the Reagan Strategic Defense Initiative (the Star Wars initiative). Some of these differences continue: for example, the two countries do not share the same view with respect to NATO's nuclear doctrine (Blanchfield, 2000) and Canada has been challenged by the US and other NATO allies to spend more on defence (Clark, 1999). As Yvon Grenier points out in Chapter 13, Cuba continues to be a source of disagreement between Canada and the US. At one level the difference over Cuba is more symbolic than substantive: in reality the island poses no threat. Grenier critically suggests that in using Cuba in an effort to distinguish our foreign policy from that of the United States, we are associating ourselves with an 'end-of-the-road' dictatorship. There is also the relatively recent issue of landmines over which the two countries differed substantially. Canada and its Foreign Minister, Lloyd Axworthy, took the lead in promoting an international ban on the production and use of landmines. In its efforts to move quickly towards an international convention, Canada demonstrated what the US felt was insensitivity to its security arrangements in Korea (Cameron et al., 1998).

Canada and the United States also have their differences about how to deal with Western corporations doing business in rogue states like Sudan. Although favouring sanctions against the Sudanese government—one of the world's most repressive—Canada exposed itself to charges of hypocrisy by allowing Talisman Energy, a Calgary-based oil giant that is a 25 per cent partner in a Sudanese consortium, the Greater Nile Petroleum Operating Company, to continue to do business even after a government-sponsored report had some unflattering things to say about Talisman's activities in helping the Sudan government's military operations in the ongoing civil war. In spite of US concerns about the way Talisman and other companies were providing hard currency to the Sudanese government, Canada resisted US pressure to get Talisman to pull up stakes (Handelman, 2000).

There are two important topics on the Canada-US security agenda. How they are resolved will have major economic, political, and defence ramifications. The first is the decision, to be made prior to November 2000 by President Clinton, on whether the US will deploy a National Missile Defense (NMD) system in 2005. The purpose of the NMD is to protect the United States against limited ballistic missile strikes. As Joseph Jockel notes in Chapter 4, some US officials predict that should President Clinton agree to the deployment of this

new defence capacity—a system with wide congressional support—
Canada would be formally invited to participate. Canada will be free
to opt in or remain out, since Canadian co-operation for the operation of the NMD is not required. No Canadian territory, no Canadian
airspace, and no Canadian military contribution will allegedly be
needed for this new defence capability. The invitation to join poses
a conundrum for the Chrétien government: Canada is a very strong
supporter of the Anti-Ballistic Missile (ABM) Treaty. The NMD is
incompatible with the ABM Treaty, which means the US would need
to abrogate it to develop and employ its new missile defence. A
Canadian refusal to participate in the NMD could mark the end of
many decades of Canada-US collaboration in continental defence
through NORAD. In reality, since the demise of the manned bomber,
Canadian participation in NORAD has been more symbolic than real;
at the same time, Canadians continue to be involved in the direction
of NORAD and a senior member of the Canadian military remains its
deputy commander. US military planning is proceeding from the
assumption that there will be a close linkage between the battle management systems for the NMD and NORAD. If Canada declines the invitation to participate in this new US defence initiative, the US might
put both systems under an all-US command.

What would it mean for Canada if NORAD, the most important
structure in the Canada-US defence relationship, were to come to an
end? At one level, as just noted, it may mean little, since Canada's contribution to NORAD at this point is very limited. A more important
consequence would be a limitation on Canada's longer-term military
capacity. The Canadian Forces have a lengthy shopping list of technologies they wish to acquire to support their activities in the modern
tactical environment. Co-operation with the US is the key to obtain-
ing much of this and NORAD is critical for enhancing Canadian access
to US space projects and space-based assets. However, with or without NORAD, Canada-US co-operation on some defence issues would
continue as a result of Canada's continued membership in NATO.

The termination of NORAD could also have an impact on the
Canada-US defence economic relationship, which was shaky
throughout much of 1999. This is the second item on the bilateral
security agenda, which highlights the intimate connection between
security and the economy in terms of the competitiveness and via-
bility of an important segment of Canadian industry. Canada and the
US have had unrestricted trade in defence products since World War

II, and consequently Canada has enjoyed a sweeping exemption from US military export controls. Canadian defence contractors sell close to $5 billion in high-tech military goods and other hardware to the US annually. Under pressure from Congress, in April 1999 the Clinton administration imposed new security regulations to keep military secrets from falling into the wrong hands. There was concern on the part of some that Canada has failed to safeguard US military technology and that there had been cases where sensitive technology had been sold by Canadian companies to purchasers in countries hostile to the US. The imposition of tough new certification rules restricting the ability of Canadian firms to receive sophisticated military technology damaged their capacity to compete for lucrative Pentagon contracts. One of the stumbling blocks was US insistence on the barring of Canadian citizens with dual citizenship from access to sensitive US military technology. The two countries announced an agreement on International Traffic in Arms Regulations (ITARs) during President Clinton's October 1999 visit to Ottawa. Essentially, the agreement restores Canada's exemption from the restrictive technology export controls. The quid pro quo is that Canada agreed to implement considerably more stringent export controls and security standards on companies using US technology (McKenna and McCarthy, 1999; Gherson, 1999).

Canada and the US have had a very close relationship on defence for over 50 years. When Canadian participation in NORAD and NATO are combined with the free trade in military equipment and technology, the Canada-US defence connection is as least as close as that recently negotiated among the EU states (Fitchett, 2000). In the past, problems such as those involving US cruise missile testing in Canadian airspace were resolved one way or another. We again find ourselves at a decision point in the Canada-US defence relationship, but with less bargaining power, since our participation in the NMD is not essential to the implementation of the system as it was in the early days of NORAD. If we are not prepared to administer technology export controls acceptable to the US, an important Canadian industry will suffer.

FOREIGN POLICY

In the more general area of foreign policy, the principal arena for Canadian activity and the projection of Foreign Minister Axworthy's new human security agenda (see Hay, 1999) has been the United Nations Security Council, where Canada is serving a two-year term that ends 31 December 2000. As Paul Knox discusses in Chapter 15, Canada's permanent representative at the United Nations has had a key impact on a range of issues using a combination of traditional and not-so-traditional diplomacy. Canada has continued to push for reform of the Security Council and to open up its decision-making processes to make the body more accountable to the UN's wider membership—though not with great success. Canada was more successful in getting the UN to pay more attention to the concept of human security, in particular, the protection of civilians in armed conflict. This was the centrepiece of an open meeting of the Security Council organized by Canada during its first presidency of the Security Council. The opportunity to put some of these ideas into practical effect came in the civilian-protection mandate for the peacekeeping force authorized by the Security Council for Sierra Leone.

In taking over the chair of the Angola sanctions committee, the Canadian representative, Ambassador Robert Fowler, led a fact-finding mission to Angola to identify ways to tighten the anti-UNITA embargo and isolate warlords and political undesirables. The report, which contained an innovative series of recommendations to revamp the sanctions regime and target individuals and groups without causing humanitarian catastrophe, was delivered to the Security Council on 15 March 2000. Canada was also instrumental in helping to break the logjam in the Security Council over weapons inspections in Iraq. At Canada's suggestion, three panels were established to examine a range of inspections and humanitarian issues. The recommendations paved the way for the Security Council resolution setting up a successor inspections body to the UN Special Commission (UNSCOM), although a number of problems will have to be resolved before the body is able to do its work.

Foreign Minister Axworthy's ideas about human security, soft power, and peacebuilding are also shaping and influencing our broader, multilateral relationships in the western hemisphere, as Brian Stevenson notes in Chapter 12. The success of this functional, as opposed to geographic, approach to hemispheric relations is evident on a number of fronts, including the ratification of the anti-personnel landmines treaty by Latin American countries (except by Cuba and the United States), growing attention to the proliferation of small arms and the drug trade, and the promotion of human rights and peacebuilding. If Canada is to expand and deepen its trade and investment ties with the region, argues Stevenson, good governance—in the form of transparent business practices, laws, and judicial procedures—will have to proceed in tandem with trade. Both agendas—the political and the economic—are critical to economic and political stability in the region.

MANAGING THE RELATIONSHIP

Critical to the Canada-US relationship is an understanding of how policy is made in one capital towards the other. Two chapters in this volume address the policy process. In Chapter 2 Andrew Cooper examines the formulation of US policy in Canada; in Chapter 3 Christopher Sands considers how policy towards Canada is made in Washington. Steven Lee, in Chapter 11, also speaks to the policy process insofar as he addresses the increasingly prominent role of domestic and international civil society in policy development.

Cooper's assessment of policy formulation in Ottawa can be summarized succinctly as 'Chrétien × 2'—in other words, the centrality of Prime Minister Chrétien and his nephew, Raymond Chrétien, Canada's ambassador in Washington, in the management of the bilateral relationship at the level of high politics. In his analysis of the Prime Minister's central role in developing and implementing the most important aspects of Canada's US policy, Cooper cites Donald Savoie's depiction of government in Canada over the last couple decades as 'court government' (1999: 635–64). In other words, the location of political power in Canada with respect to Canada-US relations (and other issues as well) rests with the Prime Minister and a small group around him, including, in the context of the bilateral relationship, Canada's envoy to the US. The Prime Minister's overall stamp on the conduct of relations with the US is clear: he came into office determined to differentiate himself from his predecessor, whom he accused of having far too close a relationship with US Presidents Reagan and then Bush. Although Chrétien and President Clinton meet often, these encounters are at international meetings, occasional visits by one to the other capital, and golf matches in the US South. There are no regularly scheduled bilateral meetings as there were in the days of Prime Minister Mulroney. Moreover, at least for public consumption, the Prime Minister continues to avoid anything that suggests a closer relationship between Canada and the

United States. Other Canadian political actors and officials play a role in the day-to-day management of aspects of the bilateral relationship, among them Foreign Minister Axworthy, Trade Minister Sergio Marchi and his successor, Pierre Pettigrew, and Defence Minister Art Eggleton, as well as their officials and officials from a range of line departments. Whether there is sufficient attention to the overall picture, including the changing character of politics in Washington, is one of the questions we leave our readers to consider.

Christopher Sands analyses the process by which policy towards Canada is made in Washington. A number of critical points emerge from his assessment. First, there is no central location of responsibility for Canada policy. In the State Department, the Bureau of Western Hemispheric Affairs now covers Canada—a change that took place in 1998. Various line departments and the Office of the United States Trade Representative (USTR) address Canada in the context of particular issue areas. Second, with the exception of border issues and security concerns, Canada is not high on the US radar screen; there are few gains politically (and potentially few losses) from taking a stance on Canadian matters. A senior official in the Canadian Department of Foreign Affairs and International Trade (DFAIT) noted recently that the FTA marked the apex of US interest in Canada. In continental terms, since NAFTA, Mexico has displaced Canada in the attention of the US. This general lack of interest in Canada in Washington is generally viewed as a good thing, since when we do pique attention, it is often the result of actions or positions with which the US takes exception. Third, as noted earlier, important demographic and regional shifts in the United States have a significance for policy formulation on Canada: the generation of US policymakers who knew Canada as a result of war and postwar experiences or who came from the US Northeast and therefore were likely to have visited Canada, and may even have had relatives in the country, is passing from the scene. This group is being replaced by a younger generation of politicians who did not share with Canadians the construction of the postwar world, who have little familiarity with Canada, and who come from the US South and Southwest, where the locus of political power now resides.

The challenge of overseeing the multifarious aspects of the bilateral relationship is perhaps the most daunting. The analysis of the components that connect the two countries suggests a penchant for sectoral or issue management, with institutions or instruments established as necessary. A range of institutions exist under bilateral and trilateral agreements, such as NORAD and the FTA and then NAFTA. Canada and the United States also participate in major multilateral institutions, which have their own principles, rules, and norms. In effect, a number of nested institutions play a significant role in managing—and massaging—relations between Canada and the United States. This sectoral management strategy reflects the historic suspicion of supranational institutions in the United States and of bilateral institutions in Canada. Management of the relationship and the lack of overarching or multi-tasked institutions most distinguish the Canada-US linkage from the European Union. In many respects, the absence of institutions with broad responsibilities for the relationship parallels what was described above as the lack of issue linkage.

The question now is whether Canada and the US continue to manage their relationship, as they have in the past, on an issue-by-issue basis with the traditional absence of issue linkage. As Sands notes, politics in Washington are not what they once were: that character might have been one of the contributing factors to the tradition. Are Canadian policy-makers sensitive to the implications for Canada of the changing locus of power in the US? Both Cooper and Sands suggest that Canada should devote more resources to making its case in Washington. The existence of NAFTA complicates the development of new modalities to manage at least the economic side of the Canada-US relationship since Mexico is also a signatory to that agreement.

At a minimum the two governments should give serious attention to the reinstitution of the regular prime ministerial-presidential meetings terminated by Prime Minister Chrétien in 1993. The quarterly meetings that used to take place between the Canadian Foreign Minister and the US Secretary of State should also be resurrected. This is not a question of politics but practicality. Regular meetings provide their own incentive to address issues and to look ahead to problems that, if left unattended, may well become serious irritants.

CONCLUSION

This introduction has reviewed some aspects of the complex Canada-US relationship. There are areas we have not addressed, where co-operation is also significant, for example on the environment and flood management (where the International Joint Commission plays a role), and on cross-border arrangements to fight forest fires and manage other natural disasters. Similarly, significant differences of opinion remain on other issues—on Canadian sovereignty in the Arctic and the definition and preservation of Canadian culture (see Acheson and Maule, 1999), to name but two.

Though cognizant of its limitations for comparative analysis in regard to the unique relationship between the United States and Canada, we have used the example of the European Union in this chapter because it is the only instance of a comprehensive, integrated, regional regime available. We are not suggesting that Canada should negotiate a more expansive bilateral agreement with the US. There is probably only a limited constituency in Canada that would support a customs union, let alone anything more comprehensive. Nor, at this juncture, is there any interest in the United States in new, more institutionalized connections with any of its trading partners, including Canada. Rather, our intent has been to highlight the depth of our linkages to the United States and to indicate the absence of any clear medium-term or long-term vision of, and strategy for managing, the deepening relationship. Unless economic circumstances change dramatically, at a minimum we are likely to see our trade and investment dependence on the US continue. Canada's economic health is now inextricably tied to that of the United States. At the same time, in the next few years as the recovery from the Asian crisis continues and the economies of that region expand, the US will account for an increasingly smaller proportion of the global economy. This could represent a conundrum for Canada: our dependence on the US is clear and our efforts to diversify our trade have met with little success. Having negotiated two free trade agreements with the United States, we are back to the first option decried close to three decades ago in Mitchell Sharp's 'Options' paper (1972)—leaving things to unfold in the Canada-US relationship as they may!

NOTES

1. Three bodies are being created—a political and security committee of ambassadors, a military committee of senior officers, and a multinational planning staff. The new structure will be intergovernmental rather than supranational: decisions to deploy troops will require the consent of all 15 members rather than being made by the European Commission or Parliament (Fitchett, 2000:4).
2. For the seminal discussions of international regimes, see Krasner (1983) and Keohane (1984).

3. Intra-firm trade is trade between plants or companies owned by the same parent; intra-industry trade is trade among companies in the same industry.
4. Mexican professionals have much more limited entry provisions to the US than do Canadians.
5. Lamar Smith, Chair of the House Judiciary Committee, represents a district from Texas.

REFERENCES

Acheson, Keith, and Christopher J. Maule. 1999. 'Battlefields and Birds: New Directions for Cultural Policy', in Fen Osler Hampson, Michael Hart, and Martin Rudner, eds, *Canada Among Nations 1999: A Big League Player?* Toronto: Oxford University Press, 155–73.

Bhagwati, Jagdish. 1984. 'Incentives and Disincentives: International Migration', *Weltwirtschaftliches Archiv* 120, 4.

Blanchfield, Mike. 2000. 'Axworthy defends NATO nuclear views after U.S. criticism', *National Post,* 8 Feb., A7.

Cameron, Maxwell, Robert Lawson, and Brian W. Tomlin. 1998. *To Walk Without Fear: The Global Movement to Ban Landmines.* Toronto: Oxford University Press.

Clark, Campbell. 1999. 'Spend More on Defence, U.S. Envoy Tells Canada', *National Post,* 12 Jan., A1.

Duffy, Andrew. 2000. 'Ottawa urges U.S. to adopt continental security ring', *National Post,* 29 Jan., A1.

Embassy of Canada/Ambassade du Canada. 1999. *United States-Canada: The World's Largest Trading Relationship.* Washington. October. Web site: http://www.canadianembassy.org

Fitchett, Joseph. 2000. 'EU Taking First Step Toward Own Military Force', *International Herald Tribune,* 1 Mar., 4.

Gherson, Giles. 1999. 'Canada hopes to end export dispute before Clinton visit', *National Post,* 7 Oct., A4.

Handelman, Stephen. 2000. 'Double Standards', *Time,* 28 Feb., 32–3.

Hay, Robin Jeffrey. 1999. 'Present at the Creation? Human Security and Canadian Foreign Policy in the Twenty-first Century', in Fen Osler Hampson, Michael Hart, and Martin Rudner, eds, *Canada Among Nations 1999: A Big League Player?* Toronto: Oxford University Press, 215–32.

Hufbauer, Gary C., and Jeffrey J. Schott. 1998. *North American Integration: 25 Years Backward and Forward.* Ottawa: Industry Canada. Canada in the 21st Century Series.

Keohane, Robert O. 1984. *After Hegemony: Cooperation and Discord in the World Political Economy.* Princeton, NJ: Princeton University Press.

——— and Joseph S. Nye, Jr. 1977. *Power and Interdependence: World Politics in Transition.* Boston: Little, Brown.

Krasner, Stephen. 1983. *International Regimes.* Ithaca, NY: Cornell University Press.

Little, Bruce. 1999. 'Canada ranks 10th in competitiveness study', *Globe and Mail,* 21 Apr., B7.

London Free Press. 1999. 'Canada-U.S. Links a Focus of Two-Day Cabinet Retreat', 29 June, A8.

McKenna, Barrie, and Shawn McCarthy. 1999. 'U.S. to enforce defence, aerospace export controls', *Globe and Mail,* 24 Apr., B11.

Rugman, Allan M., John Kirton, and Julie Soloway. 1997. 'Canadian Corporate Strategy in a North American Region', *American Review of Canadian Studies* 27, 2: 199–219.

Savoie, Donald. 1999. 'The Rise of Court Government in Canada', *Canadian Journal of Political Science* 32, 4 (Dec.): 635–64.

Schwanen, Daniel. 1997. *Trading Up: The Impact of Increased Continental Integration on Trade, Investment and Jobs in Canada.* Toronto: C.D. Howe Institute Commentary, no. 89, Mar.

Sharp, Mitchell. 1972. 'Canada-U.S. Relations: Options for the Future', *International Perspectives* Special Issue (Autumn): 1–24.

US Embassy, Ottawa. 1999. Joint Statement on Border Co-operation, US-Canada Partnership Forum, 14 Oct. http://www.usembassycanada.gov/outreach/ca1015a.htm

US House of Representatives. Committee on the Judiciary. Subcommittee on Immigration and Claims. 2000. 25 Jan. http://www.house.gov/judiciary

Part One

The Bilateral Relationship

2

Waiting at the Perimeter:
Making US Policy in Canada

ANDREW F. COOPER

By virtue of its importance, US policy should be at the top of the international policy agenda in Canada. In form, Canada's entanglement with the US remains a deep and intricate one. The multi-dimensional features of this relationship exemplify the model of complex interdependence, replete with a vast set of 'networks, flows and complexes' (Hurrell, 1995: 334). In scope, the relationship encompasses the economic core (including more than $1 billion US of trade between the two countries on a daily basis) as well as myriad other connections ranging from cultural influence to the arrangements covering the defence/strategic alliance. Although the other aspects of Canada's foreign policy remain highly salient in reinforcing a unique Canadian role in the world, from the criteria of national interest the US is Canada's first, second, and third priority. As Denis Stairs suggests, there is 'only one imperative in Canadian foreign policy. That imperative is the maintenance of a politically amicable, and hence economically effective working relationship with the United States' (Stairs, 1993).

The Chrétien Liberals have managed the US relationship in a more positive fashion than might have been expected before they came into office. There has been no return to the deep chill experienced between the Trudeau government and the Reagan administration over the National Energy Program (NEP) and the Foreign Investment Review Agency (FIRA). Contrary to the expectations of many of its critics (and some of its nationalistic supporters), the Chrétien government has accepted the basic terms on which the Canada-US relationship rests. While continuing to display a 'posture of independence' (Clarkson, 1968: 257) on a variety of issues, signs of autonomous actions have been directed for the most part towards selected and specialized niche areas. The reversal in attitude to the US is highlighted not only by the Liberals' accommodation towards the Canada-US Free Trade Agreement (FTA) and the North American Free Trade Agreement (NAFTA) but also by the disavowal of the traditional 'Third Option' approach based on diversification with alternative economic partners. As Sergio Marchi stated in 1998 when introducing a new trade document, the priority of the Liberal government's policy has caught up to realities on the ground by targeting 'our best customer before jetting off to exotic lands' (Marchi in Morton, 1998).

The sense of tranquility experienced through the course of the Chrétien years has been associated with the easing of many of the traditional trade irritants in Canada-US relations. The vast majority of these issues either run relatively smoothly or at least have become depoliticized. Joseph Jockel, in writing on Canada-US relations in 1996, emphasized the atmosphere of calm that had come to mark the bilateral, government-to-government relationship (Jockel, 1996: 111). Moreover, the suggestion was made that this mood was not just a temporary feature but becoming firmly embedded. As Jockel concluded, Canada-US relations have 'entered into a period of enduring calm' (ibid., 112).

Nonetheless, the prospect of a sustained peace in the Canada-US relationship cannot be taken for granted. Where many older individual sources of tension have faded away, newer issues have risen in intensity. At the top of this emergent agenda is the question of the overall status of Canada on the perimeter of the US. Although still somewhat ad hoc and ill-defined, choices are beginning to be imposed about whether Canada is inside or outside this perimeter. On economic issues, the pressures are still largely self-imposed, as in the case of whether Canada should move forward on projects such as a customs union or dollarization. In the critical sphere of security, pressure has been exerted in a more direct manner from the US. The end of the Cold War has not brought with it a sense of comfort vis-à-vis potential threats to the sole remaining superpower. On the contrary, the world is perceived by the US as being full of real and volatile danger. Coincidentally, the dominant American political perspective has shifted from internationalism to expressions of a defensive localism. Even a long-standing partner with the pedigree of Canada no longer enjoys the degree of tolerance it hitherto possessed to disagree or to differentiate itself from US policy on an issue-by-issue basis. Inexorably, Canada is being compelled to decide whether it belongs inside or outside a North America within a more comprehensive and well-defined format. As Gordon Giffin, the current American ambassador to Canada, has warned, the rules of Canada's main game have changed: 'Our mutual relationship is [no longer] contained on an à la carte menu. Rather, at this North American restaurant, it is necessary to take the whole dinner' (Giffin in Trickey, 1998).

This changing game poses a very different test for the Chrétien government. As personified by Chrétien's attitude towards the Canada-US relationship, the management approach of the Liberal government had built into it a considerable degree of calculated ambivalence. The substantive importance of the relationship and the means of handling it politically have been well recognized. In stylistic terms, though, the specific way Prime Minister Chrétien shaped the tone of this relationship was designed to play down the significance of this main game. To put political distance from the Mulroney record, the bilateral relationship was deemed in declaratory terms to be 'good' but 'not cozy' (Chrétien in Fraser, 1997a). While Prime Minister Mulroney openly and unequivocally embraced the US relationship, Prime Minister Chrétien has distanced himself from this connection through a number of signalling devices.

In more general operational terms, the management approach to the Canada-US relationship highlights the duality found in the workings of governance adopted by the Chrétien government. To be sure, two very divergent images have been presented about the mode of policy-making of the Chrétien government. The first of these images, in tune with the model of complex interdependence, remains that of fragmentation in which multiple actors have a presence and a voice.[1] The second is what Donald Savoie has termed 'court government', that is, the concentration of powers and responsibilities within the ambit of the Prime Minister and a small cohort of 'carefully selected courtiers' (Savoie, 1999).

In retrospect, this duality has provided the Chrétien government with a number of strengths in managing the Canada-US relationship through the 1990s. Fragmentation built up a vigorous push-pull effect of competing objectives. At the political level, activist ministers such as Lloyd Axworthy and Sheila Copps have been provided with enough space to push their own agendas. The result is a valuable (if awkward) sense of equipoise, in which resistance as well as accommodation to the US has been allowed. At the bureaucratic level, the emphasis has been on the distribution of activities within and across various layers of administration. While much of this work has become routinized, new ideas about how better to manage the Canada-US ties with respect to early warning and lobbying are allowed to filter through and up the system. Concentration, in turn, facilitates bursts of intervention from the apex of power. While designed to impose discipline, the trigger for this type of intervention usually comes when an issue within the ambit of the bilateral relationship becomes either controversial and/or wrapped up with the central priorities of the government.

Looking forward, however, the weaknesses contained in this mode of decision-making stand out. Faced with the challenges posed by the new perimeter concept, the combination of fragmentation and concentration appears to be a recipe for immobilization. As the stakes become higher, the search for balance between autonomous action and integration at the political level becomes much more difficult. By pushing a cluster of initiatives with like-minded countries, Foreign Minister Axworthy faces accusations by some of his critics of neglecting the main game of Canada-US relations at the expense of a series of noisy but distracting (and unproductive) sideshows.[2] Yet, when Axworthy has pulled back with the support of his department to advocate constructive solutions to the changing bilateral context, he has been accused by Canadian nationalists of 'selling out'. A similar dilemma exists with respect to Prime Minister Chrétien's 'court government'. As revealed by some of the recent proposals put forward by Raymond Chrétien, Canada's ambassador to the US and the Prime

Minister's nephew, this clustered élite has the capacity to rethink the nature of the Canada-US relationship. If increasingly stretched, the well-developed skills of the Canadian foreign service can also be harnessed productively to this effort. The difficulty for the Chrétien government, or more precisely for Prime Minister Chrétien himself, will be to demonstrate that it has the will to put any new ideas into practice. Having done well politically by avoiding raising the US to the top of the list of the government's priorities, innovative policy in this area will likely remain subordinated to the cautious dictates of process. By this refusal to acknowledge the extent of these new problems in the relationship, and thereby risk controversy and debate, the Chrétien government risks being overtaken by an agenda that will be increasingly difficult to manage.

CLOSE BUT NOT TOO CLOSE

The tone of Canadian policy-making with respect to the United States has clearly been set at the apex of power. Nowhere is the 'compact economy model' of Prime Minister Chrétien's diplomacy more evident than in his approach to the US. Rather than going in a sharp new direction, Chrétien has tried to build on many of the older habits of the past in the Canada-US relationship. In many ways, Chrétien's style echoes the approach used during the Pearson era, i.e., quiet diplomacy and the use of formal institutional mechanisms and multiple contacts to temper US action. In other ways, the approach replicates in a more low-key fashion the informal mechanisms (with a heavy usage of telephone diplomacy) favoured by Prime Minister Mulroney.

The stylistic hallmark of Chrétien's approach has been a reluctance to acknowledge publicly the privileging of the US relationship in Canadian policy-making. This sense of calculated ambiguity did not in any way preclude the eventual establishment of a good personal relationship between Prime Minister Chrétien and President Clinton. As witnessed by a number of symbolic and instrumental episodes, the two leaders have built up a warm personal chemistry. Chrétien wished Clinton 'good luck' when the American President became embroiled in the White House sex scandal. Clinton asserted himself vigorously into the Canadian national unity debate on behalf of Chrétien. In the Eisenhower/St Laurent tradition the two leaders even began to play rounds of golf together.

However close, Prime Minister Chrétien has avoided being seen as too close to the US President. To distance himself from the image of Mulroney cosying up to President Reagan at the 1985 'Shamrock Summit' or to President Bush at the President's summer cottage at Kennebunkport, Maine, Chrétien delayed one-on-one meetings with Clinton. Indeed, as Kim Nossal notes: 'it was not until 23–24 February 1995 that Clinton paid an official visit to Canada, addressed the House of Commons, and had his first bilateral summit with Chrétien' (Nossal, 1997: 206). Chrétien did not reciprocate with an official visit to the US until April 1996. Although it is true that Clinton and Chrétien met quite frequently in the gap between the time they were elected to office (November 1992 and October 1993, respectively) and their bilateral summits, these earlier meetings were held under a multilateral cover, such as the Seattle summit (of the Asia-Pacific Economic Co-operation forum) in December 1993.

This sense of calculated ambivalence is reinforced by the determination of Chrétien to balance Canada's role as a partner to the US with its role as an autonomous actor free to say and do what it likes in the domestic and international arenas. Externally, this signalling device was ingrained, albeit often unintentionally delivered. An illustrative case in point is the 'open mike' episode at the July 1997 Brussels North Atlantic Treaty Organization (NATO) summit, when Chrétien displayed his double-edged feelings about the US to the Belgium Prime Minister: 'I like to stand up to the Americans. It's popular. But you have to be careful because they're our friends' (Chrétien in Gwyn, 1997).

Domestically, Chrétien has gone to great lengths to differentiate the Canadian and American political and social systems. This signalling technique was demonstrated in the Prime Minister's speeches to US audiences. In an April 1997 address to the National Press Club, for example, Chrétien played up the differences in the cultures of the two countries, emphasizing 'our cherished public health-care system' and the introduction of 'one of the toughest gun-control laws in the Western world' (Chrétien in Greenspon, 1997). A similar set of themes was delivered in a variety of off-the-cuff remarks. As revealed on issues such as NATO expansion and the Helms-Burton legislation, Chrétien displayed a sharp public frustration with the entrenched localism displayed in US politics. From a more defensive perspective, the Prime Minister has gone on record to deny the validity of charges that the much publicized 'brain drain' between Canada and the US was a result of higher taxes and excessive regulation.

BETWEEN DEVOLUTION AND CONCENTRATION

While Prime Minister Chrétien has set the tone of the management approach in Canadian policy-making towards the United States, considerable room has been left for ministerial responsibility. Guided by his own formative experience from the Pearson government of 1963–8, Chrétien refrained from extensive micromanagement. So long as they did not make mistakes, ministers were allowed in usual circumstances to run a long way with their own policy initiatives. As a general principle, and usually in specific practice, the goal has been not to tighten but to 'relax central control over the government by farming power back to individual ministers' (Greenspon and Wilson-Smith, 1996: 46).

Evidence of this devolution of responsibility during the span of the Chrétien government is provided most compellingly by the international agenda pursued Lloyd Axworthy. On issues such as landmines and the International Criminal Court (ICC), Axworthy worked closely not with the US but with loose coalitions of like-minded countries. On issues such as Helms-Burton and NATO nuclear strategy, Axworthy was prepared to give the US what one commentator described as a 'stick in the eye' (Pearlstein, 1999).

In declaratory terms, this mission-oriented diplomacy reinforced the impression of Canada's independent posture. As Axworthy declared about the Canadian and US approaches to international affairs: 'We follow our own paths, which allow us to play to our own strengths and our own unique role in the world' (DFAIT, 1997: 8). Still, in operational terms, the conclusion that this strategy represented a decisive shift from accommodation to resistance can only be taken so far. For one thing, the extent of Axworthy's own anti-Americanism should not be overblown. From his graduate school days at Princeton, Axworthy has been thoroughly engaged by American political issues. On landmines and the establishment of the International Criminal Court, most notably, Axworthy found common cause with Jody Williams and a variety of other American activists. On other foreign policy issues, such as Haiti and Kosovo, his thinking was quite akin to that of President Clinton and Secretary of State Madeleine Albright. Axworthy's differences are not with the US *per se*, but with Republican ideological/partisan values personified by Jesse Helms and others on the right of the American political system.

Furthermore, it can be said that there are two Axworthys. The first of these is the Axworthy featured outside of North America and personified through the above-mentioned initiatives. The second Axworthy is the one whose policy initiatives have begun to focus not so much on resistance but on closer integration with the US. Indeed, in a series of recent speeches, Axworthy has begun to lay out an ambitious vision for a 'North American community'. Breaking with the status quo in a speech in Chicago, Axworthy talked of a deeper engagement and harmonization beyond trade in the areas of security, environmental and emission standards, and possibly the creation of continental transportation corridors. As he suggested on another occasion, 'We have a host of common concerns which we need to address together, but many of these mechanisms we have developed piecemeal over the years are simply out of date or not up to the task' (Axworthy in McCarthy and Scoffield, 1999).

In any case, clear parameters were imposed on Axworthy's freedom of action by the 'court government' component of the institutional design within the Chrétien government. Axworthy's relative autonomy on 'sideshows' such as landmines and the International Criminal Court, for example, could not only be tolerated but were actively embraced by the Prime Minister and his key advisers within the Prime Minister's Office (PMO) and the Privy Council Office (PCO). But on specific 'main-game' issues, the discipline imposed from the centre of the structure of governance was absolute. One illustration of this top-down control came with the Chrétien government's decision to reverse course on NAFTA soon after it was first elected. Rather than opening up the NAFTA issue to a wide-ranging discussion in cabinet, Chrétien chose, decisively, to close the issue once and for all. Acting on the policy advice of such senior trade officials as Allen Kilpatrick and John Weekes, and supported by the logistical expertise of key PMO/PCO advisers, including Jean Pelletier, Eddie Goldenberg, and Jim Judd, Chrétien moved towards accommodation with the Clinton administration's priority of not letting NAFTA fall. The narrative provided by Greenspon and Wilson-Smith of the meeting between Chrétien and the then American ambassador to Canada, James Blanchard, to discuss the NAFTA issue underscores the influence of prime ministerial intervention. When Blanchard wondered whether the new Trade Minister would agree with the Prime

Minister's decision, Chrétien replied that the appointee would or 'I will have a new trade minister' (Greenspon and Wilson-Smith, 1996: 48). Another illustration that reinforces the notion of top-down discipline involved Prime Minister Chrétien's own mission-oriented diplomacy on the 1996 Zaire/Great Lakes episode, where Canada was tasked to head a multinational force to intervene in a growing humanitarian crisis. Although some considerable space was allowed for ministerial/bureaucratic involvement during this initiative, the management function involving the Canada-US relationship was held exclusively by the Prime Minister and his key central agency advisers. Decisions were made through one-on-one telephone calls between Prime Minister Chrétien and President Clinton. Operational details were handled primarily via meetings between a small US administrative team led by Tony Lake, Clinton's national security adviser, and members of an exclusive Zaire Interdepartmental Task Force headed by a PCO official (Cooper, 2000; Kirton, 1997: 42–4).

Questions of national unity demonstrate even more strikingly the extent of the authority imposed by Prime Minister Chrétien and his close advisers. In accordance with the notion of 'court government', a power triangle consisting of the Prime Minister, a close-knit group of central agency officials, and selected Canadian diplomats in the Canadian embassy in Washington acted as the guardian of the Canada-US dimension of this dossier. Determined to keep issues of national unity in safe hands, this clustered élite tightened its control of this sensitive area of governance in the run-up to the October 1995 Quebec referendum. Individual cabinet ministers, such as Axworthy, were largely sidestepped by this process. Commitments were made either at the leadership level or in meetings between trusted delegates such as Ambassador Blanchard and Raymond Chrétien.

To suggest that this capacity for intervention remains available on a selective basis, however, is not to say that that this approach was deployed on a consistent or rapid basis. At least in terms of Canada-US affairs, the impression one gains from the record of the Chrétien government is a tendency towards intermittent and sometimes quite delayed forms of intervention rather than a systematic tilt over to the application of discipline. The controversy over cultural protection, with specific reference to 'split-run' magazines, highlights the extent of this awkward equipoise between devolution and concentrated control in Canada-US policy-making. As has been the case with Axworthy on a variety of foreign policy issues, Sheila Copps has had considerable leeway to develop an autonomous policy. One key example is the setback Copps faced following a negative World Trade Organization (WTO) ruling on an approach that used high excise taxes and tariffs on imported magazines to stymie US publishers from establishing Canadian editions. Copps was allowed to persist with an alternative in terms of Bill C–55 centred not on the regulation of the magazine industry *per se* but on the regulation of advertising. Indeed, it was not until an enormous amount of countervailing pressure built up both externally (in the form of threats of US retaliation) and internally (with pressure from other Canadian economic sectors being targeted by the Americans) that Prime Minister Chrétien and his central advisers stepped in. Once reined in, however, Copps was reined in hard. Faced with a disintegration of bilateral relations, Chrétien signalled that he was ready to intervene personally through a phone call to President Clinton to defuse the magazine issue (McCarthy, 1999). More to the point, PMO officials met with Copps to force a compromise and get the negotiations with the Americans back on track.

BUREAUCRATIC DECLINE AND ADAPTATION

Canadian bureaucratic agency generally, and the role of the Department of External Affairs and International Trade (DFAIT) more specifically, towards the US may be seen in terms of both decline and adaptation. On the one hand, many of the changes in the administrative structure dealing with the US have contributed to some erosion in status and/or resources. Traditionally, the US desk at DFAIT had been at the centre of Canada's US policy-making. As Assistant Deputy Minister (ADM) for the US, Derek Burney took on the role as the major policy entrepreneur in the formative stages of the free trade policy formulation process. This capacity has been cut back during the time of the Chrétien government. No longer is there an ADM position in the DFAIT hierarchy exclusively for the US. Furthermore, the specific bureaus responsible for the management of Canada-US relations (the US Transboundary Relations Division, the US General Relations Division, and the US Business Development Division) have shrunk in relative terms. In part, this reduction has gone hand in hand with the wider cuts inflicted on DFAIT as part of the Chrétien government's budgetary review. However, it has been accentuated by the shift in emphasis in DFAIT away from a geographic orientation towards functional units.

On the other hand, these same changes reveal the skill with which DFAIT has adapted to the new environment. By design, the appointment of an ADM for the Americas allows greater flexibility in responding to the deepening and widening NAFTA and NAFTA-plus agenda. The filtering of the complex array of bilateral dossiers through and around the foreign policy apparatus cuts down on the competition experienced in the past between the geographic and functional sides of DFAIT. Some of the centralization of past eras remains visible. This is evident in the intervention on NAFTA at the outset of the Chrétien government, as well as in the magazine case where the Deputy Minister of International Trade, Robert Wright, took on an important role in crisis management. Nonetheless, much of the day-to-day work on Canada-US matters has been passed down to the level of directors general and directors. On top of this vertical movement, a good deal of horizontal rejigging has become necessary because the relationship between Canada and the US is simply too large for DFAIT to handle by itself. As some 20 departments have a stake in the bilateral relationship, the need to share information and authority is vital for coherent problem-solving.

Outside Ottawa, increasing responsibility for Canada's relationship with the US has been delegated to the Canadian embassy in Washington. Structurally, the embassy has taken on the shape of what Derek Burney has called a 'mini-government' on the front line with the US (Burney in Greenspon and Fraser, 1997). Situationally, the embassy has benefited from the presence of Raymond Chrétien as Canada's ambassador to the US. Ambassador Chrétien could make use not only of his extensive experience as a senior Canadian foreign service officer, but also of his reputation for being plugged into the power centre of Canadian decision-making. In terms of application, therefore, Raymond Chrétien could extend the tactics of public diplomacy and advocacy programs built up by his immediate predecessors. In a similar fashion to Allan Gotlieb and Derek Burney before him, Raymond Chrétien concentrated a good deal of his efforts on supplementing traditional points of contact through lobbying not only the executive, but also the legislative branch of government. As he stated in one interview, playing the game in Washington meant putting together winning coalitions on an issue-by-issue basis: 'I can push the envelope very far in Washington—as long as I can convince the politicians . . . that what I am proposing has something in it for their own interest' (Chrétien in Fotheringham,

1997). As the nephew of the Prime Minister, though, Raymond Chrétien's name alone signalled to the Americans that the embassy should be treated in a serious manner. With unique access to the 'boss' in Ottawa, Raymond Chrétien could claim considerable authority about his own ability to speak for Canada in the US. As he declared at the time of Prime Minister Chrétien's first official visit to the US: 'It's been my job for the last three years, to keep the [relationship] smooth' (Chrétien in Fraser, 1997b).

Much of the work done by Raymond Chrétien and his embassy staff has had a highly defensive tinge to it. This was true of basic trade issues. On the question of Canadian wheat exports, for instance, Ambassador Chrétien was able to play what Micky Kantor, the former US Trade Representative, termed a 'valuable role' as a fixer in 'smoothing the edges' and working out a compromise (Boustony, 1996). This pattern of activity was also evident in highly charged political/constitutional matters. As mentioned earlier, Raymond Chrétien remained an important interlocutor between the Prime Minister and his core advisers on the question of national unity in the run-up to the October 1995 Quebec referendum. As part of a well-organized campaign, Ambassador Chrétien was instrumental in priming Clinton for his February address to the Canadian Parliament during the American President's official visit to Ottawa. Certainly, the Canadian ambassador was highly effective in making sure that Clinton got the message 'right', i.e., that Clinton deliver a speech extolling the virtues of the Canadian model of federalism.

Still, over time, this activity has taken on a more forward-looking dimension. To a considerable extent, this different orientation has come about because of multiple problems in co-ordinating Canadian policy-making with respect to the US. In a diffuse environment where multiple actors with varied needs and interests have to be taken into account, this task had become increasingly complicated. In a general sense, this problem was restated in regard to the objective of applying resources to objectives, when turf tensions remained at the bureaucratic level. The problem was exacerbated, however, by two specific conditions under which the Canadian embassy had to work. The first of these was that significant elements of the Canadian business community continued to bypass the embassy to do their own lobbying. The second was the ingrained habit among Canadian ministers of meeting with their executive counterparts rather than working at the legislative level. In order to move beyond these co-ordination questions, Ambassador Chrétien pushed hard for the implementation of a more coherent and aggressive Canadian public diplomatic strategy. Indeed, this was one of the key recommendations he brought to the table when invited to the special cabinet retreat in June 1999 focusing on the Canada-US relationship.

The primary impetus towards a change of approach has come from the type of issues moving to the core of the bilateral relationship. Looking backwards, the onus of the embassy's work in terms of process has been on detailed micromanagement with the aim of defusing specific crises and potential embarrassing situations before they occur. Looking forward, Ambassador Chrétien and his staff have begun to take on a catalytic function in terms of signalling the future trajectory of the bilateral relationship. This bellwether effect surfaced most dramatically in a speech delivered at the Woodrow Wilson Center on 29 April 1999, in which the Canadian ambassador asked how best 'Can we deepen and fine-tune our bilateral trade relationship to maximize the prosperity and security of North America'? (Chrétien in Scoffield, 1999). Although cast in a very speculative fashion, the release of such a trial balloon signified an appreciation of how fully the bilateral agenda was being transformed.

THE FORCE OF THE CHANGING AGENDA

The nature of the issues on the emergent agenda of the Canada-US relationship differs fundamentally from what was found on the old agenda. For all their difficulty, the traditional economic issues could be handled through protracted negotiation with trade-offs and concessions. The ascendant issues, concerned as they are with Canada's status on the perimeter of the US, contain less room for compromise. Canada is either in with the US in a more tightly defined North America or it is to return outside of this orbit. To be sure, there is a highly significant economic dimension to this new agenda. This component centred on a deeper form of integration through such initiatives as monetary union or dollarization; tax harmonization; a full-fledged customs union with one market governed by the same set of rules and similar external tariff; and a move towards a free flow of people. Although the implications of any move in these directions can be appreciated, in terms of a vanishing border, any decision on these questions still remains a 'made in Canada' one. The increased momentum in favour of these economic aspects of the new agenda comes from voices on the Canadian side of the border, voices found especially within the Canadian business community, such as the Business Council on National Issues (BCNI) and John Roth of Nortel, and Canadian think-tanks, most notably, the C.D. Howe Institute (see, e.g., Courchene and Harris, 1999). In contrast, it remains unclear whether US interests favour such a deepening process or not.

The immediate force of the new agenda from the US side of the border concerns an array of non-traditional security matters. One cluster relates to the general issue of illegal movement of people across the border. Largely as a spillover from the NAFTA connection, the Canadian border has been targeted for greater scrutiny in terms of incursions on the perimeter. In tracking down foreign nationals who abused the 1986 waiver program, Canada has faced the threat of losing its differential status under Section 110 of the 1996 Illegal Immigration Reform and Immigration Responsibility Act. A second intersecting cluster relates to cross-border activities of a criminal nature. Most commonly, this involves drug smuggling. From a US perspective, Canada is increasingly perceived as being soft on the drug issue through lax reporting from financial institutions, poor interdiction and enforcement, and light sentences. In a more rarefied manner, the Canadian connection has been brought into the spotlight in at least one case involving questions of fund-raising abuse within the American political system. This case was the so-called Huang affair in which a prominent friend of President Clinton was accused of making calls and sending faxes into Canada soliciting funds while pursuing other illegal activities (*Globe and Mail*, 1997). These issues helped prompt the introduction of US measures in which American customs officers were authorized to frisk individuals, seize illegal goods, and impose fines on those who make false declarations. A third cluster of issues relates to what many US politicians see as a looseness in Canadian scrutiny over the diversion of sensitive technology to restricted or 'rogue states'. This concern was related to the question of targeting individuals handling sensitive military technology by nationality. New US regulations not only threatened to end Canada's special status for export licensing under the US International Traffic in Arms Regulations (ITARs) but would require special permits for Canadians with dual citizenship (Alden, 1999).

If somewhat amorphous when put together, all of these issues had two common characteristics. In causation, all have been put on the agenda by pressure developing in the US about the porous nature of the Canadian border. In terms of policy effect, they acted to extend and tighten the perimeter controls on a unilateral basis. Nor, must it be added, does it appear that this policy will be easily reversed. On top of everything else, the shift in thinking and actions has been reinforced by increased (if arguably exaggerated) concerns in the US about threats of terrorism emanating from Canada, in other words, the use of Canada as a transit point or staging ground. One well-publicized case centred on what was interpreted as an attempt by two Palestinians to blow up the New York subway system because the men accused of this plot were arrested after entering from Canada. Indeed, as revealed by the case of Ahmed Ressam (an individual with refugee status in Canada who was arrested as a suspected terrorist crossing into Washington state) just prior to the celebrations for the new millennium, fears in the US of this sort of scenario have become obsessive. Lamar Smith, the Republican Chair of a Congressional Subcommittee on Immigration, called the Ressam arrest a 'wake-up call about our porous shared border' (Smith in Gatehouse and Morton, 1999).

Canadian state officials possess the confidence and expertise to adjust to this new agenda. The full repertoire of lobbying techniques has been used to try to delay, deflect, and/or temper the US push on cross-border controls. On the question of Section 110 implementation, the focus of the Canadian effort has been to point out the adverse effect of this legislation on the already congested traffic at entry points between the two countries (McKenna, 1997). To hammer home this point, Canadian officials worked closely with American partners through the Canadian-American Border Trade Alliance. On the question of the application of ITARs, Canadian state officials tried to win a reprieve from the protracted new review process by highlighting the need for co-operative bilateral solutions to the problems associated with the diversion of sensitive military technology, not the disruption of the integrated nature of the defence industries in North America. Raising their game from routinized activity, Canadian state officials also took on the role of idea entrepreneurs. In sync with the efforts of Raymond Chrétien, ideas began floating through DFAIT concerning how best to address Canadian-US perimeter (or CUSP) issues in a more creative and systematic fashion.

Administrative capability, however, is not enough to address this new agenda in an effective fashion. Despite all of the work by Canadian state officials, the issues at the centre of the new agenda have proven to be extremely hard to manage by the traditional techniques of lobbying and deal-making. Although it appeared that Canadian officials had won a delay on the introduction of the new border controls until March 2001, Section 110 remains a live issue with no guarantee of settlement. Nor has a final deal been worked out on ITARs. Although an effective compromise seemed to be within reach, this issue not only has dragged on but has become more intrusive given the extensive revisions needed in Canadian legislation for Canada to meet US requirements on export controls (McKenna, 2000).

Therefore, besides an impressive administrative skill set, political will is needed at the apex of power. Signs of how far strides have been made in the process of rethinking the Canada-US relationship can be scoped at the ministerial level. Stimulated in good part by the perceived lack of a coherent game plan by the government on the magazine issue, Sergio Marchi had called for a discussion of the future of bilateral affairs (including the issues pertaining to a customs union and labour mobility) before he exited from the position as Trade Minister (McCarthy and Scoffield, 1999). Moreover, as noted above, Lloyd Axworthy had moved to take on a creative (if somewhat surprising) role as change agent for greater harmonization of border controls in the North American context. The approach of closer bilateral management put forward by Axworthy contained a blend of loosening and tightening of controls, based on the objective to develop borders 'which are seamless and straightforward for legitimate trade and movement of people, but which present effective barriers to crime, terrorism and the drug trade' (Axworthy in Thompson, 1998).

As a result of this combined pressure, Prime Minister Chrétien demonstrated a willingness to move the Canada-US relationship up the Liberal government's priority list. A cabinet retreat on the relationship was held at Meech Lake at the end of June 1999, just prior to the summer recess. This made good instrumental sense, in that interventions on various aspects of the bilateral relationship in regular cabinet meetings had become increasingly time-consuming. Devoting a good proportion of the retreat to the vast array of economic and diplomatic matters thus sent a clear signal that the new agenda was being grasped. The fact that Raymond Chrétien came in from Washington, amid the publicity emerging from his Woodrow Wilson Center speech, reinforced this message. Symbolically, among the attractions of this change in format was that open discussion downplayed the image of concentrated decision-making associated with 'court government', emphasizing instead cabinet consultation and responsibility. The various ministerial voices wanting to be heard were allowed space beyond the confines of normal cabinet protocol.

If willing to talk about the new agenda facing Canada-US relations, Prime Minister Chrétien remained reluctant to do anything in a dramatic fashion to address them. As opposed to the stylistic message, the substantive signal from the cabinet retreat was that it was business as usual in terms of bilateral matters. In declaratory terms, the Prime Minister was reluctant to acknowledge that anything about the relationship was in the process of changing. The mantra remained: 'We have an excellent relationship with [the US] at this time. There are very few problems' (Chrétien in Walker, 1999). Any notion of a grand vision in terms of rethinking the relationship was played down. The security dimension of the new agenda remained invisible. Any prospect towards a deepened form of economic integration by way of bold steps, such as a customs union or dollarization, was denied. The focus was on ways the two countries could work more closely together to loosen cross-border controls, such as by streamlining and modernizing Canadian and US customs procedures, and on routine forms of trade facilitation. In institutional terms, there was no talk of reviving the regular quarterly meeting between key ministers to oversee and seek solutions on the new agenda. The management of the Canada-US relationship was left to an ad hoc and open-ended process. The only procedural change to come out of the cabinet retreat was the decision to act on the recommendation of Raymond Chrétien that ministers take a more aggressive and diversified approach when travelling to the US, i.e., that they break with tradition and meet influential members of Congress as well as with their executive counterparts.

The risks attached to the Canadian government altering its mind-set (and the way it operates) with respect to the US should not be minimized. Any further fundamental change in terms of how this main game is played raises profound questions about identity and the future institutional makeup of Canada. From this domestic political perspective, the stance of calculated ambivalence taken by the Chrétien government remains an attractive one. A cautious approach plays well to the logic of closer integration with the US while reducing the prospect of new controversies over a 'sellout' of national sovereignty. From an external perspective, incrementalism helps reduce both the level of misunderstanding and the problem inherent in any situation in which Canada has to negotiate inside the American political system without direct electoral representation.

At the same time, though, the Chrétien government faces the prospect of being a prisoner of its own success for handling the Canada-US relationship. As the general atmosphere of calm and tranquility is intruded upon by specific issues contained within the new security-cum-economic agenda, the ingrained techniques of bilateral management are no longer enough. Tactical improvisation through ministerial rethinking, due diligence to process at the bureaucratic level, and an emphasis on good personal chemistry between Prime Minister and President cannot be substitutes for strategic and creative leadership. The top-down approach imposed by Prime Minister Chrétien and his close advisers, so effective when deployed in vital matters of the main game in the past, has become the core of the current blockage problem. Given their origins, scope, and impetus, it appears unlikely that the pressures within the US to impose tighter controls on its borders will ebb in the near future. By choosing not to make a clear choice about whether Canada will be inside or outside of what appears to be an evolving and redesigned North American fortress, Canada will in all likelihood find itself faced with a *fait accompli* in which its wriggle room for negotiation is substantively reduced. Rather than being able to use its (albeit limited) diplomatic space as it has in the past, under this type of problematic scenario Canada will become increasingly subject to American dictate. Waiting at the perimeter for the US to change its mind, rather than taking matters into its own hands, is a recipe for marginalization and anxiety.

NOTES

1. The classic expression of this model remains Keohane and Nye (1977).
2. For a more general discussion of this theme, see Cooper (1999).

REFERENCES

Alden, Edward. 1999. 'Tighter US arms controls anger Canadians', *Financial Times* (London), 22 Apr.

Boustony, Nora. 1996. 'The Ambassador's Splitting Headaches', *Washington Post*, 31 Jan., D1.

Clarkson, Stephen, ed. 1968. *An Independent Foreign Policy for Canada*. Toronto: McClelland & Stewart.

Cooper, Andrew F. 1999. 'Coalitions of the Willing: The Search for Like-minded Partners in Canadian Diplomacy', in Leslie A. Pal, ed., *How Ottawa Spends, 1999–2000*. Toronto: Oxford University Press, 221–50.

————. 2000. 'Between Will and Capability: Canada and the Zaire/Great Lakes Initiative', in Andrew F. Cooper and Geoffrey Hayes, eds, *Worthwhile Initiatives? Canadian Mission-Oriented Diplomacy*. Toronto: Irwin (forthcoming).

Courchene, Thomas J., and Richard G. Harris. 1999. *From Fixing to Monetary Union: Options for North American Currency Integration*. Toronto: C.D. Howe Institute, June.

Department of Foreign Affairs and International Trade (DFAIT). 1997. 'Notes for an address by the Honourable Lloyd Axworthy, Minister of Foreign Affairs, to the World Affairs Council, Canada and the United States in a Changing World', 97/14, Los Angeles, 14 Mar.

Financial Times (London). 1999. 'Ottawa starts to test the waters for further economic and trade agreements with the US', 25 May.

Fotheringham, Alan. 1997. 'Raymond Chrétien a mover in world's most powerful town', *Financial Post*, 15 Nov., 29

Fraser, Graham. 1997a. 'No hot buttons in Chrétien visit', *Globe and Mail*, 7 Apr. A1.

————. 1997b. 'Chrétien adjusts warmth dial', *Globe and Mail*, 10 Apr., A1.

Gatehouse, Jonathon, and Peter Morton. 1999. 'U.S. turns up millennial terrorist vigilance', *National Post*, 20 Dec., A1.

Globe and Mail. 1997. 'Canada may be tied to U.S. problem', 16 July, A1, A11.

Greenspon, Edward. 1997. 'PM upholds the difference of Canada', *Globe and Mail*, 10 Apr., A5.

———— and Graham Fraser. 1997. 'On the Fairway of Foreign Policy', *Globe and Mail*, 5 Apr., D1, D3.

———— and Anthony Wilson-Smith. 1996. *Double Vision: The Inside Story of the Liberals in Power*. Toronto: Doubleday.

Gwyn, Richard. 1997. 'So what if PM's remarks smacked of Machiavelli?', *Toronto Star*, 16 July, A19.

Hurrell, Andrew. 1995. 'Explaining the resurgence of regionalism in world politics', *Review of International Studies* 21, 4 (Oct.): 331–58.

Jockel, Joseph T. 1996. 'Canada and the United States: Still Calm in the "Remarkable Relationship"', in Fen Osler Hampson and Maureen Appel Molot, eds, *Canada Among Nations 1996: Big Enough to be Heard*. Ottawa: Carleton University Press, 111–31.

Keohane, Robert O., and Joseph S. Nye. 1977. *Power and Interdependence: World Politics in Transition*. Boston: Little, Brown.

Kirton, John J. 1997. 'Foreign Policy Under the Liberals: Prime Ministerial Leadership in the Chrétien Government's Foreign Policy-Making Process', in Fen Osler Hampson, Maureen Appel Molot, and Martin Rudner, eds, *Canada Among Nations 1997: Asia Pacific Face-Off*. Ottawa: Carleton University Press, 21–50.

McCarthy, Shawn. 1999. '"It's up to the PM" as trade war nears', *Globe and Mail*, 20 May, A1.

———— and Heather Scoffield. 1999. '"Inward-looking" U.S. threatens Canada's interests, ministers told', *Globe and Mail*, 30 June, A4.

McKenna, Barrie. 1997. 'Ottawa fights U.S. visa legislation', *Globe and Mail*, 16 Sept., A1.

———. 2000. 'Canada-U.S military access talks bog down', *Globe and Mail*, 7 Jan., B1.

Morton, Peter. 1998. 'Ottawa shifts trade focus to embrace U.S.', *Financial Post,* 2 Nov., C1.

Nossal, Kim Richard. 1997. *The Politics of Canadian Foreign Policy*, 3rd edn. Scarborough, Ont.: Prentice-Hall Canada.

Pearlstein, Steven. 1999. 'Canada's New Age of Diplomacy: Foreign Minister Unafraid to give Americans Occasional Poke in the Eye', *Washington Post*, 20 Feb., A13.

Savoie, Donald J. 1999. 'The Rise of Court Government in Canada', *Canadian Journal of Political Science* 32, 4 (Dec.): 1–30.

Scoffield, Heather. 1999. 'Canada pushed on several fronts towards integration with U.S.', *Globe and Mail*, 4 June, A2.

Stairs, Denis. 1993. 'Canada in the New International Environment', notes for presentation to inaugural meeting of the Canadian Consortium on Asia Pacific Security (CANCAPS), York University, 3–4 Dec.

Thompson, Allan. 1988. 'Axworthy plan comes under fire', *Toronto Star*, 14 Sept., A6.

Trickey, Mike. 1998. 'U.S. ambassador warns ties are a "two-way street"', *National Post*, 5 Nov.

Walker, William. 1999. 'PM seeks freer trade in Americas', *Toronto Star*, 30 June, A1.

3

How Canada Policy Is Made
in the United States

CHRISTOPHER SANDS

The United States' relationship with Canada is one of the most successful and popular in US foreign relations history. It is conditioned by a high degree of economic and societal integration between the two countries, which has resulted in a significant degree of direct participation in the relationship by Americans at all levels. The complex linkages between Canadian and US interests make it difficult to distinguish between the two sides in many cases and can lead US policy-makers to stumble across Canada inadvertently in the course of domestic decision-making. The US relationship with Canada is so close that it can appear domestic to Americans, prompting policy responses more commonly seen in the rivalry among US communities. Yet in the intimacy of US-Canada relations there is also great opportunity for co-operation and collaboration to an extent not conceivable elsewhere in international relations.

Given the integration of Canada and the United States, is it possible for the United States to operate a Canada policy? This chapter argues that it is possible, and offers a model to explain the formation of policy within such a diffuse relationship. The most important variable within this model is knowledge, and policy-making bodies in the United States can be differentiated by their approach to acquiring and using knowledge in decision-making, particularly in light of modern information technology.

The model alone does not account for the remarkable consistency of the US approach to Canada for much of the twentieth century. This consistency is discussed and attributed to the existence of a broad consensus among Americans about Canada as a neighbour and ally. This consensus substituted for lack of knowledge of Canada and Canadian interests and thereby reinforced the general model. However, evidence indicates that this consensus is now eroding in the face of changes in American society. Thus, the chapter concludes with a consideration of the bilateral relationship without the former consensus, and looks ahead to the options for US and Canadian policy-makers who will have to grapple with the challenges of mutual interdependence and integration in the twenty-first century.

WHAT IS CANADA POLICY?

'Canada policy' is a term that can be applied to a wide array of policies made in the United States that address either Canadian interests directly or incidentally. For most analytical purposes, it is wise to narrow the scope of Canada policy to include a more consistent range of policies, for example, US foreign policy towards Canada made by the federal government, or US trade policy towards Canada, which can be identified with the Office of the United States Trade Representative (USTR). These policies naturally demonstrate patterns because the same institutions make them. But US relations with Canada also include, for example, a decision made by the Detroit City Council regarding parking tickets received by Canadian visitors to Detroit Tigers baseball games. They can be affected and shaped by a law passed by the Alaska state legislature on the migration of caribou across the border from the Yukon Territory. In these cases, democratically elected officials are responding to their constituents, who are direct participants in this relationship.

Policy is generally thought to be made primarily by governments, but non-governmental organizations (NGOs), companies, universities, and other collective groupings of citizens can make important policy decisions that affect Canadian interests. A professional association may deliberate on the equivalence of a degree from a Canadian university in a particular field. US corporations make decisions about the location of plants and facilities in Canada. An environmental group with chapters in both countries may plan a joint action to draw attention to pollution in a river that crosses the border on its way to the sea. Unlike government organizations, for which citizenship is a prerequisite for participation in policy-making, groups such as these are frequently made up of members from both countries, and so the decisions they take may affect Canadian interests without being solely American. This is the complexity of US-Canada relations.

Although there are advantages to narrow definitions of Canada policy, these inevitably result in a limited analysis that is useful in explaining only part of the relationship between Canada and the United States. Government policy made at the federal level can be influenced by problems that emerge at a local level, and local officials certainly take note of the general tone and direction of federal policies when considering local options. In addition, the role of organizations in society, from interest groups to associations and corporations, can be determinative of the decisions made by governments; this is particularly true in the context of deep integration between these two countries.

Using such a broad definition of what decisions and which decision-makers the term 'Canada policy' encompasses is logical, but what can this wide variety of policies have in common? It is true that US policy-makers do not share agendas or definitions of organizational interests, and the policies being considered take diverse forms, from legislation to administrative rules to simple statements. Yet all of these policies take shape in an environment of profound integration, and this lends a considerable observable consistency to how Canada is perceived and addressed by various policy-makers in their decision ambit.

Therefore, it is not a narrow definition of *what* Canada policy is, or of *who* makes it, that unites US policy-making and its effect on Canadian interests. Instead, it is *how* Canada policy is made in the United States—a consistency in the process of policy-making—that is important in understanding the American approach to Canada. The first step to modelling policy behaviour in this area is to consider the motivations that lead US policy-makers to make Canada policy and, subsequently, to categorize the manner in which they may proceed.

A MODEL FOR DIFFUSE POLICY-MAKING

Policy-making bodies in the United States approach problems and opportunities in similar ways, and where Canada is concerned, the pattern of policy options available to US policy-makers is consistent across all levels, from non-governmental organizations to national foreign policy. Where the various policy-making entities differ most significantly is in their approach to the acquisition and application of knowledge in their decision processes.

US policy affecting Canadian interests shares much in common with American policy-making in general, at least in the sense that it originates in similar ways to other policies. Policy-makers are motivated to make decisions on any subject for one of three basic reasons. The first is a constituent demand, a motivation arising from a group that may or may not include the decision-maker as a member. For government policy-makers, constituents are generally the voters (or their parents who vote). For corporations, constituents include shareholders and customers. Non-governmental organizations respond to volunteers and key sources of funding. Universities may react to students, faculty, or alumni. Professional associations may act as a result of a request from their memberships.

A second motivation for policy-making can be structural, due to delegation from another policy-making body or the assignment of policy-making responsibility to the policy-maker through a constitution or charter. Action may be taken because it is considered to be within the proper mandate of a particular actor.

In addition, individual policy-makers may become self-motivated to act in a particular area, through a personal inspiration that such action would be beneficial or worthwhile. The role of individual motivations is frequently underestimated in modelling policy-making behaviour.

These three motivations for policy action help to determine the level of analysis for the model. It is important to begin by distinguishing among policy-making that occurs as a result of group-specific, structural, and individual responses and actions. These distinctions can apply at all levels of US policy-making, from federal to local government and the non-governmental policy-makers mentioned earlier. For example, farmers concerned about the effect of imports of low-cost Canadian grain on US grain prices may demand action from their state and federal governments to block Canadian imports, to fix prices in the market, or to provide a subsidy to help farmers. The farmers will also likely turn to farm organizations to organize protests and to make representations on their behalf to both the US government and even the Canadian government. They will also lobby grain buyers—large firms in the US—not to purchase the Canadian grain, either through their own farm organizations or through their elected representatives. This constituent demand from farmers would motivate policy decisions (which may or may not reflect the farmers' wishes) by government, corporations, and organizations, and the consequences would redound to Canadian grain exporters.

In another example, a prosecutor may face the questions of how to indict a Canadian citizen for a crime committed in the United States and what penalty to seek from the courts if the individual is convicted. US law provides the prosecutor with certain responsibilities and constraints, but the consequences of his or her decision will have implications for the individual's family and friends in Canada, and could establish a precedent for future cases where Canadians are suspected of similar offences. The US prosecutor might also have to decide how to respond if Canadian authorities choose to intervene by requesting the extradition of the individual to face trial, or perhaps to serve out a prison sentence, in Canada. The prosecutor in such a case does not set out to make Canada policy. Instead, the motivation for all of these decisions by the prosecutor comes from the structure of his or her job as a prosecutor, as set out in US law.

Individual policy-makers can and do act on their own inspiration. For example, a parent who volunteers as head of a local youth soccer league might decide to invite Canadian teams to participate in a big tournament at the end of the season, transforming the event into an international competition. The invitation may lead to a reciprocal invitation from the Canadian youth league and a regular series of tournaments bringing together children and parents from both countries, thereby fostering new friendships and rivalries. At the league banquet, another parent notes that it was all thanks to the one parent who had a good idea and followed through to make it happen. But that idea clearly had positive consequences for US-Canada relations.

Motivations for US policy-makers to venture into the realm of Canada policy clearly vary, as do their responses to these motivations. In general, it is possible to categorize US policy actions in three ways, as indifferent, reactive, or neighbourly. Within these three categories two distinctive types of response can be differentiated.

Policy-makers may take decisions indifferent to (or unaware of) the fact that they are contributing to Canada policy. Indifferent Canada policies can be of two types: accidental or irredentist. An accidental Canada policy action can come from an indifference to the consequences of the action for Canadians. Managers at a video rental store chain might select new software that requires a Social Security number to identify individual customer records, unaware that this will block Canadian customers from continuing to rent movies and video games at their outlets. A US philanthropic foundation may decide it will only consider funding applications from organizations that qualify for charitable status under the federal tax code, intending to exclude individuals and local government groups from submitting applications, but unintentionally excluding Canadian applications at the same time. The US Environmental Protection Agency could promulgate new groundwater quality standards that do not address runoff and other pollution from Canadian sources, thereby making the standards less effective for US communities and encouraging polluters to relocate to the Canadian side of the border—posing an additional challenge for Canadian regulators.

Irredentist (or expansionist) American Canada policy actions stem from policy-makers seeking to expand their area of jurisdiction or legitimate activity, indifferent to what this could mean for Canada. A US association of material science engineers, whose members work with advanced composites and other high-tech materials, may decide to issue new guidelines for its members designed to foster recycling and then campaign to have these practices accepted as an industry standard. Canadian material science engineers would then face pressure to adopt US standards from their employers and customers. A state legislature might adopt a new law requiring that small watercraft be inspected before owners can receive a permit to operate in inland lakes, only to find that the largest group of citations issued by state police for boating without a permit was due to Canadian tourists unaware of the new requirement.

Canadians often respond effectively to indifferent policies affecting their interests by pointing out to US policy-makers the unintended consequences of their decisions. In some cases, an exemption for Canadians is ordered or the application of the new policy is adjusted to accommodate Canadian concerns.

The second category of Canada policy is reactive. Unlike indifferent actions, reactive policies reflect awareness of Canada and Canadian interests on the part of policy-makers. Reactive policies can be of two types, reflecting their orientation: defensive and offensive. Defensive policy actions are intended to protect US interests in reaction to a perceived problem related to Canadians or Canadian interests. For example, county hospitals in Florida recently sought relief from the state legislature for the costs of treating uninsured Canadian retirees. These elderly Canadians believed that Canada's health-care system would cover the costs of health care in Florida, but changes in provincial health-care policies left them without any coverage and county hospitals were being forced to absorb the costs of their treatment without compensation. The state legislature responded by passing a new law denying free public health care for non-citizens. In another case, the US Congress approved a law, signed by President Clinton, designed to curtail Canadian investment in property in Cuba expropriated by the Castro government without compensation to the legitimate US titleholders. This law, popularly known as the Helms-Burton Act, was intended to prevent a further dilution of the American claims by threatening penalties for the executives of Canadian firms involved in profiting from the use of these properties.

Offensive policy actions, in contrast, seek to take advantage of an opportunity related to Canadians or their interests. A service club in a border community, to encourage Canadians to attend, may decide to accept Canadian money at par with US funds for its monthly luncheon admission fees. An on-line retailer may offer special discounts on shipping to encourage Canadians to use an e-commerce Web site originally designed for US customers. A hospital in the United States might choose to recruit medical professionals in Canada, aware that they are typically well trained and less well paid than their American counterparts under the Canadian health-care system. In 1999, a bill before Parliament to protect Canadian magazines from US competition faced little domestic opposition. The Office of the USTR threatened retaliation against unrelated Canadian exports to the US in order to raise the political stakes for Ottawa, exploiting an opportunity to prevent the passage of the bill. The Chrétien government modified the legislation before it was passed to accommodate the concerns of the US entertainment industry, thereby heading off a small trade war.

Canadians attempting to respond to reactive US Canada policies must contend with policy-makers who are often well informed about Canadian realities. Disagreements over reactive policy measures are frequently among the most difficult to address. Canadians resent the need to defend their decisions to American policy-makers or attempt to treat disputes as misunderstandings by the American side—in effect, treating a reactive Canada policy measure as though it were an indifferent one. The assumption of US ignorance is of limited value in these cases. Specific US policy-makers may be ignorant in many ways about Canada, but reactive policies are adopted in response to concrete problems and opportunities, and Canadian responses need to address these concerns directly if they hope to alter the US policy.

One method used by Canadians in response to such reactive policies has been to ally with like-minded US constituent groups, higher-ranking authorities in the United States friendly to the Canadian position, or individual policy-makers willing to support Canadian appeals. This can undermine the position of the US actor through new pressures from within their own system, creating a window for negotiation or dialogue to address the original concerns without unnecessary damage to Canadian interests.

The third and final category of US Canada policy action is neighbourly. The rich interaction and shared values among Canadians and Americans can make the politics of neighbourly actions attractive to US policy-makers, and historically such efforts have often been successful in addressing US concerns. In contrast to indifferent and even reactive policies, neighbourly policy requires a more extensive knowledge of Canada and Canadians on the part of the US policy-maker or an active working relationship with Canadian counterparts. Neighbourly Canada policy actions are of two types: comparative and co-operative.

The incidence of comparative policy pressures in Canada and the US is growing, as individuals communicate across the border about their experiences. This leads to an inevitable 'comparison shopping' effect, as one community's approach is cited as a model—or a cautionary tale—for another. Thus, Canada's experience with gun control is cited in city council chambers and legislatures across the country, and public health officials in the United States study the ineffectiveness of steep Canadian taxes on cigarettes in reducing the incidence of smoking beyond a certain level. US tax rates are praised by Canadian business, and welfare reform is studied for its implications for Canadian social policy.

While comparative policy has been a part of domestic policy-making for some time, it is also increasingly a factor in American policy formulation. For example, when the Red River flooded its banks in Minnesota, North and South Dakota, and Manitoba there was a tremendous combined US-Canada effort to contain the flooding and aid people in the flood plain. Subsequently, US officials expressed admiration for the earthworks around Winnipeg designed to prevent the city from flooding, and efforts were made in the US to copy Winnipeg's preparedness. Environmental groups in the Pacific Northwest states of Washington and Oregon have shared advice on protest techniques and fund-raising with similar organizations in British Columbia. US health officials cited Canada's tragic national experience with infected blood in its national blood system as a reason to adopt stringent testing and screening of blood and blood products.

Thus far, the US Canada policy actions identified have shared a common characteristic—they were largely unilateral. The second type of neighbourly Canada policy action is co-operative. Where US policy-makers have a sufficient knowledge of Canada to identify appropriate partners and develop working relationships with them, joint action has the potential to be the most effective means of addressing US interests and related Canadian interests. If deepening economic and societal integration makes co-operative action easier, it also makes co-operation more necessary.

Canada and the United States have established numerous institutions to facilitate and, to an extent, formalize bilateral policy collaboration, particularly among government policy-makers. The International Joint Commission (IJC) addresses shared environmental concerns. The North American Aerospace Defense (NORAD) agreement provides for co-operation between the US and Canadian air forces. Regional US state governors' associations invite Canadian premiers to attend their regular meetings. Selected members of Congress and of the Canadian Parliament meet every year in the US-Canada Inter-parliamentary Group conferences. For corporations and non-governmental organizations, a more common approach is to become transnational—accepting Canadians and Americans into their ranks and organizing co-operation within their own structures and rules.

With this description of the elements of a model for diffuse US-Canada policy-making in mind, it is now possible to place the motivations for American policy action (the levels of analysis) in a common framework with the modes or categories of US policy action. Figure 3.1 illustrates these relationships as a matrix.

Using this model to analyse the formation of US Canada policy begins with an assessment of the motivation behind the action. Given that policy-makers and policy-making groups in the US must be responsive to these motivations in some fashion, the next step is to consider the action proposed or taken. The greater the knowledge of Canadian interests or Canada in general on the part of the particular policy-makers, the more modes of US Canada policy open to them. This suggests that access to appropriate information is the key independent variable in moving US Canada policy away from unilateral actions and towards co-operative ones. It is not always certain that this will be the preferred path, depending on the position of the observer using the model, and so no normative judgement is offered in the arrangement of the options in Figure 3.1.

Figure 3.1

Model for the Diffusion of Canada Policy in the United States

Mode of US Canada Policy

	INDIFFERENT		REACTIVE		NEIGHBOURLY	
	Accidental	Irredentist	Defensive	Offensive	Comparative	Co-operative
Constituent demand *(group)*						
Delegated *(structural)*						
Originates with policy-maker *(individual)*						

(left axis label: Motivation for US Canada Policy *(Level of Analysis)*)

INCREASING KNOWLEDGE OF CANADA NECESSARY

Information flows in the current environment of deep integration and Internet communication render a strategy of information control as a means of influencing US Canada policy difficult if not impossible to achieve. Decision-makers at all levels in the US have access to numerous sources of information. The challenge for American policy-makers is to sort through the available information and draw on the useful knowledge that it may contain. This means that the role of experts—academics, staff advisers, consultants, technical specialists and professionals, researchers, and individual Canadians and Canadian sources of analysis known to the policy-maker—can be particularly important in shaping policy relating to Canada.

THE ROLE OF KNOWLEDGE IN DIFFUSE POLICY-MAKING

To this point, the model has not distinguished among types of policy-makers: government, corporations, non-governmental organizations, and others are all considered to follow the same path towards participation in the making of Canada policy. There are important differences among these types of decision-making actors, the most significant relating to the manner in which they manage information.

Governments at all levels have relatively formal processes for acquiring, considering, and applying information in policy-making. The policy-making process for NGOs and corporations varies. In all these, however, the larger the policy-making entity, the more formal the process used to acquire and process information for decision-making is likely to be.

The first consideration for policy-makers when it comes to information sources is simple accessibility. A source is irrelevant if the policy-makers do not know that it exists. The Internet makes many sources newly accessible for decision-makers at various levels at little or no cost. The news media also call attention to information that may be useful or may help to shape the political dimensions of the policy choice facing the decision-maker. In this regard, Canadian media sources, particularly newspapers and broadcast media, are accessible through Web sites that permit policy-makers in the US to track reactions to issues and options by the Canadian public or those who shape opinion in the media. This improvement in the accessibility of information about Canada, however, is often balanced by time pressure on policy-makers since it raises the expectation on the part of policy-makers that they should be able to obtain relevant information very rapidly. This expectation favours Internet-based information in many cases, simply due to the convenience of this format rather than because of the potential reliability of the information contained on various Web sites. As a result, a thoughtful book on a relevant subject may be considered less accessible (and therefore not considered) than a news wire story that comes up on a search by staff.

The second and in many ways most important criterion for policy-makers in choosing information sources is the credibility of the source of information. The determination of credibility is a necessarily subjective judgement, but this will be influenced in the case of American policy-making relating to Canada by the motivation of the policy-making entity for acting in this area. If the pressure on the policy-maker comes from constituents, then the information used by the policy-maker must be credible to these constituents. For example, a US farm lobby group must be cautious in using information from the Canadian Wheat Board, but may find Statistics Canada an acceptable source. If there are structural motivations for the policy-maker to act, or the responsibility has been delegated to the policy-maker, the information used must satisfy the delegating authority or the structural requirements of the policy-maker's position. In the case of a US prosecutor, legal precedents are useful but must be from American jurisprudence. International law arguments may be considered, but these will not bind the prosecutor. An individual policy-maker may choose among information resources based on a personal assessment of their credibility or with a view to persuading others to follow the policy-maker's lead (either fellow policy-makers or constituents).

An important and occasionally frustrating aspect of the credibility of information in US policy-making is the widespread tendency at all levels to view information with a suspicion of its inherent biases. Some may credit this to cynicism, but whatever its rationale, it is necessitated by the very open US policy process in which decisions are regularly and openly challenged. In American policy-making focused on Canada, this means that information *from* Canada—especially from official sources, such as the Canadian embassy or Canadian consulates around the country—can be considered as partisan and therefore irredeemably biased towards Canada. This taint to Canadian information can make it impossible for US policy-makers to justify decisions using Canadian sources, regardless of the veracity of the information itself.

Such suspicions extend to many US sources, although in a slightly different way. Within the executive branch of the federal government, the Department of State must compete with numerous other government agencies for the attention of the President, and is not frequently viewed as the most persuasive source of information or analysis on foreign issues. The Central Intelligence Agency, too, has had its credibility undermined in recent years due to notable oversights and misjudgements that have, fairly or unfairly, brought all of its assessments into question. Congress often views administration sources as hostile to congressional intervention in international policy, and congressional oversight and budget responsibilities encourage representatives of the executive branch to become guarded in communication with Congress. State governments alternate between respect for federal information sources and suspicion that Washington policy-makers wish to discourage state activism in international arenas. Corporate decision-makers approach government information similarly suspicious of the motives of its providers. In many ways these suspicions are structural, built into a system that sets powers against one another and has traditional institutional rivalries that colour the policy process.

In practice, policy-makers in the US generally approach the biases inherent in information sources by relying on multiple sources in every decision—seeking, in effect, second and third opinions to avoid becoming captive to a particular perspective. Canadian information is thus balanced by US information, and government sources are weighed against independent experts. This approach, reflected in the political culture and in the popular culture by the news media, establishes the credibility of sources through contrast rather than based on the authority of a particular source.

This notion leads to a third consideration for policy-makers choosing among information sources, that is, a determination of the compatibility of the information with the needs of the US policy-making entity. The determination of compatibility is largely subjective, as is the determination of credibility. It proceeds as policy-makers raise a series of questions about the information. For example, does it take account of the official US government view or of American perspectives? Does the information speak generally, or directly, to the issue at hand? Does the consideration of this information lead to a feasible course of action or a practical recommendation for action? Can the information as found be adapted to the decision at hand?

Certain sources of information for US policy-making are particularly influential because they are interactive for policy-makers, that is, they can respond to specific questions or problems. For formal information evaluation systems, such as those operated by US corporations and state and federal government bodies, interactivity is particularly prized. Such processes employ expert opinions solicited from individuals or organizations that demonstrate the necessary accessibility and credibility. A corporate vice-president considering a Canadian problem may turn to a trusted consultant, lawyer, or think-tank scholar for a quick primer on the issue at hand and the options worth reviewing. Members of Congress may seek testimony from individuals whose views are consistent with their own in order to build support for their position in a hearing.

In the diffuse policy process described by this model, and with myriad possible sources of information and knowledge now available to US policy-makers, the influence of integration on the US Canada policy process is evident. Yet even before integration had deepened to the present extent, bilateral co-operation was an important part of US policy towards Canada. With limited means for interaction among policy-makers and before the revolution in information technology, the dynamics of this model operated much as it does today. In fact, a sustained coherence was achieved in US Canada policy at all levels (with few exceptions) for most of the twentieth century.

For much of the past century, the evaluation of policy options and the consideration of information in decision-making related to Canada policy were influenced by the presence of a remarkable consensus in the United States about Canada's place among US international relationships. This consensus was largely unacknowledged during this period, and yet it has become more obvious as it has faded. In effect, we can only consider the role of this consensus in the preceding model now that it no longer plays such an important role. In the following sections, the role of the US consensus on Canada will be described in detail.

THE INFLUENCE OF CONSENSUS

Previous attempts to theorize about the nature of Canada-US relations have considered the question of why the two countries have consistently favoured close co-operation. US scholars have generally agreed that linkages between the two societies (rather than an adroit Canada policy managed by the US government) explain the success of bilateral diplomacy. Keohane and Nye (1977) attribute the relative equality within the relationship between these two disparately powerful states to the effects of complex interdependence. Their argument anticipates the effects of economic social integration on US Canada policy, but it addresses only the state-to-state relationship as managed by the governments in Washington and Ottawa and does not consider the implications of interdependence on local governments and other organizations (such as corporations and environmental groups) that participate in the relationship. Doran (1984) argues that political, psychosocial, and economic linkages made the postwar partnership possible, but notes that the relationship was weakened when not fostered by institutions. Lipset (1990) confirms Doran's argument about the linkages between the two countries as a foundation for good relations by documenting, with demographic data, many commonalities and differences between the societies and citizens of Canada and the US, and suggests that these may explain the closeness of bilateral relations.

Although focusing on different aspects of the bilateral relationship, all of these authors agree that there has been a consistent, positive tone to US policy-making where Canada is concerned. The model described in this chapter accounts for similarities in process, but the consistency of approach results not from process or the influence of common information sources. With the end of the Cold War, an additional explanation for the consistency of US Canada policy to date can be made, building on the observations of interdependence, societal linkages, and common heritage. This coherence stems from the existence of a broad societal consensus on Canada that guided decision-makers at virtually all levels throughout most of the last century. Four principal elements support this consensus and the resulting coherence of US Canada policy at all levels: goodwill, self-restraint, the tradition of good relations, and the dominance of professionals (rather than specialists on Canada) as policy-makers.

The first element, goodwill, comes from a wide acceptance of Canada as a friend and ally with whom Americans *ought to* get along and co-operate. The data on these attitudes are limited but consistent. The Chicago Council on Foreign Relations (Reilly, 1999) conducts a survey each year to determine the attitudes of Americans towards other countries around the world. Since the poll began in 1974, Canada has consistently ranked well ahead of other countries as a reliable friend and ally of the United States. The US public clearly sees Canada as a particularly likeable country and a good neighbour.

The second element of the American consensus on policy towards Canada, self-restraint, derives from the observation of the disproportionate size and power of the US vis-à-vis Canada. The American sense of fair play translates directly into a feeling that it would be unfair to bully Canada, which has always been smaller, less populated, and less wealthy. Once viewed as a stronghold of the occasionally menacing British Empire, on its own Canada has posed no threat to the security of the United States. Canadians have generally played to this image of themselves and invoked US might before it could be used against them.

The third ingredient in the US policy consensus is a tradition of good relations with Canada that has taken on mythical proportions in American society. American attitudes towards Canada are shaped by the widespread personal experience of ordinary citizens who have engaged in co-operative ventures with Canadians. Professional associations, labour unions, youth soccer and hockey leagues, civic organizations from the Kiwanis to Rotary, church and synagogue exchanges all contribute to a long-standing intertwining of the institutions of Canadian and American civil society. These ties were established through proximity in border states, but also encouraged by the family ties that cross the border. What pushed these linkages to new levels, and beyond the border states, was a combination of technology (which made travel and communication cheaper and easier) and historical crisis.

Both countries were transformed by the unforgettable societal upheavals of the Great Depression and World War II. For those who lived through these events, habits of a lifetime—frugality, hard work, collective action, and modesty—were formed. And who else shared the experience with Americans? Canadians, like Americans, went to another continent to sacrifice much to restore peace to Europe; moreover, the Canadian participation was proportionately significant. Americans in public service trying to revive the economy during the Great Depression communicated with their Canadian counterparts dealing with the same farm crisis, the same unemployment lines. Wartime leaders and ordinary servicemen and servicewomen could look at US allies and find the Canadians the most like themselves. For thousands of enlisted personnel, the war was their first experience outside the United States, their first direct encounter with foreign cultures, making Canadians stand out as people like themselves. And it was from this powerful, personal experience that the Canadians became known to many Americans.

In the institution-building and organization-creation that followed the war, Canadians were included in numerous groups that sustained the close contact and common bonds between individuals in the two countries. In addition, the postwar period saw many large US companies with subsidiaries in Canada expand those operations and in many cases promote Canadian staff to headquarters or other international operations. The commercial ties between Canadians and Americans, as one another's suppliers and customers in a massive expansion of interfirm trade, continued and expanded the personal contact between individual citizens of both countries.

From this experience the US gained the third element of its consensus regarding Canada: tradition. It became possible to argue, from the halls of Congress to city council chambers across the country, that the Canadians should be treated differently from other foreigners because they were easier to work with, not true outsiders to the United States. It was also argued that Canadians received different treatment because that was the way things had always been done, or the way they were done in other areas—even though there had been and would continue to be friction and conflict between the two countries. The tradition of good relations was a self-sustaining myth, a reason for policy-makers to practice self-restraint and goodwill in approaching Canadian interests.

This idea of an unstated notion that influences policy-making at many levels is not unique to the Canadian context. The noted American journalist Walter Lippmann wrote during this period of the virtues of policy-making guided by a 'public philosophy' made up of societal values that informed the public's perception of what was desirable and appropriate (Lippmann, 1955). Successful leaders, he argued, would have an intuitive sense of this values set, and would be guided by it. The most successful policies would be articulated in terms resonant of the public philosophy, as when during the Cold War the US was able to sustain a broad consensus against Soviet totalitarianism. Lippmann's critics argued that his 'public philosophy' was unquantifiable, and for scholars in the positivist school this immeasurable, intangible values set was suspect at best and meaningless at worst. Yet this notion, applied in the context of US relations with Canada, offers an explanation for the remarkable coherence of US policies affecting Canadian interests after World War II and until relatively recently.

A final common factor in traditional US policy-making regarding Canada is important to note. With few exceptions, policy-makers are professionals, not Canada specialists. In other words, they are trained for their functional expertise as lawyers, legislators, civic leaders, agricultural economists, financial analysts, military planners, or health professionals. They are not, typically, Canadianists. They cannot rely on knowledge of the Canadian system of government, the cycles of the Canadian macro economy, the history of the relationship dating back to the American Revolution, or Seymour Martin Lipset's latest book to inform their decisions. It is not that they do not want to know these things—many US policy-makers develop a fascination with Canada on the job and take time to study it further. But the individual who finds him or herself thrust into an assignment that involves making some Canada policy decisions, or who is confronted with a decision with implications for Canadian interests, rarely has the benefit of Canada-specific knowledge or expertise. This explains why the role of intuitive factors is so important. The predispositions to goodwill, restraint, and respect for the tradition of close co-operation play a critical and often unconscious part in the options that will be considered and those that will be rejected out of hand by such a policy-maker.

These four elements have combined in the postwar period to foster a remarkable consistency and even coherence in what may be considered Canada policy made in the United States, even when a broad application of that term is employed. There are, of course, specific examples of conflicts that have departed from the consensus. At work in these cases are other elements, such as specific Canadian actions that are inconsistent with the US expectation of Canadian behaviour. The consensus behind Canada policy that is being claimed here is a kind of default position, a baseline set of attitudes for decision-making that shape the equilibrium of bilateral relations at various levels. The foundations of this consensus, however, are not immutable. Even now, it is visible mainly in hindsight.

THE EROSION OF CONSENSUS

An unease in the US-Canada relationship has received attention among diplomats in both countries and has been the subject of commentary in the news media. Judging from the statistics that show unprecedented peace and prosperity, things have never been better in North America. Yet something has changed, adding surprising tension to the management of bilateral issues.

The broad consensus that gave consistency to US policies at various levels of government when they concerned Canadian interests has eroded considerably. The Cold War and the prominence of the generation that experienced the Great Depression and World War II in public life in the US fostered the consensus. Today, in the post-Cold War environment and as the members of this influential generation retire from public service, Canada's place in US international relationships is being reconsidered. The erosion of this consensus is easiest to see in the traditional diplomatic relationship between Ottawa and Washington, but the effects seen at this level are also reflected in corporate and NGO relationships. Tensions between the two countries influence the framing of policy issues at all levels of US Canada policy-making, as well as the process of evaluating information and selecting policy options. Without the historical consensus, the model described in this chapter should operate predictably, but a consequence of the erosion of the former consensus may be a negative colouring of issues due to changing expectations of Canadian behaviour by Americans and their policy-makers.

As Andrew Cooper notes in Chapter 2, Canadian attitudes are also changing as Canadians struggle on their own with their place in the post-Cold War world. This re-examination of the relationship occurs during a period of profound change driven by accelerated economic integration between the two countries, globalization, and technological advances that are transforming the societies of both countries. It is worth considering the impact of each of these factors in turn and the effect they have in shaping the new environment for bilateral relations.

First of all, technology and economic integration have created new pressures on both societies. Advances in technology (and the lowering cost of sophisticated equipment that once was available to a relative few) have made the continental neighbourhood in the global village feel much smaller. In on-line chat rooms—sharing in cultural events like the release of a new hit single or monitoring tragedies such as the Columbine shooting—Canadians and Americans interact as if the border did not exist. The 'Letters to the Editor' section of virtually any US magazine includes letters from Canadian readers. Accompanying the intensification of economic integration between the two countries, the quantitative and qualitative growth in interaction among Canadians and Americans has changed the way we learn about one another—and the way in which our political leaders may make policy. A particular challenge is comparison shopping. Not long ago, Democrats in the US had to contend principally with Republicans and maybe the occasional third-party challenge. American voters would generally refer to conditions in other parts of the country in their appeals for new policies. Today, US city leaders will point to the loss of NHL franchises in smaller Canadian cities as a cautionary tale, and debates over Spanish-language education in California and Texas feature references to the language policy problems in the province of Quebec. It is possible in many states to find Americans discussing the merits of Canadian health care as a model for improving US health policy.

The same trend affects Canadian politicians. The federal and provincial governments now face pressure for tax cuts and debt reduction, an agenda familiar to many Americans. The experience of US state governors has influenced provincial political agendas across Canada, from Ontario's Progressive Conservative government to the NDP government in Saskatchewan.

Indeed, the US is increasingly becoming a familiar part of Canadian domestic politics. The Liberal majority in the House of Commons has been faced with a divided opposition that has been ineffective in presenting itself as an alternative 'government in waiting'. As a result, domestic interests in Canada seeking to influence the agenda of the Chrétien government have increasingly attempted to invoke the United States in their arguments in order to gain the government's attention. For example, the Business Council on National Issues has complained that competitive pressure from the US renders the need for tax cuts in Canada acute. Provincial governments seeking to meet the health-care needs of their citizens arrange for treatment in selected US hospitals and, in doing so, call on Ottawa to restore fiscal transfers for health care. In perhaps the most striking recent example, advocates of increased Canadian spending on law enforcement and immigration system administration took their case to Washington, raising awareness for their issues in Canada by testifying before a congressional subcommittee on the dangers posed to the United States by lax law enforcement and counter-terrorism efforts, as well as a liberal refugee system in Canada.[1]

To an extent that neither US nor Canadian politicians and public servants are comfortable acknowledging, voters are increasingly comparing Washington and Ottawa, Victoria and Sacramento or Austin. As with most such trends, the effects of this change are felt disproportionately in Canada.

The second factor affecting bilateral relations is that Canada is a less significant global economic player than it was two decades ago. Once its GDP ranked it among the larger national economies. Today the largest economies in the developing world have grown larger in terms of aggregate GDP than the smallest economies in the developed world, such as Canada. This is a good thing, but it makes Canada in some ways a relatively smaller player even though it has continued to grow. Developing countries, and many smaller developed countries, are better able to participate in the numerous international forums where once Canada was a champion of their concerns.

However, it is also true that a significant part of Canada's decline in world affairs is self-inflicted. Canada's military has shrunk so badly that it cannot serve much more than a symbolic role—even in disaster relief efforts around the world. The Canadian Foreign Service is shrinking (and the entire public service is losing talented people through attrition and downsizing) and attracting fewer of Canada's best and brightest. Canada cannot field the strong team it once could on the international scene. The diplomats Canada has are excellent, but they are starved for resources and overwhelmed by the burgeoning number of international talks, commissions, and negotiations.

A third important factor changing the climate of bilateral relations is an overall shift in the US attitude in the post-Cold War era. During the Cold War, the US was focused on the Soviet threat. What it needed from its friends and allies was a solid commitment against Soviet expansionism and the spread of communism in general. Canada was an outstanding ally in this regard. At the same time it was understood by Washington's policy-makers that the allies would need to demonstrate to their voting publics that they were not merely acting like puppets of the United States. The allies needed to demonstrate their independence by taking policy positions at odds with the American line. US presidents and senior officials would play along by expressing just enough outrage to give political cover to Canadian politicians when, for example, Canada courted Fidel Castro or negotiated grain sales to the Eastern bloc.

In the years since the Cold War ended, the US attitude has changed, along with the circumstances in which the United States must now operate. As the only remaining superpower, the US has many suitors. Inevitably, many of the world's problems, great and small, are presented on the US doorstep along with demands for action of some kind. Under the Clinton administration, US diplomacy has become a constant search for coalitions, contact groups, and nations with resources to contribute to the resolution of the crisis of the day. Canada, with considerable expertise and modest but still available resources, has been a crucial contributor on a number of fronts, from Haiti to Kosovo to East Timor. The dilemma for Canada has been a corresponding rise in impatience in Washington with flagrant expression of policy disagreements.

As Yvon Grenier describes in Chapter 13, the Chrétien government seemed genuinely surprised at Washington's reaction to its overture to Cuba's Communist government, which after all was consistent with Canadian positions during the Cold War. To Washington, Canada was not a team player on Cuba (that is, working with the United States rather than against it), and was grandstanding on an issue that has long been a sore point in US politics.

Canada's generally positive US policy under the Chrétien government has been undermined by other Canadian foreign policy initiatives that have seemed anti-American. Part of the problem is a US conceit that it must be involved in the resolution of major international issues—if not leading, then at least on board. Convinced that vast US resources are the *sine qua non* for all situations, US policymakers expect to be courted, pleaded with, and cajoled into involvements. So when Canada hosted a conference to foster a treaty banning the use of landmines, a cause for which President Clinton and many of his advisers had general sympathy as well as specific reservations, Washington leaders were pleased. Canada surprised the US by insisting that countries proceed with a timetable that left the United States no option to sign the treaty.[2]

The fourth and final factor in the context of the current bilateral relationship is the generational change in US leadership. US relations with Canada were once managed in the context of the Anglo-American connection. This began to change during the first half of the twentieth century. The generation that defined US policy towards Canada included those who entered government during the 1930s and those who came of age during World War II. These individuals came to know Canada as a stalwart ally in Europe during both wars, an ally that, like the United States, was separated from Europe by an ocean, making its sacrifices in these European wars all the more noble. Americans knew the Canadians better than most around the world, and shared with them the experiences of the Great Depression and the settlement of vast continental frontiers. After the war, the US was an unabashed Canada-booster, encouraging Canada to play an important role in many international organizations, from the United Nations to the Bretton Woods institutions.

Many of the clichés of the relationship, like the 'world's longest undefended border', are this generation's handiwork. They express the reasons why Canada should have a special place in US relationships with other countries. It is worth noting that for most of the post-war period this presumption of Canada's exceptional nature was not seriously challenged. The institutions of the relationship were also formed by this generation, from the Defence Production Sharing Agreement and the Permanent Joint Board on Defence to the Auto Pact and ultimately the Canada-US Free Trade Agreement—and this is to mention only the most prominent.

Today, younger people, the baby boomers and generation X-ers, run Washington, from the White House through Congress and into the ranks of the bureaucracy. Most US governors and legislators, mayors, and city and county officials belong to these generations, too. Their rise is overthrowing many of the stable assumptions about American politics that stood firm during the Cold War era.

One of the assumptions no longer made by American policy-makers is that Canada is unique among US allies. Canada is now a country like the others. Thus, Americans struggle with the question of why Canada should be treated differently from Mexico when it comes to border controls. They can no longer assume Canada is any less a security risk than any other North Atlantic Treaty Organization (NATO) ally when it comes to defence-related technology transfer. And US officials contend that they cannot abide Canadian cultural protectionism, which if tolerated is sure to inspire imitators.

At the beginning of the twenty-first century, integration draws Canadian interests into the ambit of US policy-makers at all levels, and the erosion of the societal consensus about Canada removes an important source of consistency in American policy responses. Stripped of the influence of the former consensus, Canada policy is made in the United States as it always has been made, through a diffuse but logical process across all levels of American society.

WHAT COMES NEXT?

Without the Canada-friendly bias in US Canada policy provided by the former societal consensus, integration will continue to deepen and Canadian interests will increasingly become subject to the direct and indirect consequences US policy-making at various levels. Decisions made in the United States are not random, but follow the rhythms of a diffuse policy-making model. But what does this mean for the future of US-Canada relations? Will the two countries continue to have a close, co-operative relationship? Without the old consensus, will there be a positive and coherent pattern to US approaches to Canada in the future?

For those citizens of the two countries seeking to foster the best possible relations, the analysis provided in this chapter suggests two paths to sustaining the broad friendship between the two countries. The first is to recognize and embrace the effects of deepening integration and diffusion in US policy-making. In practice, this means that the need for accessible, credible, and adaptable information for US policy-makers at all levels will be enormous in the coming years. The limited number of available sources poses a serious challenge. Educational institutions in the United States must anticipate this need for knowledge through the incorporation of Canadian study in all curricula: research institutes and private consultancies, even those not previously constituted around an international mandate, need to consider Canada within the context of their work. Professionals, from lawyers to medical specialists, need to be aware of developments in Canada in their field. The US news media must consider coverage of Canada, particularly since demand will push consumers towards Canadian news media as alternatives should US sources fail to meet this need. As the participation in the relationship by private citizens grows, word of mouth will play an important role in establishing the value of information, and will more or less favour information on its merits and not by its sources. As a result, the Canadian government must let go of the notion that Ottawa can manage the relationship with the United States. Under diffusion, it has already lost control, but it can still do considerable damage by attempting to resist provincial, private-sector, or NGO participation. Moreover, there is no long-term alternative to the need for Americans to develop their own sources of information and expertise about Canada. These need not be contentious with Canadian viewpoints, but they must be credible in the US policy context and reflect an American perspective.

The second path is more difficult, but could prove highly beneficial to both sides: the rediscovery of consensus. In the rush of change in world affairs at the end of the twentieth century, new generations of US leaders have abandoned the consensus forged by the World War II generation. But its elements—goodwill and self restraint towards Canada and an appreciation of the tradition of constructive co-operation that has marked this relationship to date—are as valid to the challenges of bilateral relations under integration as they have ever been. Reclaiming the former consensus requires that we demystify it, see it for what it was, and value it for its salutary effects in a diffuse policy environment. While today's policy-makers did not fight alongside Canadians abroad, they are likely to have encountered Canadians in the struggles that marked their youth and their adult lives—integration increases the likelihood of this happening—raising the potential for the experience of continental integration itself to be the common bond that brings Americans and Canadians together in policy-making, from the local youth soccer league to the US Congress.

NOTES

The author would like to thank the editors of this volume, Maureen Appel Molot and Fen Osler Hampson, for the invitation to contribute this chapter. Particular thanks are due to Molot for her helpful comments and suggestions along the way. Responsibility for any shortcomings rests exclusively with the author.

1. A hearing of the Subcommittee on Immigration and Claims of the US House of Representatives Committee on the Judiciary, held 26 January 2000, heard testimony on the question of border security, international terrorism, and Canadian policy from several witnesses, including this author.
2. Canada was believed to be friendly to US security interests and was counted on by many in the Clinton administration to undertake the necessary diplomacy to bring the United States into the international consensus. Canadians, it was thought, would surely get the others to accommodate the US position on retaining mines in the Korean demilitarized zone and allow Clinton administration officials time to win over the Pentagon sceptics. This did not happen.

REFERENCES

Doran, Charles F. 1984. *Forgotten Partnership: U.S.-Canada Relations Today*. Baltimore: Johns Hopkins University Press.

Keohane, Robert O., and Joseph S. Nye. 1977. *Power and Interdependence: World Politics in Transition*. Boston: Little, Brown.

Lippmann, Walter. 1955. *The Public Philosophy*. Boston: Little, Brown.

Lipset, Seymour Martin. 1990. *Continental Divide: The Values and Institutions of the United States and Canada*. New York: Routledge.

Reilly, John E. 1999. *American Public Opinion and U.S. Foreign Policy, 1999*. Chicago: Chicago Council on Foreign Relations.

4

US National Missile Defense, Canada, and the Future of NORAD

The United States moved markedly closer during 1999 towards deciding to put into place a National Missile Defense (NMD) to protect itself against limited ballistic missile strikes. It may proceed further in 2000 towards deployment, despite persistent Russian objections, and later invite Canada to participate in operating the new defences. The US still hopes that an agreement with Russia can be reached on missile defences. If not, Ottawa could face a difficult choice between its arms control convictions and its interest in the long-term continuation of the North American Aerospace Defense Command (NORAD).

No final decision on NMD has yet been taken by Washington. But in January 1999, Secretary of Defense William Cohen announced that in the Clinton administration's view, the potential ballistic missile threat to the US posed by countries such as North Korea, Iraq, and Iran warranted a new defence. At the same time, he said that spending on missile defence would be increased significantly over the next several years in order to provide the potential basis for NMD deployment. He also confirmed that after taking into consideration the results of scheduled tests of missile defence technology and other factors, President Clinton would be making a formal decision in June 2000[1] on whether to begin deploying NMD in 2005.

Cohen's announcement was followed in spring 1999 by votes in both the US Senate and House of Representatives to endorse NMD. The majorities were large: 97 to 3 in the Senate and 317 to 105 in the House. In the words of a critic of the US missile defence program, the congressional votes 'exploded like thunderclaps across the American national security landscape' (Isaacs, 1999: 26).

Canadians scarcely heard that thunder. But if, as now seems likely, President Clinton decides in favour of going ahead despite Russian objections, the issue is bound to become controversial in Canada, especially once Ottawa faces the thorny issue of whether to participate. Some US officials predict that about a year after a decision by the President to proceed further with NMD, a formal invitation to participate would be tendered to Ottawa. But on this matter, as well, no formal decision has been reached by the US.

Canada will be quite free to decline the invitation. Although US officials certainly are hoping that it would accept, there is most unlikely to be any real pressure exerted on Ottawa by Washington. Canadian co-operation is not necessary, for neither Canadian territory, waters, or airspace nor any contributions by the Canadian military would be needed by the US for the operation of NMD.

Ottawa might well say 'no' to the US invitation because of arms control concerns that in recent years have been close to the heart of Canadian foreign policy. The greatest worry for the Canadian government is that in order to deploy its new missile defences, the US will abrogate the 1972 Anti-Ballistic Missile (ABM) Treaty, which has been fervently supported by successive Canadian governments. NMD would not be compatible with the treaty as it now stands. Discussions between Washington and Moscow, the treaty's other signatory, over amending it to accommodate NMD have thus far gone nowhere.

Canada's saying 'no' to NMD would probably also mean eventually having to say 'goodbye' to NORAD. Since its creation in 1957, NORAD has been a Canada-US command, with a US Air Force general as its commander-in-chief, a Canadian general as its deputy, and a Canada-US staff. As such, it has been the most important structure of bilateral defence relations.

'We have developed', said NORAD's commander-in-chief in 1999, 'an NMD Concept of Operations with a key assumption being NMD would be a logical extension of NORAD's . . . mission' (Byers, 1999). In particular, US military planning is now proceeding from the assumption that the battle management system for NMD should be intimately linked to the process of warning of a nuclear attack on North America and assessing it, which today is NORAD's central function. Canada's declining to be involved in NMD would almost inevitably lead to the US eventually placing not only NMD but also the linked warning and assessment responsibilities under an all-US command. This would bring NORAD in fact, if not in name, to an end.

The NORAD issue is already on the bilateral agenda, inasmuch as the current NORAD agreement expires in March 2001. In the spring of 1999, Foreign Affairs Minister Lloyd Axworthy travelled to Colorado Springs to be familiarized with NORAD. Naturally, the NMD issue featured prominently in his discussions there.

Canadian and US officials had hoped to insulate NORAD temporarily from the anticipated Canadian public debate over NMD by quietly renewing the agreement, with the text all but unchanged, in early 2000, thus well before the President's decision on NMD. The agreement could, if necessary, be adjusted—or terminated—several years later, depending on the outcome of decisions on NMD. By the end of 1999, the strategy of quick and quiet renewal had been thrown into doubt as Canadian officials grew reluctant. They no doubt worried that they might later be charged in public with allowing Canada to be dragged into NMD. Similar groundless charges were hurled at their predecessors in the early 1980s when it was noticed that a clause in the NORAD agreement expressing Canada's intent not to participate in missile defence had been removed. In reality, the absence of such a clause in the current agreement does not in any way lock Canada into future participation in NMD.

In addition to NMD, the US has also been pursuing a parallel Theatre Missile Defense (TMD) program to develop weapons, such as the Patriot missile of Gulf War fame, to protect its overseas forces and its friends and allies against ballistic missile attack. TMD has generally been less controversial than NMD, on which this chapter solely focuses.

FROM SDI TO NMD

For many people, Canadians certainly among them, ballistic missile defence evokes memories of President Ronald Reagan's Strategic

Defense Initiative (SDI) and its sobriquet, 'Star Wars'. During the mid-1980s, SDI was highly controversial in Canada. Unfounded charges were continually hurled at the Mulroney government that through NORAD it was allowing Canadian air defences to be linked to SDI. The Tories, for their part, picked their way carefully around the issue, declaring that while they endorsed SDI research by the US, the Canadian government would not participate in it, although Canadian private companies and citizens were free to do so. With the end of the Cold War, and with it fears of nuclear annihilation, Canada's potential relationship to US missile defences ceased to be a public issue. Many Canadians will no doubt be surprised over the next year or so that not only has ballistic missile defence research continued in the US during the 1990s, but that it now may be ready to bear fruit.

NMD certainly is a lineal descendent of SDI in the US ballistic missile defence research and development program. However, 'NMD is not SDI in disguise' (Fergusson, 1998: 59). The differences between the two are significant. NMD will be much smaller in scope than the vast defences envisaged under SDI, and will also be directed against a different threat.

The SDI research program was driven by Reagan's famous dream of rendering nuclear weapons 'useless and impotent', which he expressed in his March 1983 speech announcing the program's establishment. Thus, its task was to research ways of developing a true strategic shield for the US, capable of blocking an attack by thousands of incoming Soviet missiles with only minimal leakage. It envisaged the eventual deployment of thousands of interceptors, both on the ground and in space. Among them would have been not only 'hit-to-kill' weapons, but potentially also such exotic weapons as space-based particle-beam devices and lasers.

Reagan's successor, George Bush, shifted the focus of US ballistic missile defence research away from such a massive strategic shield for the US and towards limited but global protection, relying on a combination of space- and ground-based interceptors for the US, its forces overseas, and its friends and allies against accidental or unauthorized missile launches. The Clinton administration further downgraded efforts for US missile defences in its early years, funding 'technology readiness' but setting no goals for deployment.

The Republican takeover of Congress in 1994 eventually led to a change of direction by the Clinton administration. Inspired by Reagan,

Republicans have mostly remained firm supporters of missile defence, convinced that American voters would approve of efforts to protect them against nuclear strikes. As promised in their 'Contract with America', the congressional Republicans adopted a bill mandating deployment of a national missile defence by 2003. The President vetoed the bill, but soon sought to co-opt the issue. As a newspaper writer later observed, '[t]he Clinton White House seldom lets a popular parade pass by without leaping to the front, or at least latching onto the last carriage. Clinton has once again joined a popular cause, this time national missile defense' (Broder, 1999). In 1996 the administration devised a so-called '3+3' program, whereby a limited ground-based system would be developed over three years, with deployment to follow in three years if in 2000 it were judged feasible

Republicans grumbled that it was a ruse, that the Democrats had no intention of ever deploying, and that '3+never' would have been a better title. Yet, as Michael O'Hanlon of the Brookings Institution has observed, '[s]upport for the NMD built up in 1998 when both Iran and North Korea surprised the intelligence community with tests that showed rapid progress in their respective missile programs' (O'Hanlon, 1998: 78). During that summer, North Korea tested a multi-stage rocket, the Taepo Dong 1. A special, bipartisan Commission to Assess the Ballistic Missile threat to the United States, headed by former Secretary of Defense Donald Rumsfeld, reported in the summer of 1998:

> Concerted efforts by a number of overtly or potentially hostile nations to acquire ballistic missiles with biological or nuclear payloads pose a growing threat to the United States. . . . These newer, developing threats in North Korea, Iran and Iraq are in addition to those still posed by the existing ballistic missile arsenals of Russia and China. . . . they would be able to inflict major destruction in the US within about five years of a decision to acquire such a capability (10 years in the case of Iraq). During several of those years the US might not be aware that such a decision had been made.
>
> The threat to the US posed by these emerging capabilities is broader, more mature, and evolving more rapidly than has been reported in estimates and reports by the Intelligence Community. (United States, 1998: 2)

Defense Secretary Cohen invoked both the Rumsfeld report and the recent North Korean missile tests in his January 1999 pronouncement that, in the administration's view, NMD deployment was warranted by the threat. At the same time he announced that the deployment date, if authorization were given in 2000, would be pushed back from 2003 to 2005.

While the chief task of the NMD would be to blunt a missile attack by a rogue state, it might also be used to respond to an accidental or unauthorized launch of several missiles from Russia or China. The number of interceptors initially to be deployed in Alaska would only be about 20, rising thereafter to about 100. This means that at first the system should be able to destroy several North Korean missiles and, later, missiles in the low tens, providing protection for all 50 states. Early in the next decade, another 100 interceptors might be deployed, presumably in North Dakota. With this second site and some additional improvements in sensors, NMD should have the ability to deal with a more complex threat, consisting of several tens of warheads, including those with penetration aids, launched from either North Korea or the Middle East.

Unlike the rich mixture of weapons envisaged by SDI, the NMD interceptors will all be both ground-based and 'hit-to-kill'. While the old term 'anti-missile-missile' probably best describes them, they bear the title Ground Based Interceptors (GBI). It is worth emphasizing that the GBIs will not carry nuclear warheads, but will destroy incoming missiles by actually striking them kinetically. Assessing whether they and the associated components of the NMD system are capable of doing so, that is, 'hitting a bullet with a bullet', is the chief object of the tests President Clinton will be considering when he makes his late summer or early fall 2000 decision.

Still, that decision date has been set by politics, not technological developments. Not all the tests will be ready then. So a 'final' decision taken then to deploy could later come undone if subsequent tests show that elements of the system are not ready.

Of the four other major elements of the NMD, three will also be ground-based, namely, upgraded early warning and tracking radars located in Alaska, Greenland, the United Kingdom, and on the east and west coasts of the US; x-band radars capable of guiding the interceptors to target, which will be located in Alaska (and, if interceptors are later located in North Dakota, at a site nearby); and the battle management/command, control, and communications (BM/C3) system, which almost certainly will be located in Colorado Springs, under a command to be determined. The final element of the system will be satellites used to detect missile launches and, when newer satellites become available, to track missile trajectories.

NMD, RUSSIA, AND THE ABM TREATY

NMD would be, as US Undersecretary of Defense Walter B. Slocombe emphasized in a November 1999 speech in Washington, 'fully compatible with the fundamental purpose of the ABM Treaty. That purpose is not to ban defenses altogether—since it does not do that—but to ensure that each party's strategic deterrent is not threatened by the missile defenses of the other party' (Slocombe, 1999). Since Russia still retains thousands of nuclear warheads atop delivery vehicles, its ability to strike at the US would not be compromised by the proposed system's capability to destroy tens of missiles, even if the US were to strike first.

The Russians, for their part, still maintain one local ballistic missile defence system around Moscow. Two such local systems, one to protect a national capital and one to protect missiles, were allowed until a 1974 Soviet-US protocol to the treaty reduced the permissible number from two to one. While the Soviet Union opted to continue to provide protection for its capital, in 1976 the US dismantled the system it briefly had in place in Grand Forks, North Dakota, to protect missiles.

Nonetheless, deploying even just one NMD interceptor site would violate the treaty, which permits only local missiles and prohibits defence of the entire national territory. There are also technical aspects of the NMD system that would not be treaty compliant, such as the upgrading of the existing ground-based radars and the reliance on space-based sensors.

The Russians have rebuffed the efforts of the Clinton administration, formally begun with a January 1999 letter from the President to President Yeltsin, to convince them to agree to amend the ABM Treaty in order to accommodate NMD. Originally, they appeared receptive, accepting that NMD was to be directed not against them but 'rogue' states. Later in the year, though, their tone turned toughly negative. 'There can be no compromise on this issue', said, for example, the first deputy chief of the Russian general staff in the fall (Manilov in Gordon, 1999). They also looked for support in the international community, introducing in the United Nations General Assembly a resolution calling for the preservation and strengthening of the ABM Treaty through 'strict compliance'. The resolution was adopted in December by a vote of 80 in favour, 4 against (the US, Israel, Micronesia, and Albania), and 68 abstentions. Among the majority was none other than North Korea, whose representative declared that his government viewed the ABM Treaty as a 'pillar of stability' (UN, 1999).

The Russians may be bluffing and posturing before finally agreeing. It seems to be a matter of wounded pride and prestige as they attempt to show that, despite their calamitous national decline and their recent humiliating inability to influence the course of events leading up to and during the Kosovo war, they still cannot be pushed around by the one remaining superpower. In that sense, the ABM Treaty is for them a symbol of their world status.

Vestigial paranoia also appears to play a role in Russian thinking about NMD. Russian spokesmen have complained that new missile defences might allow the US to establish in the future clear-cut nuclear superiority with which to coerce Moscow, especially if the US later were to expand its missile defences. While surely this is a misreading of US motivations, the notion that NMD is only a precursor to a much more extensive missile defence 15 or 20 years from now is not fanciful, and is certainly shared by many US missile defence enthusiasts.

When it was signed in 1972, the ABM Treaty was intended to prevent an unbridled offensive-defensive arms race. If it were terminated, there is little chance of such a race today, especially given Russia's penurious condition. However, it apparently would not be beyond Russia's means to expand its nuclear arsenal by placing multiple warheads back onto older missiles or atop missiles of a new type that are planned for deployment. This would undo recent progress in strategic arms reduction.

The Russian Duma has ratified the Strategic Arms Reduction Talks (START) II accord, which should lower the number of Russian strategic nuclear warheads from about 7,000 to about 3,000, with parallel reductions for the US. While the US declined to enter into formal START III negotiations until START II was ratified, START III levels informally agreed upon by the Russian and US administrations would reduce the Russians to 2,000–2,500 warheads.

A petulant Russia might walk away entirely from these deals. As the deputy chief of the Russian general staff also asserted, '[a]ny attempt to withdraw from the 1972 ABM Treaty would destroy the entire system of treaties dealing with the restriction

and reductions of weapons of mass destruction. All these agreements can be implemented on as a single whole' (Manilov in Gordon,
1999).

Throughout 1999, various US officials repeated again and again
that the ABM Treaty was a cornerstone of US policy and that they
ardently hoped and fully expected that the Russians eventually would
agree to its amendment. Nonetheless, the ABM Treaty provides for its
own abrogation by either party if its 'supreme interests' have been
jeopardized. Undersecretary Slocombe warned in his November
speech that 'we will not permit any other country to have a veto on
actions that may be needed for the defense of our nation', specifically adding that if the Russians persisted in refusing to negotiate,
'then the United States will have to face a very difficult question,
which is to withdraw from the treaty' (Slocombe, 1999).

Was he bluffing? It is, of course, impossible to say. Republican
supporters of missile defence fear that he was and worry that if no
agreement with the Russians is reached by the time the President
makes his decision, he will, on arms control grounds, back away
from authorizing NMD deployment. Abrogation of the treaty would
be unpopular with many congressional Democrats, who successfully
attached an amendment to the March 1999 votes on NMD calling for
arms control to be a consideration in the June 2000 decision. The
President might fear, though, that if he backs down on deployment in
the face of Russian intransigence and thus appears soft on defence, he
would threaten Vice-President Gore's chances in the November 2000
elections—assuming Gore is the Democratic nominee. In Washington
it is sometimes joked these days that the main purpose of the NMD
program is not to protect the US against North Korea but Gore against
Republicans.

Two potential outcomes in 2000—abrogation and deployment or
rejection of deployment on arms control grounds—could throw the
NMD issue into the vagaries of both the presidential and congressional
elections. The likely Republican presidential candidate, George W.
Bush, ardently supports NMD—and abrogation, if necessary. Gore,
the Democratic presidential candidate, supports the 1999 approach,
favouring deployment depending on the outcome of the tests and
negotiations with the Russians.

Should the US, in the face of Russian intransigence, decide to
abrogate and deploy, then there are steps Washington could take to
limit the ensuing damage in Russian-American relations, with a view

especially towards encouraging Russia to continue to reduce its strategic nuclear weaponry. It will be important to demonstrate to Moscow that the US has no intent of pursuing nuclear superiority and dominance. One strong possibility would be for the US unilaterally to begin to reduce its forces to the levels set in START II even before Russia ratifies the agreement and then to propose even lower levels for START III, on the order of 1,000 warheads. As has recently been championed by several arms control and weapons experts, the US could also lower the alert of many if not all of its nuclear forces to show that it has no intention of launching a sneak attack through Russia's deteriorating warning system. While both the US and Russia have announced that neither 'targets' the other, retargeting can be fairly swiftly accomplished. Removing warheads from atop missiles would further, and quite demonstrably, reduce alert levels. De-alerting down to the projected START III levels might be an option. The US government could, as well, help finance the repair of the Russian early warning network, especially the replacement of satellites that Russia can no longer afford (O'Hanlon, 1999: 81). Finally, it can be assumed that the US will want to keep on the table offers it made in the fall of 1999 to co-operate with Moscow in the development of a Russian NMD capability to deal with North Korean, Iraqi, and Iranian threats.

CHINA AND NMD

China has also strongly opposed NMD deployment by the US, though its ire is also directed at TMD out of concern that the US might provide Taiwan with missile defences. NMD could effectively negate China's current capability to strike the US with intercontinental ballistic missiles.

China has only a very small inventory of some 20 aging, fixed-site missiles capable of reaching the US. Its strategy has been based on minimum deterrence, that is, hoping that being able to strike an adversary's homeland with just a couple of missiles would give that adversary most serious pause. Since its weapons would be vulnerable in a crisis to attack, the Chinese have plans to replace them with those that would be mobile and easier to launch. How extensive those plans are and whether the Chinese might ever abandon minimum deterrence are the subject of some debate among outside experts. China's apparent theft through espionage more than 10 years ago of the design of the most advanced US miniature nuclear warhead, the W-88, appears to give it the capability to place many modern warheads on missiles.

NMD might very well precipitate an expansion of the Chinese nuclear modernization efforts to the point where the Chinese would regain the certainty that they could strike the US. In so many words, they repeatedly have warned of such a possibility. As the senior Chinese arms control official said in April 1999 when discussing NMD, 'China is not in a position to conduct an arms race with the US and does not intend to do so, particularly in the field of missile defense. However, China will not sit idly by and watch its strategic interests being jeopardized without taking necessary countermeasures' (Sha Zukang, 1999). The Chinese may well also share the suspicion with the Russians that NMD is but a prelude to the construction of a more extensive system.

CANADA AND ABROGATION OF THE ABM TREATY

No one doubts that the Chrétien government, like every Canadian government before it since 1972, firmly supports the ABM Treaty. The real question is what Ottawa will do if the US abrogates it.

With the Clinton administration still asserting that it hopes and expects to achieve an accord with Russia on modifying the treaty, there has been no incentive for the Chrétien government to tip its hand—or even reach a decision—on what it will do in the event of abrogation. Nor has it taken an official position in public on whether the potential North Korean, Iraqi, and Iranian threats to US security warrant NMD deployment. Rather, it has understandably sought shelter in the trite, but undeniably useful, classic diplomatic formulation, '[t]he Government of Canada is closely following these developments but has made no decision' (Department of National Defence, 1999). The government also refused to be drawn into the ABM Treaty drama staged at the UN by Russia, abstaining on the voting. And a November 1999 speech in Boston by the Minister of Foreign Affairs was so carefully formulated in regard to the issue that it forcefully reiterated Canada's strong support for the treaty while seeming to rule nothing else out:

> Respect the ABM Treaty. Both Russia and the US say this is the cornerstone of strategic stability. It should not be undermined with changes that are incompatible with its intent. In the effort to accommodate the possibility of an eventual National Missile Defence, great care should be taken not to dam-

age a system that, for almost 30 years, has underpinned nuclear restraint and allowed for nuclear reductions. (Axworthy, 1999)

The current government, in its 1994 defence White Paper, formally removed the Mulroney government's ban on official Canadian participation in US missile defence research. In small numbers, Canadian defence scientists have been working on missile defence projects within Canada and in the US. As well, Canadians in NORAD have been participants in NMD simulations, which have also been observed by other Canadian officials. But all this provides no real clue as to what Ottawa will decide to do if research turns not only to deployment but to deployment after abrogation.

Like previous governments, the Liberals have made arms control and disarmament a major element of their foreign policy. Their energetic Foreign Minister led what many perceive as a major arms control success, namely the Ottawa Process leading up to the 1997 treaty globally banning anti-personnel mines. He has also launched or helped to launch a number of other arms control initiatives, among them one calling for the North Atlantic Treaty Organization (NATO) to rethink its nuclear options. Canada has been a strong supporter of both Russian-US nuclear weapons accords and multilateral instruments, especially the 1968 Non-Proliferation Treaty and the Comprehensive Nuclear Test Ban Treaty. Axworthy called the test ban treaty's rejection by the US Senate in October 1999 'a significant step backwards—a repudiation of 50 years of US leadership on the nuclear non-proliferation front and a devastating blow to global arms control efforts' (Axworthy, 1999).

Because of Canada's long-standing efforts and Axworthy's apparently very strong feelings about them, it is hard to avoid the conclusion that he would find US abrogation of the ABM Treaty in favour of NMD an all but intolerable jeopardizing of arms control, especially after the US Senate's rejection of the test ban accord. He and the cabinet (the Prime Minister presumably taking a pre-eminent role in the deliberations) might also conclude that Canada's international credibility would be jeopardized if it were to acquiesce in the termination of a treaty it had so long and so ardently supported. Canada might well be in allied company. Most of the European allies, among them the French, the British, and the Germans, have also been sceptical about NMD. This seems to mean that there could be a terrible row within the alliance.

However, the Canadian government would no doubt have to ask itself what the point would be of feuding with the US over the issue, once Washington already had taken the decisive step of terminating the treaty for purposes of its own national defence. Rather than complaining, it would be far more useful for Ottawa to continue to encourage the US to take steps, along the lines of the ones mentioned above, that might assure the Russians that Washington was not intent on strategic superiority. Ottawa would then face the decision of whether to participate in operating the NMD system.

NORAD IN QUESTION

When NORAD was created in 1957 under its original name, the North American Air Defense Command, Canadian air defence efforts and Canadian geography were central to North American security. This is no longer the case. As a result, NORAD today is more important to Canada than Canada is to NORAD.

Canada lay beneath most of the routes Soviet manned bombers would have travelled to strike at the US. Sweeping air defences were put into place. Two vast radar systems and a third detection chain based on alternative technology were stretched across the country, and the Canadian Air Force flew at home no fewer than nine squadrons of fighter aircraft dedicated to continental air defence. It only made sense to place these efforts under the same command as the extensive air defences of the US.

Just as NORAD was getting under way, the Soviet threat began to shift away from the manned bomber and towards the intercontinental and submarine-launched ballistic missile. North American air defences began their long decline, which, interrupted briefly during the early 1980s, continued with the end of the Cold War. Today, they are the palest shadows of earlier efforts. Radars in Canada have been reduced to peripheral coverage in the Arctic (by the North Warning System, successor to the old Distant Early Warning Line) and along the east and west coasts, with practically no military radar coverage in the interior. On a day-to-day basis, only four CF-18 fighter aircraft are kept on alert status in Canada, two in the east and two in the west. Throughout NORAD there are 20 fighters on alert at all times. With these reduced resources, the focus has shifted from air defence to 'air control' over Canadian and US sovereign airspace, in conjunction with civilian air traffic and law enforcement agencies. These limited efforts provide the core around which a somewhat more robust air defence might be reconstituted, if it ever were needed.

While Canadian geography and efforts have declined in importance for North American air defence, they never have held any importance for detecting or tracking ballistic missiles. None of the US missile detection or tracking systems has ever been located in Canada or operated by the Canadian Forces. It might seem as if the US deliberately avoided Canadian territory. But as a glance at a map, or much better, a globe, will show, the Alaskan, Greenland, and UK locations provide better fan coverage towards the former Soviet Union. Sites located on the US east and west coasts provide capability to detect submarine-launched ballistic missiles.

With no Canadian missile detection and tracking systems, and with Canadian air defence efforts having vastly contracted, it might be expected that the Canadian personnel at NORAD have been reduced to an unimportant role. On the contrary, though, NORAD's core function has remained a joint Canada-US responsibility. This is to provide what NORAD calls Integrated Tactical Warning/Attack Assessment (ITWAA). In fact, a much more descriptive, although certainly clumsy name for the command, based on what it does today, would be the 'North American Integrated Tactical Warning/Attack Assessment and Air Control Command'.

To be able to warn of and assess an attack on the continent, a NORAD staff relies on information drawn from the US missile detection and tracking systems and from US and Canadian air surveillance networks. An attack would have to be confirmed by what NORAD calls an 'assessor', who is always a US general or admiral or a Canadian general. Because of the speed of ballistic missiles, time would be short; it would be a matter of minutes between the first detection of incoming missiles and the assessor's being asked to confirm that the continent was under attack.

In 1985 the Pentagon created US Space Command, located it at Colorado Springs, and placed it under the same commander-in-chief as NORAD. It co-ordinates the use of US Air Force, Army, and Navy space assets (including providing NORAD with information on ballistic missile launches and trajectories) and plans for future military use of space. The two commands share facilities, including the famous operations centre deep in Cheyenne Mountain. Reflecting sensitivities at the time on both the Canadian and US sides, US Space Command posts were originally to be limited exclusively to US personnel. But with NORAD and US Space Command working so closely together and with Canadians at the heart of NORAD, many (although still not all) of the restrictions have been lifted in recent years. Today, Canadian Forces personnel will be found in Colorado Springs working in NORAD, US Space Command, and dual NORAD-US Space Command entities.

The US would trust no other ally in a role so intimately linked to its security. It is a bit of a mystery why Canadians have remained so welcome in Colorado Springs when their geography and their direct contributions to North American aerospace defence have so greatly declined in strategic importance to the US. There are several possible explanations. The simplest is that the Canadians have, over the decades, become trusted and liked by their American NORAD partners. The Canadian Forces also tend to send skilled and well-prepared personnel to NORAD, at a time when even the mighty US military is feeling a bit of a personnel pinch. Traditional air defence, while today of very limited importance, still cannot be overlooked entirely and NORAD remains the best way of effecting it. Finally, why should the US change an arrangement that has worked well and has become symbolic of Canada-US co-operation if there is no good reason to do so?

A decision by the government of Canada not to participate in NMD would be just such a reason, since the US military's planning assumption is that the battle management of NMD would be closely linked to ITWAA. In particular, the 'assessor' would be given the additional responsibility of deciding whether to authorize use of the NMD interceptors. This only makes sense, since there would only be minutes available for decision-making. So if Canadian Forces personnel could not be involved in NMD, they also could not fully participate in attack warning and assessment.

IF NORAD ENDS

Structurally, the end of NORAD would be easy to engineer. Arrangements have long existed whereby a US command, today US Space Command, could take over ITWAA. At NORAD's dissolution, should it come to that, the current US Space Command could assume this responsibility permanently, although the US might then take the opportunity to reshuffle further its major command arrangements.

Canada-US air defence co-operation would still be necessary. Conceivably, a small Canada-US air defence command could be created, which would also provide information to US Space Command or whichever US command had been given ITWAA. It might even continue to bear the NORAD name in order to smooth over the rupture. But such an air defence command would hardly be necessary; the sorts of close Canada-US air defence co-operation that existed before 1957 without a joint command would do.

Since the US pays about 90 per cent of NORAD's costs, it might appear that its dissolution would oblige Canada to spend a lot of money to create and operate new command and control structures of its own. But this really would not be the case. In fact, for Canada there probably would be short-term budgetary savings arising from NORAD's demise, since Canada's role would be reduced to conducting air defence operations. For these, there already are adequate command and control facilities at the current 1 Canadian Air Division Headquarters located in Winnipeg (which now also is the headquarters of the Canadian NORAD Region), along with the underground Sector Air Operations Centre at North Bay, Ontario.

In fact, to stay in NORAD might actually cost the Canadian government some additional money. In all probability, the US would not expect Canada to help pay for NMD, but it might expect Canada to make what is being called by Canadian defence officials an 'asymmetric contribution' to some other aspect of North American aerospace defence that the US might value. The Canadian military has also identified an area in which Canada might make such a new contribution: surveillance of space. Canada might become what a policy paper calls a 'full partner' in the US Space Command's Space Surveillance Network, which tracks all objects in orbit around the earth. It serves several functions, not the least of which is warning of objects whose orbits have decayed and that are about to enter the atmosphere. It can also be used to warn when spy satellites are overhead. Space surveillance was a Canadian speciality in NORAD until the 1980s, when new technology rendered obsolete sensors located at Cold Lake, Alberta, and St Margaret's, New Brunswick. The Canadian military hopes to reinvigorate this capability (Department of National Defence, 1998).

Nonetheless, there could also be real, longer-term costs to Canada if the most important structure in the Canada-US defence relationship were dissolved (in essence, if not in name), potentially beginning with limitations on Canada's future military capabilities. Space is increasingly important to the military. The Canadian Forces have a lengthy (and expensive) list of space capabilities they wish to acquire simply to support the army, navy, and air force in modern tactical environments. These include communications, navigation, search and rescue, intelligence, weather, and mapping projects. To achieve much of these, co-operation with the US is key. As James Fergusson of the University of Manitoba argued in a comprehensive 1998 study of NMD commissioned by the Department of Foreign Affairs and International Trade, NORAD, especially because of its siamese-twin relationship to US Space Command, is critical for enhancing Canadian access to US space projects and space-based assets. Thus, if Ottawa declines to participate in NMD, 'it is difficult to see how Canada could continue to participate in other key space-related activities in a joint way with the United States. . . . In other words, Canada's future involvement in space may be at issue, with a wide range of possible political and budgetary implications' (Fergusson, 1998: 70). There would also be some ripple effects into other areas of Canada-US relations, beyond the military sphere. At the very least, the bilateral defence economic relationship, recently so badly roiled by differences over certification rules and the capacity of Canadian companies to bid on US defence contracts, probably would become shakier as it became harder to justify special exemptions for Canadian firms.

Canadian influence in Washington would decline. Great care has to be taken not to exaggerate here, for the influence argument has tended to be overstated since NORAD's very beginning and it has sometimes led to Canadian disappointment. As famously discovered by Prime Minister John Diefenbaker during the 1962 Cuban Missile Crisis, a scant five years after he agreed to NORAD's creation, the pledges made in the NORAD agreement for the two countries to consult can mean little in a true emergency. It would also be very difficult and probably impossible to identify any fundamental aspect of the US defence posture that, over the years, has been altered by Canada's exerting influence through NORAD.

With or without NORAD, through NATO Canada would be a member of the Western alliance with a seat at the table. Canada-US defence co-operation, including on air defence, would also continue. Still, it is hard to avoid the conclusion that if NORAD were to go, Canada's long-term standing as a close ally whose views on matters of international security needed to be listened to and whose interests needed to be given most serious consideration would diminish, and not just with the US military but also with the State Department, intelligence agencies, senior administration officials, and members of Congress. Washington might not be piqued or miffed at Canada, unless, of course, Ottawa tried to lead a crusade to denounce NMD and the abrogation of the ABM Treaty. The two governments probably would work hard to smooth over any short-term symbolic damage the end of NORAD might cause. But over the years, Canada would not count quite as much with the US government and so would not be viewed in quite the same fashion.

Canada's global standing could also be affected, the same caution about exaggeration being kept in mind. Some countries might be impressed with Canada's having loosened a security tie with the US. Others, especially those in NATO, would not, knowing that Canada had lost the most important part of its special security relationship with the US, which had provided it with uniquely intimate access to and knowledge of the US defence establishment.

CONCLUSION

The NMD issue might not lead to differences between Washington and Ottawa after all, at least not for the next several years. There certainly are plenty of possibilities. (1) Russia may at the last minute agree to an amendment to the ABM Treaty. This would free the Canadian government to swallow whatever doubts it may have about the necessity of deploying an NMD system to respond to North Korean, Iraqi, and Iranian threats and also allow Ottawa to act to preserve NORAD. (2) The NMD tests scheduled for 2000 may fail, allowing the President to put off deployment, although in such a case no one in Canada should think that US missile defence efforts then will just go away. (3) President Clinton might decide that preserving the treaty is more important than NMD, although here, too, the issue will not, under Republican pressure, go away. (4) Finally, Canadians and their government might even come to agree with the US administration that since NMD does not threaten the intent of the ABM Treaty, it is not reasonable to give Russia a veto over actions needed for the defence of the US. They might even come to the conclusion that defending North America against missile attacks by countries such as North Korea, Iran, and Iraq is not such a bad idea.

In recent years we have grown steadily used to the increasing integration of Canada and the US, especially in terms of the bilateral economic relationship. This integration is reflected in many of the other chapters of this volume. For purposes of defence, though, geography no longer ties Canada and the US quite as closely together as in the past; in the case of NORAD, a measure of institutional disintegration is conceivable. If the outcome over the coming year or so is abrogation of the ABM Treaty and deployment of NMD over the continuing objections of not just Russia but of Canada, the Canada-US relationship will be strained. Perhaps then some satisfaction is to be had for both Canadians and Americans in that both countries will be free to choose on this matter, each according to its priorities.

NOTE

1. The decision may be slightly delayed but will be taken prior to the November 2000 election.

REFERENCES

Axworthy, Lloyd. 1999. 'Notes for An Address by the Hon. Lloyd Axworthy to Accept the Endicott Peabody Award', Boston, 22 Oct., Department of Foreign Affairs and International Trade, Statements and Speeches 95/54.

Broder, John M. 1999. 'Clinton's Flip-Flop, President's Reversal on Missile Bill Denies G.O.P. Foes a Campaign Issue', *New York Times*, 18 Mar., A22.

Byers, Richard B. 1999. 'Statement of General Richard B. Mayers before the Senate Armed Service Committee, Strategic Forces Subcommittee on Military Space Programs', US Space Command, 22 Mar.

Department of National Defence. 1998. 'A Canadian Military Space Strategy', Directorate of Space Development, 21 Apr., Ottawa.

———. 1999. 'Canada's Policy on Ballistic Missile Defence', 19 Aug., Backgrounder BG-99,055. Ottawa.

Fergusson, James. 1998. 'Canada and Ballistic Missile Defence: Issues, Implications, and Timelines', Department of Foreign Affairs and International Trade, Non-proliferation, Arms Control and Disarmament Division, Ottawa.

Gordon, Michael R. 1999. 'Russians Firmly Reject U.S. Plan to Reopen ABM Treaty', *New York Times*, 21 Oct., A3.

Isaacs, John. 1999. 'Missile Defense: It's Back', *Bulletin of the Atomic Scientist* (May-June): 26–8.

O'Hanlon, Michael. 1999. 'Star Wars Strikes Back', *Foreign Affairs* 76, 6 (Nov.-Dec.): 68–82.

Sha Zukang. 1999. 'Can BMD Really Enhance Security?', Remarks by the Ambassador, Director-General, Department of Arms Control and Disarmament, Ministry of Foreign Affairs of the P.R. of China at the Second U.S.-China Conference on Arms Control, Disarmament and Nonproliferation, Monterey, Calif.: Center for Nonproliferation Studies, Monterey Institute of International Studies, Apr.: cns.miis.edu/cns/projects/eano/conf/uschina2/report.htm#remarks

Slocombe, Walter B. 1999. 'National Missile Defence Policy', Remarks by the Undersecretary for Defence Policy at the 'Statesmen's Forum', Center for Strategic and International Studies, 5 Nov., Washington.

United Nations, General Assembly. 1999. Press Release GA/9675, 1 Dec.

United States, Commission to Assess the Ballistic Missile Threat to the United States. 1998. 'Executive Summary of the Report', 15 July.

5

The Role of Dispute Settlement in Managing Canada-US Trade and Investment Relations

MICHAEL HART

Relations between Canada and the United States seem, once again, to be going through a period of strain. The forces unleashed by deepening integration are adding to the ever-present challenge of managing relations between the lone remaining superpower and its closest neighbour. Despite the fact that the US economy is firing on all cylinders, many Americans remain besieged by self-doubt about their role in the world and their capacity to lead and compete. A bumbling Clinton administration, unsure of the direction in which it wants to take US foreign trade and economic policy, closed out the year by presiding over its third trade policy failure in as many years. Following its inability to gain fast-track trade negotiating authority in 1996–7, and its throwing in the towel on the ill-fated multilateral investment negotiations at the Organization for Economic Co-operation and Development) (OECD) in 1998–9, it proved incapable of brokering the successful launch of a new round of multilateral trade negotiations at Seattle in December (see Chapter 16 by Curtis and Wolfe in this volume). More ominously, few pundits and opinion moulders in the United States seem overly concerned with these signs of faltering international economic policy leadership.

For Canadians, increasingly dependent on bilateral trade and investment—annual two-way trade and investment flows are now equivalent to nearly three-quarters of Canada's total gross domestic product—these developments appear worrying. Nevertheless, unlike during previous bouts of US parochialism, newspaper stories over the past few years suggest surprisingly few lingering conflicts. More than a hundred Canada-US trade stories can be found in a quick perusal of Canadian newspaper indexes for the period May 1998 through March 1999, but they largely revolve around a few familiar issues. US restrictions on Canadian exports of softwood lumber and US complaints about Canadian restrictions on advertising in split-run periodicals take pride of place. In addition, there are stories about state troopers harassing Canadian truckers carrying farm exports in the Dakotas, about state restrictions on the sale of Canadian beer, about the US initiating a countervailing duty on Canadian beef, and about fallout from the World Trade Organization (WTO) panel decision regarding Canadian subsidies on exports, and restrictions on imports, of dairy products.

Other news sources, such as InfoGlobe-Dow Jones and *Inside US Trade,* while providing perhaps more in-depth and specialized coverage, do not materially change the impression of relative tranquility in Canada-US trade and economic relations. That tranquility, of course, may only reflect good economic times. Should the current nine-year economic expansion in the United States weaken or end, Canadians may be reminded once again of how ugly US trade politics can become, how much Canada relies on good rules and procedures to keep US protectionism in check, and how the increasing sophistication and reliability of those rules and procedures have provided Canada with the capacity to resist US protectionist pressures.

For both Canada and the United States, but particularly for Canada, binding dispute settlement procedures are proving their worth in managing relations between the two countries. Considerable negotiating coin was used by Canada in the Canada-United States Free Trade Agreement (FTA), the North American Free Trade Agreement (NAFTA), and the WTO negotiations in order to strengthen dispute settlement procedures by making access more automatic, ensuring the independence of panellists, making panel rulings more binding, providing the process with greater institutional support, and otherwise establishing rules and procedures that would help to reduce the disparity in power between Canada and its major trading partner. In all three instances—FTA, NAFTA, and WTO—Canada claimed that the dispute settlement procedures had greatly strengthened the rule of law in relations between Canada and the United States.

The record of the past decade seems to justify this confidence in rules and dispute settlement procedures. While there may be problems in the relationship, they do not stem from failure to address and resolve the day-to-day irritants of the rapidly growing trade and investment flows. Canada has benefited from a more principled approach to resolving conflict. This chapter looks at the record of the past decade, examines the extent to which dispute settlement has made a difference, and considers whether additional efforts along the same lines would pay further dividends.

CONTRASTING VALUES AND PERCEPTIONS

As Andrew Cooper and Christopher Sands illustrate in Chapters 2 and 3, Canada and the United States may share a common heritage, but their forms of government are fundamentally different, and these differences give rise to tensions and conflicts that casual observers of the relationship sometimes have difficulty understanding. These differences tend to be accentuated in trade relations because of the competitive or adversarial nature of trade and the artificial intrusion of borders into what are essentially transactions between private parties. Objectionable behaviour within a country is applauded when it involves an international transaction. Economic nationalism may not be theoretically sound, but it is a creed to live by and, intuitively, most politicians live by it. As a result, governments are often prepared to champion the interests of their own producers at the expense of foreign producers, even in matters that clearly suggest that broader societal interests are being sacrificed.

The US separation of powers accentuates this internationally antisocial behaviour. The assignment of the trade policy-making authority to Congress virtually ensures that US policy will be more attuned to narrow rather than broad interests and will be more adversarial than is the case for most other countries. International trade rules and institutions and the trade agreements negotiated under their auspices seek to curb these natural tendencies. They seek to reduce discrimination, but they always represent an uphill struggle. Even though the United States has long been a leader in the negotiation of international trade rules that seek to make national trade policies less discriminatory and more liberal, US politicians, particularly in Congress, consistently characterize such rules as stacked against US interests and seek ways to neutralize their impact.

It is thus not difficult to appreciate why there is sometimes conflict between Canada and the United States and why such conflicts can be very confrontational. Most Canada-US trade disputes, of course, are not between Canada and the United States but between private parties in Canada and the United States. They may involve government programs or policies, as in a subsidy or countervailing duty case, or they may involve governments as champions of their producers, as in antidumping cases.[1] Bilateral trade disputes may require that the government take sides on an issue in which there are conflicting interests within Canada, for example, between producers and consumers. In all such cases, it is important not to confuse the vigorous defence of specific interests in a dispute with a country's broader public policy interests. Like conscientious lawyers, governments will vigorously defend domestic firms or policies, but a loss does not necessarily mean a loss for the country as a whole.

Conflict, of course, can be regarded as a healthy sign of a dynamic relationship. In a tough, competitive world, individuals, firms, industries, and countries will work hard to gain and maintain advantage. It is not unusual in such circumstances to see conflict. At any one time, dozens of issues may be disputed by Canadians and Americans and defended or pursued by their governments. The fact that there is a border between the two countries staffed by customs agents, for example, is often enough to spark a conflict. What is surprising is not that there are conflicts, but that relatively few are so controverted and difficult as to require formal dispute resolution mechanisms.

Canadians, traditionally, have not liked this adversarial approach to bilateral issues. They prefer a more consensual approach. The parliamentary system of responsible government concentrates tremendous authority in the executive, which is thus much better equipped to negotiate international trade agreements and to address problems in international trade relations. As a result, Canada has shown a strong preference for quiet rather than public diplomacy.

Given that conflicts are likely to be addressed aggressively between Canada and the United States, the challenge is to ensure that appropriate substantive rules and procedures are in place to allow such conflicts to be resolved on the basis of law and due process rather than on the basis of power and the entrenched interests of the moment. That challenge has been the thrust of Canadian trade policy for the past 60-plus years, still more so as the US decision-making process has become more and more fragmented and unpredictable.

THE RULES

Any system of rules or laws starts with substantive rights and obligations. The international trading regimes set out in the WTO, NAFTA, and other agreements involve hundreds of pages of detailed rules governing the exchange of goods, services, capital, and technology and agreed-upon exceptions to those rules. These rules have become increasingly more reliable as a result of the evolution of procedures for the settlement of disputes. In effect, the procedures help to bring the rest of the rules together into a coherent and enforceable whole.

Over the years, governments have experimented with a variety of techniques to help them resolve conflicts and ensure compliance with international agreements. These techniques can be classified as follows:

- transparency: provisions that ensure all applicable rules and procedures are known to traders, investors, and other governments reduce opportunities for misunderstandings and arbitrary behaviour;
- consultations: provisions for notification, consultation, and negotiation facilitate efforts by the parties to resolve disputes themselves;
- objective support: procedures involving third-party good offices, fact-finding, and inquiry may help the parties to a dispute find a basis for its resolution;
- mediation: procedures providing for third-party mediation and conciliation between parties to the dispute can provide a basis for finding a mutually acceptable resolution;

- adjudication: provisions setting out mandatory procedures for third-party arbitration and adjudication ensure that difficult issues can be resolved.

As the role of international trade and investment in national economies has grown and rules have expanded and become more detailed and intrusive, governments have increasingly seen benefit in procedures that go beyond simple consultative or objective support models to mediation and even adjudication. Because these have greater implications for the exercise of national political autonomy, they tend to be more difficult to negotiate and to assume an increasingly larger role in negotiations.

Where governments have been prepared to go further than consultative arrangements, they are more likely to do so on the basis of substantive rules. Dispute resolution without such rules is a mug's game because there is no mutually accepted basis for conciliation, arbitration, or adjudication. Conversely, rules without an effective mechanism to resolve disputes about their interpretation and application are less likely to inspire confidence and create a stable trading environment. The importance of both good rules and good procedures is well illustrated by Canada's experience this decade in addressing US complaints about exports of durum wheat and the operations of the Canadian Wheat Board. After a series of studies in 1992–3 failed to find any basis for addressing US producer complaints under existing US trade laws, American officials used the threat of legislative action to strong-arm Canada into restraining exports of durum wheat in 1993–4. Canadian authorities agreed because international rules governing trade in agricultural products were weak. US efforts to maintain the restraints failed the following year in the face of Canadian intransigence. The successful implementation of the WTO, its Agreement on Agriculture, and its improved dispute settlement procedures provided Canada with the rules and the procedures to resist US pressure tactics.

The General Agreement on Tariffs and Trade (GATT), the basic international trade agreement from 1948 through 1994, provided a fairly simple framework of procedures to help governments resolve conflicts. In addition to the transparency requirements laid out in Article X and the consultation provisions of Article XXII—both aimed more at dispute avoidance than dispute settlement—Article XXIII set out procedures giving parties the right to complain and seek redress when others failed to live up to their obligations. Over the years, GATT members experimented with varying techniques to make these provisions operative and by the late 1970s these had settled into an accepted pattern of customary practice. These procedures worked reasonably well except that they were based more on convention than established obligations, and they required consensus at every decision point.[2]

The FTA, NAFTA, and WTO negotiations all provided opportunities to build on the GATT experience and codify it into a more binding and transparent set of procedures geared to ensuring full compliance with the rights and obligations set out in the rest of the GATT agreement. For Canada and the United States, these three sets of negotiations provided critical opportunities to ensure that the rules governing their intensifying trade and economic relationship would function to their mutual benefit.

The FTA/NAFTA Dispute Settlement Rules and Procedures

In general, the FTA provided a code of conduct for the two governments in their regulation of both private firm behaviour and their own economic policies. It covered trade in all goods and most services as well as many investment transactions and most business travel. The most extensive obligations covered trade in goods and included obligations regarding tariffs, rules of origin, quotas, customs procedures, safeguards, unfair trade remedies, government procurement, national treatment, technical barriers, and exceptions.

In the two chapters setting out the procedures for the settlement of disputes, an effort was made to build a basis for a more ambitious agreement for the future, particularly in the chapter devoted to settling disputes involving trade remedies. The general dispute settlement chapter (18) established a range of institutional obligations to avoid and settle all but disputes between the parties related to trade remedies and financial services. They included:

- mandatory notification of any measure affecting trade and investment;
- compulsory provision of information to the other party on request regarding any measure, whether or not it had been notified;
- consultations at the request of either party concerning any measure or any other matter affecting the operation of the

Agreement, with a view to arriving at a mutually satisfactory resolution;

- referral to a Canada-United States Trade Commission, should resolution through consultations fail; and
- use of dispute settlement procedures should the Commission fail to arrive at a mutually satisfactory resolution.

The dispute settlement procedures included:

- compulsory arbitration, binding on both parties, for disputes arising from the interpretation and application of the safeguards provision;
- binding arbitration in all other disputes where both parties agree; and
- panel recommendations to the Commission, which, in turn, is mandated to agree on a resolution of the dispute.

Special provisions for the resolution of disputes related to the application of trade remedies were set out in Chapter 19. Producers in both countries continued to have the right to seek redress from dumped or subsidized imports, but any relief granted could be challenged and reviewed by a binational panel that would determine whether domestic laws were applied correctly and fairly. Such bilateral panels took on the judicial review function of the Court of International Trade in the United States and the Federal Court in Canada. Canadian producers who had complained that political pressures in the United States disposed US officials to side with complainants could, on the basis of these procedures, appeal to a binational panel. Findings by a panel would be binding on both governments. Should the panel determine that the law was properly applied, the matter was closed. If it found that the administering authority (the Department of Commerce or the International Trade Commission in the United States or the Department of National Revenue or the Canadian International Trade Tribunal in Canada) erred on the basis of the same standards as would have been applied by a domestic court, it could send the issue back to the administering authority to correct the error and make a new determination.

The provisions of both Chapter 18 and Chapter 19 are carried forward into the NAFTA as Chapters 20 and 19, respectively—with some relatively minor but interesting improvements and modifications. In addition, NAFTA adds innovative new procedures to settle disputes between foreign investors and host governments in Chapter 11—the investment chapter. In cases of conflict with a host government, investors may take their disputes to international arbitration for resolution. A panel of three arbitrators, one picked by the complaining investor, one picked by the responding government, and a chair selected jointly, will hear such investor-state disputes. In the event the disputants cannot agree on an arbitrator, the Secretary-General of the International Centre for the Settlement of Investment Disputes (ICSID) serves as the appointing authority. For Canada, enforcement of arbitration awards takes place under the New York Convention (the UN Convention on the Recognition and Enforcement of Foreign Arbitral Awards, signed at New York on 10 June 1958). In addition, disputes relating to investment measures can also be resolved through the state-to-state dispute settlement procedures contained in Chapter 20.[3]

WTO Basic Obligations and Procedures

The Uruguay Round of GATT negotiations (1986–93) provided a further opportunity for Canada and the United States, together with the rest of the international trade community, to build on the GATT experience and codify GATT practice into a detailed set of rights and obligations. The result can be found in the Understanding on Rules and Procedures Governing the Settlement of Disputes (DSU) annexed to the agreement establishing the new World Trade Organization. The WTO provides the organizational framework within which members can pursue rights and obligations set out in three main agreements: an amended General Agreement on Tariffs and Trade, dubbed the GATT 1994, a new General Agreement on Trade in Services (GATS), and a new Agreement on Trade-Related Intellectual Property Rights (TRIPs).

The DSU is an integral part of the single undertaking that establishes the WTO and its constituent agreements. The dispute settlement provisions set out in the DSU, as well as in some of the agreements, can be summarized as follows:

- Governments are required to make their laws and policies publicly available so that traders, investors, and other governments can find all necessary information about rules and procedures that affect trade and investment.

- Every member has the right to consult with any other member on any matter, and every member is obliged to listen 'sympathetically' to the concerns of any other member. The purpose of such consultations is to try to resolve any matter in dispute between members on an amicable basis.
- Dispute settlement procedures can only be triggered by members in response to the failure of other members to implement their obligations, in response to members' taking action inconsistent with their obligations, or in response to members' otherwise 'nullifying or impairing' anticipated benefits. The GATT procedures were originally envisaged as ensuring a balance of rights and obligations: failure to act or acting inconsistently might upset the balance, and successful dispute settlement would restore the balance. Balance remains important as an underlying principle of the WTO, but the DSU places it on a much firmer, more judicial footing. Under WTO Article XVI:4, each member has a positive obligation 'to ensure the conformity of its laws, regulations and administrative procedures with its obligations as provided in the annexed Agreements.'
- If consultations do not resolve an issue, any member can ask the Dispute Settlement Body to appoint a panel to resolve the issue by establishing facts and determining applicable rules and thus help the members as a whole in making a finding. Other members with an interest in the issue may participate in panel proceedings as third parties. The rules seek to conclude proceedings within a year from the establishment of a panel. Throughout, the panel has the assistance of legal advice from the Secretariat and works closely with officials from the involved parties to ensure that it has a clear understanding of the facts and the legal issues involved. The report of the panel is circulated to members and is adopted unless a dissatisfied party to the dispute can organize a consensus to reject the report.
- A dissatisfied party to a dispute can request that the report of a panel be reviewed by a permanent Appellate Body on matters of law and interpretation. Findings by the Appellate Body are final.
- The purpose of WTO dispute settlement is to resolve problems between a complaining member and a defending member and thus ensure that members' laws and policies are in compliance with the rules of the WTO and its constituent agreements. Panel

procedures provide a basis for the members as a whole to help the members in dispute resolve a problem between them on the basis of the rules of the agreement. Throughout the dispute settlement process, procedures aim to bring the issue being litigated to a mutually satisfactory conclusion. To that end, for example, members can also seek the good offices of the Director General to appoint a mediator to help resolve an issue.

- Members are expected to implement findings by a panel or the Appellate Body and, where appropriate, to take such steps as may be necessary to bring their laws and regulations into conformity with the WTO as determined by the panel within a reasonable period of time (considered to be within 15 months of the adoption of the panel's or Appellate Body's report).

These procedures have now been tested for five years and, on the whole, have proven their value. During the course of a substantive review conducted by WTO members over the course of 1998–9, members agreed that there was room for improvement in a number of areas, many of which are likely to be considered during the next round of multilateral negotiations, but there was also broad consensus that the system was working well.[4] As of the end of 1999, members had raised 144 matters for consideration under the DSU's procedures; 32 cases were active; 26 had been completed; and 39 matters had been settled or were inactive.[5] Canada and the United States have been among the most active participants in the process, either as litigants or as third parties.

THE BILATERAL RECORD

Over the past decade Canada and the United States have both made extensive use of the full range of dispute settlement procedures available to them, including consultations that were held pursuant to these provisions but that did not lead to panel proceedings. The availability of panel proceedings often has a salutary effect on consultations and helps them to reach mutually satisfactory conclusions. While it would be difficult to demonstrate specific instances in which the existence of binding panel procedures has led to resolution of an issue on the basis of consultations alone, the impression of officials in both capitals certainly confirms the view that the existence of such procedures has a prophylactic effect.

The availability of these improved procedures has led to a marked reduction in the number of festering bilateral issues and an increase in the number of conflicts resolved on the basis of mutually accepted rules. These circumstances help to explain the current relative tranquility in bilateral trade and investment relations. In the 41 years between the entry into force of the GATT and the entry into force of the FTA, Canada and the United States made sparing use—12 times—of the dispute settlement provisions of the GATT, in large part because Canadian governments had more confidence in their capacity to settle on the basis of consultation than litigation. Since 1989, Canada and the United States have used the general litigation procedures of the GATT/WTO and FTA/NAFTA Chapters 18 and 20 a total of 17 times and have used the more specialized provisions of Chapter 19 a total of 55 times. By any measure, this frequency suggests a very high level of mutual confidence, even if some cases end up creating temporary political discomfort and other cases, such as softwood lumber, prove too difficult to resolve.

From a Canada-US relations perspective, what counts is the extent to which the two governments have been prepared to live with the results of the dispute settlement process, regardless of whether their point of view has prevailed. The record to date suggests a remarkable level of acceptance and compliance.

FTA/NAFTA Chapter 19

FTA Chapter 19 introduced innovative procedures allowing binational panels to review the application of domestic law in trade remedy cases, in effect substituting binational panel review for judicial review of US and Canadian administrative tribunals. As indicated in Table 5.1, over the course of the five years that the FTA was in force, i.e., until its replacement by NAFTA, some 30 cases were reviewed under Chapter 19 procedures. In addition, the United States launched three extraordinary challenge procedures of determinations by Chapter 19 binational panels (pork, live swine, and lumber).[6]

Canada and the United States were generally pleased with the way Chapter 19 operated. As a result, NAFTA made it a permanent feature of the agreement and extended it to Mexico. Since its entry into force on 1 January 1994, the pace has slowed somewhat, as have the number of bilateral antidumping and countervailing duty cases. Nevertheless, to the end of 1999, the two countries had used NAFTA Chapter 19 proceedings to review 25 cases. Neither Canada nor the

Table 5.1

US and Canadian Resort to FTA/NAFTA Chapter 19, 1989–1999

	Reviews of US determinations	Reviews of Cdn determinations
FTA 1989–93		
Antidumping	8	4
Subsidies/countervail	6	–
Injury	5	7
Extraordinary challenge procedures	3	–
NAFTA 1994–9		
Antidumping	10	5
Subsidies/countervail	2	–
Injury	–	8
Extraordinary challenge procedures	–	–

Source: www.nafta-sec-alena.org/english/index.htm

United States used the extraordinary challenge proceedings under NAFTA during this period.

Over the course of a decade of cases, panels sustained some decisions by administrative tribunals and remanded others, seeking either clarification or stronger justification for the decision rendered or, in the absence of justification, determining that the decision be vacated. Experts reviewing the reasoning in such cases have generally agreed that three- or five-person panels, familiar with the economic and legal concepts, have performed their tasks ably and professionally and often more thoroughly than had been the case by the domestic courts. With the exception of the celebrated dissent by Judge Malcolm Wilkie from the majority decision of an Extraordinary Challenge (EC) panel dealing with softwood lumber, Chapter 19 cases have raised little controversy and been widely accepted. Judge Wilkie's dissent in the softwood lumber decision gained extra cogency because the luck of the draw provided that each of the three EC panels was made up of two Canadian judges and one US judge. As noted below, however, the charge of national bias has no foundation in fact. The other two EC panels reached unanimous conclusions. William Davey concludes that Judge Wilkie's reasoning had little merit (Davey, 1996: 225–50).[7]

The US challenges of three panel determinations under the FTA's extraordinary challenge procedures, all of which were dismissed, must be understood as illustrative of the political difficulty faced by US authorities in rejecting an available channel of appeal. In the United States, as long as litigants are unhappy and a channel of appeal exists, there is likely to be an appeal unless it has been clearly demonstrated that the chances of success are marginal at best. The three challenges involved countervailing duty cases on pork, swine, and softwood lumber, all high-profile cases brought forward by politically powerful industries. In all three cases, the US Trade Representatives, Clayton Yeutter and Carla Hills, were unprepared to face the wrath of Congress and three powerful industries without having demonstrated a willingness to exhaust all possible remedies.

From a Canadian perspective, US use of the challenge procedures proved beneficial because the three-judge panels in all three cases ended up setting a very high standard that appellants must satisfy. The decisions confirmed what for Canada had been the purpose of the procedure: a safety valve in cases of aberrant decisions or tainted panels; they were not meant to be used as a routine form of appeal. For Canada, this was a highly satisfactory result in ensuring that dispute settlement procedures would play their role in depoliticizing the management and resolution of conflict, an objective the US shares in the abstract but has difficulty applying in specific instances. As noted, none of the 25 Chapter 19 cases pursued under NAFTA since 1994 has been appealed to an EC panel.

US critics of Chapter 19, including Judge Wilkie, have charged that the process is unsatisfactory because it allows foreign nationals to determine how US laws should be administered. They also charge that the bias of foreign participants in favour of their own litigants, as well as their lack of knowledge of US law and procedure, has tainted and discredited the process. While the first criticism is, of course, correct and forms the basis of the Chapter 19 procedures, the second charge is wholly without foundation. Of the 69 Chapter 18/20 and Chapter 19 panel decisions involving Canada and the United States rendered by the middle of 1999, only two involved a determination split along national lines, both involving softwood lumber. Fifty-four panels made their determinations unanimously. The remaining 13 panels involved dissent by one or two panellists, with all decisions involving majorities of mixed national origin (Stevenson, 2000).

By any measure, the process has demonstrated a very high level of professionalism and lack of bias and, with the exception of a small number of high-profile cases discussed further below, has succeeded in resolving disputes on a more principled, less political basis. For the smaller, less powerful partner, this is a highly desirable outcome.

FTA Chapter 18/NAFTA Chapter 20
Chapter 18 of the FTA (replaced by Chapter 20 in NAFTA) provides the general dispute settlement provisions of the agreement. Modelled on procedures developed under the GATT, but with a number of important innovations aimed at making the procedures more certain and credible, Chapter 18/20 provides the basis for resolving complaints arising from conflicting interpretations of the agreement.

Canada and the United States used the FTA procedures five times over the course of the five years that the FTA was in force: three times by Canada and twice by the United States. In all five cases the procedures succeeded in settling the dispute (see box below). In addition, Canada and the United States used the FTA's consultation provisions to resolve a number of other issues on a basis that fell short of formal panel proceedings.

Since the entry into force of NAFTA, Canada and the United States have used the revised provisions of Chapter 20 only once. The United States complained that Canadian tariffication of import quotas on supply-managed dairy and poultry products implemented pursuant to the WTO Agreement on Agriculture was inconsistent with Canada's NAFTA obligations. The complaint was dismissed by a panel of five law school professors. The United States expressed deep disappointment but accepted the verdict. At the same time, it has vowed to continue to keep the heat on Canada to make changes in policies protecting its dairy and poultry sectors and has successfully challenged some aspects of these policies at the WTO.

Similar to the experience with Chapter 19, panels under Chapter 18/20 have proven highly professional. Both governments have exercised care in picking qualified, able, and experienced individuals to serve on panels and have provided them with sufficient resources to hire staff to support their efforts. The issues in most of the cases raised difficult points of law and policy and required a sophisticated understanding of both, as well as a capacity to develop reasoning that would ensure acceptance of the decisions rendered. The use of experienced former officials and law school professors has invested the process with a high degree of credibility. The decisions rendered, however, have not been without controversy. Canada was deeply disappointed in the lobster decision, convinced that it had a good case. Similarly, US officials were confident that they would prevail in the dairy and poultry supply management case. In both instances, however, governments accepted the decision of the panel, thereby clearly signalling their determination to live with the results of the process.

Canada-United States Trade Dispute Settlement Cases, 1989–1999

1989	FTA	US complaint regarding salmon and herring landing requirements—sustained and settled following further consultations.
	FTA	Canadian complaint regarding US lobster size restrictions—dismissed.
	GATT	Canadian complaint concerning the imposition of countervailing duties by the United States on imports of fresh, chilled, and frozen pork from Canada—sustained and implemented.
1990	GATT	US complaint regarding the import, distribution, and sale of certain alcoholic drinks by provincial marketing agencies—sustained in large measure, and required changes largely implemented.
1991	FTA	Canadian complaint regarding US application of automotive rules of origin (Honda engines)—sustained and the offending practice rescinded and then clarified during NAFTA negotiations.
	GATT	Canadian complaint regarding measures affecting the distribution and sale of alcoholic and malt beverages in the United States—sustained in large measure, but not yet fully implemented.
	GATT	US complaint about a Canadian countervailing duty case involving grain corn—sustained and the offending measure withdrawn.
	GATT	Canadian complaint regarding US initiation of a countervailing duty involving imports of softwood lumber from Canada—sustained in part and implemented.
1992	FTA	US complaint regarding Canadian subsidies on exports of wheat (pricing and other practices of the Canadian Wheat Board)—dismissed.
	FTA	Canadian complaint regarding Puerto Rican standards affecting imports of UHT milk (ultra-high temperature) from Canada—sustained and the offending practice rescinded.
	GATT	US complaint regarding antidumping duties on beer imported into British Columbia—suspended.

1995   NAFTA   US complaint that Canadian tariffication of supply-managed commodities (dairy and poultry products) was not required by the WTO Agriculture Agreement and was inconsistent with Canada's NAFTA obligations—dismissed.

1996   WTO   US complaint regarding Canadian measures affecting the importation and distribution of split-run periodicals—sustained and upheld by the Appellate Body; the panel ruling provided the basis for a negotiated settlement of the issue.

1997   WTO   US complaint regarding measures affecting the importation of milk and the exportation of dairy products—sustained and upheld by the Appellate Body; Canada has agreed to make the required changes in Canadian practice.

1998   WTO   Canadian complaint regarding state measures (South Dakota and others) affecting the importation and shipment of cattle, swine, and grain—suspended.

1999   WTO   US complaint regarding the term of patent protection in Canada—active.

      WTO   Canadian complaint regarding the initiation of countervailing duty proceedings by the United States against live cattle—active.

Sources: www.wto.org/wto/dispute/bulletin.htm and www.nafta-sec-alena.org/english/index.htm

GATT/WTO Disputes

Despite the entry into force of the FTA on 1 January 1989, both Canada and the United States continued to exercise their GATT rights. Before the GATT was subsumed into the WTO on 1 January 1995, each used the GATT complaints procedures three times following the FTA's entry into force. The FTA specified that for issues covered by both the FTA and the GATT, the complaining party has the option of choosing the forum where it wants to pursue the issue; once a forum has been chosen, however, the complaining party cannot change its mind and take the issue to the other forum.

With the entry into force of the binding dispute settlement provisions of the World Trade Organization, both Canada and the United States have shown a marked preference for these procedures to settle general trade disputes between them, as well as with other parties. Similar to the FTA, NAFTA Chapter 20 provides that the complaining party has the right to choose the forum for issues covered by both agreements. By the end of 1999, Canada had formally invoked WTO procedures twice and the United States had used them three times to address bilateral issues. Again, some of the cases litigated proved difficult and controversial. Two reined in excesses in the increasingly protectionist US trade remedy system and helped to keep two highly politicized industries—pork and softwood lumber—in check. The two cases involving alcoholic beverages are part of an ongoing saga of ensuring compliance with trade agreement obligations by sub-federal authorities. To date, Canada has proved more willing or able to exercise its responsibility under the federal state clauses of the GATT/WTO and FTA/NAFTA, but each case has established important precedents for the principle that the rule of law in trade relations extends beyond national governments. The periodicals and supply-management cases, arguably the most politically difficult trade cases faced by Canada in the 1990s, were each resolved as a result of panel determinations, one under NAFTA, the other under the WTO.

Like the FTA/NAFTA panels, GATT/WTO panels have proven highly competent and professional. While the Appellate Body has shown a penchant for amending panel determinations, it has done so on the basis of relatively esoteric points of law and treaty interpretation, often adding nuances aimed at strengthening the role of precedent and ensuring more uniform interpretations. The existence of a permanent body of officials with legal training to assist panels and the Appellate Body has added to the quality of panel decisions and made them increasingly more judicial in tone. A continuing weakness is the insistence of government lawyers, driven more by political than by legal considerations, on using every possible argument in presenting a case, regardless of its merit, and the willingness of panels to take these arguments seriously. As a result, determinations are now running well over a hundred printed pages, often diluting their potential policy impact.

The overall impression of this record of litigation between the two countries over the past decade under both the FTA/NAFTA and the GATT/WTO is one of commitment to the rule of law. Both sides have used the procedures roughly equally. Both have succeeded and failed in pressing their complaints. Both have generally accepted the results of panel proceedings and implemented the required changes in law and policy, although not always with enthusiasm and grace. On occasion, some additional pressure is required to resolve the issues. On other occasions, the resolution of one dimension of an issue has led to a flare-up of a related issue. In general, however, the two governments have been prepared to make full use of the system and to live by its results.

Concluding that the dispute settlement provisions of the WTO and NAFTA are working well, of course, does not mean that there is no room for improvement. After a decade of experience, a number of flaws have become apparent, not least of which is the difficulty of finding sufficient numbers of qualified candidates willing and able to serve on panels. Token payment, a high level of required commitment of time and resources, and strict conflict rules make it difficult to find panellists, let alone convince them to serve more than once. The obvious solution is for governments to agree to establish permanent tribunals rather than to continue to rely on rosters of ad hoc panellists. These and other deficiencies are likely to form an important part of future bilateral and multilateral negotiations. In most cases, however, these are the shortcomings of success rather than failure. They attest to the fact that governments have expressed confidence in the system through its frequent use and that frequent use has created strains and stresses that need to be addressed.

NAFTA Chapter 11

Chapter 11 of NAFTA, which sets out the three countries' rights and obligations related to foreign direct investment, also includes an innovative set of provisions to address disputes between foreign investors and the host government. Unlike the state-to-state provisions of Chapters 19 and 20, Chapter 11 provides for mandatory arbitration between an investor and the government. After a slow start, investors have begun to make increasing use of these provisions, particularly to challenge regulatory policies that, in their view, have had discriminatory and negative impacts on investor interests. By the end of 1999, only one arbitral panel—between a US investor and Mexico—had concluded its work and made an award. About a dozen cases have been initiated; some have been settled before an arbitral panel could make a ruling. The cases involving Canadian or US governments in disputes with US or Canadian investors include:

1996   Ethyl Corporation (US: Virginia) complaint regarding Canadian restrictions on imports of the gasoline additive MMT; the issue was settled on the basis of proceedings under the Canadian Internal Trade Agreement, without formal resort to arbitration under NAFTA; the Canadian government amended the offending regulations and offered Ethyl a financial settlement.

1998   S.D. Myers (US: Ohio) complaint regarding a Canadian ban on the export of hazardous wastes; the ban was withdrawn, but arbitration procedures are continuing to settle the claim for damages.

1998   Loewen (Canada: BC) complaint regarding court antitrust harassment/ settlement in the state of Mississippi—active.

1998   Sun Belt Water Inc. (US: California) complaint regarding the conduct of the government of British Columbia in a court case arising out of its withdrawal of permission to export bulk shipments of water; its Vancouver joint venture partner—Snowcap Waters Ltd of Vancouver—was compensated by the BC government; Sun Belt claims it was not—active.

1999   Methanex Corporation (Canada: BC) complaint regarding restrictions applied by the state of California on imports of the gasoline additive MBTE—active.

1999   Pope and Talbot (US: Washington) claim against Canada for damages arising as a result of the bilateral softwood lumber agreement—active.

1999   Mondev International (Canada: Montreal) complaint regarding Massachusetts court ruling on a real estate contract with the City of Boston—active.

It is still too early to reach any firm conclusions on the operation of Chapter 11. Some of the early cases have involved the issue of 'regulatory takings'. Complainants have launched procedures when, in their view, government regulatory action has been tantamount to an expropriation or forced divestiture of their assets in that jurisdiction. Some of the US complaints against Canada have raised the issue of standing, given the lack of clear evidence of direct investment in Canada. Canadian complaints have all revolved around court rulings rather than governmental measures. All the cases, therefore, raise complex issues regarding the intent of the governments in establishing the investor-state provisions that the arbitral panels will need to sort out.

In the first two complaints against Canada involving environmental regulatory measures, critics charged that the procedures had the effect of undermining Canada's capacity to protect the environment. The legal arguments advanced by the complaining parties also raised concerns that the concept of a 'regulatory taking' might prove rather vague and elastic. In both cases, however, the Canadian government found itself in an uncomfortable position because the offending measures were difficult to defend. Both were clearly inconsistent with the elemental national treatment requirement of NAFTA; both involved discriminatory restrictive trade measures. In the Ethyl case, the necessary legal requirements to take action to protect Canadian health were absent, leading to action under less onerous environmental legislation. In both cases, the Minister of the Environment chose to act despite advice that the measure would be inconsistent with Canada's international trade obligations and despite serious reservations by experts that the measures served any useful policy purpose. In short, the Canadian measures fell well short of the standards set out in the agreement. As it turned out, the first also fell short of the standards set out in the Agreement on Internal Trade, which provided the basis for the settlement of the case.

The one arbitral panel that has concluded its work, in regard to a complaint by a US firm that a Mexican regulatory decision was tantamount to an expropriation, dealt with an environmental matter. The panel, in a withering ruling, dismissed the case as frivolous and vexatious, and would have awarded costs to the Mexican government but for the novelty of the proceedings. More importantly, the panel clearly established a high benchmark for future cases alleging regulatory takings, indicating that any harm done to private parties by governments in exercising their normal regulatory authority should not give rise to Chapter 11 litigation. Some of the remaining cases may further clarify this critical dimension of Chapter 11.

CONCLUSION

To the extent that governments have been prepared to use available rules and procedures, it is clear that the new, more binding procedures have helped the management of Canada-US relations. The existence of international agreements does not mean that there will not be conflicts, only that there is a better basis for resolving them. They make it possible to bring conflicts to an end and to resolve contentious issues. A profound misreading of the FTA and NAFTA led to popular Canadian complaints about the rash of Canada-US trade disputes in the late 1980s and early 1990s. The existence of rules and procedures does not end disputes and, in fact, may increase the number of issues that need to be resolved. Canadians benefit from this process. As the rules become clearer, trade and investment conditions become more stable and predictable, and the capacity of governments to favour local producers is constrained.

The FTA at first seemed to multiply disputes, as players on both sides of the border tested the will of the two governments to live by the new rules. In all of these cases, however, the application of clear rules within a set of binding procedures greatly facilitated the management of relations between the two countries. Canada has not won all the cases, in part because Canada's policies have not always been consistent with its obligations. The purpose of dispute settlement is not to guarantee 'wins' but to ensure that conflicts are resolved on the basis of mutually accepted rules and procedures rather than on the basis of power and politics.

Nevertheless, there are limits to governments' willingness to cede control to international rules and procedures, as illustrated by the continuing saga of softwood lumber. Originally written out of the FTA, the issue has bedevilled Canada-US relations for the last two decades. Canada's current (1996) agreement to restrain exports of softwood lumber appears to have been based on the judgement that while Canada had right on its side, the cost of proving this point, both economically and politically, outweighed the benefits of restraining exports. Canada's decision to restrict its softwood exports to the United States ensured peace in the industry for five years, keeping the scarcity rents in Canada. Reasonable people can differ about the wisdom of this political judgement and its long-term impact on the integrity of a rules-based approach to managing relations.

The softwood lumber exception seems to have an echo in a number of high-profile WTO cases similarly remaining to be resolved despite the benefits of panel proceedings. In the case of such high-profile matters as the tuna-dolphin and shrimp-turtle cases, in which GATT and WTO panels invalidated US embargoes on imports of tuna and shrimp because the harvesting methods employed by foreign fishermen harmed dolphins and sea turtles, respectively, US authorities respected the decisions of the panels and rescinded the offending embargoes, despite criticism from environmental groups that the system was insensitive to environmental issues. On the other hand, in two high-profile US-EU cases, beef hormones and bananas, EU authorities have determined that they would rather face the wrath of their trading partners than that of the public, and have not taken satisfactory action to implement the decisions of WTO panels.

Much progress has been made over the past decade and a half in enshrining into international trade agreements better rules and procedures to settle disputes, but international rules and procedures remain some distance from the level of certainty expected from domestic rules and procedures, particularly in politically controversial issues involving the policies of one of the major players, such as the EU or the US, or in bilateral cases involving stakes as high as those in softwood lumber. In the coming years, as efforts to expand and strengthen the rules keep pace with deepening integration, it will be important to pay equal attention to the concomitant need to ensure that the procedures for the settlement of disputes are sufficiently robust to make the rules enforceable and thus provide traders and investors with the confidence to make the best of the close ties between Canada and the United States.

NOTES

1. Countervailing duty is a duty imposed in response to a duty imposed by another country. Antidumping rules are imposed when one country sells goods in another country at prices below production cost, and the other country then applies a duty to the imports to bring them up to a 'normal value', thus reducing the damage being done to its domestic industry.
2. The most detailed examination of GATT dispute settlement can be found in Hudec (1990, 1993). See also Thomas (1996) and Plank (1987). More generally, see the relevant chapters of Jackson (1998), Johnson (1995), and Trebilcock and Howse (1999) for descriptions of the dispute settlement provisions of the GATT, WTO, and NAFTA.
3. In addition to the general sources cited above, see Dearden (1995).
4. See Forton (1999) and *Journal of International Economic Law* (1998), which contains a number of articles by participants in the review process.
5. See www.wto.org/wto/dispute/bulletin.htm for a regularly updated report on the state of play in WTO dispute settlement cases. The numbers do not add up because of the consolidation of 'matters' raised by various complainants into 'cases' with multiple litigants.
6. The complete record of Canada-US dispute settlement under the FTA was examined by Davey (1996). Davey was director of the WTO dispute settlement division from 1995 to 1999. He concluded that 'the dispute settlement mechanisms of the [FTA] have worked reasonably well, particularly the binational panel review process. The basic goal of trade dispute settlement . . . is to enforce the agreed-upon rules. By and large, these dispute settlement mechanisms have done that' (288–9).

7. The details of the case and of Judge Wilkie's dissent are discussed in Trebilcock and Howse (1999: 88–93). See also Howse (1998). Howse concludes that the FTA/NAFTA regime works tolerably well for routine cases, but that the WTO regime places Canada in a better position for highly politicized cases, such as the perennial softwood lumber issue. Howse completed his analysis before the limits of WTO dispute settlement were suggested in beef hormones, bananas, and other high-profile cases, indicating that, as discussed further below, his conclusion about the limits of FTA/NAFTA dispute settlement may also apply to the WTO process. It is also important to keep in mind that the NAFTA Chapter 19 procedures, on the one hand, and NAFTA Chapter 20 and WTO DSU procedures, on the other, are not interchangeable. Chapter 19 litigation replaces domestic appeal procedures. Litigation under NAFTA Chapter 20 or the DSU allows governments to settle disputes arising as a result of differing interpretations of the rights and obligations set out in NAFTA and the WTO. The difference is important and should not be confused.

REFERENCES

Davey, William J. 1996. *Pine and Swine: Canada-United States Trade Dispute Settlement: The FTA Experience and the NAFTA Prospects.* Ottawa: Centre for Trade Policy and Law.

Dearden, Richard G. 1995. 'Arbitration of Expropriation Disputes between an Investor and the State under the North American Free Trade Agreement', *Journal of World Trade* 29, 1 (Feb.): 113–27.

Forton, Heather. 1999. 'Defusing Conflicts in International Trade: Making the WTO Rules Work,' in Fen Osler Hampson, Michael Hart, and Martin Rudner, *Canada Among Nations 1999: A Big League Player?* Toronto: Oxford University Press, 55–72.

Howse, Robert. 1998. *Settling Trade Disputes: When the WTO Forum Is Better than the NAFTA.* Toronto: C.D. Howe Commentary, no. 111, June.

Hudec, Robert E. 1990. *The GATT Legal System and World Trade Diplomacy,* 2nd edn. Salem, NH: Butterworths.

———. 1993. *Enforcing International Trade Law: The Evolution of the Modern GATT Legal System.* Salem, NH: Butterworths.

Jackson, John H. 1998. *The World Trading System: Law and Policy of International Economic Relations,* 2nd edn. Cambridge, Mass.: MIT Press.

Johnson, Jon. 1995. *The North American Free Trade Agreement: A Comprehensive Guide.* Aurora, Ont.: Canada Law Book, 1995.

Journal of International Economic Law. 1998. Vol. 1, no. 2.

Plank, Rosine. 1987. 'An Unofficial Description of How a GATT Panel Works and Does Not', *Journal of International Arbitration* 4, 4: 53–102.

Stevenson, Matthew. 2000. 'Bias and the NAFTA Dispute Settlement Process: Controversies and Counter-Evidence', *American Review of Canadian Studies.*

Thomas, J. Christopher. 1996. 'Litigation Process under the GATT Dispute Settlement System—Lessons for the World Trade Organization', *Journal of World Trade* 30, 2 (Apr.): 53–81.

Trebilcock, Michael J., and Robert Howse. 1999. *The Regulation of International Trade,* 2nd edn. New York: Routledge.

6

Catching Up Is Hard to Do: Thinking About the Canada-US Productivity Gap

DANIEL SCHWANEN

In the 1998 Doug Purvis Memorial lecture, former Canadian deputy finance minister David A. Dodge said that a major aim of Canadian fiscal policy in the coming years had to be that of 'preparing ourselves for our collective old age'. But fiscal prudence alone could not get us there. He added: 'To secure rising real incomes per capita, we will require a sharp increase in productivity.'

Although Canada's productivity performance has in fact been slightly better than that of the United States since the 1960s overall, all of the relative gains occurred from the mid-1960s through the late 1970s (Wells, Baldwin, and Maynard, 1999). The more recent numbers are both disappointing and puzzling. In spite of major policy shifts predicated on a more efficient use of resources, Canada's productivity did not pick up noticeably in the 1990s from its performance of the late 1970s and 1980s, remaining sluggish even in relation to

the generalized slowdown in the United States and many other industrial economies after the oil price shock of 1973. And in manufacturing, where productivity was supposed to be boosted by a
combination of better access to a larger market and increased competition generated by the Canada-US Free Trade Agreement (FTA), it
has continued to lag behind US performance since the FTA came into
effect in 1989 (see Table 6.1).

Thus, the well-documented, large absolute gap in productivity
between many Canadian and US industries (see OECD, 1998: 70) has
not closed, which strongly suggests that we are not using our
resources to their best potential and not preparing as well as we can
for our collective old age.

To be sure, over periods of a few quarters or years, which typify
business cycles, other factors may obscure the fact that productivity
tends to be by far the most important long-term determinant of standards of living. Thus, the widening gap in incomes between
Canadian and US residents in the 1990s can also be attributed to a
decline in Canada's employment relative to the working-age population (see Sharpe, Chapter 7) and to other significant upheavals in
the economy in the past decade, such as falling commodity prices
and rising levels of taxation. But the only way to surmount these difficulties in the long run is to improve on Canada's productivity.

In this Chapter I will summarize a conceptual framework, proposed by Harberger (1998), which is useful for understanding the

Table 6.1
Canada and US Labour Productivity:
Real GDP Per Working Hours

Productivity growth (% per year, annualized)	Canada	United States
Total Economy		
1977–88	0.9	1.1
1988–98	1.1	1.1
Manufacturing		
1977–88	1.3	3.1
1988–98	1.9	2.7

Source: Sharpe (2000: table 9).

process of productivity growth. I will then list a number of factors the literature and recent debates on Canada's economic performance identify as potentially important for productivity growth, divided into two groups along the lines of Harberger's analysis—the 'yeast' group and the 'mushrooms' group of factors—and will briefly comment on Canada's performance in each. Discussion will then turn to whether Canada has focused on the right policies to allow the factors most important to productivity growth to emerge.

In brief, Canadian governments should probably stop worrying about correcting symptoms of lagging productivity, such as the weak Canadian dollar or Canada's falling share of total foreign direct investment in North America, and instead concentrate on the factors that may hold back the dynamism of the Canadian economy. These factors are of three types:

- those about which we cannot do much in the medium term— the inherent (or at least inherited) importance of natural resources to the Canadian economy being a prominent factor here;
- those that seem essential to high productivity and standards of living (although it is difficult to see them as the primary factors behind Canada's sluggish productivity performance), such as education, research and development, and infrastructure;
- barriers that prevent the best possible use in Canada of education, research and development (R&D), and infrastructure, such as remaining barriers to accessing North American markets for Canadian firms, but also including the incentives (or lack thereof) to grow, innovate, and ultimately maintain a business and employment in Canada.

While it is important to maintain an adequate 'stock' in regard to infrastructure, R&D, and education, productivity and standards of living would receive a bigger boost from paying close attention to incentives and trade barriers.

THE PROCESS OF PRODUCTIVITY GROWTH

Harberger's (1998) framework distinguishes between two possible types of productivity-enhancing factors. In his framework some factors act like 'yeast'. Just as yeast causes bread to rise evenly, these factors are said to support the overall productivity of all sectors of the economy (or of an industry). Other factors cause productivity 'mushrooms' to 'pop up' in uneven growth spurts, both across various industries in the economy and across firms within a particular sector.[1] These productivity mushrooms, by their nature, are not predictable, resulting from myriad decisions taken by managers within firms to attempt what Harberger calls 'real cost reductions' at different points in time. But their existence can be measured, or at least inferred, from the data. While high-productivity countries also tend to be characterized by heavy investments in education and R&D, these factors are more akin to 'yeast', in that they are necessary to high levels of productivity but do not guarantee further progress. Such progress occurs through mushrooming, which will occur particularly in contexts in which valuable innovations are rewarded.

Harberger's concept is supported by Tremblay's (1998) analysis of productivity growth at the level of individual paper mills in Canada and India. While these two economies obviously operate at very different levels of development, the mills in both countries produced similar outputs and used similar process technologies. Tremblay found that in neither country was the productivity growth process uniform among firms. Nor could it be explained by a firm's human resources (degree qualifications of technical and managerial staff). He did find a strong link between productivity growth and what he calls the 'wider organizational dimensions' of the firm, such as variables describing 'motivation and commitment' and 'information flow' within each firm. He found in-house training to be a significant motivator of productivity gains. Overall, such organizational variables seem to operate similarly between Canadian and Indian firms. External factors, on the other hand, and even the degree of competition, were not very important in predicting the emergence of a process of productivity growth.

While Harberger's framework is more suitable for micro-level analysis, it is powerfully echoed in the evidence from aggregate Canadian industry data. When this framework is applied at that level, the continuing emergence of mushrooming sectors that pull the economy along, while productivity in other sectors stagnates or even declines, is indeed revealed. Typically, a few productivity 'leaders', which may account for less than 30 per cent of economic output at any given time, will account for the equivalent of an economy's entire productivity growth performance over a given period. Note, however, that industries in the lead typically vary from period to period. The recent Canadian experience in this respect is illustrated in Table 6.2.

Table 6.2
Canada: High Productivity Growth Industries

1984–8	1989–92	1993–7
Plastic & synthetic resin	Steel pipes & tubes	Tobacco products
Vegetable oil mills	Refined petroleum & coal products	Rubber hose and belting industries
Other transportation equipment	Office, store, & business machines	Office, store, & business machines
Office, store, & business machines	Sign and display	Commercial refrigeration & air
Jewellery	Soft drink industry	Paint & varnish
Fruits & vegetables	Non-ferrous metal smelting & refining	Foamed & expanded plastic products
Ready-mix concrete	Other plastic products industries	Clay products, abrasives & lime
Aluminum rolling, casting, & extruding	Tire and tube industries	Vegetable oil mills
Ornamental & architectural metal products	Sugar & sugar confectionery	Plastic & synthetic resins
Fabricated structural metal products	Wine industry	Primary textiles
Copper rolling, casting, & extruding	Other wood product industries	Wire & wire products
Agricultural Chemicals	Plastic film & sheeting industry	Office furniture
Plastic film & sheeting industry	Cement	Textile products
Communication & other electronic equip.	Battery & misc. electrical products	Fish products
Electrical industrial equipment	Distillery products industry	Scientific & professional equip.

Continued

Table 6.2—*continued*
Canada: High Productivity Growth Industries

1984–8	1989–92	1993–7
Other rubber products	Heating equipment	Soap & cleaning compounds
Communication energy wire & cable	Iron foundries	Other furniture & fixtures
Refined petroleum & coal products	Other metal fabricating	Other converted paper products
Foamed & expanded plastic products	Ornamental & architectural metal products	Machine shops
Concrete products	Major appliances	Other metal fabricating
	Communication & other electronic equip.	Motor vehicles
		Heating equipment
		Other chemical products

Note: The industries listed in each column together accounted for 100 per cent of productivity growth in manufacturing during the period specified.

The upshot is that if, as seems to be the case, productivity growth over any period of time is characterized more by the unpredictable 'mushrooming' of certain industries and firms within industries, of which all we know for sure is that it does happen, and if the abundance of 'yeast' factors seems less important than internal 'motivating' factors for generating productivity growth, the right policy prescriptions for increasing productivity would seem to be more in the nature of removing barriers to potential growth and innovation in individual firms or sectors than in attempting to kick-start productivity in hand-picked sectors or encouraging an abundance of 'yeast' factors in the economy as a recipe for increasing productivity *per se*.

Harberger almost concludes from his observations that a single factor, such as 'education' or 'social capital', is unlikely to explain the heart of the process by which productivity gains emerge. If R&D, or education, or even the scale of an industry were key to explaining productivity improvements, would such gains, as he puts it, 'jump wildly around from one industry to the next, from period to period?'

However, evidence that productivity gains are typified by a mushrooming process does not mean that we should be unconcerned with 'yeast' factors. One possible interpretation of the process is that 'leading' firms or even industries do not remain in the lead forever, because poorer competitors drop off and others learn from the leading firms. Thus, success itself, once it is known and appreciated, becomes the 'yeast' for the next generation of technical and managerial personnel within that industrial cluster or even within the economy as a whole (e.g., the spread of 'just-in-time' delivery). This leads to what I might call an augmented 'mushrooming' process: success in enhancing productivity must not only be able to take place somewhere, it must also be allowed to spread, and here factors identified as 'yeast' for economic growth have a key role to play.

DOES CANADA HAVE ENOUGH 'YEAST' FOR PRODUCTIVITY GROWTH?

An educated population, scientific and technical knowledge acquired through R&D, and public infrastructure are key 'yeast' factors that contribute to high standards of living in advanced economies. An interesting question within the Harberger framework, in relation to Canada's productivity gap with the United States, is whether these factors are inadequately abundant in Canada relative to the US, and if so, should governments intervene to ensure they are in increased supply, or, rather, are we not using what 'yeast' we have to the best of its potential to produce productivity 'mushrooms'?

Education and Human Capital
In a highly technological world, math and science education takes on a significant place in desirable educational achievements. Here, Canada may be lagging. Canadian business leaders are less likely than those in 23 other countries (out of 53) to agree with the statement that 'The school system in your country excels in math and basic science education' (WEF, 1998: 261, table 5.02).

Does Canada have a problem with education levels or with social capital, relative to the US? (I will defer comment on this question here. However, studies on the comparability of US and Canadian educational achievement levels, as well as on the still murkier issue of social capital, suggest that we are not doing especially badly on either count.) Canada ranks highest in the World Economic Forum (WEF) survey in terms of tertiary education enrolment.

The issue therefore does not appear to be education levels, but whether and how these are converted into high value-added activities in Canada. Here, in spite of the ongoing debate about its importance or what causes it, the question of the 'brain drain', and of its impact on average productivity levels in Canada, must be raised again. The WEF survey ranks Canada 12th on the question, 'Your country has a large pool of competent scientists and engineers (ibid., 266, table 5.12), while the US is 3rd. When the statement is 'Engineering as a profession greatly attracts young talent', Canada is a dismal 15th, but not far behind the US at 10th.

Porter (1998: 58, n. 11) finds that:

> The available human resources variables, largely concerned with the quantity and quality of schools, have only a modest relationship to the level of GDP per capita [bivariate regression]. National investment in schools and universities *per se* appears insufficient to explain differences in national productivity without parallel mechanisms to foster the development of skills meaningful to companies and to create demand in companies for more skilled employees. Interestingly, the variable measuring attention to skills training, which is linked directly to companies, has a considerably higher R2 than any of the other human resource-related measures in the level [of GDP, as opposed to growth] analysis.

The Bundesbank considers that while some aspects of public 'investments' do not boost productivity, other government expenditures classified as consumption do have productivity-enhancing effects. 'This applies, in particular, to spending on education and science, which to some extent may be regarded as an investment in human capital. Spending on health care has a similarly mixed character . . . it maintains and promotes the efficiency of the factor labour' (Deutsche Bundesbank, 1999: 40).

Basic Research and Development

As is well known, Canada ranks low among other industrial economies in R&D spending as a share of total economic activity (GDP). In 1997–8, Canada ranked 15th out of 47 countries surveyed by the World Economic Forum and for which data were available. Spending on R&D in top-ranked Sweden was more than twice what it was in Canada (3.6 per cent vs 1.6 per cent). Spending on R&D in Japan, Korea, Switzerland, Finland, and the US (all between 2.5 per cent and 2.8 per cent of GDP), and in Germany, France, Israel, the Netherlands, and Denmark (2–2.4 per cent of GDP), was also substantially higher than in Canada (WEF, 1998: 290, table 5.20).

In an earlier survey by the same organization, Canada ranked even lower in terms of patents granted per 1,000 employees: in 22nd place with 0.68, not so far behind the United States however (0.81), but well behind the leaders, Switzerland (5.38), Sweden (5.22), and Belgium (5.20), and indeed all of the EU except Portugal (which tied Canada) and Norway (ibid., 270, table 5.19).

Indicators collected by the OECD suggest a similar picture. In both Canada and the US, about 32 per cent of R&D was financed by governments, although in the US more R&D is performed by industry than in Canada (74 per cent vs 63 per cent), while in Canada more is performed by educational institutions (21 per cent vs 14 per cent) and by government (14 vs 8 per cent). There are major differences between countries regarding the share of R&D performed by domestic firms as opposed to foreign affiliates. In general, there are signs that R&D is becoming a more globalized activity, with the share of inventions made by non-residents rising in the average OECD country (from 6 to 8 per cent from the mid-1980s to the mid-1990s). In many countries, if the local research capacity is attractive enough, foreign firms will conduct research there and contribute to the stock of domestic inventions.

How important is this gap for Canada's relatively poor productivity performance? Does Canada lack in this crucial activity or in the potential to perform it? And if it is important, what is its origin and how can policy help to close it?

The evidence that low levels of R&D and patent activity are holding back productivity growth is sketchy. Certainly, the potential decoupling between the R&D activity and the economic success flowing from it is widely acknowledged. The question becomes whether any factors lead Canada to under-invest in R&D (and whether these can be corrected by policies, for example, increased incentives for R&D), or whether R&D expenditures are simply not our comparative advantage, or even whether low R&D expenditures are a symptom, rather than a cause, of Canada's disappointing productivity perfor-

mance. Answers to these questions may be delineated by considering the following facts:

- Canada's tax incentives for R&D are already among the most
  generous in the world.
- While measurements showing Canada as having one of the
  highest ratios of corporate R&D spending as a percentage of
  sales refer to our top three firms only, the World Economic
  Forum survey puts business-sector R&D intensity in Canada just
  slightly below that of the Netherlands, France, and the UK,
  albeit at quite a distance behind Switzerland, Japan, Sweden,
  Finland, the US, and Germany, and ranks Canada fairly high
  (7th) in terms of collaboration between universities and industry (ibid., 263).
- Canada seems able to absorb new technologies from abroad
  relatively fast, thanks to high foreign direct investment (FDI).
  Indeed, the WEF surveys rank Canada 8th in terms of the
  importance of FDI as a source for technology transfer (ibid.,
  265).
- Canada ranks 6th in terms of protection of intellectual property, while the US is 3rd (ibid., 266).
- In terms of the raw materials of the 'knowledge-based economy', Canada does not at first glance seem to suffer from an
  imbalance in terms of exchanges with the rest of the world, at
  least not if one looks at Canada's trade balances in what I would
  call 'knowledge' items (R&D, patents, royalties) and in knowl-
  edge-intensive services (e.g., computer services). That balance
  has remained stable and even improved in recent years.
- The WEF surveys indicate that Canadian responses to the statement 'Scientific research institutions in your country are truly
  world-class' place Canada 9th out of 53 countries, in the same
  class as Germany or Japan, and not far from the respondents'
  assessment of the US in terms of public commitment to non-
  military R&D (ibid., 262, tables 5.03, 5.04). Interestingly, this
  may suggest that military R&D, or R&D dedicated to addressing
  particular issues (rather than by sector), may be the way to go.
  Canada does less well in terms of business-sector spending on
  R&D, ranking 11th, well below the US in 5th place (ibid., 263
  table 5.05). In turn, the US is below Switzerland, Japan,
  Sweden, and Finland.

- Research collaboration between university and industry is deemed to be less close in Canada than in the US (7th place vs 2nd), Canada being behind the Scandinavian countries and Switzerland in that respect but well ahead of many other competitors (ibid., table 5.06). Canada ranked 8th in ability to transform academic ideas into commercially viable new products, with Israel and Japan vaulting ahead of us on that question (and Norway falling below). But there is a wide gap here between the US's top score (5.62 on a scale of 7) and Canada's (4.57) (ibid., 264, table 5.07). Canada also ranks behind the US (5.47 vs 6.11), but ahead of other competitors, when the question relates to the ability of companies to absorb new technologies (ibid., table 5.08).

- In response to the statement, 'Overall, your country is a world leader in technology', the answers of Canadian business leaders for the 1998 *Global Competitiveness Report* averaged 5.64 out of 7, resulting in Canada being ranked 6th out of 53 countries, behind the US, Japan, Israel, Germany, and Finland (ibid., 261). Two observations here. First, Canada is only ahead of the 11th place country by 0.17 points, whereas it is behind the number 1 country, the US, by 0.91 points. Second, if business leaders understood the question to refer to their own industry, then differences in 'technological leadership' due to a more dynamic industrial structure ('more computer chip plants') may not be picked up by this kind of question.

- In general, those surveyed for the WEF ranked Canada low (17th, behind, e.g., Ireland, Chile, New Zealand, and even Mexico, but ahead of Australia in 28th, the US in 32nd, and France in 41st) when questioned about government's ability to direct its subsidies towards 'future winners' (ibid., 213, table 2.03).

- Canada ranked 3rd in the world in 1997 in terms of computers per 1,000 persons, at 364, behind the US at 450 and Australia at 366 (ibid., 268, table 5.16). The same ranking obtained in terms of computer processing power (ibid., 271, table 5.22).

A tentative conclusion to be drawn is that these factors are all crucial to growth in standards of living, yet attempting to produce economic growth by stimulating one of these factors is more akin to 'pushing on a string'. For example, more R&D spending in Canada may well guarantee that we will have more ideas to sell, which in itself is not a bad thing. But will it guarantee that we will have commensurate long-run economic activity here?

Public Infrastructure

A similarly fuzzy link exists between public expenditures on physical infrastructure and productivity growth. In part, this is because the definition of 'infrastructure' is itself elastic. Certain types of investments made by governments, such as in schools, hospitals, or conservation areas, can legitimately be considered infrastructure, although they also have a significant consumption aspect (Deutsche Bundesbank, 1999), and in some cases (e.g., schools) are not expected to produce a particularly noticeable payoff in terms of national productivity over anything less than long periods (Gramlich, 1994).

While some authors use an expansive view of productivity, I prefer to discuss only physical infrastructure here, as education, another 'opportunity' variable, is discussed separately, and I analyse R&D as an 'entrepreneurship' component. Furthermore, my focus here is on infrastructure more closely related to business functions, but whose particular features (natural monopolies, etc.) make them valuable as a network, over and above the value of a particular segment, and beyond that which business can be expected to provide for (roads, tourism).

Even if we knew what the contribution of such infrastructure to productivity is, it is far from clear where Canada's problem might lie. The WEF survey ranks Canada generally high in terms of public infrastructure, although interestingly, Canada nevertheless ranks behind the US both in the quality of overall infrastructure (8th vs 3rd) and on the matching of road infrastructure to 'business requirements' (10th vs 6th) (WEF, 1998: 243, tables 4.01, 4.02). But Canada outdoes the US when the availability and efficiency of railroads, air transport, ports, and even telephones and fax machines are considered (ibid., 244–5, tables 4.03–4.06). Canada also beats the US in terms of affordability of international telephone services (1st vs 5th) (ibid., 246, table 4.08). Both Canada and the US rank low in terms of the priority given by government budgets to infrastructure spending (20th and 23rd, respectively), but Canada is well behind the United States in terms of private-sector participation in infrastructure projects (18th vs 8th) and cost of domestic air travel (32nd vs 4th).

Not surprisingly, many authors have found a generally positive correlation between the infrastructure available for use within a country and productivity levels. But does this mean that spending on public infrastructure is sufficient to generate productivity gains ('if you build it, they will come'), or does it mean more simply that potential productivity gains in specific areas need supporting public infrastructure to be realized ('if it is needed, then it should be built')? And does the answer vary according to the type of infrastructure spending? These two questions are key to the role of public infrastructure spending in boosting productivity and standards of living.

Much recent work points to infrastructure spending as not being sufficient to generate higher productivity, but being very project- and location-specific, and not being uniform across various types of infrastructure. Indeed, much evidence also points to the linkage between productivity and infrastructure as running in both directions: richer countries often choose to acquire more infrastructure. In fact, one area where there is least controversy is that 'mature infrastructure systems can produce high rates of return when growth creates bottlenecks', although even then:

> in Canada, recent studies, including those of the Royal Commission on National Passenger Transportation, were more inclined to recommend first getting the current infrastructure priced and used correctly, and then evaluating new investment projects in these more informative circumstances. A very important part of this strategy was to get environmental and safety costs fully included in infrastructure use and investment decisions, and especially to do this equally across all modes of transport. (Helliwell and McCallum, 1995: 466–48)

Fernald (1999) found that the construction of the US interstate highway system, from the 1950s to the early 1970s, was correlated with rising productivity growth in vehicle-intensive industries relative to the economy's average productivity growth. The conclusion is that more roads indeed contributed to productivity growth. Fernald calculates this contribution to be 1 per cent per year to economy-wide growth before 1973, substantial enough that he associates the decline in productivity growth since then to the fact that almost no new addition was subsequently made to the highway stock. However, because of the 'network' nature of this type of spending, Fernald is also clear on the following point: this was a one-time boost to productivity growth and it is not reasonable to expect that another program of road-building would have a similar, or even a positive, social rate of return.

Intuitively, the results of the Fernald study suggest that public infrastructure spending can be most productive when it facilitates the spread or use of a new, existing technology, rather than as a means to increase output in old industries or to invite new industries that otherwise are not developing. In the case of US highways, growth in miles driven substantially exceeded that in new highways for six of the postwar years, before building started to catch up (ibid., Figure 1). Another way of saying this is that infrastructure can be productive if it relieves existing or building congestion.

This fits with the observation that perhaps some subsidy programs are worth the money, but others are not. Gramlich found, for example, that it is much more economically sensible for the US federal government to provide matching grants to help states maintain highways up to a basic standard than to support new highway construction. He notes that, 'like other public goods, a large share of the benefits of infrastructure capital involve improved security, time saving, improved health, a cleaner environment, or improved outdoor recreation, magnitudes that are difficult to measure and that are not included in official measures of national output' (Gramlich, 1994: 1178). He adds that the utility value of outdoor recreation is not counted in national output, and that 'many of the benefits of highway investment will also involve the time saving of private individuals, which will generally not be reflected in national output' (ibid., 1186). Finally, Gramlich concludes that 'Even if there were no doubt of an infrastructure shortage, it is not clear what infrastructure policy or policies should be changed. By the same token, finding no evidence of shortage would not mean that *no* policy should be changed' (ibid., 1189–90).

In a recent study of the financing of public-sector investments, Germany's central bank noted that public investments include consumption-related assets, such as sports amenities and nursing homes. The bank noted that while this type of investment constitutes 'an integral part of the provision of basic public services, it does little to improve the prospects for macroeconomic growth' (Deutsche Bundesbank, 1999: 40), implying that it would best be financed out of current tax revenues rather than by borrowing. Likewise, it concludes that a similar type of reservation must be made:

even in the case of public infrastructure capital formation. Thus capital formation for the sake of environmental protection, notwithstanding its necessity, is less 'productive' in the customary sense. Moreover, government
capital formation includes capital goods that could be more efficiently provided and maintained by private suppliers. In general it can be said that public sector capital goods are more likely to promote growth if they
complement private sector capital formation. Their influence is thus dependent on the specific overall economic framework. (Ibid., 40)

The emerging conclusion on public infrastructure, then, seems to
be that it matters very much what it is that we are calling 'infrastructure'. As the Bundesbank noted: 'Studies on the effect of public infrastructure capital formation in Germany during the past years come to
relatively divergent conclusions. On balance, however, such investment is said to have a productivity enhancing tendency' (ibid., 41).

In short, many public investments fall under the definition of
'infrastructure' and can be justified on the merits of social equity,
environmental cleanup, or even macroeconomic stabilization. However, these should not be viewed as productivity-enhancing. In other
cases, such as investments in health care and education, productivity effects are more pronounced. In general, however, it is not likely
that infrastructure investment *per se* will generate productivity
enhancements, unless it (1) relieves congestion or is necessary for
existing use or (2) facilitates the emergence of new ways of doing
things. And even for relieving congestion, pricing should be gotten
right before expanding the infrastructure, and for facilitating something new, a commercial demand should be identified before going
ahead.

Summary: Do We Have the Right Tools, and Are They Enough?
When considering the impact of social capital, education, R&D, and
public infrastructure on productivity growth, similar questions
emerged in each case about causality (i.e., does the factor being considered drive productivity, or is it a symptom of productivity?).
Quantitative impact, of course, is another issue.

Perhaps the best way to appreciate the relative importance of
'yeast' factors is to cite Porter (1998: 43):

> While the accumulation of factors is necessary, the path and composition of
> accumulation takes precedence over the sheer quantity of factors developed.

Clearly, a preoccupation with factor accumulation is misguided in a world where many factors can be sourced internationally. Various factors must be developed or improved in sequence or firms will lack the types of inputs that correspond to their state of competition, and deficiencies in more basic factors will undermine the value of more advanced ones.

On 'yeast' generally, Porter (ibid., 47-8) also notes:

there must be alignment between the competitive environment and the capacities and needs of companies. Government must anticipate (because of the lead times involved) and put in place somewhat ahead of time the infrastructure, institutions and policies needed for the next level of competition. Yet moving too far ahead of firms' strategies and capabilities will not only deprive them of the types of inputs and supporting conditions they really need, but will confuse and demoralize the nation's institutions and citizens. . . . Not only will investments fail to bear fruit, but confidence in the entire development agenda can be undermined.

'Mushrooms', the other part of the Harberger model, are also considered by Porter (ibid., 45):

In wealthy economies, the challenge is to maintain the vitality of rivalry. Doing so seems to require healthy new business formation and the growth of entrepreneurial companies that shake up established rivals. . . . Highly developed sources of private equity capital and a system that rewards risk taking become governing factors in advanced economies.

IS THERE SUFFICIENT 'MUSHROOMING' OF PRODUCTIVITY IN CANADA?

Canada has a similar pattern to that of the US for productivity 'leaders', but the weight of 'laggards' in the Canadian economy seems much more onerous than in the US. Productivity is not only about producing more of what we are already producing, albeit with a more parsimonious use of factors of production. It is also about the ability to shift swiftly towards the production of new types of goods and services. This has possibly been underplayed in the discussions of Canada's productivity quandary, although it finds an echo in the literature on how standard measures of productivity growth tend to underestimate, sometimes dramatically, the improvements in well-being due to the appearance on the market of entirely new goods or services.

Part of Canada's productivity problem is related to the structure of the economy, which is more heavily weighted towards industries that, on a North American scale, are on average experiencing slower than average productivity growth. Based on the experience so far under the Canada-US Free Trade Agreement and NAFTA, one avenue for weaning the Canadian economy from its dependence on these sectors is to pursue even greater opening of the North American markets to Canadian firms. Clearly, however, opportunities to trade have already markedly expanded over the 10 years that the FTA has been in place. If the low level of the Canadian dollar, the vagaries of FDI flows, and the 'hourglass' structure of the Canadian economy in terms of the size of businesses are, as I suggest, symptoms but not culprits, what, then, can explain Canada's persistent underperformance, even in the face of expanded opportunities?

Many factors are involved, including the importance of social cohesion, property rights, and equity. As John Kenneth Galbraith (*Globe and Mail*, 1999) has said, 'nothing so ensures hardship, poverty and suffering as the absence of a responsible, effective, honest polity.' On that score, Canada ranks 10th in terms of public-sector competence in the WEF survey, well ahead of many key competitors, including the United States.

Industrial Structure

It is possible for two countries to be equally productive on an industry-by-industry basis and yet experience considerably divergent standards of living as a result of their different industrial structures—one country will be more heavily weighted in industries in which demand and/or productivity is rising more rapidly than in other industries, whereas the other's economic structure will be biased towards industries that are experiencing slow productivity growth in both countries. Indeed, the differences in industrial structure seem to explain a sizeable share of Canada's lacklustre productivity performance over the past 10 years. If Canada had been a region of the US, it would have tended to see a declining income per worker relative to the rest of the United States.

The Scale of Firms and Markets

The managers in larger Canadian plants have reported better results on the international competitiveness of their production technology than have those in smaller plants (Baldwin and Sabourin, 1998: 6). Indeed, when actual technology adoption was compared between Canadian and US plants in five industries for which comparable data were available, small Canadian establishments exhibited the largest differences in terms of adoption of at least one advanced technology compared with their US equivalents. By this measure, there was no difference between large Canadian and large US establishments, with the inter-country gap in technology adoption beginning to open at the level of the medium-sized establishment. In both countries, technology adoption is positively linked to the size of an establishment. 'Because of this, a country like Canada that has a greater proportion of small establishments will have a lower overall technology adoption rate even if each class size adopts technologies at the same rate' (ibid., 11).

The FTA may have helped, since the technology adoption gap, which was 16 percentage points in 1989, was halved to 8 per cent in 1993, that is, the incidence of advanced technologies grew at a faster rate in Canada than in the US during that period (ibid., 12). Apart from the FTA allowing better intra- and inter-industry specialization and concomitant efficiency gains, free trade was also supposed to allow Canadian firms to reap economies of scale from having such a vast, integrated market to serve. In principle, free trade would free manufacturers from being constrained to operate in Canada with smaller product runs than their US counterparts.

In a context of free trade, Daly (1999) has noted that while one might have expected small Canadian firms to begin growing by closing the productivity gap between themselves and large Canadian and foreign firms, this has not been happening. Puzzling as this is, it would be even more so if firms operating in Canada were in fact enjoying unfettered access to the US market. But in practice, firms continue to face significant barriers in their access to the United States market: rules of origin, continued significant restrictions to accessing public procurement contracts (in particular at the state level), and the threat of antidumping or countervailing duties make the home market a much more attractive target for expansion, albeit a more limited one than the US market. This interpretation is consistent with the well-known results obtained by Helliwell and

McCallum (1995), and others since, to the effect that the 'border still matters'. A recent study by the Canadian Chamber of Commerce shows that interprovincial trade (and not the sometimes more geographically intuitive north-south pattern) remains a particularly important expansion platform for small businesses. In addition, the share of the bilateral Canada-US trade accounted for by intra-firm trade has not dropped significantly since the FTA came into effect. All told, it may be that remaining trade impediments may continue to account in part for the 'hourglass' structure of firm sizes in Canada.

Canada ranks low in the WEF survey in terms of emphasis on product design capability, below Denmark, Italy, the US, Japan, and even Taiwan, but, surprisingly, ahead of France and the UK (WEF, 1998: 274, table 6.02).

Entrepreneurship

Canada ranks high (3rd) when decision-makers are asked whether 'the quality of management in your country is truly world-class', behind only the US and Sweden. Many countries have scores not far behind Canada's, but Canadian managers ranked well ahead of those in the UK, France, Italy, Australia, and Japan (ibid., table 6.01). In response to the statement, 'Total quality management is strictly applied in your country', Canada ranked 10th, the US 7th. The top three were Japan (by far), Germany, and Switzerland, followed by Taiwan, Sweden, and Denmark.

This issue can be linked to that of the industrial structure of the economy. Porter (1998: 54) finds that Canada is one of those countries 'whose business environment is ahead of company practice. . . . Many of these are countries whose leading companies are still heavily involved in natural resource extraction or original equipment manufacture (OEM) production despite relatively advanced business conditions.'

The WEF survey ranks Canada 6th, but well below the United States, on whether 'Firms in your country are very strong at marketing', and also 6th on whether firms paid close attention to customer satisfaction and on whether managers know how to attract, retain, and motivate high-quality staff, but in both cases quite a bit closer to the US first place (ibid., 276–7, tables 6.05, 6.06, 6.08). Canada also ranks low in terms of companies' emphasis on staff training, 13th, although it is not noticeably behind the US in 9th (leaders are Japan, Germany, Denmark, the Netherlands, and Sweden). While Canada ranked well in terms of competency of financial managers, effectiveness at controlling costs, and effectiveness of corporate boards in monitoring management performance (ibid., 279–81, tables 6.12, 6.13, 6.15), it ranked significantly lower on the question of whether it was common for owners to appoint outside professional managers (8th, as opposed to the US in 3rd, behind Norway and Sweden). While Canada was ranked 3rd among 53 countries, there was a significant gap between the scores of Canadian and US business schools, ranked in first place (ibid., 281, table 6.16). Canada outperformed the US in terms of managers' language skills and international experience, although both countries ranked low by international standards (28th and 46th out of 53). The UK, Australia, and New Zealand were 47th, 48th, and 49th (ibid., 282, table 6.17). Canada is second only to the United States (roughly the same score) in linking pay with job performance (ibid., 279, table 6.11).

The fact that self-employment has accounted for over half of Canada's job growth in the 1990s, in sharp contrast to the United States, though it has yet to be fully explained, probably should be brought into the productivity picture when discussing the persistent effect of small businesses on Canada's productivity performance (see Sharpe's analysis in Chapter 7). Manser and Picot (1999) suggest that high tax rates could be an explanation for mushrooming self-employment in Canada relative to the US, along with other factors such as relatively high immigration rates to Canada.

Technological and Product Innovation

Innovation immediately drives progress in living standards. R&D is often seen as a component of innovation, presumably because of the 'development' component, which by no means constitutes the costlier one. As the OECD puts it, 'Large complementary investments in equipment, training, licences, marketing and organisational change are needed to make innovation work' (*OECD Observer,* 1999: 63). However, more advanced 'template' technology does not necessarily equate to productivity growth. It does when it is able to deliver more or better products, at lower costs; otherwise, it is just a different way of doing things. Nevertheless, it may be a matter of life and death in terms of not falling behind with one's customers: companies still must adapt to the new way of doing things.

Most Canadian manufacturing plant managers surveyed in 1993 reported that their production technologies (encompassing the use of computer or micro-chip in four functions: design and engineering, fabrication and assembly, automated material handling, and inspection and communications) were superior or equal to those of their most significant foreign competitors (Baldwin and Sabourin, 1998: 5). This, however, seems at variance with the findings of the WEF survey, in which Canada ranked 12th on the statement: 'Production processes generally employ the most efficient technology.' The US was in 5th place.

IS THE CANADIAN POLICY ENVIRONMENT SUFFICIENTLY SUPPORTIVE OF PRODUCTIVITY GROWTH?

It is important to understand why Canada's productivity performance has not significantly improved vis-à-vis that of the United States, in spite of a number of policy changes in the late 1980s and 1990s explicitly meant to raise Canadians' standards of living. In particular, we need to understand whether these policy changes have actually had the desired impact, at least qualitatively, but were then obscured by other, countervailing factors pulling Canada's performance down, or whether they have failed to have the desired impact altogether, in which case policy prescriptions surely have to be revised.

The Impact of Free Trade
One of the key such policy developments of the late 1980s in Canada was the FTA, which came into effect in 1989 and was augmented, from the point of view of the bilateral Canada-US relationship, by NAFTA in 1994. Eleven years on, the sharp increase in two-way trade between Canada and the United States is there for all to see and has been well documented. In particular, a significant part of this increase was due to faster trade growth in those sectors that were liberalized under the FTA (Schwanen, 1997).

What is the link between this increase in trade and Canada's productivity performance? Prior to the FTA, studies had concluded that Canadians would see a rise in their standard of living as a result of tariff elimination between Canada and the United States. The manufacturing sector was expected to register a major increase in productivity, which, while not creating jobs in that sector, would spill over through lower costs to create jobs in other industries. Recent studies have shown that the reduction in tariff barriers faced by industries on both sides of the border has indeed had an impact on

Canada's productivity performance in those industries, which is positively linked to the size of the tariff barriers preceding the agreement (Trefler, 1997, 1999).

Another way of looking at the impact of the FTA on Canada's productivity performance would be to ask whether Canada's specialization pattern in the US market has shifted, under the agreement, towards industries that have since experienced faster productivity growth. In fact, it has, with the most dramatic upward shifts occurring within the group of industries 'liberalized' (i.e., moved from positive to zero tariffs) under the FTA. Subsequent analysis will attempt to link this changing specialization pattern to that of productivity growth in Canada since the FTA came into effect. If confirmed, this evidence would add to the conclusion that free trade has increased the productivity of Canada's manufacturing sector.

Note that Canada could do a lot more on this front, according to the World Economic Forum's *Global Competitiveness Report*. Canada ranks 27th out of 53 countries in how serious an impediment tariffs and quotas are to accessing foreign materials and equipment, and 22nd on the question of whether import barriers are an important problem, which is quite extraordinary when considering that the survey was taken nine years after the FTA came into effect. On both counts, Canada ranked well behind the United States and most EU countries (WEF, 1998: 202, tables 1.01, 1.02). (Canada did rank very high on accessibility to foreign exchange for importing, on export policy generally, and on import credits and insurance, but 34th on whether the exchange rate 'properly reflects economic fundamentals' and 32nd on expected exchange rate volatility, albeit 2nd on whether exchange rate policy was 'favorable to export expansion'!)

The Role of (Gross and Net) Foreign Direct Investment (FDI)

It has sometimes been suggested that Canada's disappointing economic performance could be linked to a problem with attracting foreign direct investment. The rationale here must be that FDI plays a special role in fostering productivity. This role, in turn, could be played through one of the following channels: increasing the stock of capital in Canada (thereby lifting labour productivity), increasing the flow of new technologies (a different type of investment), or helping to provide scale economies through increased access to foreign markets (trade disputes, for example, tend not to occur in sectors where cross-border ownership of industries is significant).

The question is: should we be concerned that Canada is missing out on any of these fronts because of a shortage of FDI? It is true that Canada's share of total FDI in North America has plummeted over the past 15 years. However, the stock of FDI has soared in absolute terms over the same period, in the United States in particular, and encompasses a large share of portfolio rather than greenfield investments. If Canada had maintained its share of the North American stock of FDI to what it was in 1980, today the share of FDI in the Canadian economy would stand at well over 50 per cent of GDP. In any event, 1998 saw a flow of inbound FDI unprecedented since at least the 1970s.

Are we missing out on some of the benefits of FDI? No doubt this is the case in some sectors that remain closed to FDI. But overall, it is not clear that Canada is wanting on that front. After all, a traditional complaint has been that subsidiaries of foreign multinationals do not provide enough of the human 'intellectual' capital required for productivity growth. If this is true, then things should have gone in the right direction in the 1990s: Canada has become less of a branch-plant economy and is now, in dollar terms, as big an investor abroad as foreign firms are here. In principle, the benefits of FDI also occur to countries that export capital, and here Canada has been making great strides in the past decade (1998 was also a record year for outbound investment). If the benefits of FDI run in both directions, it would be equally puzzling as to why the large increase in Canadian FDI abroad has not by now also contributed to an increase in productivity at home.

At least with respect to the quantity of fixed capital installed, it is possible to say that Canada's share of either total private machinery and equipment spending or private spending on structures (plants, oil rigs, etc.) in North America (whether the investment is made by a domestic or foreign firm is not relevant) has not dropped below its historical average. While Canada has not done as well when its share of *combined* machinery and equipment and structures spending is calculated, I would suggest that this is yet another phenomenon resulting from the composition of our economy: traditionally, investment in Canada has been oriented relatively more towards structures than towards machinery and equipment. But in the past 15 years, the structure of fixed capital spending in North America has shifted dramatically towards machinery and equipment.

Ultimately, the question is not one of attempting to raise even further the level of FDI in the Canadian economy. The key question regarding the link between FDI and productivity remains whether large multinational firms—Canadian or foreign-owned—face barriers to generating highly productive (in the sense of high value-added) activities in Canada—and, more generally, to growing in Canada. The question takes on a practical aspect when two major Canadian corporations are near the top of the list of the United Nations 'transnationality' index, indicating that while they are Canadian-owned, most of their operations are conducted from abroad. Viewed from this angle, the question is not one of too little openness to FDI, but rather one of attractiveness for Canada as a place from which to operate large multinational corporations. In turn, this would likely depend on the regulatory environment, the attractiveness of location for the personnel, the presence of foreign barriers, the local infrastructure, and the size of the domestic market.

Other factors here may also include the stability of political institutions, a factor for which Canada ranked only 11th in the 1998 *Global Competitiveness Report* (212, table 2.01), and the pervasiveness of administrative regulations that constrain business, on which Canada ranked 16th (behind Ireland and in the same league as Chile and New Zealand, but ahead of the United States and Australia). In terms of management time being spent dealing with the bureaucracy, Canada's ranking is low (17th) but comparable to that of the US (19th). Interestingly, Canada ranks much higher than the US in terms of policy independence from special interest groups (13th vs 40th) (ibid., 212, 214, tables 2.01, 2.02, 2.05, 2.06).

Of course, one way of enhancing Canadians' incomes would be to permit them greater access to foreign investments. A measure of agreement to the statement, 'Citizens of your country are free to invest in . . . other countries', ranked Canada 21st out of 53 in the *Global Competitiveness Report* (US, 15th), 22nd when the question concerned inward investment (US, 14th), 19th when the question was about freedom to negotiate cross-border ventures (US, 11th), 18th in regard to protection for foreign investment (US, 14th), and 35th on 'Foreign investors are free to acquire control of domestic companies' (US, 14th). On the other hand, the more objective 'number of types of capital restrictions, out of 12' showed Canada with only one, tied for 4th place, and the US with three, tied for 18th. In both the US and Canada, approval for the statement 'Public sector contracts are open to foreign bidders' was low, ranking them 25th and 29th, respectively (behind Vietnam in 24th!). According to the WEF,

Canada's average tariff rate in 1997 was 4.00 per cent (26th), vs 3.30 per cent (13th) for the US.

The Canadian Dollar and Manufacturing Productivity

Free trade has not been a panacea in terms of closing the gap with American productivity performance. Other factors must have held Canada's productivity performance back. One often mentioned as a potential explanation is the low and falling Canadian dollar. It is argued that the falling 'real' (after inflation differentials are factored out) value of the currency allows plant managers to be complacent vis-à-vis potential productivity improvement, since they can maintain their share of the US market without being forced to compete on such a basis: the falling dollar shields them from productivity improvements (and hence, lower prices in US dollars) made by their competitors. In the long run, this attitude is detrimental to Canadian standards of living, as Canada gets 'hooked' on competing on the basis of cheap prices on world markets (and increasingly expensive prices for what we purchase abroad), rather than through more efficient production.

While one intuitively understands that managers would more strongly perceive the need to improve the efficiency of their operation in the context of heightened foreign competition—which would indeed result from a stronger currency—there are nevertheless serious problems with relying on the 'lazy manufacturers' hypothesis as an explanation for Canada's lagging productivity growth. One problem is that, to the extent that Canada's productivity has lagged, it appears to have been only in manufacturing. Productivity growth in services, in contrast, seems to have been more solid. Yet, services are also tremendously exposed to international competition, both directly, as evidenced by a growing share of tradeable services in the economy, and indirectly, as manufacturers increasingly rely on a growing army of service providers for activities that are, for all intents and purposes, satellites to the manufacturing operations.

Another problem with the dollar explanation is that the performance of Canada's manufacturing industries, relative to that of their US counterparts, is far from uniform (Sharpe, 2000). Indeed, according to Sharpe, Canada's performance is only lagging in a few sectors, albeit sectors that make a huge contribution to overall US productivity growth. The question then arises as to why a handful of sectors in the economy would be markedly 'lazier' than others as a result of the falling currency.

Note also that one of the areas in the WEF survey in which Canada ranks the highest (4th, though still considerably behind the UK and the US) is the need for managers to take the possibility of hostile foreign takeovers into account (WEF, 1998: 232, table 3.08)

Different measurement methods in Canada and the United States can also skew the Canada-US comparison, making any observed correlation between the two countries' relative productivity levels correspondingly suspect. Trefler (1999) has noted that in the past comparisons have erroneously been made between a Canadian measure of productivity, relying on GDP in manufacturing, and a different type of measure of US productivity, relying on gross manufacturing output netted out of purchases between manufacturing firms. The latter measure will therefore implicitly include productivity gains that, by a GDP measure, would be factored out of manufacturing GDP (in particular, services purchases). The Deutsche Bundesbank (1998) has noted that similar problems hamper the comparability of manufacturing labour cost data for the purpose of calculating 'real' exchange rates.

SUMMARY AND POLICY IMPLICATIONS: HOW TO CLOSE THE GAP?

This chapter has surveyed some of the evidence and made a number of observations related to the process of productivity growth as Canadians have experienced it over the past decade. Its conclusion amounts to a plea that our search for higher productivity and standards of living be focused on the elements that are the most likely obstacles to the emergence and blossoming in Canada of high-productivity manufacturing and services activities.

I have suggested that, by and large, the decline of the dollar and the vagaries of FDI flows are not the place to look for an explanation of Canada's lagging productivity performance. Although they may well be symptomatic of the larger problem, artificially raising the value of the dollar or scurrying about the world to attract FDI is not likely to solve Canada's fundamental productivity problem.

In contrast, the evidence is fairly solid that the 1989 FTA has had a positive influence on productivity growth. Unfortunately, Canadian firms continue to face many barriers when attempting to access North

American markets. In the context of evaluating policies that will improve productivity, Canadians must discuss the extent to which they are prepared to engage the United States and other markets in providing better access to Canadian-based firms, in spite of the apparent public exhaustion with the process of greater economic integration between countries. In the meantime, one should also repeat, and act upon, the importance of an open internal Canadian market for the growth process of small and medium-size firms in our economy.

But open markets alone cannot ensure adequate growth in living standards. The discussion and evidence presented here inevitably lead to a consideration of tax, institutional, and even regulatory factors that might prevent Canadians from enjoying a higher standard of living, and from enticing firms, both Canadian and foreign, to locate high and growing productivity activities in Canada.

NOTE

1.   I am indebted to Bill Robson for bringing the Harberger article to my attention.

REFERENCES

Baldwin, John, and David Sabourin. 1998. *Technology Adoption: A Comparison between Canada and the United States.* Ottawa: Statistics Canada, Analytical Studies Branch Research Paper No. 119, Aug.

Daly, Donald J. 1999. 'Small Business in the Canada-U.S. Manufacturing Productivity Gap', mimeo, Mar.

Deutsche Bundesbank. 1998. 'The indicator quality of different definitions of the real external value of the Deutsche Mark', *Deutsche Bundesbank Monthly Report* (Nov.).

————. 1999. 'Development of public sector investment, and its financing', *Deutsche Bundesbank Monthly Report* (Apr.).

Fernald, John G. 1999. 'Roads to Prosperity? Assessing the Link between Public Capital and Productivity', *American Economic Review* 89, 3 (June).

Globe and Mail. 1999. 'John Kenneth Galbraith's World Tour', 6 July, A13.

Gramlich, Edward M. 1994. 'Infrastructure Investment: A Review Essay', *Journal of Economic Literature* 32, 3 (Sept).

Harberger, Arnold C. 1998. 'A Vision of the Growth Process', presidential address delivered at the 110th meeting of the American Economic Association, 4 Jan. *American Economic Review* 88, 1 (Mar.).

Helliwell, John F., and John McCallum. 1995. 'National Borders Still Matter for Trade', *Policy Options* (July-Aug.).

Manser, M., and G. Picot. 1999. 'The Role of Self-Employment in Job Creation in Canada and the United States', *Canadian Economic Observer*, Statistics Canada, Cat. no. 11–010–XPB, Mar.

Organization for Economic Co-operation and Development (OECD). 1998. *OECD Economic Surveys: Canada*. Paris: OECD.

———. 1998, 1999. *OECD Economic Surveys: Canada*. Paris: OECD.

———. 1999. *OECD Observer*.

Porter, Michael E. 1998. 'The microeconomic foundations of economic development' and 'Measuring the microeconomic foundations of economic development', in WEF (1998).

Schwanen, Daniel. 1997. *A Growing Success: Canada's Performance Under Free Trade*. C.D. Howe Institute Commentary 52. Toronto: C.D. Howe Institute, Apr.

Sharpe, Andrew. 2000. 'The Stylized Facts of the Canada-U.S. Manufacturing Productivity Gap', paper presented at the Centre for the Study of Living Standards Conference on the Canada-US Manufacturing Productivity Gap, Ottawa, 21 Jan., mimeo.

Trefler, Daniel. 1997. 'No Pain, No Gain: Lessons from the Canada-U.S. Free Trade Agreement', in *Incomes and Productivity in North America, Papers of the 1997 Seminar*. Dallas and Lanham, Md: Commission for Labor Cooperation and Bernan Press.

———. 1999. 'The Long and Short of the Canada-U.S. Free Trade Agreement', paper prepared for the Micro-Economic Policy Analysis Division, Industry Canada, revised 16 Feb., mimeo.

Tremblay, Pierre J. 1998. *Technological Capability and Productivity Growth: An Industrialized/Industrializing Country Comparison*. Montreal: Centre interuniversitaire de recherche en analyse des organisations, Série Scientifique 98s-07, Mar.

Wells, J.S., J. Baldwin, and J.-P. Maynard. 1999. 'Productivity Growth in Canada and the United States', *Canadian Economic Observer* 12, 9 (Sept.).

World Economic Forum (WEF). 1998. *The Global Competitiveness Report 1998*. Geneva: World Economic Forum in collaboration with the Harvard Institute for International Development.

7

A Comparison of Canadian and US Labour Market Performance in the 1990s

ANDREW SHARPE

The gap between Canadian and US living standards widened in the 1990s. Americans, on average, were 14 per cent better off in terms of real personal income per capita in 1999 than in 1989, while Canadians experienced no increase in real incomes. The thesis of this paper is that this divergence to a large degree has its roots in the different labour market performance of the two economies and that Canada's inferior performance reflected cyclical factors associated with poor macroeconomic performance rather than structural factors.

The paper is divided into three main parts. The first section examines general economic and labour market developments in Canada and the United States in the 1990s, looking at trends in real income, population, labour force, employment, unemployment, output, and productivity. The second looks at the common trends in the two labour markets, including the concentration of employment growth in services and in managerial and professional occupations, growing wage inequality, and the downward trend in the non-accelerating inflation rate of unemployment. The third examines divergent trends in the two labour markets, including the widening of the unemployment rate gap, the emergence of a participation rate gap, and greater self-employment and part-time employment growth in Canada.

ECONOMIC AND LABOUR MARKET DEVELOPMENTS IN CANADA AND THE UNITED STATES

Real Income Trends

The most relevant measure of income trends is personal income per capita, measured in real terms (excluding inflation). In 1999, per capita personal income in Canada, expressed in 1992 Canadian dollars, was $22,378, virtually identical to the level of $22,381 in 1989.[1] In other words, there has been no increase in real incomes for Canadians in the 1990s. In the United States, per capita personal income, expressed in 1992 US dollars, was $24,022 in 1999, up from $21,042 in 1989. Americans on average enjoyed a 14.2 per cent total increase or a 1.33 per cent average annual increase in living standards in the 1990s (Table 7.1).

International comparisons of real income levels or living standards are more difficult than comparisons of growth rates (which use domestic or own-country currencies) because they require the use of purchasing power parity exchange rates, which are subject to a margin of error. According to Statistics Canada, the bilateral Canada-US purchasing power parity in 1992, the base year, was 1.23 Canadian dollars per US dollar (US$0.813 per Canadian dollar). This means that

Table 7.1

Trends in Real Per Capita Income, 1989-1999
(average annual percentage rate of change in real per capita terms)

	Real GDP	Personal Income	Disposable Personal Income
Canada	1.05	0.11	−0.33
US	2.03	1.33	1.09
Canada-US	−0.98	−1.22	−1.42

Source: Statistics Canada, Bureau of Economic Analysis and Bureau of Labour Statistics.

per capita personal income in Canada in 1989 was 86.5 per cent of the US level, but by 1999 it had fallen to 76.6 per cent (Figure 7.1).

A second definition of living standards is per capita personal disposable income, or income after taxes. According to this definition, Canada's relative standard of living fell even more in the 1990s, as real per capita disposable personal income declined at a 0.33 per cent average annual rate between 1989 and 1999, compared to a 1.09 per cent average annual increase in the United States (Table 7.1). The gap between growth in personal income and personal disposable income is explained by the rising proportion of personal income going to taxes in the 1990s (Figure 7.2).

In absolute terms, personal disposable incomes in Canada fell from 77.7 per cent of the US level in 1989 to 67.5 per cent in 1999. One limitation of this definition of living standards is that it only captures the private consumption possibilities; it excludes the provision of public services such as health and education that are financed with tax revenues. Individuals are not necessarily worse off when tax increases lower disposable income but result in a greater supply of public services.

Figure 7.1

**Relative Aggregate Income Trends in Canada
(Canada as % of US)**

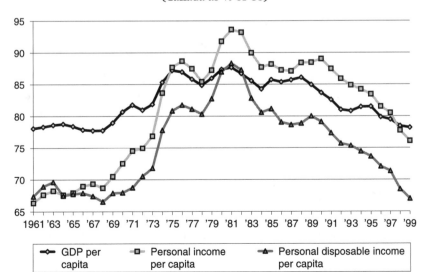

Figure 7.2

**Personal Disposable Income as Share of
Personal Income in Canada and US**

A third definition of living standards is real gross domestic product (GDP) per capita. According to this measure, living standards in
Canada advanced by 1.05 per cent per year in the 1990s, compared
to 2.03 per cent in the United States (Table 7.1). Real per capita GDP
growth in Canada was thus considerably faster than personal income
growth. This discrepancy is largely explained by the greater increase
in the consumer price index (CPI), which is used to deflate personal
income, than in the GDP deflator, which is used to deflate GDP. The
CPI grew at 0.7 per cent faster than the GDP deflator (2.19 per cent
vs 1.54 per cent) between 1989 and 1999 because of the fall in the
price of investment goods, driven by very large price declines in computers. Slightly more rapid nominal GDP growth than personal
income growth (3.76 per cent vs 3.34 per cent) also accounted for
some of the discrepancy between real GDP per capita and real personal income per capita.

The rate of increase in per capita real GDP is determined by the
rate of change in the number of workers in relation to the total population and the amount of output each worker produces, or worker
productivity. This per capita GDP term can in turn be broken into the

Table 7.2

Sources of GDP Per Capita Growth in Canada and the United States, 1989–1999
(average annual percentage rate of change)

	Canada	US	Canada-US
GDP per capita	1.05	2.03	–0.98
Output per worker	1.04	1.73	–0.69
Employment/total population	0.0	0.30	–0.30
Working-age population/ total population	0.25	0.09	0.16
Employment/working-age population	–0.24	0.21	–0.45

ratio of the working-age population to the total population, and the employment rate, that is, the ratio of employment to the working-age population. The employment rate is a function of the labour force participation rate and the unemployment rate.

In Canada, the 1.05 per cent average annual increase in real GDP in the 1990s can be decomposed into a 1.04 per cent rise in output per worker and no change in the share of employment in the total population. The stability of this latter figure reflects two offsetting trends, the increasing share of the population of working age (0.25 per cent) and the decreasing employment-population ratio (–0.24 per cent) arising from the falling labour force participation rate (–0.24 per cent).

In the United States, the 2.03 per cent average annual rate of increase in real GDP per capita over the 1989–99 period can be decomposed into a 1.73 per cent increase in output per worker and a 0.30 per cent increase in the proportion of the total population at work. This latter category in turn reflects a 0.09 per cent increase in the relative importance of the working-age population and a 0.21 increase in the employment rate or employment/working-age population ratio. The decline in the unemployment rate and the rising labour force participation each contributed equally to the growth of the employment rate (Table 7.2).

Canada experienced 0.98 percentage points slower real GDP per capita growth in the 1990s relative to the United States (2.03 per cent vs 1.05 per cent per year). Nearly half of this differential (–0.45 points) was due to the relative worsening of labour market conditions in Canada and two-thirds (–0.69 points) was due to slower productiv-

Table 7.3

**Labour Market Developments in Canada and the United States, 1989–1999
(average annual percentage rates of change unless otherwise indicated)**

	Canada	US
Working-age population	1.38	1.09
Participation rate	−0.24	0.10
Labour force	1.13	1.19
Employment	1.13	1.30
Unemployment rate (total percentage point change)	0.02	−1.05
Employment/population ratio	−0.24	0.20
Real output	2.19	3.05
Output per worker	1.04	1.73

ity growth. More favourable trends in demographic structures in Canada offset somewhat (0.16 points) these negative developments for trends in relative living standards.

Working-Age Population

The working-age or source population is defined as the population 15 and over in Canada and 16 and over in the United States.[2] In Canada in the 1990s, the source population advanced at a 1.4 per cent average annual rate, compared to 1.1 per cent in the United States (Figure 7.3). Canada's higher population rate growth reflected the greater relative importance of immigration in Canada than in the United States (average annual gross immigration represented 0.8 per cent of the total population over the 1990–8 period in Canada compared to 0.4 per cent in the United States).

Annual variation in source population growth in Canada also was largely due to variation in immigration levels, with population growth peaking at 1.5 per cent in the 1990–2 period when immigration levels averaged 250,000 per year. With the decline in immigration levels after the early years of the decade, source population growth fell off to 1.3 per cent by 1999.

Participation Rates

The participation rate is defined as the proportion of the working-age population in the labour force, that is, either employed or unemployed and looking for work. The participation rate in Canada fell significantly

Figure 7.3

Working-Age Population in Canada and the United States, 1989–1999

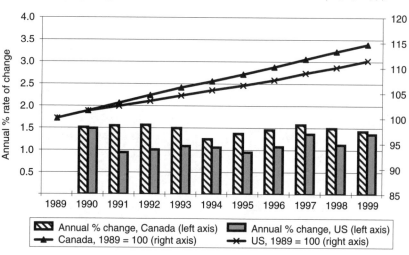

in the 1990s. From a peak of 67.2 per cent at the 1989 cyclical peak, it hit a trough of 64.7 per cent in 1996 before rebounding somewhat to 65.6 per cent in 1999. The average annual rate of decline over the 1989–99 period was 0.2 per cent. In contrast, the participation rate in the United States rose over the decade. While it initially declined from 66.5 per cent in 1989 to 66.2 in 1991, it then advanced slowly, reaching 67.1 in 1999 for an average annual growth rate of 0.1 per cent.

Labour Force

Labour force growth is determined by the growth of the working-age population and participation rate. Labour force growth in Canada (Figure 7.4) averaged 1.1 per cent per year in the 1990s (1.4 per cent source population growth and -0.2 per cent participation rate growth). It was much weaker in the first half of the decade when the participation rate experienced large declines. Labour force growth picked up after 1996 when the participation rate levelled out and began to regain lost ground, averaging a strong 1.8 per cent per year. Labour force growth in the United States was nearly identical to that in Canada in the 1990s, at 1.2 per cent per year, but the sources of the growth were somewhat different, with working-age population contributing 1.1 per cent and participation growth 0.1 per cent.

Figure 7.4

Labour Force in Canada and the United States, 1989–1999

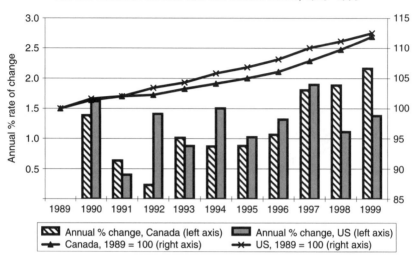

Employment

Employment growth averaged 1.1 per cent per year in Canada in the 1990s (Figure 7.5), with great variation within the decade following the business cycle. In 1991 and 1992 employment fell in absolute terms because of the recession. In the 1993–6 period it showed modest annual gains in the 0.8 to 2.0 per cent range. It has only been since 1996 that employment growth has been consistently strong, averaging 2.6 per cent per year.

In the United States, employment growth over the decade—at 1.3 per cent per year—was only slightly above that in Canada, but the pattern of growth differed from that experienced in Canada. The decline in employment was smaller in the United States in the early 1990s, reflecting the less severe impact of the recession. Equally, the pace of employment growth during the recovery and expansion of the 1993–7 period was stronger, again reflecting the more robust economic growth. Only in 1998 and 1999 has the United States been outperformed on the employment front, with the rate of increase at 1.5 per cent per year, over one percentage point slower than in Canada. The dwindling of the supply of unemployed workers may in part account for this deceleration of US employment growth from the 1.9 per cent pace of the 1994–7 period.

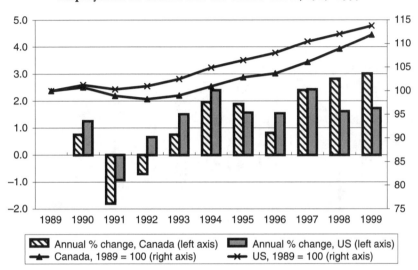

Figure 7.5

Employment in Canada and the United States, 1989–1999

Unemployment Rate

The unemployment rate in Canada in the 1990s averaged 9.6 per cent, the highest decade average since the 1930s, but there has been much cyclical variation within the decade (Figure 7.6). The rate rose from a low of 7.5 per cent at the peak of the last business cycle in 1989 to a high of 11.4 in 1993. It declined in 1994 and 1995 as the recovery progressed. But this downward trend stopped in 1996 when the unemployment rate actually rose, reflecting the slowdown in the pace of economic growth that year. Since then the unemployment rate has continued its downward track as the economic expansion has picked up, reaching 7.6 per cent in 1999, virtually identical to the pre-recession rate 10 years earlier.

Changes in the unemployment rate reflect the relative rates of growth of the labour force and employment, with the rate rising when the former exceeds the latter and vice versa. The constancy of the unemployment rate over the 1989–99 period in Canada (but not within the period) reflects the similarity in employment and labour force growth (1.1 per cent per year).

The unemployment rate in the United States in the 1990s averaged 5.8 per cent, below that experienced in the 1970s and 1980s but above that of the 1950s and 1960s. The US rate rose from a cyclical

Figure 7.6

Unemployment in Canada and the United States, 1989–1999

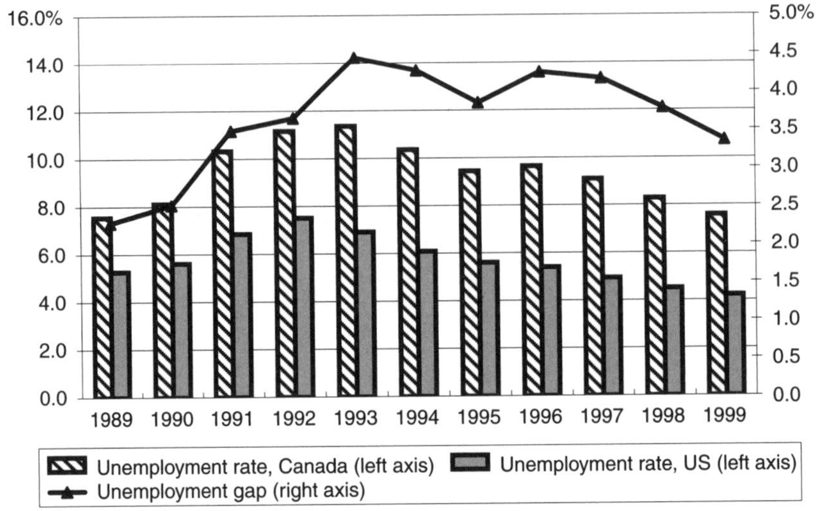

low of 5.3 per cent in 1989 to peak at 7.5 per cent in 1992 because of the recession of the early 1990s. With strong economic growth it then started a steady and continuous decline, reaching 4.2 per cent in 1999, the lowest rate since 1969. The 1.1 percentage point decline in the unemployment rate between 1989 and 1999 was due to the slightly faster pace of employment growth over the period (1.3 versus 1.2 per cent)

Employment/Population Ratio

The employment/working-age population ratio or employment rate is the proportion of the working-age population that is employed. This ratio plummeted in Canada in the early 1990s, falling from 62.1 per cent in 1989 to 58.0 per cent in 1993 because of the decreasing labour force participation and rising unemployment. By 1999 it had rebounded to 60.6 per cent due to the return of the unemployment rate to the pre-recession level and the rising participation rate. But it was still 1.5 percentage points below the 1989 level since the participation rate was still this amount below the pre-recession level.

In the United States the employment rate fell in the early 1990s from 63.0 per cent in 1989 to 61.5 per cent in 1992 and then recovered strongly with the fall in the unemployment rate and rising labour force participation, reaching 64.3 per cent in 1999. By 1999 there was a 3.7 per cent gap in employment rates between the two countries, compared to only 0.6 points in 1989.

Output

Real GDP advanced at a 2.7 per cent average annual rate in Canada in the 1990s (Figure 7.7). The decade started out very poorly, with 0.3 per cent growth in 1990 and a 1.6 per cent decline in 1991, and a weak recovery in 1992 and 1993. The economy picked up steam in 1994 but faltered in 1995 and 1996. Only in 1997 did sustained robust economic growth emerge, with increases averaging 3.7 per cent per year over the 1997–9 period.

The United States enjoyed annual average growth of 3.1 per cent over the 1990s. It also experienced a recession in the early years of the decade, albeit more shallow than that experienced in Canada. Its recovery from the recession was also slightly more robust. Since 1995 economic growth has averaged a very strong 4.1 per cent per year. The 0.9 percentage point gap in growth rates between the two countries in the 1990s means that over the 10-year period a 9 per cent gap in growth levels has emerged.

Figure 7.7

Real GDP in Canada and the United States, 1989–1999

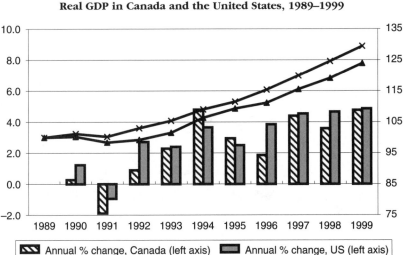

Productivity

Productivity, defined as output per person employed in the aggregate economy, rose at a 1.0 per cent average annual rate in Canada in the 1990s (Figure 7.8). Productivity growth was weak in the early years of the decade because of the recession, but picked up in the second half of the decade when stronger economic growth resumed.

In the United States, productivity advanced at a 1.7 per cent average annual rate in the 1990s. Between 1989 and 1995 it advanced at a tepid 1.3 per cent average annual rate. Since 1995 it has picked up to a strong 2.4 per cent rate. This development is seen by many observers as evidence of an upward structural shift in trend productivity associated with the information technology revolution. Canada has not yet seen this burst in productivity growth, which in part may account for the stronger employment growth.

COMMON TRENDS IN THE CANADIAN AND US LABOUR MARKETS

Concentration of Employment Growth in Service Industries

In both Canada and the United States, employment creation has been highly concentrated in the service sector. Between 1989 and 1999, employment in services-producing industries in Canada increased 16.3 per cent and accounted for 94.0 per cent of net employment

Figure 7.8

Real GDP per Worker in Canada and the United States, 1989–1999

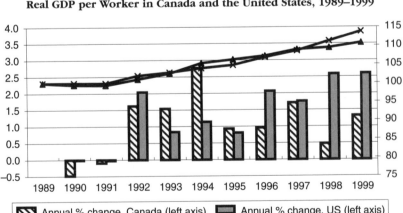

growth. Employment in goods-producing industries only rose 1.9 per cent. In the United States, employment in the service sector grew 25.1 per cent over the 1989–99 period, accounting for 100 per cent of net employment growth.

This common pattern reflects the influence of a number of factors. First, and most important, it results from intrinsic limits on productivity improvements in many service-sector industries because of the personal nature of the services, resulting in slower productivity growth in the service sector relative to the goods sector. For a given rate of output growth, employment growth is thus greater in the service sector than in the goods sector. A second factor may be the greater income elasticity of services, which with real income gains leads to faster demand growth for the output of service industries. A third, less important factor may be the contracting out to firms in the service sector of service-type functions (e.g., legal services) previously performed within goods industries. The concentration of employment gains in the service sector represents an employment shift comparable to the fall in the share of employment in agriculture over the 1940–70 period, a structural development that also affected both countries.

Concentration of Employment Gains in Managerial and Professional Occupations

Managerial and professional occupations have accounted for the greatest employment gains in the two countries. Between 1989 and 1999 in Canada, employment in managerial and professional occupations (defined as management occupations; professional occupations in business and finance; natural and applied sciences and related occupations; professional occupations in health; occupations in social science, education, and government service; and occupations in art, culture, recreation, and sport) rose 26.9 per cent and accounted for 58.7 per cent of net employment growth. Their share of total employment rose from 26.0 per cent to 29.5 per cent.

In the United States, employment in managerial and professional occupations rose 33.1 per cent over the same period and accounted for 48.6 per cent of net employment growth. Their share of total employment rose from 28.2 per cent to 31.5 per cent.

This common pattern is explained by the increasing importance of the knowledge-based skills possessed by managers and professionals and the declining importance of blue-collar occupations made redundant by skills-biased technological change.

Increased Labour Market Inequality

The United States has experienced a marked increase in wage or earnings inequality in recent years, and Canada has experienced the same trend to a lesser degree. This development has resulted in a significant increase in total income inequality in the United States, but not in Canada due to the offsetting influence of government transfers.

The causes behind the increase in labour market inequality in North America are still poorly understood. Explanations include skills-biased technological change, increased competition from low-wage countries, deregulation, reduced value of the minimum wage, and lower unionization. Whatever their relative importance, it appears that the factors have been operating in the same direction in both countries to increase inequality.

Downward Trend in the NAIRU

The most surprising development in the US economy in recent years has been the fall in the unemployment rate without a rise in inflation. By December 1999 the unemployment rate had reached a 24-year low of 4.1 per cent, yet the rate of increase in the CPI was still below 2 per cent. In the past, inflation has picked up at a higher rate of unemployment, a rate that economists call the non-accelerating inflation rate of unemployment (NAIRU). The conventional wisdom was that this unemployment rate was around 6 per cent.

There is a vigorous academic debate as to whether the current situation is temporary in nature or represents a permanent development. Those that take the former position argue that positive supply shocks, such as low commodity prices, account for the failure of low unemployment to ignite wage and price pressures and that if the current unemployment rate persists, we will soon see a resurgence of inflation (Gordon, 1998). Others argue that the economic world and, more particularly, labour markets have changed and the NAIRU estimates based on past experience are no guide to future developments. The changes that have led to a decline in the NAIRU include:

- an upward shift in trend productivity due to information technologies, which has reduced the rate of increase in unit labour costs for a given increase in wages;
- the aging of the labour force, with older workers having lower unemployment rates than younger workers;

- better labour market matching and hence lower frictional or job search unemployment due to the proliferation of Internet-based labour exchanges;
- the perception of increased job insecurity on the part of workers, which dampens wage expectations;
- reduction in the social safety net (e.g., the abolition in the US of the Aid to Families with Dependent Children Act in 1996), which has increased the supply of workers seeking employment and keeps wage increases down;
- the continued decline of union coverage, which has tempered wage demands;
- increased international competition due to globalization, which has limited the ability of firms to raise prices.

In Canada there has been less debate on the NAIRU because, at least until recently, the unemployment rate has not gone below the standard NAIRU estimate of around 7.5 per cent. Now that the unemployment rate has dropped below 7 per cent, the issue of whether the NAIRU has fallen takes on a new urgency for policy-makers. A case can be made that the forces outlined above that may have reduced the NAIRU in the United States have also been at play in Canada (with the possible exception of reduced union coverage and the substitution of UI/EI [Unemployment/Employment Insurance] reform for welfare reform). Hence, the current NAIRU in Canada may be in the 5–6 per cent range or even lower.

DIVERGENT TRENDS IN THE CANADIAN AND US LABOUR MARKETS

Despite the similarities in trends in the Canadian and US labour markets noted in the previous section, there have been a number of divergent developments in the two labour markets, including the widening of the Canada-US unemployment rate gap, the emergence of a participation rate gap, and greater non-standard employment growth in Canada.

The Widening Canada-US Unemployment Gap
In 1989 the unemployment rate in Canada, at 7.5 per cent, was 2.2 percentage points above that in the United States (5.3 per cent). In the early part of the 1990s this gap widened dramatically, peaking at

4.5 percentage points in 1993. It remained in the 3.8–4.2 percentage point range for the next five years, before falling to 3.4 percentage points in 1999 (Figure 7.6).

Labour economists have devoted considerable effort to explaining this unemployment rate gap (Riddell and Sharpe, 1998). Differences in the measurement of unemployment between Canada and the United States have been found responsible for about one-fifth of the gap (Zagorsky, 1996). In Canada, the definition of the unemployed includes persons engaged in only passive job search, namely, looking at help wanted ads. In the United States these persons are not counted as unemployed. The Canadian unemployment rate in 1997 was 0.9 percentage points lower when the US definition of unemployment was applied to Canada (Statistics Canada, 1998).

Canada's more generous social safety net, including UI/EI and social assistance, has been found to result in somewhat higher structural unemployment, although the generosity gap between Canadian and US social programs has been falling in the 1990s. These institutional factors are estimated to explain about one-quarter of the gap.

The most important factor behind the Canada-US unemployment gap has been found to be the cyclical weakness of the Canadian economy in the 1990s. Aggregate demand growth has been weaker in Canada than in the United States since 1989, with the result that labour demand growth has been weaker, and unemployment rose more in Canada during the recession of the early 1990s. It is estimated that Canada's poorer macroeconomic performance has been responsible for about one-half the gap.

Canada's relatively weak economic growth since 1989 reflects the impact of tight monetary policy associated with the pursuit of low inflation and, in mid-decade, tight fiscal policy used to eliminate government deficits. The weakness of domestic expenditure growth compared to exports testifies to the made-in-Canada nature of our macroeconomic weakness (Fortin, 1996).

The Emergence of a Participation Rate Gap

In 1989, the aggregate labour force participation rate in Canada was 67.2 per cent, 0.7 percentage points above that in the United States at 66.5 per cent. By 1999, the participation rate in Canada had fallen to 65.6 per cent, while that in the United States had risen to 67.1 per cent, creating a 1.5 percentage point gap in favour of the United States (Figure 7.9).

Figure 7.9

**Labour Force Participation Rate in
Canada and the United States, 1989–1999**

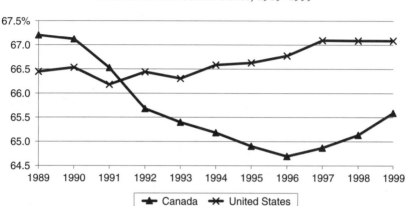

Like the widening of the unemployment rate gap, the emergence of the participation rate gap is largely a macroeconomic phenomenon (Sharpe and Grignon, 1999). When unemployment is high and employment opportunities are limited, individuals, particularly youth and older men, are more likely to leave, or not enter or re-enter, the labour force. The greater rise in the unemployment rate in Canada relative to the United States in the early 1990s consequently resulted in a greater decline in the participation rate, and the continuation of high unemployment until late in the decade discouraged persons from joining the labour force.

Greater Non-standard Employment Growth in Canada
Standard employment is defined as paid full-time positions, while non-standard employment includes part-time employment and self-employment. In the 1990s, growth in both part-time and self-employment has been much stronger in Canada than in the United States.

Self-employment in Canada advanced 36.6 per cent between 1989 and 1999, accounting for 42.7 per cent of net job creation. Self-employment rose from 13.9 per cent to 16.9 per cent of total employment. The unincorporated self-employed with no paid help accounted for nearly three-quarters of this increase in self-employment. In contrast, self-employment in the United States grew a meagre 0.8 per cent in the 1990s, accounting for well less than 1 per cent of net employment growth, and declined from 9.3 per cent of total employ-ment in 1989 to 7.8 per cent in 1999.

Many persons enter self-employment when paid employment opportunities are scarce. The boom in self-employment in Canada in the 1990s is in part linked to the limited paid job opportunities caused by the laggard economy. In contrast, the almost non-existent growth in self-employment in the United States in the 1990s testifies to the ample paid employment opportunities in that country.

Part-time employment grew 23.1 per cent in Canada in the 1990s, accounting for 32.6 per cent of net employment growth. As a share of total employment, part-time employment increased from 16.7 per cent to 18.5 per cent between 1989 and 1999. Over half of the increase in part-time employment has been involuntary in nature as persons took part-time positions because they could not find full-time work. The rate of part-time employment growth has been similar in the United States (up 21.8 per cent in the 1990s), but because of much stronger full-time employment growth, it has only accounted for 16.2 per cent of total employment growth, close to its share of total employment (14.6 per cent in 1999, up from 14.3 per cent in 1989).

Again this divergent development in the area of non-standard employment reflects the different macroeconomic performance of the two economies. With weaker labour demand, Canadians have accepted second-best employment situations, such as precarious and poorly remunerated self-employment and part-time positions. With stronger labour demand in the United States, relatively fewer Americans have been forced into these types of positions.

CONCLUSION

The 1990s have been in many ways a lost decade for the Canadian economy. Economic growth has been weak by historical standards, unemployment has been very high, and real personal income growth has been nil. A key question is whether this performance reflects structural impediments to growth or, rather, the cyclical weakness caused by restrictive macroeconomic policies. This paper argues strongly that it is the latter factor.

An examination of the performance of the Canadian and US labour markets reveals similarities in trends in a number of structural variables, including the industry and occupational composition of unemploy-ment, earnings inequality, and the NAIRU or the structural unemployment rate, but differences in trends are found in a number of variables influenced by aggregate demand conditions, namely, the unemployment rate, the participation rate, and non-standard employment. This finding supports the view that the problems in Canada's labour market in the 1990s have been largely macroeconomic in nature. Had Canada enjoyed the same pace of economic growth as the US in the 1990s, it is likely that there would have been no increase in the Canada-US unemployment rate gap, no emergence of a labour force participation rate gap, and slower growth in non-standard employment.

The precipitous decline in Canada's standard of living in the 1990s relative to that in the United States has its roots in both our poorer labour market performance and weaker productivity growth. In terms of the decline in relative level of real GDP per capita, about three-quarters is directly attributable to the relative decline in the employment/working-age population ratio and one-half to weaker productivity growth. These contributions sum to more than 100 per cent because of the positive contribution of trends in Canada's demographic structure to real GDP per capita. Both the falling employment rate and lagging productivity growth are a reflection of the high level of underutilized capacity that has characterized the Canadian economy throughout the 1990s.

Over long periods economies have certain equilibrating tendencies, with the poor performance in one period setting up conditions for strong rebound in the following one. For this reason there may be a possible silver lining in the dark clouds of poor economic performance in the 1990s. The conditions may now be ripe for solid and sustained economic growth. For example, weak labour market conditions in the 1990s resulted in many younger Canadians enrolling in post-secondary education, giving Canada the highest enrolment rate among OECD members. This increased supply of human capital may serve Canada well in the future and contribute greatly to economic growth. Such positive developments do not, of course, justify policy decisions that contributed to poor economic performance in the 1990s, but they do illustrate the complex nature of the long-term economic growth process.

NOTES

1. Supporting tables for the data presented in the paper are posted on the Centre for the Study of Living Standards Web site, under reports: www.csls.ca

2. The data sources used in this paper, unless otherwise specified, are the Labour Force Survey for Canada and the Current Population Survey for the United States. Canada's Labour Force Survey was rebased for the 1976–99 period in early 2000 and these revisions have been incorporated.

REFERENCES

Fortin, Pierre. 1996. 'The Great Canadian Slump', *Canadian Journal of Economics* 29, 4 (Nov.): 761–87.

————. 1999. 'The Canadian Standard of Living: Is There a Way Up?' Benefactors Lecture. Toronto: C.D. Howe Institute.

Gordon, Robert J. 1996. 'The Time-Varying NAIRU and Its Implications for Economic Policy', NBER Working Paper no. 5735, Aug.

————. 1998. 'The Foundations of the Goldilocks Economy: Supply Shocks and the Time-varying NAIRU', *Brookings Papers on Economic Activity* 2: 297–333.

Katz, Lawrence F., and Alan B. Krueger. 1999. 'The High-Pressure U.S. Labor Market in the 1990s', *Brookings Papers on Economic Activity* 1: 1–65.

Riddell, Craig. 1999. 'Canadian Labour Market Performance in International Context: Presidential Address to the Canadian Economics Association', *Canadian Journal of Economics* (Nov.).

———— and Andrew Sharpe, eds. 1998. 'CERF/CSLS Conference on the Canada-U.S. Unemployment Rate Gap', Special Issue of *Canadian Public Policy* (Feb.).

Sharpe, Andrew. 1999. 'The Nature and Causes of Unemployment in Canada', in Ken Battle and Sherri Torjman, eds, *Employment Options for Canada*. Ottawa: Caledon Institute for Social Policy.

———— and Louis Grignon, eds. 1999. 'A Symposium on Canadian Labour Force Participation in the 1990s', Special Issue of *Canadian Business Economics* 7, 2 (May).

———— and Tim Sargent, eds. 2000. 'Structural Aspects of Unemployment in Canada', Special Issue of *Canadian Public Policy* (forthcoming).

Statistics Canada. 1998. 'Labour Force Update: Canada-U.S. Labour Market Comparison', Cat. no. 71–005 (Autumn).

Zagorsky, Jay. 1996. 'The Effects of Definitional Differences on U.S. and Canadian Unemployment Rates', *Canadian Business Economics* 4, 2 (Winter): 13–21.

8

Friendly, Familiar, Foreign, and Near

ROBERT BOTHWELL

Once upon a time, in an attempt to promote American tourism to Canada, the Canadian government coined the slogan 'Friendly, familiar, foreign, and near'. As jingles go, it was inspired: enticement mingled with obfuscation. Americans should not worry: visiting Canada was 'familiar' and 'friendly'—just like home. 'Near'? Self-evident, at least to the (probably) northern readers of the periodicals that carried the ads, and reassuring to a generation that worried about European plumbing and other unfamiliar customs, and the expense of an overseas boat-ride. 'Foreign'? Sure, technically correct, but denatured by familiarity, friendliness, and proximity. Visiting Canada was less strenuous than visiting parts of the United States (White, 1996).

Put in cultural as opposed to touristic terms, over the years Canada has enjoyed assets in dealing with the United States that no other country has. Canadians (the English-speaking variety) speak with the same flat North American accent. They read the same things, listen to the same music, can talk about the United States with the same superficial familiarity as the average American, and sprinkle their speech with the same reassuring banalities about sport, technology, and daily life that denote sameness and safety. When Americans make goods and services available, 'and Canada' is the usual suffix to their printed or electronic blandishments. Canadians, they assume, will respond in about the same way as Americans when it comes to consumption. And what goes for consumption can be extrapolated, even to politics. 'Foreign'? Perhaps, but then again perhaps not: Canada exists, where the United States is concerned, in a state of sovereign ambiguity. It is a state that most of the time has conveyed mutual advantage.

To begin with, there was no ambiguity, and the experience was unhappy. Canadian-American relations go back further than any other foreign relations of the United States, back to a time when future Canadians and future Americans were neighbours in fact, and not just in rhetoric. In the 1770s, neighbours could be next door, even though they might disagree on the dominant political issue of the day, whether Americans could or should be British. Those who held differing views on the subject eventually took up arms. The Revolutionary War that established the United States was a civil war that ended with the suppression or emigration of the losing side; and many of the losers, as is well known, moved to what is now Canada. But because the war left these Americans, or pre-Americans, on the western side of the Atlantic, and because the British retained some colonies along the United States' northern frontier, the peace that ended the war was more like a truce than a genuine completion. (Consider contemporary analogies: East and West Germany, North and South Korea, North and South Vietnam, all cases where ideological division was supplemented by geographical severance.)

The American Revolution was an affair of a whole generation, neither side forgiving the other, each plotting the eventual downfall of the other, both stimulated by paranoid fantasies of what the erstwhile enemy and former neighbour might do. It took the War of 1812, so unsatisfactory in some respects, so very satisfactory in others, to dissipate the political venom. The major point of satisfaction to later generations was that the war was inconclusive: both sides could claim victory, and did. Where clarity had failed—the clear enmity of rebels for Loyalists and vice versa—ambiguity in the form of double meaning succeeded. Muddle proved to be a fertile soil for a new relationship.

For another generation, encouraged by a flow-through of American emigrants moving west through the fertile lands around the Great Lakes, Canada remained relatively prominent in the American mind. But as the frontier of settlement moved west rather than north, and as Americans became preoccupied by different political issues, Canada receded into a backwater, familiar but unthreatening, and definitely not where the action was (Stuart, 1988). The question of slavery, the Civil War, and then Reconstruction preoccupied the American mind. And if the Revolutionary War and the War of 1812 were shared experiences, as between British Americans and American Americans, the war between the northern and southern states clearly was not.

Canada and the United States became politically distant in the mid-nineteenth century, which was not true of culture or economics. Trade between the states and the provinces was always fairly lively, a trade in goods but also in ideas and fashions. Americans found they could move easily to Canada, and Canadians often found the United States more inviting than their own small country—federated into a larger British colony in 1867 but still tiny in population and under-developed in infrastructure. Waves of Canadians left for the United States—both English and French Canadians—in the late nineteenth century, and again in the 1920s, so that at one point, early in the twentieth century, about a quarter of native-born Canadians actually lived in the United States (Bothwell, 1992). The process contributed not so much to *knowledge* about Canada—that was easily dated and, given the character of most of the emigrants, limited—as to a *sense* of Canada. It was a good place to leave, certainly, but a good place nevertheless.

It was also a good place to visit, as American tourism spread into the lakes and rivers of central and eastern Canada. The American summer encouraged migration to cooler and more scenic climes, far from the city: President William Howard Taft to the lower St Lawrence, President Franklin D. Roosevelt to Campobello off New Brunswick. One southern magnate, unable to forgive the Civil War, built a summer mansion modelled after Mount Vernon in southern Quebec, and travelled there in a railway carriage with the blinds drawn. Travel was at first by railway and steamer, and later by automobile, which brought a whole new class of summer visitors to the roadside cabins of interwar Canada. (Even Richard Nixon spent his honeymoon in Victoria, BC.)

Canada was also becoming slightly more important in the American scheme of things: trade with Canada surpassed trade with Great Britain in the 1920s, and Canada has ever since remained the United States' largest trading partner. (In the 1920s and 1930s the United States and Great Britain alternated as the largest destination and source of Canada's exports and imports.) Investment followed the same pattern: in the 1920s the United States became the largest source of foreign investment in Canada.

Political connections were not quite as close. Canadians repudiated the notion of a special, though not especially close, trade deal with the United States in a general election in 1911. The election was notable, on the winning side, for its anti-American rhetoric and fervour, and its effects lingered for a generation—in fact, several generations (Bothwell and Kirton, 1983). Politicians and diplomats as late as the 1960s assured each other, on both sides of the border, that it was unwise to awaken the sleeping dragon of Canadian nationalism, as too close a public connection with the United States was bound to do (ibid.). What could not be done by treaty could be handled informally—producing a marked preference for lower-level but effective bureaucratic contacts as opposed to substantial political links.

The 1911 Canadian election and its lingering political aftermath, from the perspective of the twenty-first century, represented not merely an assertion of Canadian autonomy and nationalist feeling, but a product of special circumstances and what are now vanished assumptions. Canadians in 1911 not only opted against the United States but for the British Empire. That Empire in 1911 was a worldwide construction on which the sun never set, whose monarch sat in dignity on a gilded throne, and whose fleet cruised the globe. These things would diminish gradually over the twentieth century, and with their disappearance some of Canadians' self-confident assertion of difference would drain away.

Canada as a British colony joined in World War I in 1914 and enthusiastically sent hundreds of thousands of soldiers to the Western Front. Again, in 1939, Canada, by then constitutionally autonomous, declared war on Germany only a week after Great Britain did; there was absolutely no serious consideration given to remaining neutral, like the United States, or, indeed, the rest of the independent Americas.

The Americans were not certain what to make of the situation. Great Britain was important to them, at least in the Northeast, from Washington to Campobello, and there was no overwhelming desire to offend the British by overtly coveting a large chunk of the British Empire. But Canadians were definitely similar, related, and, to American eyes, mostly friendly. President Taft, an enthusiast for the Anglo-Saxon legal tradition and a promoter of international arbitration, chose Canada for one of his forays. To Taft, arbitration worked best if parties to a dispute were already linked by a common tradition and were culturally and legally alike. An International Joint Commission, the by-product of a treaty dealing with waterways and pollution, was negotiated in 1909. The Commission had broad powers, potentially covering any Canadian-American question, though with a special mandate for transboundary waters. Taft regarded the Commission fondly, and placed it in his vision of the Washington hierarchy close to the Supreme Court. (Its members were invited to his annual reception for the judiciary.) The International Joint Commission was the first, but not the last, bilateral body that attempted to place Canadian-American relations in a predictable institutional setting. It still exists, but it exists because it selected a niche covering water and the environment for its activities. It relied on expert opinion and consensus to operate—on shared cultural assumptions, in other words. It did not venture forth into the larger fields of Canadian-American relations—into politics, or multilateral relations, or, more dangerous still, economics.

The two countries finally exchanged legations in 1927, as Canada extended and formalized its sovereign status in the 1920s. Treaties in 1935 and 1938 eased trade relations. (This became possible because the United States changed its approach to tariffs and trade in the 1930s, handing much of the effective tariff-making power from Congress to the executive.) Canadian prime ministers began to drop in on American presidents. President Franklin D. Roosevelt in particular found his Canadian contemporary, Mackenzie King, congenial and relatively undemanding—two qualities he greatly appreciated. Roosevelt sympathized with Canada's entry into the war in 1939 and, when it was imminent, in August 1938, publicly promised that the United States would protect Canada from invasion by any hostile power. Mackenzie King, a few weeks later, made a reciprocal pledge.

Without exactly intending to do so, and with their minds elsewhere, Canada and the United States had formed a limited alliance (Stacey, 1981).

King and Roosevelt had Europe on their minds. Both men accepted a cultural and strategic link to Europe as natural and even supremely important. The mastery of the Atlantic and the coasts of Western Europe concerned them as it eventually did the majority of their fellow citizens. World War II was thus strategically very much a shared enterprise, prosecuted by two countries closely linked by culture and experience.

There were differences, however, in size, money, and power. The United States had more money, more resources, and more people than Canada. It was an alliance leader and there were more important countries than Canada in the alliance. In the 1930s Mackenzie King had been virtually the only foreign head of government to drop in regularly on Washington; in the 1940s he was but one among many, and certainly not the most important one.

The emergence of the United States as alliance leader sat uneasily on Canada. On the one hand, postwar Canada strongly favoured an alliance that would bind the United States, and its crucial resources, to a Western alliance. On the other, Canadian considerations receded in a Washington preoccupied with Berlin or Vietnam or Cuba. Bilateral relations did not so much suffer as migrate to a lower plane. An abortive scheme for Canadian-American free trade in 1948 originated inside the American bureaucracy, for example. In Canada, it was a subject for anxious consideration by the Prime Minister—still Mackenzie King—and his most senior ministers and advisers. In the United States, it barely reached the Undersecretary of State and was never seriously considered by the President—if, indeed, Harry Truman ever knew about it. In Ottawa, Prime Minister Mackenzie King reflected that a special arrangement with the United States would compromise Canada's relations with Great Britain, and forbade any further discussion of the matter. It was almost the last appearance of the British alternative; henceforth Canada would be on its own. What was crucial to Canada—a matter of sovereignty and identity—was much less so to the United States (Bothwell and English, 1977: 219–20).

Nor did the Canadians have better luck engaging the Americans on large alliance questions. With a complicated system of internal diplomacy at home in Washington, American representatives sometimes had little patience for the intricacies of external diplomacy. Canadian complaints about the wheat trade in the 1950s or uranium in the 1960s or lumber in the 1980s got short shrift in Washington, where these commodities were primarily and essentially a matter of congressional politics and outside the realm of easy diplomatic horse-trading.

Questions of alliance strategy were also difficult to pin down. Had there been a Warsaw Pact attack on NATO during the 1950s, the American response was clear: nuclear retaliation, and within days if not hours. There would be no time for serious consultation with most of the allies, and certainly not with Canada. Yet Canadian attempts to secure what we might call 'pre-consultation'—discussing or modifying American strategy before it was needed—only revealed that the United States government did not want to be tied down. These Canadian efforts were not, as political legend has it, confined to the 'nationalistic' Conservatives of John Diefenbaker: they were regular features of Canadian-American diplomatic discourse throughout the 1950s under External Affairs Minister Lester B. Pearson.

The Canadian government reacted as one might expect. An atomic confrontation would be beyond its ability to control, and so Canadian advice and reactions became consistently 'dovish'. A prime example, though not the only one, was Canadian skittishness over the Cuban Missile Crisis in 1962. And yet the more reluctant Canada became, the less inclined were the Americans to consult it.

Even on Europe there was a difference of opinion, or at least of emphasis. The United States favoured and promoted European integration as a key to the problem of Germany and, more broadly, European recovery. A healthy Europe made for a healthier NATO. Canada was not quite so sure. A unified Europe might be an exclusive Europe, and one inspired not by Canada's closest European connection, Great Britain, but by France or Germany. The difference in perception no doubt flowed from the difference in size and responsibilities between Canada and the United States, but what is more interesting is that there was practically no effort to bridge the gap in analysis or to formulate a common policy.

Latin America might have been another field of difference, and from time to time it was, but Canada's southward policy tended not to look beyond the United States—'our American squint', as one of our ambassadors once put it. There were spasmodic trade missions—one in 1956, another in 1968, and some later—but there was little governmental or popular interest. Occasionally the United States tried to engage Canadian diplomacy or Canadian money—notably President John F. Kennedy in 1961 with his Alliance for Progress—only to meet Canadian reluctance if not resistance. Sometimes, too, there was a difference of view between Canadian representatives on the spot and the home office in Ottawa—as in 1973 when the Canadian ambassador in Chile could barely contain his enthusiasm for the Pinochet coup, while Ottawa exerted itself to admit Chilean political refugees. In neither the enthusiasm nor the lack of enthusiasm for Latin America was there a real difference in the spectrum of Canadian and American reactions (though there certainly would have been between, say, Prime Minister Pierre Trudeau and President Richard Nixon or Secretary of State for External Affairs Allan MacEachen and Secretary of State Henry Kissinger). But Latin America was not an item that Canadians pressed in bilateral talks.

The widest divergence between Canada and the United States occurred over Asian policy. Canada had been a very minor player in Asia both before and during World War II, and the postwar period did little to alter the situation (Bothwell, 1998). Both countries participated in the Korean War, the Americans massively, the Canadians respectably—and with relief because the war was an officially sanctioned UN operation. Europe remained the main theatre for Canada, and while the Canadian brigade in Korea was withdrawn as soon as possible after the war, the Canadian brigade and air division in Europe remained until 1992.

American adventures in and around Taiwan were guaranteed to raise Canadian blood pressure in the 1950s, but on the whole Canada was satisfied to leave American China policy be. In addition, the Canadian government bowed to American pressure and refused to recognize the Chinese Communist government in Beijing or vote for its admission to the United Nations. There was harmony of a kind over Indochina during the 1950s, where Canada sat on a tripartite truce supervisory mission and where Communist behaviour towards non-Communists was guaranteed to raise Canadian indignation. The Canadian government did not see Indochina as a field of opportunity for the anti-Communist cause and lacked only a reasonable excuse to pull its diplomats and their escorting soldiers out. The excuse was never offered and so the Canadians reluctantly stayed, sympathizing with American anti-communism while frequently deploring the means the Americans chose to implement their policy.

Despite the anti-communism of Canadians stationed in Indochina, they did not especially approve of American efforts to ratchet up the war, and reported gloomily to Ottawa that there was no light at the end of the tunnel in any of the Indochinese states—but especially Vietnam. That was worrisome enough for the government in Ottawa, but more worrisome was the importation to Canada of Vietnam as an issue that could move and disturb the public. The origin of much if not most Canadian opinion on the Vietnam War was, of course, the United States.

We should bear in mind that ever since the 1770s currents of opinion in the United States have produced their eddy in Canada. The sociologist Seymour Martin Lipset has observed that in public opinion polls Americans and Canadians have agreed most of the time, more, apparently, than any other two nationalities in the world (Lipset, 1990: 212).[1] Canadians joined the Americans in participating in the consumer society of the 1950s, followed American styles, adopted American management techniques, worshipped American royalty such as the Kennedy family. It was not surprising—it was depressingly predictable—that Canada should import in the 1960s American anti-Americanism. Lacking draft boards, Canadian demonstrators concentrated on American consulates and for six or seven years American diplomats in Canada could count on being bombarded with a steady and noisy diet of the counterculture—a horse whose intellectual feedbag was back in the United States.

Canadian ministers and officials, in discussing Vietnam with their American counterparts, pointed to the unfavourable impact the subject was making in Canada. They could not wholeheartedly support American policy even as they hesitated, wholeheartedly, to condemn it. The American response was to limit the transfer of information to the Canadians—even as they used Canadian auspices to bear messages from Washington to Hanoi in 1964 (Logevall, 1999: 158).[2]

The 1960s and 1970s were periods of strong Canadian nationalist feeling, tempered in the seventies by confusion over the energy crisis and by uncertainty over the sudden absence, after 25 years, of a strong American anti-Communist lead. The Canadian Prime Minister of the day, Pierre Elliott Trudeau, proclaimed the end of a special relationship with the United States, a point echoed in December 1971 by American President Richard Nixon. Canada, he said, would be treated equally—just like any other country. And yet that very summer of 1971, when Nixon had attempted to cancel a special auto-

mobile trade agreement between Canada and the United States—using
the principle of equal treatment—his officials successfully reversed
the move. They reversed it so quietly and effectively that even the
Canadians did not know what had happened (Bothwell and Kirton,
1983: 108–27).

Perhaps Trudeau would not have cared. Of all Canadian prime
ministers, he was perhaps the one most intellectually and emotion-
ally removed from the United States. Nor was economics particularly
his specialty. He sat atop his government for well over a decade, but
during that time Canadian-American relations seldom kept him occupied, unless they could be linked to his central concern, the maintenance of Quebec inside the Canadian federation. Recognizing, after
a separatist provincial government came to power in Quebec, that
the United States could have a tremendous impact in persuading
Quebecers to vote for or against separation, Trudeau adroitly culti-
vated American concerns and was pleased to find that the US government had concluded that an independent Quebec had no appeal,
while a familiar and united Canada did (Bothwell, 1992).

As far as Canadian-American relations were concerned, the 1970s
came to an unexpected climax. In October 1980 the Trudeau government capped its nationalist agenda by introducing a series of measures designed to harvest energy rents from the presumably rising
price of oil, while expanding Canadian control in the oil industry at
the expense of American interests. The measures were ill-timed. For
one thing, they became a first item on the agenda of the incoming
Reagan administration, which was itself more nationalist and more
assertive than the preceding Carter presidency. For another, the price
of oil began to fall precipitately, negating all the anticipated benefits
from the Trudeau strategy. Finally, the Canadian economy entered a
sharp recession that took the wind out of the sails of economic
nationalists who had wished to define an economic destiny apart
from that of the United States (Granatstein and Bothwell, 1990: 315ff.,
327ff.).

The Trudeau government, by 1983, had reversed course and was
exploring instead the idea of sectoral free trade with the United
States. This would have been a difficult project at the best of times,
but its chances were not increased by coolness between Liberal
Ottawa and Republican Washington. Trudeau had become worried
and upset by growing tension between the Soviet Union and the
United States, and he set out, even-handedly, to bring the two back

together. Trudeau's round-the-world peace mission in the fall of 1983 accomplished little, except to irritate the Americans, who resented Trudeau's implicit characterization of them as trigger-happy (Trudeau later confirmed their impression in his foreign policy memoirs) (Bothwell and Kirton, 1986: 299–317).

'We put up with Trudeau for so long', one American official groaned, after Trudeau was gone. In his place there was the Conservative Brian Mulroney. If anything was clear about Mulroney's election platform, it was that he would improve relations with the United States. This he did, capitalizing on his ability to charm Reagan and by aligning Canadian external policy with that of the United States to a degree not seen since the 1950s (Morris, 1999: 661).[3] Though he did not originally have free trade with the United States in mind when he became Prime Minister, he grasped the opportunity and despite a lengthy and discouraging set of negotiations managed to bring home an agreement that over a decade abolished tariffs between Canada and the United States. Strongly supported and financed by the Canadian business community, Mulroney then won a federal election in 1988 on the issue.

The 1988 election was a turning point in Canadian-American relations. Fought squarely on the question of a Free Trade Agreement with the United States, the election produced victory for closer relations. Canadian trade with the United States grew absolutely and proportionately, and so did Canadian acceptance of the inevitability of a free trade regime. Only gradually did it become apparent how much Canada had come to depend on a regular and uninterrupted flow of goods over the border. To safeguard this trade, the Free Trade Agreement included a provision for binational panels to interpret Canadian and American trade law fairly—to take the issue to some extent out of the realm of active politics. As with the International Joint Commission many years before, there was a sense that Canada and the United States were sufficiently similar, culturally, for such institutions to work.

Mulroney subsequently succeeded in inserting Canada into the NAFTA negotiations between the United States and Mexico, making it a tripartite rather than bilateral arrangement. Again, he capitalized on good relations with the American President, George Bush. Although Mulroney left office before the NAFTA negotiations were completed, his successor, the Liberal Jean Chrétien, found it inadvisable to back out.

Although the Mulroney government did have points of differ-ence with Washington, for example over Central American policy, Canadian opinion tended to ignore these in the extravagance of his pro-American rhetoric. It is therefore possible that disapproval over Mulroney's pro-American performance played a role, and not merely among Canadian nationalists, in the repudiation of his party in the 1993 general election. Certainly the incoming Liberals, while careful not to mimic the Trudeau nationalism of the 1980s, kept a careful public distance from the sun of the American presidency.

The timing of the Liberal victory coincided with the realization that international relations suffered a sea change. At the time this was obscured in a natural preoccupation with bilateral issues. Mulroney's last three years in office focused on the great bilateral issue of trade relations with the United States. There was the Gulf War of 1991, to which Mulroney had sent troops to fight beside the Americans in the face of Liberal criticism. Simultaneously, the Cold War came to an end and the Soviet Union disintegrated. The context of Canadian-American relations abruptly changed. The great mutual enemy had vanished. Mulroney took advantage of the situation to withdraw Canadian troops from Europe, although Canada remained a member of NATO, which had suddenly become an alliance in search of a mis-sion. From the American point of view, the allies suddenly became more marginal, less essential. Mere alliance, with its promises of aid or co-operation against a known enemy, faded as a positive consid-eration for American policy-makers.

After Mulroney's international adventures, the Chrétien govern-ment at first kept its focus at home, working on the challenging top-ics of national unity and the national deficit. NATO and political relations with the United States could wait. The Clinton administra-tion made sympathetic noises on national unity, as its predecessors had 20 years before. Relations on the political level were cordial but moderately distant under Chrétien's first Foreign Minister, André Ouellet, who did not practise a particularly active diplomacy. Under Ouellet's successor, Lloyd Axworthy, there was both more engage-ment and more disputation, perhaps because Axworthy, a veteran of the activism of the 1960s, was more engaged in American causes, or at any rate the causes that interest some members of the Ivy League foreign policy élite in the United States. That élite has traditionally taken a friendly attitude towards Canada and Canadian concerns;

unfortunately, by the 1990s its dominance over American life and politics was becoming uncertain.

The balance of population and wealth in the United States has been shifting south and west, away from Canada. The Cold War, which defined security interests and provided a rationale for alliance relations, is over. Canada is very remote for a southern politician like the Republican majority leader in the Senate, Trent Lott of Texas; Mexico is closer and, on the whole, more important. (It was an attitude shared by George W. Bush in his presidential campaign in 2000, in which he spoke of 'the neighbourhood' and its importance to the United States. By 'neighbourhood' he meant Latin America.) Generation by generation, Americans know less about Canada, and care less. Canada does not fit in a mental universe that, even among the élite, thinks in categories like 'America and Europe' or 'the Americas'. There is less scholarly activity dealing with Canada in the 1990s than there was in the 1940s. Canada is both less familiar and more foreign to a generation of leaders for whom the Cold War, allied solidarity, and a sense of common political identity are an increasingly distant memory.

The consequences, unintended but nevertheless real, have already been seen in the question of border transit. A regulation intended for the fortified Mexican border would have been applied willy-nilly to Canada, strangling trade and limiting access. The problem was postponed, but only after frantic lobbying. Southern (and especially Texan) politicians are irritated, and the question has returned in the form of immigration control. Canada is alleged to be a major conduit for illegal immigration. Or drugs. Or spies. Or terrorists. Why should Canada have privileged access to American defence data? Why should Canada (and Canadians) have privileged access to the United States? To politicians anxious to close the border against Mexicans, there is a pleasing symmetry in equal treatment for Canadians.

When to this is added a pronounced tendency to unilateralism in international relations, enhanced by the end of the Cold War, a worrisome pattern emerges. Unilateralism encourages some Americans to deal with Canada in power terms that are at a ratio of ten to one or more.

This raises in a pointed form the problem of living in the same neighbourhood as the United States. It is difficult to establish and maintain variations in policy from the policies of the United States.

Canadians and Americans adopted income tax at roughly the same time. Canada could maintain conscription in World War I and World War II because the United States also had it; the fact that Canada did not have conscription in the 1960s complicated American recruiting policy for Vietnam. Trade in military items was eased during war and Cold War by confidence in mutual objectives. American complaints over porous borders or too liberal immigration in Canada are in this sense nothing new; but they are a complication that exposes the ambiguity in Canada's sovereignty.

There is another complication. Canadians know (and knew) more about the United States. Most of what they see they like, and like quite a bit. They certainly consume a lot of it, from television to automobiles to industrial machinery. Year by year, they consume more. They measure their achievements by an American standard and study the rise and fall of the Canadian dollar in American currency. Yet it is also true that there is a thread of anti-Americanism in Canadian life, occasionally noted by puzzled Americans as a Canadian sense of superiority. And, of course, there is a border—'the border', since Canada has no other.

In the 1988 election campaign, in a famous television ad, John Turner's Liberals depicted the Canadian-American free trade negotiations ending with an American hand reaching over and erasing the border on a map. The ad proved very successful—and it is probably one of the best-remembered features of the 1988 election. It was successful—had resonance—because many Canadians find the border a nuisance and in one sense or another would like to see its restrictions disappear. Naturally, this is not a sentiment that gets much publicity, but it has shown up in polls, and it is a factor in Canadian-American relations. It helps remind the government that it cannot go too far in dealing with the United States without irritating or alienating a significant number of Canadians.

The free trade encounter with the United States did produce, or revive, the idea of a joint body that would arbitrate a carefully limited series of questions related to bilateral trade. (The International Joint Commission, referred to above, did much the same thing for many years in questions related to boundary waters and the environment, while the Permanent Joint Board on Defence, created in 1940, was a less successful precedent in the field of defence.) Throughout the 1990s, joint panels have examined and pronounced on whether American or Canadian trade law has been fairly applied. If Canadian-American relations can be raised—or lowered—to a judicial plane, then the legal traditions of both countries will act as a safeguard—a legal analgesic, lowering the political temperature, if only temporarily.

The questions that evoke quasi-judicial bodies staffed with expensive binational talent are traditional and all too familiar problems, with familiar solutions from a historian's perspective. They rely for their success on a sense of commonality, while their purpose is simultaneously to keep similarity from becoming identity. This problem of sovereign ambiguity dates back to the eighteenth century—to the origins of both countries. Through size and wealth, the Americans have transcended their side of the ambiguity. Canadians have not. Relations with the United States—how close is too close—go to the heart of Canada's sovereign existence. Combined with American unilateralism and an increasing tendency to focus attention south, they suggest that Canada will have increasing friction with the United States at a time when Canada's contacts with the United States are fraying, generationally and geographically.

Canada's relationship with the United States has traditionally balanced similarity against autonomy. Canadians feel uneasy with the United States, because it is so large, overpowering, and successful, but at the same time they feel an identity based on culture and proximity. Disparate size has been a factor in Canadian-American relations especially since World War II, by diverting American attention from the neighbourhood to larger problems where Canada has little to say. Canadian governments since the 1940s have worried that American neglect may translate into negligence, and have worried, as they continue to do, that the very size of American concerns may prove the negation of Canadian sovereignty.

NOTES

1. Lipset (1990: 212) emphasizes differences between Canada and the United States. He also comments: 'At the same time, the two [countries] resemble each other more than either resembles any other nation. . . . Their differences, as we have seen from many public opinion polls, are often in the range of 5 to 10 percent.'
2. 'Canadian reservations about a wider war had led America's top diplomat [Secretary of State Dean Rusk] to conclude that Washington would have to be circumspect in its discussions with Ottawa' (Logevall, 1999: 158).
3. 'Brian Mulroney . . . called to boast that of all the G7 Western leaders "I was the one Ronnie felt closest to"' (Morris, 1999: 661).

REFERENCES

Bothwell, Robert. 1992. *Canada and the United States*. New York and Toronto: Twayne.

———. 1998. 'Eyes West: Canada and the Cold War in Asia', in Greg Donaghy, ed., *Canada and the Early Cold War*. Ottawa: Department of Foreign Affairs and International Trade, 59–70.

——— and John English. 1977. 'Canada Trade Policy in an Age of American Dominance and British Decline', *Canadian Review of American Studies* 8 (Spring): 52–65.

——— and William Kilbourn. 1979. *C.D. Howe: A Biography*. Toronto: McClelland & Stewart.

——— and John Kirton. 1983. 'A Sweet Little Country: American Attitudes Toward Canada', *Queen's Quarterly* 90, 4 (Winter): 1078–1102.

——— and ———. 1986. 'A Very Necessary Country: American Attitudes towards Canada, 1976–1980', *Queen's Quarterly* 93, 2 (Summer): 299–317.

Granatstein, J.L., and Robert Bothwell. 1990. *Pirouette: Pierre Trudeau and Canadian Foreign Policy*. Toronto: University of Toronto Press.

Lipset, Seymour Martin. 1990. *Continental Divide*. New York: Routledge.

Logevall, Fredrik. 1999. *Choosing War: The Lost Chance for Peace and the Escalation of War in Vietnam*. Berkeley: University of California Press.

Morris, Edmund. 1999. *Dutch: A Memoir of Ronald Reagan*. New York: Random House.

Stacey, C.P. 1981. *Canada in the Age of Conflict II*. Toronto: Macmillan.

Stuart, Reg. 1988. *United States Expansionism and British North America, 1775–1871*. Chapel Hill: University of North Carolina Press.

White, Stephen. 1996. *Harm's Way*. New York: Viking.

9

Economic Integration and Harmonization with the United States: A Working-Class Perspective

NANCY RICHE AND ROBERT BALDWIN

Economic integration with the United States is a long-standing reality of Canadian existence. Canadian participation in the Canada-US Free Trade Agreement (FTA) and the North American Free Trade Agreement (NAFTA) both reflected and reinforced that integration. But the period since the implementation of these agreements has been one of decline in the economic and social situation of Canada's workers. There has been a process of harmonization in the situation of Canadian and US workers that has worked to our disadvantage. This process reflects both the effects of the specific provisions of the agreements and, more importantly, intense lobbying by Canadian business to undermine the social and labour protections of Canadian workers. The FTA and NAFTA and the harmonization with which they are associated reflect a particular ideological and class approach to trade.

Workers in Canada and in other countries are allying themselves with other popular organizations to resist purely commercial approaches to trade agreements, economic integration, and harmonization. The basic elements of alternative approaches are beginning to emerge through the debates on the World Trade Organization (WTO) and the Multilateral Agreement on Investment (MAI).

A CANADIAN ADVANTAGE THAT IS UNDER ATTACK

For working people there are important advantages to living on the Canadian side of the Canada-US border. Despite the well-known fact that average incomes in the United States are about 10 per cent higher than those in Canada, the less well-known fact is that the average Canadian actually enjoys a higher after-tax real income than his or her American counterpart. What explains this seeming paradox is the fact that all of the income advantage in the US comes at the very highest end of the income spectrum. In fact, if Canadians from the midpoint of the Canadian income spectrum downward are matched with their US counterparts, the Canadians have higher incomes (Osberg, 1999; see also Wolfson and Murphy, 1998). But the income advantage that working Canadians enjoy is only part of the story of Canadian advantage.

Above and beyond the income advantage, Canadian workers also have an advantage in terms of access to income security and public services. Employment Insurance (EI) and medicare are, and have been, particular sources of advantage for Canadian workers. There is also a substantial advantage in terms of access to union membership, which brings with it not only higher wages and benefits, but also the rule of law at the workplace and real advantages in terms of access to statutory rights under employment standards and human rights law. Unionization rates in Canada are about double the US rates (approximately 35 per cent versus 17 per cent of non-agricultural workers). Moreover, employment regulation is somewhat stronger in Canada and Canadians work fewer hours than their US counterparts. Canadians also face somewhat lower threats to their person and property as a result of criminal activity. Finally, there is an advantage in living in a more equal society in regard to health, the quality of community life, and avoiding the risk of poverty.[1]

While the advantage of being Canadian is real, the US has done a much better job than Canada in recent years of providing work to all who are willing and able to work. The Canadian problem in this area is largely the product of government policy.[2] Two broad strands of public policy thinking are putting the advantage of Canadian workers at risk. First, macroeconomic policy has been conducted for many years on the basis that a substantial degree of slack has to be maintained in Canadian labour markets to make sure that Canada does not face wages-driven inflation. This approach to the conduct of economic policy has clearly been designed to have a negative impact on any possible wage advantage of Canadian workers. It has also accounted for a significant part of Canada's weaker performance on the unemployment front.[3]

One of the theoretical underpinnings of macroeconomic policy has been a view that if labour markets are deregulated, wages will drop to a market clearing level and full employment will be attained at a lower level of wages and salaries. This perspective has led to and/or reinforced a view that the protection afforded to workers through social security, especially Employment Insurance, as well as collective bargaining and labour standards legislation, will increase unemployment and raise wages 'artificially'. Thus, the concomitant of tight macroeconomic policy has been repeated attacks on unemployment insurance (and social assistance at the provincial level) and a period of general stagnation in terms of workers' rights.

The other major strand of policy thinking that has led to an undermining of the advantage of Canadian working people is a view that places Canada's competitiveness in terms of exports and attracting foreign investment as being at the centre of Canada's economic growth process. This view tends to treat the improved living standards of workers as a threat rather than a sign of success. While this line of thought is distinct from that which underlies macroeconomic policy, it leads to the same conclusions at a lower level of policy generalization and program change.

The central currents of economic policy thinking just noted have made a very important contribution to making the 1990s, the free trade era, a very bleak one for Canadian workers. We will return to this point below. Let us first note several points. Average wages and salaries have stagnated, and so have family incomes. Earned income and total income have become more unequal. At the same time that incomes have become restrained, social programs and public services have been cut and little or no progress has been made on statutory rights. Unemployment has been high and work has become more precarious and stressful (see Jackson and Robinson, 2000).

FREE TRADE AS A FORM OF INTEGRATION (AND HARMONIZATION) WITH THE US

The Canada-US Free Trade Agreement and NAFTA represented a particular approach to the long-standing reality that the Canadian and US economies are highly integrated. Business supporters of the FTA said they needed secure access to the US market and a more reliable process for resolving trade disputes than existed at the time. Economist supporters of the FTA argued that access to the US market would bring with it productivity improvements that would support higher incomes for Canadian workers. Both the Economic Council of Canada and the federal Department of Finance estimated that Canada would experience a 2.5 per cent increase in gross domestic product (GDP) over a 10-year period thanks to the productivity-enhancing effects of free trade (Jackson, 1999).

Opponents of the agreement focused their concern on the likelihood that it would result in the downward harmonization of Canadian labour and social conditions to US levels. In response, proponents of free trade argued that flexible exchange rates would permit Canadian governments to pursue an independent fiscal agenda that could include substantially stronger social programs. Besides, as the Finance Minister of the day argued, higher Canadian incomes that would result from free trade would make it easier to finance stronger social programs. Critics of the proposed agreement also argued that it would not be a trade agreement in the normal sense of the term. It would go far beyond an agreement on tariffs, and the non-tariff parts of the agreement would limit the capacity of Canadian governments to manage the economy.

In the free trade election of 1988, a majority of voters voted for parties opposed to the FTA, but the party that won the election supported it. In 1993 voters elected a party opposed to NAFTA. Canada's participation in the FTA and NAFTA are, nonetheless, realities.

As predicted by its critics, the FTA proved to be a much broader agreement than one would normally associate with a trade agreement. In addition to the elimination of tariffs on a wide range of goods and services, it included an energy agreement that guaranteed the US access to Canadian energy, even in emergencies; rules that would govern the introduction of state monopolies; rules on government procurement that would prohibit giving preferential treatment to local suppliers; provisions that committed Canada to what were basically US positions on trade-related investment measures and trade-related intellectual property rights in the General Agreement on Tariffs and Trade (GATT) negotiations that were under way at the time; and dispute resolution rules.

Both through its commissions and omissions, two things stand out about the FTA: first, the raw power of the US in the negotiating process; and second, the overwhelming predominance of a purely commercial view of trade issues. During the period of the FTA negotiation, there was a point when the negotiations almost collapsed. Canada's chief negotiator walked away from the table in frustration at Canada's inability to extract any concession from the US on the key issue of subsidy and countervail (Ritchie, 1997). US trade law on subsidy and countervail had played a key role in blocking Canadian exports of softwood lumber, steel, and agricultural products. Intervention at the ministerial level was required to get the negotiations back on track. But when the agreement was signed, there was still no agreement on subsidy and countervail—merely a commitment to try to negotiate one over the next 10 years.

The inability to move the US on the subsidy and countervail issue may be the most striking example of the difficulty of negotiating in a very unequal bargaining relationship. One might also cite the agreements on energy, procurement, state monopolies, and bargaining positions at the GATT as further manifestations of the same reality. The related attack on Canada's drug patent legislation illustrates the same point.

By the time the FTA was negotiated, the European Union (EU) had already established a precedent for trying to address the potential negative side effects of trade agreements on labour and social conditions. While the effectiveness of the measures has been subject to dispute, the EU did establish a general principle of levelling up social and labour conditions, and it created a regional development fund both to offset negative effects of the common market on specific regions and to allow the relatively less-developed regions to compete on a more even plane. Moreover, the EU has also provided the auspices under which labour and business have been engaged to develop directives that apply across the EU on a range of labour issues, including the creation of works councils in large firms, parental leave, and equal pay and benefits for part-time workers. These directives are binding on all EU countries unless they specifically opt out, as the UK has done on several occasions.

The EU experience highlights the absence of any such measures in the FTA. Indeed, aside from the never-fulfilled claim of the Prime Minister of the day that Canada would establish the most generous adjustment programs in the world for workers who lost their jobs due to the FTA, the social issues related to changing patterns of trade were ignored by the Canadian government. Moreover, much of the text of the agreement establishes rights for commercial actors, but for no one else.

The extension to corporations of the right to sue governments under Chapter 11 of NAFTA is the most extreme manifestation of the class-specific nature of the rights protected by the FTA and NAFTA. However, it also has to be noted that by the time NAFTA was signed, a Democratic President had been elected in the US with the backing of the US labour movement. The new President insisted that labour and environmental side deals be grafted on to what was a basically commercial agreement. The labour side deal committed the three participating governments to uphold both core labour rights and their own laws, which was not unimportant in the case of Mexico. Experience with the labour side deal is still emerging and reactions to it vary substantially. It has been useful in highlighting and even changing some particularly egregious violations of labour rights, but it falls very short of a systematic effort to raise labour standards. It neither establishes common standards nor includes a mechanism for redressing the denial of labour rights.

The effects of the FTA and NAFTA are difficult to separate from the effects of other policy initiatives undertaken at the time: contractionary monetary and fiscal policies and domestic market liberalization through privatization and deregulation. Nonetheless, a few things can be said definitively. First and foremost, the FTA did not usher in the era of prosperity that its advocates predicted. This point has already been documented above. What bears special emphasis is that the period of the FTA and NAFTA has seen a decline in Canada's economic performance in relation to that of the US. From 1989 through 1998, Canada's average annual rate of economic growth has been 1.8 per cent compared to 2.5 per cent in the US. In the manufacturing sector, which is highly responsive to the trade environment, US annual increases in productivity outpaced Canada's by 1.8–2.8 per cent over the period from 1989 to 1996 (Jackson, 1999; see also Chapter 6 in this volume).

These differences reflect both macroeconomic and structural factors. Canada's monetary policy was much more stringent than that of the US during most of the 1990s, with the Bank of Canada seeking 'zero inflation' under Governor Crowe from 1988 to 1993. At the same time, the US Federal Reserve accepted inflation of 3 per cent and tested the limits of low unemployment in the late 1990s. Canada's lower output and productivity growth also reflect continued under-development of capital goods and high-tech manufacturing, which have been high-growth sectors. Electrical and industrial machinery and equipment combined contribute 34.8 per cent of booming US manufacturing output. The structure of Canadian manufacturing has changed little under free trade, which should reopen the question of whether active industrial policies are needed to shape Canada's comparative advantage. This was, indeed, a key question in the 1988 FTA debate.

Canadian and US workers have shared much in common over the period of the FTA and NAFTA—increased inequality of earned and total income, increased precarious work, and increased intensity of work. But there were some important differences, too. Throughout the period the US has maintained a lower unemployment rate. After years of maintaining very similar unemployment rates, a gap in rates opened up in the early 1980s and it grew wider again in the 1990s. The US unemployment rate reached a 1990s peak of 7.5 per cent in 1992 and has been under 6.0 per cent since 1994. The Canadian rate exceeded 9.0 per cent from 1992 to 1997 (see also Chapter 7 in this volume). For most of the decade Canadian and US workers also shared stagnating wages, but the persistence of a low unemployment rate in the US is finally producing some real wage gains that are positively affecting the low end of the wage spectrum. It should be noted, too, that during the 1990s the advantage Canadian workers previously enjoyed in terms of UI/EI protection while unemployed has been eliminated. During the decade the portion of the unemployed who qualify for such social insurance has fallen from more than 85 per cent to roughly one-third.

Moreover, if one focuses on the narrower business concerns of access to the US market and a more reliable method of solving trade disputes, there is a mixed story to tell. It is certainly true that Canadian exports to the US have increased dramatically over the FTA period, doubling as a share of national income from just over 20 per cent to just over 40 per cent of GDP. At the same time, the US share of Canada merchandise exports increased from 73 to 83 per cent. Moreover, as evidence of the high degree of integration of the two economies, more of Canada's manufactured goods are now produced for the US market than for the Canadian market; East-West trade is now significantly less than North-South trade, which is the reverse of the situation at the time the FTA was signed.

At the same time, however, in certain sectors the US still effectively manages its imports from Canada, including such traditionally managed imports as softwood lumber, steel, and agricultural products. It would be a mistake to pretend that all of the increase in trade with the US is attributable to the FTA and NAFTA. Canadian merchandise exports had been growing very rapidly over the decade prior to the introduction of the FTA, indeed, at a pace that was not far off that attained between 1988 and 1998. In addition, more than 20 per cent of the increase in exports to the US ($42 billion out of $178 billion) over the 1988–98 period was accounted for by autos, and the FTA has had little bearing on trade in that sector. Moreover, as is evident from the treatment of the Canadian dollar in financial markets, the FTA and NAFTA have made little or no contribution to overcoming the traditionally narrow, resource-dependent base of the Canadian economy.

The increased integration of the Canadian and US economies has not eliminated the importance of the border between the two countries. Indeed, it is always important to bear in mind that much of Canada's international trade amounts to a shuffling back and forth across the border of manufactured inputs and final products. In the auto industry, which accounts for much of this cross-border shuffling, the process is occurring within single firms. That having been acknowledged, however, there has been a real reorientation of the Canadian economy from an East-West to a North-South axis. This reorientation seems to have contributed to a declining willingness in the Canadian political sphere to treat Canada as a single economic unit. This change in attitude seems particularly pronounced in Ontario.

One area where Canadian business and government seem relatively pleased with the results of the FTA and NAFTA is with respect to dispute resolution mechanisms (see Chapter 5 in this volume). However, it has been argued that the strengthening of dispute resolution procedures with the creation of the WTO in 1994 has reduced the significance of what was accomplished in the FTA and NAFTA (Howse, 1998). What *has* accompanied the FTA is a substantial process of harmonization with US social and economic conditions of the sort that opponents of the FTA had feared. In this process, the specific provisions of the FTA and NAFTA have played a less important role than the demands for policy change by Canadian business interests.

Although the FTA and NAFTA are new institutions whose full implications are far from clear in early 2000, a few things directly associated with their operation deserve mention as forces of harmonization. It appears that a combination of three features of the NAFTA environment may create strong pressures to harmonize the institutional framework within which business takes place: first, a broadening of the notion of what constitutes a subsidy, from direct payments by governments into the realm of regulatory law; second, a broadening of what constitutes effective expropriation to include almost all forms of government activity that might reduce a company's prospective profits; and, third, the investor-to-state dispute settlement mechanism.

In this context, it is worth underlining that two areas of long-standing dispute between Canada and the US on trade issues revolve quite specifically around the unwillingness of the US to accept Canadian institutional arrangements that differ from those of that country. This is the case with regard to softwood lumber, where the Canadian property rights regime is not accepted, and in agriculture, where Canadian supply management is not accepted.

The FTA and NAFTA have also limited the use of a number of tools of public economic management. Provisions such as those dealing with energy, government procurement, state monopolies, and the NAFTA investment chapter all have this effect. Thus, the participating countries have limited the options for offsetting the destabilizing and unbalanced nature of market-based economic development.

In addition, for both Canadian and US workers in the highly competitive manufacturing sector, wage growth has not kept pace with productivity growth. In other words, workers are claiming a smaller share of value-added in this sector; in Canada the decline was from 31 per cent to 27 per cent over the 1988–95 period. The reason for this, it has been argued, is that the FTA and NAFTA have increased competition in the manufacturing sector, which consequently has intensified employers' pressure for labour cost reductions. Moreover, within the region as a whole, union power has declined compared to what it was in Canada prior to the FTA and NAFTA, and in the US prior to NAFTA. One of the traditionally important roles that unions play is to ensure that the benefits of productivity improvement are broadly shared, a role that has been difficult to play effectively in the face of a highly competitive continental market (Jackson, 1999; Betcherman et al., 1994).

While there have been some discernible harmonizing effects of the free trade agreements themselves, these have been less important than the major assault by business on the social and legal protection of Canadian workers. Barely a week goes by without business-backed think-tanks like the C.D. Howe Institute or Fraser Institute launching a public attack on worker protection, while more overtly business organizations such as the Business Council on National Issues (BCNI) and Chamber of Commerce carry on the same attack with politicians.

It may be argued that the desire to harmonize social and economic conditions with the US is not the only explanation for this behaviour and that the realm of possible explanations allows for other possibilities. Yet, the desire to avoid being put at a disadvantage compared to US competitors has been heard too often as a rationale for business proposals to lower social and labour conditions to ignore the role of a deliberate desire to harmonize with the US. Moreover, the recent business clamour about the brain drain and the need to lower taxes to US levels is, in fact, an argument both for constraining the fiscal capacity of Canadian governments based on a US model and for making sure that it is upper-income Canadians—i.e., those participating in the brain drain—whose taxes are cut. These proposals would create a strong move in the direction of harmonization with US social conditions. The proposal to adopt the US dollar as Canada's currency, which is now being mooted by some business think-tanks, would further limit Canada's capacity to pursue an independent fiscal policy.

The point cannot be made too strongly that the harmonization taking place with the US in the context of an increasingly integrated economic market is simply one particular variety of harmonization. It is harmonization around a particular conservative world view within which liberalized markets hold pride of place and take priority over all other economic considerations (e.g., full employment) and over other social and community values and interests. It is a harmonization process being driven by a particular social class on both sides of the border—i.e., employers. It is also a process that has had extremely adverse effects on Canadian workers.

The FTA and NAFTA are among the effects of the market liberalizing philosophy and, as has just been noted, they have made both direct and indirect contributions to its further development. Moreover, the ministers who championed the FTA understood very well that it was part of a wider project of reshaping the relationship between government and business. During the 1988 election campaign, Tory cabinet ministers boasted to business audiences in Edmonton that with the passage of the FTA, further National Energy Programs would be made impossible.

ALTERNATIVE APPROACHES TO INTEGRATION AND HARMONIZATION

Concern about trade agreements that focus entirely on commercial interests is not exclusive to the FTA and NAFTA, nor is it a uniquely Canadian concern. In 1998 and 1999, respectively, the proposed MAI and the next round of WTO negotiations ran into strong international opposition from trade unions and other popular groups (see Chapter 16). Both projects, as conceived by their proponents, had to be scrapped. There is, then, an important sense in which the Canada-US issues discussed here are applicable on a much broader scale.

Fundamental to the disputes over purely commercial trade agreements is a difference of views on the relationships among market transactions, the achievement of economic objectives, and the achievement of social and community goals. It cannot be said that all participants in the trade debates have expressed specific views on these relationships. Nonetheless, it is implicit in much of the critique of the purely commercial agreements that critics see the need to supplement market transactions with active economic management by government in order to achieve acceptable economic outcomes (in context, trade is a subordinate part of economic policy), and further that economic activity and objectives need to be subordinated to a wider set of social and community goals. Thus, in the recent debate on the WTO many of the opponents of a new round of negotiations to liberalize trade argued that trade agreements should be subordinated to such international instruments as the UN Universal Declaration of Human Rights, the platforms of action that emerged from the Beijing UN 4th World Conference on Women and the Copenhagen World Summit for Social Development, and international environmental accords.

For its part, the international labour movement has focused a great deal of energy and attention on attaching core labour rights to international trade agreements. One important way to look at this proposal is that it is a first and extremely important step in trying to build a social framework that would make the operation of markets safe for workers, communities, and the environment. It is a particularly important step in that the recognition of core labour rights achieves three things: first, it begins to remove the possibility of using a reduction in labour and social standards as a way of improving the competitive position of firms and nations, and forces competition onto more positive grounds such as the achievement of technical and administrative efficiencies, improved product quality, and improved customer service; second, it strengthens domestic demand in exporting countries; and third, it creates a force in the form of organized workers who will almost inevitably push for measures (collective bargaining rights, labour standards, and social programs) that will ensure the broad diffusion of the benefits of trade and economic activity.

Clearly, the critics of the purely commercial agreements would take a very different point of departure for the development of international agreements on trade (and they would represent different parts of society, too). That having been said, there are some real dilemmas in trying to move from this different point of departure to the implementation of a clear alternative.

The standard of living enjoyed by many workers in high-income countries requires the achievement of substantial economies of scale not available in most national markets.[4] This reality cannot justify the wilful abandonment of national economic regulation, nor does it reduce all international economic issues to purely commercial issues. But it clearly indicates that closed national economies are not compatible with workers' well-being.

There is a clear need to supplement national economic regulation with international regulatory mechanisms to facilitate trade without compromising labour, community, and environmental interests. Moreover, the substantive challenge that this implies is coupled with major process challenges. There are serious problems of a lack of transparency and accountability on the part of both the international economic institutions now in place and the national governments that participate in them. These institutions tend to be inaccessible to labour, and non-élites generally, and they tend to be disconnected from each other and from supranational political authority.

National economic regulation will remain an important element of economic management that is absolutely vital as long as the nation-state remains the only viable way of imposing social restraint on the market. But from a working-class perspective, the exercise of national economic management cannot be allowed to yield results that simply move jobs and income generation from one side of a border to the other. There is little likelihood of building international solidarity among workers on trade issues if national regulation is used in this fashion.

For Canadians there is a particularly difficult issue to resolve, that is, the choice between a regional (North American or hemispheric) as opposed to a global basis for trying to resolve trade and related issues. Each has advantages and disadvantages. Given the high degree of integration of the Canadian and US economies, it would seem to make sense to place a priority on regionally based rules. The broad similarity between Canadian and US living standards and cultures would also argue for a regional focus. But the prospects for creating a counterweight to US predominance are less likely in a regional forum than in a global one where Canada is more likely to find significant economic powers that share a view that differs from that of the US. Finding an ally in France in Canada's desire to exempt culture from the proposed MAI is a case in point.

CONCLUSION

Whether one is dealing with the economic integration of Canada and the United States or the wider process of economic globalization (bearing in mind that important parts of the globe are left out of key parts of the process of economic globalization), raising the living standards of the lowest-income parts of the world is the strongest protection that workers can have against getting whipsawed by employers in the economic and political arenas. This consideration bears most clearly on relations between the highest-income and lowest-income countries, but it is also relevant to Canada-US relations. The large number of low-paid jobs in the US, the absence of minimum-wage laws in some states, and union density rates of 4 per cent in the Carolinas pose the same threats to well-paid workers in Canada (and the US) as do the same conditions in other parts of the world. Indeed, the threats posed are more immediate, as many of the other conditions that would make low-wage states in the US attractive sites for capital investment (e.g., proximity of suppliers and markets, skilled labour supply, etc.) are more present in the low-wage states than in locations outside the US. From a working-class perspective, economic integration should be accompanied by instruments that raise the bottom end of the distribution of income and wealth and ensure its broad diffusion among all parts of the population.

This is clearly a rather distant goal at present. It implies change not only to international trade agreements that are hard enough just to conceptualize, but also in the ideological and class perspectives brought to bear in the definition of national interests in trade agreements. To date, Canadian interests as expressed by the government of Canada have been dominated by business interests, especially those of exporters. It is not surprising, then, that the harmonization that has emerged from our economic integration with the US has not had a positive effect on the economic and social conditions of Canadian working people. Indeed, the government's track record in recent years raises serious concerns about its capacity to respond to interests other than business interests.

Notwithstanding the magnitude of the challenge that faces a working-class perspective on economic integration, there is a growing international understanding of the perverse effects of purely commercial trade agreements and harmonization around a declining set of social and labour conditions. That was demonstrated in Seattle at the WTO ministerial meeting. The basic elements of a more worker-friendly process of integration and harmonization are emerging; indeed, the EU is providing some guidance on an alternative approach to integration and harmonization. Moreover, new energy and enthusiasm are animating the long-standing practice of trade union solidarity across borders, and this opens the door not only to a critique of and opposition to purely commercial agreements and integration processes, but also to a more positive articulation of alternative approaches. In the period immediately ahead, the issues of harmonization with the US and the continued emergence of purely commercial trade agreements will have clear focal points in the national and international arenas.

Bearing in mind that the harmonization issue is fundamentally an issue of domestic politics, two current issues are of profound importance to the progress of harmonization. The first is what has been cast as the issue of how the federal budget surplus should be applied. While there are many particular dimensions to the debate, it is fundamentally a debate about the scope of state activities in Canada. A clear US-based model is being carried forward by the tax-cutters. (It is noteworthy, too, that roughly half of the surplus at stake comes from the EI account and is directly attributable to benefit cuts.) The other issue to which harmonization is central is possible coverage of private hospitals by Alberta's medicare program. If Alberta succeeds in opening the door, NAFTA will spread the seed across the country. The destruction of medicare as we know it would eliminate one of the main sources of social protection that Canadian workers have enjoyed that has not been available to their US counterparts. UI/EI, which used to share this distinction, has already been trimmed back to US levels.

In the international arena, the focal point for commercially based trade agreements and harmonization is likely to remain at the WTO for the time being. In light of what happened in Seattle, not only on the streets but in the meeting rooms where the less-developed countries just said no to a comprehensive new round of negotiations, it is somewhat unbelievable but true that there are still forces pushing for a comprehensive new round of talks aimed at further liberalization. Moreover, even if there is no new round, the issues that were carried over from the Uruguay Round of GATT negotiations will likely proceed. These include areas of vital interest to Canada—agricultural trade and trade in services. These are areas where traditional Canadian interests and concerns are likely to clash directly with US interests. The US wants to get rid of Canadian supply management in agriculture and it wants access to all countries' markets for education and health care.

The manner in which the government of Canada handles these issues will be hotly contested. If business organizations continue to dominate both the public consultation process and the substance of the Canadian bargaining positions, Canada will join the call for a new round of liberalization talks at the WTO and will offer little resistance to US demands in the areas of health and education. Canada has already developed its own education and health entrepreneurs and the government of Canada appears to see its role as being limited to supporting exporters. The government will, of course, face a strong challenge from labour and other popular groups that will demand an end to the pure liberalization agreements. They will demand the construction of a social framework for trade and they will want to test the limits to which economic integration can be made compatible with a social model that differs from that of the US.

NOTES

1. For an overview of labour standards in Canada and the US, see Block and Roberts (1998).
2. The approaches to economic policy described immediately below are reflected in a comprehensive way in Department of Finance (1994).
3. It would be appropriate to note that the broad contours of economic policy have been similar in the United States and Canada—and indeed in much of the industrialized world—in recent years. But it would have to be noted, too, that both monetary and fiscal policy have been less contractionary in the US than in Canada for some years and that goes a long way towards explaining lower unemployment in the US.
4. Sometimes this reality leads directly to talk of the need for globalization. However, there are few goods or services for which the entire global market is required to capture most available economies of scale.

REFERENCES

Betcherman, Gordon, Kathryn McMullen, Norm Leckie, and Christina Caron. 1994. *The Canadian Workplace in Transition*. Kingston: Queen's University Industrial Relations Centre, 1994.

Block, Richard N., and Karen Roberts. 1998. 'Measuring and Quantifying Labor Standards: The Cases of the United States and Canada', paper presented to the conference 'Globalization and Its (Dis)Contents: Multiple Perspectives', East Lansing, Michigan State University, 3–4 Apr.

Department of Finance. 1994. *Agenda: Jobs and Growth*. Ottawa: Department of Finance.

Howse, Robert. 1998. *Settling Trade Remedy Disputes: When the WTO Forum is Better than the NAFTA*. Toronto: C.D. Howe Institute.

Jackson, Andrew. 1999. 'From Leaps of Faith to Lapses in Logic', *Policy Options* 20, 5 (June).

———— and David Robinson, with Bob Baldwin and Cindy Wiggins. 2000. *Falling Behind: The State of Working Canada, 2000*. Ottawa: Canadian Centre for Policy Alternatives (forthcoming).

Osberg, Lars. 1999. 'Long Run Trends in Economic Inequality in Five Countries—A Birth Cohort View', paper presented to the CRESP Workshop on 'Equality, Security, and Community', Vancouver, 21 Oct., and the Jerome Levy Economics

Institute conference on 'The Macro Dynamics of Inequality in Advanced and Developing Countries', Annandale on Hudson, NY, 28 Oct.

Ritchie, Gordon. 1997. *Wrestling with the Elephant: The Inside Story of the Canada-U.S. Trade Wars*. Toronto: Macfarlane Walter and Ross.

Wolfson, Michael, and Brian Murphy. 1998. 'New Views on Inequality Trends in Canada and the US', *Monthly Labour Review* (US Bureau of Labor Statistics), Apr.

10

Canada, the United States, and the World: Making the Most of Global Opportunities

THOMAS D'AQUINO

The forces driving globalization—technological change, faster and cheaper transportation and communications, the freer flow of goods, services, people, capital, and ideas—have had an enormously positive impact overall. The benefits have not always been evenly distributed, but globalization has boosted economic growth, raised standards of living worldwide, accelerated the spread of technology, expanded consumer choice, raised environmental standards, and contributed to social progress and democratic development.

Canada has a huge stake in making globalization work and in making the most of its opportunities. As a mid-size power with 80 per cent of its economy linked to imports and exports, it must try to prevent any backsliding towards protectionism. At the same time, more open and strengthened markets worldwide, underpinned by strong and enforceable international trade rules, will ensure continued improvement in the competitiveness of Canadian enterprises.

To fear open borders is to allege that Canadians just do not have what it takes. As a country, we should have more confidence in ourselves. The experience of the past decade surely demonstrates that Canadians and their enterprises are more than capable of flourishing amid open markets, across North America and around the world. The ability to continue taking on the best in the world and to keep winning is the key to future growth in the incomes of Canadian families.

Despite the setback in Seattle in November 1999, the agenda for action under the umbrella of the World Trade Organization (WTO) remains both urgent and ambitious. What the world needs is a powerful reaffirmation of rules-based market policies throughout individual economies and a revival of the principles of open trade.

Since the Seattle meeting, the WTO General Council has agreed to launch negotiations on liberalizing trade in services and agricultural products. Also agreed is the need to address the concerns of developing countries with respect to agreements on intellectual property and investment measures. Progress in these areas should, in turn, help to advance other key issues on the global agenda, such as the need to curb non-tariff measures and abuse of antidumping, countervail, and safeguard actions.

The business community continues to support the goal of raising labour and environmental standards around the world. But the WTO is not the best place to accomplish these objectives. Other institutions, such as the International Labour Organization (ILO), are more appropriate venues for exploring ways to ensure that trade respects global concerns about labour standards and human rights.

In this context, trade strategy remains an important tool for Canada's economic development. The attainment of an effective set of global rules under the umbrella of the WTO must be our top priority. Under that umbrella, we must continue to reach out aggressively for strategic markets in Europe, Japan, China, and Latin America.

Canada's relationship with the United States, however, will remain our dominant concern on the trade strategy front, especially in the short term. There is not the slightest doubt that the Canada-United States Free Trade Agreement (FTA) has been a powerful catalyst in improving our economic performance. Now we must make fresh efforts to engage Americans in a common cause.

The FTA and the North American Free Trade Agreement (NAFTA) may have left many Canadians with the feeling that little is left to be done. The very names of these agreements, referring as they do to 'free trade' rather than freer trade, contribute to this perception. There are highly visible irritants (such as wheat and softwood lumber), but these are seen as relatively minor exceptions marring an otherwise open border. Canadians have come to take open access to the United States for granted.

In reality, the range of barriers that add to the cost or risks of serving the continental market from the Canadian side of the border is both significant and growing. Canada's share of foreign direct investment within the NAFTA zone has declined. Border effects, both real and perceived, are having a continuing impact on Canada's ability to attract investment in operations with continental mandates.

The most damaging border issue in recent months has involved the flow not of goods or people, but of that most mobile of inputs, information. American security concerns led to severe restrictions in defence-related industries that even curtailed data flows and personal contacts between American companies and their wholly owned subsidiaries in Canada.

This kind of issue, if left to fester, can have severe consequences for Canada. In addition to lost business opportunities for Canadian firms, restrictions such as those put in place last year in the defence sector can lead easily to a shift of key functions and operations south of the border. They certainly create powerful new reasons not to grant new or expanded world product mandates to Canadian subsidiaries.

The defence and security issue highlights the need for early and serious bilateral discussions on the question in principle of whether Canada wants to be inside or outside the American tent. The urgency of such discussions would be reinforced if American political portrayal of Canada as a conduit for illegal immigrants and terrorists leads to rigorous controls on cross-border movement. The resulting congestion and delays would be felt personally by all those who cross the border frequently. More dangerously, they would reinforce the perception of investors that Canada is definitely not the place to invest if most of a company's customers are or will be in the United States.

The defence and immigration issues might by themselves foster useful discussion on the benefits of a continental security perimeter, but they would not necessarily be linked to talks that would further ease restrictions on trade in goods and services. However, it would be difficult to imagine any productive negotiations on trade issues, such as government procurement or trade remedies, until the security concerns are resolved. A new round of comprehensive trade talks could not proceed quickly enough to deal effectively with the defence and security issue. The real question is whether Canada should attempt to use American defence and security concerns as a catalyst for broader progress on erasing the remaining barriers to the movement of goods, services, and people across our common frontier.

In the absence of any broad and visible threat to cross-border access, the Canadian public is unlikely to see any compelling need to enter into major negotiations that might require Canada at least to talk about such hot-button issues as culture, water, or health care. There would be clear support for obvious measures to improve access through border facilitation, but the potential remains for a great deal of opposition to a comprehensive effort to erase most or all of the remaining border barriers.

Canada certainly must seek every opportunity to eliminate impediments at the border. In addition, we should consider moving beyond the NAFTA rules to common standards; to non-discrimination in government procurement; to further liberalization in services; and, yes, even to common rules about competition and subsidies. The effect of such broad changes would be to bolster Canadian growth, productivity, innovation, and investment.

If a trilateral negotiation including Mexico were to prove feasible, Canada should support such a course. But given widespread scepticism about NAFTA in the United States and Mexico, and given the immigration and security issues that dominate American concerns at the moment, it would appear difficult to develop much appetite in the United States for a wide-ranging negotiation involving all three countries.

Negotiations to remove the remaining barriers limiting the flow of goods, services, people, and investment across the Canada-US border could be of significant benefit to Canada. But for Canada to take advantage of the resulting opportunities, it first has to pull up its socks domestically.

In particular, Canada needs to cut personal and corporate tax rates, remove regulations that still restrict companies in many sectors, and encourage Canadian firms to achieve the scale needed to compete globally. In the absence of such domestic policy reforms, even

a successful comprehensive effort to erase the border will be insufficient to achieve much impact on investment location decisions and
might actually accelerate the southbound flow of skilled people, key
jobs, and strategic assets.

It is vital to note that while policy convergence and harmonization may be key phrases in any bilateral negotiation, Canada's goal
must not be to imitate the United States. We certainly need to reduce
the tax gap and it may be to our advantage to harmonize policies in
certain fields, but such proposed changes merely accentuate the need
to develop a distinctively different and better model of economic and
social development. Canada must make itself the preferred location
for people to live and work and for companies to invest in operations serving the continental and global markets. As the smaller country, Canada must offer advantages that are clear and substantial
enough to offset the inevitable economic gravity of the larger market to the south.

Canada therefore should take the initiative in moving forward, just
as we did in the formative stages of the process leading to the
Canada-US Free Trade Agreement. First we must build a consensus
for the scope and goals of such an initiative in Canada, and then we
must convince the Americans of the wisdom of such a course of
action. As Canada enters the twenty-first century, the opportunities
are extraordinary. Two factors will be critical to achieving our full
potential—a strong and effective, rules-based global trading system,
and an even more open, two-way economic relationship between
Canada and the United States.

Part Two

Multilateral and Regional Relationships

11

Real Borders in a Not So Borderless World

STEVEN LEE

Not all borders are disappearing and, in fact, they may be increasingly important as we begin the twenty-first century. Four hundred people die every year on the Mexico-US border, according to Canada's ambassador to Mexico, Stan Gooch. Some US legislators want a tighter Canada-US border to address a fear of 'come-on-down' migrants and drug flows (*National Post*, 2000). The son of Nazi parents and an influential right-wing Austrian political leader, Joerg Haider has successfully campaigned for a new curtain between East and West Europeans.

There are more states than ever before, many of them new and small or micro states. 'During the last half of the twentieth century there has been a trend toward more and smaller states. . . . in an era of globalization, the secessionist impulse knows no geographical boundaries' (Enriquez, 1999: 30). Local identities, including national and regional, are reviving in many places, and not only in Balkan states. With a chilling whiff of the ghetto, concentration camp survivor Leon Zelman says, 'When I saw these people cheering Haider, this made me very depressed. He is waking up deep, hateful feelings.' Asked whether he is still proud to be an Austrian, he replies with a sad smile: 'I am not so much an Austrian. I am more a Viennese' (*Globe and Mail*, 2000).

Communications, the movement of people and capital, consumer identities, and increasingly well-connected civil societies are transborder, integrative, and global. Signs of rebellion against global production, trade, and investment are visible. 'Anticorporatism is the brand of politics capturing the imagination of the next generation of trouble makers' (Klein, 2000: xviii). It is likely that even well-accepted policy goals, such as humanitarian interventions (global values and help applied to local crises), will run into the wall of traditional national sovereignty and very real borders.

'Global versus local' will be critical in the future of Canada-US relations, in North American relations with Mexico, and in the shaping and conduct of much of Canada's foreign policy, including the core of Foreign Affairs Minister Lloyd Axworthy's foreign policy: human security. Global and local can be defined by borders. There are three kinds of borders worth attention at the moment: territorial borders create our national space; borders create division between rich and poor societies; and there is the changing boundary between citizens and the state. Let us turn first to the borders that define us as Canadians.

THE CANADA-US BORDER

No border is more important for Canadians than the Canada-US border. That border has played a central role in defining who we are and what we do for two centuries, and it continues to present us with a wide range of challenges. First, there are unresolved territorial issues. The maritime boundary between Canada and the United States off the British Columbia coast (Dixon Entrance and adjacent waters) has not been settled and remains a sore point. Canada's Arctic Ocean boundaries have never been recognized by the United States, and the Americans have breached Canadian boundaries and sovereignty with provocative military and commercial exploits. Transboundary water and resource issues have provided points of both conflict and co-operation in the past (acid rain, the St Lawrence Seaway, the Columbia River). Today, the Pacific fisheries boundary (quotas for salmon catches) remains a major point of international contention, and water diversions between North Dakota and Manitoba and between Yukon and Alaska are challenges to neighbourly relations. Should a future United States government deploy an anti-ballistic missile system, a Canadian government may (or may not) face a space-age border and sovereignty dilemma.

However, the Canada-US border signals much deeper challenges than these ongoing territory-related issues. The Canada-US border has always been at the heart of 'us and other' for Canadians. Divided in the past by religion, language, region, and distance (and European settler/Aboriginal peoples differences), 'The Border', a concept that helps to shape our mindset, our *mentalité*, our difference, has provided one of our few commonalities and enabled the creation of non-American space and spaces for Canadians to survive, flourish, and experiment. Though our identities as Canadians are diverse and have changed over time (pre-contact, New France, new Britain, linchpin of Empire, frontier of fish, fur, and railways, immigrant haven, multicultural mosaic, deconstructed social-history salad), we have used The Border to build an alternative North American society, a society outsiders have no trouble recognizing. British travel author, Jan Morris, says:

> The more often I have visited this country, the more clearly I have come to realize that Canada is unique. It is pure nonsense to say that it might as well be part of the U.S.A.—almost nowhere in Canada could I suppose for a moment that I was on American soil. Not only is there the utterly distinct French element, not only are the political and social systems quite different, but the whole temper of life in Canada, its manners, its looks, its values, I think, are unmistakably Canadian. Few would deny that it is less exciting than the United States, but Americans often themselves concede that in fundamental ways it is superior. (Morris, 1999: xiii)

Canadians, it seems, want to keep it that way. According to a poll carried out by Pollara, 82 per cent of Canadians 'believe the quality of life to be better in Canada' than in the US. A surprisingly low 18 per cent anticipate anyone from their family moving to the US in the foreseeable future (down from 22 per cent in 1998) (*National Post*, 2000). According to polling for *Maclean's* , 90 per cent of Canadians agree Canada has a unique identity, 81 per cent say we should not try to become more like Americans, and more than half (54 per cent) say the federal government should 'do more' to oppose Canada becoming more like the United States (Wood, 1999).

Notwithstanding the deepening economic relationship, omnipresent US cultural products and their consumption by Canadians, travel and tourism, and corporate buyouts and mergers, Canada and the US are not following the path of European Union spillover integration through trade, cultural contact and education exchanges, and common regulatory and other functions. The new American interest in the Canadian border is based on new perceived sources of threat to US security from terrorists and others. The Border may be as important as it has ever been since 1812 when, on the eve of war, Congressman Henry Clay encouraged President Madison, 'I verily believe that the militia of Kentucky are alone competent to place Montreal and Upper Canada at your feet' (Morton, 1994: 42). It was that conflict, more than any other single event, that created The Border of today, in all its forms: 'the geopolitical tradition that gave Canada its organizing principle is rooted in the war of 1812' (Camp, 2000).

For Americans The Border is no less real—their sense of Other includes Canada as part of a vague, increasingly unfriendly, and potentially threatening world outside the US. The Chair of the House Subcommittee on Immigration, Lamar Smith (R. Texas), said in January this year: 'Countering the threat of terrorism tops the agenda of the US Congress this week and our country's porous border with Canada may be the place to start cleaning house. Americans want increased security in an increasingly unfriendly world' (Smith, 2000).

Today, for some political activists in Canadian civil society, The Border provides the space to challenge a wide range of perceived threats and undesirable (from some points of view) phenomena, from Starbucks to US magazines to 'globalization'. 'Never has there been such a variety of initiatives and confrontations. Seldom has there been such a need for communication, dialogue and even new strategies between civil society actors', according to John W. Foster of the NGO Common Frontiers (Foster and Anand, 1999: 133). Far from prompting the erosion of the Canada-US border, civil society activists (often Canadian nationalists) seek to maintain The Border.

Much of the history of Canada can be seen as the establishment, maintenance, and adjustment of our border, in the largest sense, with the United States. The border is not eroding, and the public on both sides may be of a mind to strengthen 'good fences, good neighbours'. That same task remains key in public policy as we begin the new century, and it remains central to foreign policy. Canadian experiments and institutions—medicare, the monarchy, or even, heaven forbid, the NHL—might come and go. It is The Border that provides us the safe space, where we can continue to experiment, make our own mistakes, and build our own evolving cultures and institutions.

While the Canada-US border has secured space for the 'Canadian project' described by John Ralston Saul as 'perfectly conscious, highly intellectual, clearly thought out and debated' from the 1840s onward, we have often ignored our other border and neighbourhood to the North (Saul, 1998).

NORTHERN BORDERS

Except for occasional romantic events or some sudden sense of wronged violation, for Canadians 'the North has been largely ignored, even as it has remained essential' (Koring, 1998: 30). In a discussion paper for the 1998 National Forum, Paul Koring (1998) notes: 'Every Canadian international boundary in the North is disputed, or open to challenge. . . . nothing Northern matters more to Canadians than the threat posed by our closest ally's icebreaker ploughing through our Northwest Passage' (ibid., 32). Yet, this may be changing. The most recent federal government throne speech set out northern goals 'to advance Canada's leadership in the Arctic region (which) enhances co-operation, helps protect the environment, promotes trade and investment and supports the security of the region's people' (Clarkson, 1999).

Since the establishment in 1996 of the Arctic Council of Circumpolar States and Select Indigenous Peoples Organizations, Foreign Affairs Minister Axworthy has promoted, provoked, and pushed the development of a northern foreign policy for Canada— 'northernness as a foreign policy template' (Axworthy, 1999). This policy development has been shaped by parliamentary committee input in 1997, by the 1998 National Forum (meeting in Whitehorse, Yellowknife, Iqaluit, Edmonton, and Quebec City), follow-up roundtables across Canada with Ambassador Mary Simon and others, extensive policy work by officials in several government departments, and close relations with Norwegians and other Nordic neighbours. 'I am working on a comprehensive, new document on Canada's northern foreign policy', Axworthy explained. In the meantime, evidence of attention to our northern border and relations with northern neighbours is mounting.

One of the key elements of evolving northern foreign policy and recognition of our northern frontier is attention to the role of citizen-to-citizen relations across this frontier and to the intrinsic role of civil society and public diplomacy in regional relations. Recommendations from the 1998 National Forum include the following:

- Canada should encourage educational exchanges.
- Northern communities should establish links with other northern communities.
- Circumpolar exchanges of Inuit/northern peoples should be a priority.
- Scientific exchanges and technology transfers with Russia should be strengthened. (CCFPD, 1998)

These kinds of calls for civil society roles in the shaping and conduct of international relations have already been reflected in preparations for a formal Northern Foreign Policy in 2000. Axworthy has also said the new policy would include attention to 'new connections between communities, shared northernness and new networks of contacts' (Axworthy, 1999).

In the context of Canada's relations with Europe (the European Union), a northern dimension of foreign policy has already taken shape. At the Canada-EU summit meeting in December 1999, with the Finns presiding for the EU, Axworthy noted, 'I am confident that northern cooperation will be part of this dialogue.' The concluding Joint Statement on Northern Co-operation included civil society activities across borders: indigenous peoples issues, children/youth education and exchanges, enhanced research co-operation, and support for a University of the Arctic.

For policy-makers, and for foreign policy-makers in particular, it is interesting to note the creation of a regional identity as 'northerners' and the articulation of 'Other' as southerners. The National Forum noted, for example, that:

- Ottawa should foster new relationships between circumpolar groups and regions.

- Northern people often feel closer to each other than to their nation.
- Canada Post and travel should not be routed via southern Canada.
- Southerners should be educated about northern issues and realities.

Perhaps the most remarkable and impressive circumpolar achievement to date is not the Arctic Council, which ultimately is the child of nation-states, but the myriad links across boundaries that have been created by northerners: First Nations, scientists, regional governments, and sub-regional entities have created a web that spans the top of the globe (Koring, 1998).

It can be argued that civil society in Canada and across the Arctic has helped to build awareness of the North and to focus attention on circumpolar issues and relations, and in doing so has increased our consciousness of and the reality of our Arctic borders (and the opportunities they provide). Canadian civil society, as reflected broadly by citizens' opinion in polls and as animated by anti-globalization groups and leaders, wants to keep the Canada-US border and would like to strengthen Canadian self-identity. In the North, citizens seek to reach out across national borders and the permanently frozen Arctic waters to create a regional, northern identity, recognizing first the long-neglected Arctic borders, and second, a new regional self-identity and a southern Other.

THE GREAT DIVIDE

The border between rich, modernized societies and the vast majority of the rest of humanity is sharper than ever, and will be a dominant factor in global affairs in the new century. Before turning to the changing boundary between the state and civil society it is important to take note of the sharp division between OECD member countries and other nations. This division can be seen at Tijuana, Mexico, at Berg, Austria, and at any number of other places around the world. Canada sits on the privileged side of this divide. Along with our immediate neighbour to the south, most of our trading partners, and our military allies, we possess the assets of the privileged: technology, resources, capital, education, health care, rule of law, and democratic stability. Nations on the other side of this divide are burdened with all the liabilities: poverty, disease, mass unemployment, migrant and displaced people, environmental disasters, collapsed states, and widespread violence. This division is a real border in some places and an absolute division across humanity. As Michael Ignatieff writes, 'Globalism in a post-imperial age permits a post-nationalist consciousness only for those cosmopolitans who are lucky enough to live in the wealthy West. It has brought chaos and violence for the many small peoples too weak to establish defensible states of their own' (Ignatieff, 1993: 13).

'Global' and 'local' take on new meanings in the face of this divide. Global is a threat to the privileged local islands of the EU, North America, and their outposts. The failed WTO talks in Seattle showed the tension between the truly global interests and these islands of local privilege. As *The Economist* (1999) notes, 'America and Europe urgently need to show more genuine commitment to free trade. . . . By trying to force labour rights on to the agenda for the new round, for instance, America and Europe are playing with fire.'

But it is not only trade that divides this global and local. There is already a 'fortress Europe' in markets and agriculture and increasingly in immigration and possibly military arrangements.

> Bluntly, globalization has not gone nearly far enough. The principal way the North could help the South is by operating its own markets, which remain especially closed to the agricultural products in which many developing countries have a comparative advantage. In this sense, the Common Agricultural Policy of the European Union is an obscenity, preventing economic growth in both the post-communist Europe and the Caribbean. (Hall and Paul, 1999: 406)

European Union President Romano Prodi says, 'borders should be tightened against illegal immigrants to reduce the appeal of right-wing politicians' (*Vancouver Sun*, 2000). In fact, there is increasing danger of a 'fortress North America' inside a wall of fear of migrants, drugs, and terrorists, protected by perimeter defences, including the illusion of a possible US National Missile Defense:

> We are moving toward a kind of Fortress North America. . . . We are already seeing that with things happening in Canada to reduce the risk of the longest undefended border. You don't have to worry about that if you have a common wall around North America. But I don't think that's sunk in. (Mulgrew, 2000)

Some view promotion of environment and labour standards by privileged countries as a smokescreen to maintain this divide. President Ernesto Zedillo of Mexico told the World Economic Forum in Davos, Switzerland, that 'A peculiar alliance has recently come into life. Forces from the extreme left, the extreme right, environmentalist groups, trade unions of developed countries and some self-appointed representatives of civil society, are gathering around a common endeavour: to save the people of developing countries from development' (Zedillo, 2000). If this division persists, and if privileged countries like Canada are not perceived to be addressing the needs of our global village, policy-makers will be confronted with a rising tide of local conflict and global stress:

> the world could evolve into a two-tiered system in which globalized elites are linked by shared values and technologies while the populations at large, feeling excluded, seek refuge in nationalism and ethnicity and in attempts to become free of what they perceive as American hegemony. (Kissinger, 1999)

CITIZENS AND THE STATE

Civil society at home and international civil society have an important role to play in shaping our response to this challenge. The state remains the sole actor on behalf of society's interests, especially where it is legitimate through a representative, democratically accountable government. Nevertheless, the state is increasingly sharing public policy space with civil society in Canada. This partnership signals a changing boundary between governors and the governed and will require increasing attention to our Westminster model of Parliament, public service, and ministers. As Cameron and Stein (1999) observe, 'The state faces the formidable challenge of redefining itself in space so that it retains political loyalty as an authoritative, legitimate, representative and accountable arena of political action. We are just beginning a new dialogue of place amidst newly opened and shifting spaces.'

The changing political culture in Canada has driven the changing relationship between the state and civil society. In the past political scientists described the characteristics of Canadian political culture in terms of deference to élites, dualism, regionalism, and federalism.

These have undergone radical change in one generation. Conflicting views of federalism have been exposed. Regionalism continues to evolve to include an empowered North and a regionally fractured party system and regionally divided Parliament (the old political parties may no longer be able to accommodate regional diversities). English-French dualism is challenged by waves of new Canadians, recognition of indigenous peoples, and other new realities. Most important for state-civil society relations, traditional élitism has given way to widespread public demand for participation in policy-making and public affairs.

This demand for participation has taken different, evolving forms over the past 30 years. Starting with a demand for basic consultation 'hear me', Canadians want a say on issues like hydro transmission routes, new roads, and the use of chemicals in agriculture. Many Canadians now demand institutional change (an elected Senate, recall of legislators, participation in constitutional changes through referenda) and participation in the development of policy (National Forum on Health, budget-making consultations, environment impact hearings). This rising demand for participation is now reaching a demand for a role in decision-making. According to Ekos Research, 87 per cent of Canadians want the government of Canada to consult citizens more, 68 per cent want problems brought to the people 'for decision-making' (50 per cent of decision-makers disagree with that idea). Canadians also want a more citizen-centred and accessible opportunity to participate in public affairs. Polling also shows that Canadians see big business and the media having too much influence in public affairs and favour a larger role for citizens, small business, community groups, religious groups, and academics (Ekos Research Associates, 1999).

The federal government has responded to this demand in a number of ways. Through parliamentary committees, stakeholder consultations, and new experiments with 'engagement' and communications technologies, the federal government has set out to 'do government better' and recently to build 'new forms of governance'.

Foreign policy and Canada's international relations are not exempt from this public demand for participation. Lloyd Axworthy has led the move to open up foreign policy-making and has promoted partnerships with civil society in international affairs.

There is dramatic change in the actors and instruments of global affairs. Civil society and non-governmental organisations are playing an increasingly important role. The internet and more rapid communications improve people's capacity to connect directly, to participate in world affairs, and to mobilise support for the less fortunate. There is, finally and perhaps most importantly, an increasing willingness to speak up—a disposition to take action on behalf of people regardless of who they are and where they are—and, in the process, to challenge the most absolutist notions of non-interference. (Axworthy, 2000)

Institutional responses include annual DFAIT consultations on human rights, peacebuilding, and, recently, nuclear disarmament. Canada has pushed for a larger role for NGOs and other experts at the UN Security Council (as recommended by the 1999 National Forum). The successful landmines and International Criminal Court partnerships between states and NGOs and experts are being built upon in other international initiatives: small arms, indigenous peoples in the Americas, humanitarian law, and a range of other issues. The Canadian Centre for Foreign Policy Development has a specific mandate to help Canadians participate in shaping foreign policy ideas and options. The CCFPD has undertaken the annual National Forum on Canada's International Relations (recent focal topics have been peacebuilding, 1996; the Asia-Pacific, 1997; northern foreign policy, 1998; human security and the UN Security Council, 1999; and war-affected children, 2000) and has organized 60 round tables across the country. Along with funding policy option projects proposed by the public, this work has provided a significant public input to policy development.

In roundtable discussions and other forums, knowledgeable citizens have joined politicians and diplomats not only to consult but actually to make foreign policy. Just days after a discussion on East Timor in February, for example, Foreign Minister Lloyd Axworthy issued a statement that followed the citizen recommendations very closely. The Canadian Centre for Foreign Policy Development is at the heart of Ottawa's efforts to include citizens as policymakers. (Walker, 1999: 1, 7)

This changing boundary between the state and civil society in foreign policy and international relations raises a number of questions.

- Who and what is civil society?
- What are NGOs? Are some NGOs really non-governmental when most of their funding comes from governments and their major activities are the delivery of government projects or programs?
- Are they transparent and to whom are they accountable?
- What are the obligations of citizens if they participate in policy formation or international activities?
- What is the role of MPs if citizens are dealing directly with government policy-makers?
- Are some parts of civil society being over-consulted?
- What is the public capacity for participation and where are the government resources for citizen engagement, including international roles?
- What is the relationship between the citizen, public servant, minister, and Parliament?

In our work at the CCFPD we use an operating definition of civil society as 'citizens acting in the public space for the public good'. We deconstruct the roles of NGOs into their components—program delivery, advocacy, partnership, policy development—and build relations with those NGOs with the interest or capacity to contribute to foreign policy development. We also create space for citizens, stakeholder groups, policy officials, ministers, and parliamentarians to come together to explore ideas and policy development. The questions, however, remain.

These are the same questions that must be faced in other countries where the boundary between the state and civil society is changing, in new democracies where civil society is taking shape, and in international civil society as it aspires to a major role in global affairs. There is no question, to quote Minister Axworthy, that 'we ignore civil society at our peril' (Axworthy, 2000). The opening border between the state and civil society will continue to make for better policy—better because there can be a wide range of ideas and policy options; better because civil society partners can help execute foreign policy objectives; better when policy is based on the broad values of society and anchored in the democratic legitimacy of public participation.

However, more work needs to be done to address the unanswered questions. More work is also necessary to assess the role and accountability of large corporations in national policy and in international affairs. It would be reassuring to believe the editors of *The Economist* when they say multinationals are run by 'well meaning, honourable folk':

> their corporate morality is a great deal better than that of the average government: most would kick out a chairman who behaved like Bill Clinton or Helmut Kohl. They are at least as accountable (to their shareholders and the law) and a good deal more transparent than the average NGO. Multinationals should continue to listen, to try to do no harm, to accept the responsibilities that go with size and wealth. Yet in the main they should be seen as a powerful force for good. They spread wealth, work, technologies that raise living standards and better ways of doing business. (*The Economist*, 2000)

But what happens when corporations don't behave honourably, accept some responsibilities, and act as a powerful force for good? The great, global multinationals can have adverse impacts at the local level, from mining waste spills to oil profits in societies at war, to instant employment and unemployment for thousands. Along with the state, civil society, and specific NGOs, the multinationals should be a factor in assessing and addressing the shifting space for the state and the changing boundaries between the citizen and the state.

More attention is necessary to address the role of nascent international civil society in international affairs, especially to determine how it can or cannot overcome the sharp division between the privileged local and the rest of global humanity. For example, there could be real danger in the 'popularization' of the United Nations, as advocated at the December 1999 Montreal meeting of World Civil Society Organizations, which could further raise the frustration level for major southern states.

Canada is indeed a fortunate country. We will remain a fortunate country, able to promote human security and other foreign policy goals, only if we pay careful attention to the borders that matter—with our neighbour, in our Arctic neighbourhood, between rich and poor—and the boundaries of citizen-state relations. Policy-makers face the simultaneous challenges of the local and the global. They face challenges of changing borders of several kinds. And both within and beyond borders, they face the challenge of identifying and shaping a truly world politics. As R.B.J. Walker (1993: 183) reminds us, 'while states are still with us, their borders offer no theoretical or practical guarantees.'

NOTE

The author wishes to thank Peter Moore for research assistance and Alison McCuaig and Marketa Geisler for their assistance.

REFERENCES

Axworthy, Lloyd. 1999. Speech to the Canada-EU Seminar on Circumpolar Co-Operation and the Northern Dimension. Aylmer, Que., 20 Oct. http://www.dfait-maeci.gc.ca

———. 2000. Speech to the Permanent Council of the Organization of American States. Washington, 11 Feb. http://www.dfait-maeci.gc.ca

———. 2000. Speech to the University of Calgary Law School on 'Canada and Human Security'. Calgary, 17 Feb. http://www.dfait-maeci.gc.ca

Cameron, David, and Janice Gross Stein. 1999. 'Globalization, Culture and Society: The State as Place Amidst Shifting Spaces', unpublished paper, Aug. (with permission).

Camp, Dalton. 2000. *The Hill Times*, 24 Jan., 5.

Canadian Centre for Foreign Policy Development (CCFPD). 1998. *1998 National Forum on Canada's International Relations*. Ottawa.

Clarkson, Governor-General Adrienne. 1999. Speech from the Throne. 12 Oct. http://www.pco-bcp.ca/sft-ddt

Ekos Research Associates Inc. 1999. 'Citizen Engagement and Globalization: Hearing the Public Voice', paper delivered at IPAC National Conference, Fredericton, NB. http://www.ekos.com

Enriquez, Juan. 1999. 'Too Many Flags?', *Foreign Policy* (Fall).

Foster, John, and Anita Anand. 1999. *Whose World Is It Anyway?* Ottawa: United Nations Association of Canada.

Globe and Mail. 2000. 'Viennese Holocaust survivor wary of rightist resurgency', 24 Feb, A13.

Hall, John, and T.V. Paul. 1999. *International Order and the Future of World Politics*. Cambridge: Cambridge University Press.

Ignatieff, Michael. 1993. *Blood and Belonging*. Toronto: Penguin Books.

Kissinger, Henry. 1999. 'Making a Go of Globalization', *Washington Post*, 20 Dec.

Klein, Naomi. 2000. *No Logo*. Toronto: Alfred A. Knopf Canada.

Koring, Paul. 1998. 'Foreign Policy and the Circumpolar Dimension', *1998 National Forum on Canada's International Relations*. Ottawa: CCFPD.

Morris, Jan. 1990. *City to City: Canada Through the Eyes of the Greatest Travel Writer of Our Day*. Toronto: McFarlane Walter & Ross.

Morton, Desmond. 1994. *A Short History of Canada*. Toronto: McClelland & Stewart.

Mulgrew, Ian. 2000. 'Israeli style security walls coming analysts say', *National Post*, 8 Jan. http://www.nationalpost.com

National Post. 2000. 'Border with Canada must be strengthened, U.S. expert says', 24 Feb, A4.

Saul, John Ralston. 1998. 'The anniversary we forgot: the birth of democracy in Canada', *Globe and Mail*, Mar. http://www.globeandmail.com (Focus & Books)

Smith, Lamar. 2000. 'Plugging our porous border', *National Post*, 24 Jan., A15.

The Economist. 1999. 'Storm Over Globalisation', 27 Nov., 19.

———. 2000. 'The world's view of multinationals', 4 Feb.

Trickey, Mike. 2000. 'Life in Canada overshadows U.S. benefits, poll shows', *Vancouver Sun*, 13 Jan. http://www.vancouversun.com

Vancouver Sun. 2000. 'Tighter borders for EU advised', 31 Jan. http://www.vancouversun.com

Walker, R.B.J. 1993. 'Inside/outside: International Relations as Political Theory', *Cambridge Studies in International Relations*.

Walker, Ruth. 1999. 'Common folks making foreign policy', *Christian Science Monitor*, 26 May.

Wood, Chris. 1999. 'The Vanishing Border', *Maclean's*, 20 Dec.

Zedillo, Ernesto. 2000. 'Can We Take Open Markets for Granted?', Plenary Session: World Economic Forum in Davos, Switzerland, 28 Jan. http://world.presidencia.gob.mx

12

Too Close to the Americans, Too Far from the Americas: A Liberal Policy Towards the Hemisphere

BRIAN J.R. STEVENSON

NATION OF THE AMERICAS

Canada is a nation of the Americas. For decades this simple statement would have been hotly debated. Even though the geographic
reality was never in question, the political, social, economic, and cultural aspects were always, to varying degrees, debatable. For the first
few decades after Confederation and well into the twentieth century,
Canada's linkages with the Americas were primarily directed towards
the United States and the Commonwealth Caribbean. Canada was not
a member of the International Union of American Republics (established in 1890), nor was it a member of its successor, the Pan-
American Union (established in 1910). Even when the Organization
of American States (OAS) was founded in 1948, Canada remained on
the outside, becoming a member only in 1990—a full 100 hundred
years after the world's oldest regional organization was founded.

For the first part of the century, Canada's diminishing ties with Great Britain, relative to the growing continental connection, created a tension between Canada's increased economic, political, military, and cultural dependence on the United States and its growing desire to diversify its international relations. In the immediate postwar period and until the end of the 1960s, this diversification was accomplished primarily through participation in and commitment to the European-centred multilateral order. This commitment, coupled with the strong political and economic links to the United States, prevented a larger hemispheric connection for Canada.

While Latin America and the Caribbean were the 'backyard' for the United States, the region was commonly viewed by Canadians and their governments to be one too closely linked to the United States to provide an effective counterbalance for Canada. In effect, Canada seemed to be *too close to the Americans but too far from the Americas*. Indeed, for most of the twentieth century, Canada was for all intents and purposes a European country. Canada fought two world wars, helped found the North Atlantic Treaty Organization (NATO), played a substantial role in other European-based international organizations, such as the Organization for Security and Co-operation in Europe (OSCE), and generally participated fully in the postwar multilateral order that linked the United States and Europe and created what came to be known as the North Atlantic Triangle. During the postwar period, Canada sought to offset the growing influence of the US by firmly establishing itself as an active diplomatic actor in multilateral affairs. Whether it was in the United Nations (UN) or through the General Agreement on Tariffs and Trade (GATT), Canada sought to pull itself out of the orbit of the United States through the pursuit of an independent foreign policy. So, for most of the century, Canada politely avoided participation in inter-American institutions, such as the OAS. Nevertheless, geography persisted. As the end of the twentieth century approached, and especially during the 1990s, Canada became increasingly closer to the Americas.

By the end of the century Canada's political, economic, and cultural ties with the region were much more intense and amounted to a genuine commitment. Beginning with Pierre Trudeau's review of foreign policy, which culminated in the publication of *Foreign Policy for Canadians* in 1970 (Department of External Affairs, 1970), through Brian Mulroney's bold move to join the OAS in 1990, and ending with Prime Minister Jean Chrétien's active participation in the Summit of the Americas process, his Team Canada trips to the region, and his unprecedented commitment to host six major hemispheric events between 1999 and 2001,[1] Canada's accelerated road towards integration with the Americas marked a profound change in Canadian foreign policy. There has also been more involvement by Canada's non-governmental organizations (NGOs) in the areas of human rights, the environment, and trade policy, and greater interest and participation by business and its organizations. In short, government, business, and civil society have all come together, as demonstrated by their interests and their activities, in a way that would not likely have been predicted as recently as the 1980s. The key questions that emerge in this context are simple: why all of this activity since 1993 and what does it mean to Canada?

With respect to the first question, Canada's relations with the rest of the hemisphere can be understood as the result of at least three interactive forces. First, there have been very significant changes in the structure of the international system, such that the link between the United States and Europe has declined and the ties between the US and the hemisphere have naturally expanded. These changes include, among other things, the end of the Cold War, the relative decline of the United States, the shifting balance between security concerns and economic matters, and the dramatic increase in democratic practices. Second, there have been coincident pressures arising from the development of regionalism, specifically, continental and hemispheric trends towards political and economic integration. Third, domestic pressures within Canada have come from governmental initiatives, NGO activism on social issues, and private-sector interest in opening markets. This interaction has created a tension between demands of the private sector for open and transparent business practices in the rest of the hemisphere and the demands for equally open and transparent good governance and the protection of human rights made by NGOs. The question that remains, therefore, is what does it mean to Canada?

My central argument is that although powerful forces pushed (and are pushing) Canada into the 'Americas orbit' and that unprecedented factors are drawing it into a closer relationship with the inter-American system, it is too early yet to determine whether these linkages can begin to challenge the more established relations with Europe, with Asia, and, especially, with the United States. Moreover, the success of a truly active relationship with the rest of the hemisphere will depend on advancements in economic and governance issues throughout the region. Nonetheless, while the economic and trade benefits may not be great in the short term and middle term,[2] it is important for Canada to foster closer relations with Latin America and the Caribbean and to be actively involved in the inter-American system at the levels of government, trade, and people-to-people contacts.

The purpose of this chapter is to explain why this is so. In doing so it will focus mainly on the role of the Liberal Party of Canada and the federal government under Jean Chrétien and look at the period especially between 1993 and the present. This chapter does not aim to provide a comprehensive account of Canada's activities in the region, as these have become too numerous and complex to be summarized or analysed briefly. Instead, my aim is to explore the increased activity in the inter-American system after 1993 and to assess both the reasons for the heightened activity and the prospects for Canada's continued development by focusing on some selected issues that are representative of the larger trends.

A LIBERAL FOREIGN POLICY TOWARDS LATIN AMERICA AND THE CARIBBEAN

Since the government of Jean Chrétien came to power in 1993, there has been a distinct and identifiable emphasis on deepening relations with Latin America and the Caribbean. The roots of this involvement can be traced to the Trudeau government's foreign policy review. The outcome of the review, expressed in *Foreign Policy for Canadians,* was the pursuit of an independent foreign policy—independent from the United States, that is. The review was organized into six pamphlets that describe a strategy of diversification both multilaterally and bilaterally. Curiously, none of the documents discusses the bilateral relation with the United States. By 1972, this direction of Canada's US policy was enshrined in the so-called 'Third Option', which proposed three distinct directions for Canadian foreign policy: maintaining the status quo at the time, closer relations with the United States, and a foreign and trade policy that sought diversification and a move away from the United States (Sharp, 1972). This Third Option policy (and the ideology behind it) influenced not only the Trudeau government, but also Liberal foreign and trade policy under both John Turner and Jean Chrétien. This was also at the heart of Liberal opposition to the negotiations for a Canada-US Free Trade Agreement (FTA) and the North American Free Trade Agreement (NAFTA).

This drive for a Third Option was also at the heart of the establishment of the Western Hemisphere Consultative Group within the Liberal Party in November 1990 by the then new leader of the Liberal Party, Jean Chrétien, and at the request of external affairs critic Lloyd Axworthy. The Group consisted of representatives from business, NGOs, and academe. Its main goal was to develop a document that would be the Liberal response to the Conservative's hemispheric policy, particularly with respect to the negotiations for NAFTA. The resulting document, 'Part of the Americas: A Liberal Policy for Canada in the Western Hemisphere', authored by Axworthy and the Liberal critic for international trade, Roy MacLaren, articulated a comprehensive alternative to Tory policy. On the fundamental issue of Canada's relations with the US, Axworthy and MacLaren (along with Chrétien, both former cabinet ministers in the Trudeau government) pursued policies reflecting the Third Option approach.

While fundamentally agreeing that Canada should have good diplomatic and trade relations with the United States, the authors state that:

> Canada should also take every opportunity to make the best of the current trade and political trends by diversifying Canada's diplomatic and trade relations in the hemisphere. If until now Canada's foreign policy was based on three pillars (the United States, Europe and Asia Pacific) we now must define Latin America and the Caribbean as the fourth pillar. (Axworthy and MacLaren, 1991: 2-3)

At the heart of Liberal criticism, therefore, was the argument that the Conservatives had drawn Canada too close to the US while not taking sufficient advantage of new multilateral or regional opportunities, such as summit diplomacy and the greater relevance of multilateralism in a post-Cold War order, to ensure an independent foreign policy. For this reason they called for a foreign policy based on Canadian interests, not on what they perceived was a foreign policy influenced by one country. The document emphasized that good trade and diplomatic relations with the US are vital and fundamental to Canada's interests, but 'this does not necessarily mean a conflict-free

relationship as Canadian and U.S. interests may diverge at times'
(ibid., 15). Although concern over the narrowing of trade partners
was central, the proposed Liberal policy towards the western hemisphere also encompassed several non-trade areas such as regional
security, bilateral relations, multilateral relations, development assistance, the environment, human rights and democratic development,
academic and cultural matters, and a new role for domestic non-governmental organizations.

With respect to trade, the document reflected MacLaren's stated
policy of diversifying Canadian trade policy and avoiding narrowing
trade relations, which was captured by his comprehensive trade policy outlook referred to as 'wide open' and which governed his later
emphasis on the completion of the Uruguay Round of the GATT, a
push for a hemispheric free trade area, and his initiative to negotiate
a bilateral free trade agreement with Chile. The major tenets of this
approach were to seek diversification in trade through any means
possible—multilateral, bilateral, or regional—but not to be caught
within the confines of the emerging and existing regional trade blocs.
For MacLaren a bilateral agreement with the US was not bad in and
of itself, but as a primary policy for trade this could be strategically
unwise. A trilateral relationship in North America was only margin-
ally better and a multilateral connection in the hemisphere was in
the right direction, but the ultimate goal would be a global approach.
The more players around the table and the more established multilateral norms and rules, the more protected Canada could feel from
the arbitrary trade actions of the US.

The document on the western hemisphere thus emphasized that
for Canada global trade is preferable to being in a regional trading
bloc, so a 'North American Free Trade zone is, therefore, the worst
case scenario' (ibid., 17). In this context, the emphasis is therefore
on the need for a free trade agreement in the hemisphere (as part of
a global approach) based on the proposals the Bush administration
was making at the time. A diversified trade relationship in the hemisphere was seen as fundamental, not only in terms of trade policy
but also in terms of trade promotion. Foreshadowing the establishment of Team Canada missions, the authors state:

> A Liberal trade strategy in the Western hemisphere should make the invest-
> ment now in educating Canadian entrepreneurs about the potential bene-
> fits of investment and trade in Latin America and the Caribbean, while

informing government and business sectors in the region about the positive aspects of Canada's trade with their countries. (Ibid.)

The political side of the Liberal policy paper focused primarily on the themes that Axworthy had been developing as opposition critic. These sought to establish what he viewed as an independent foreign policy and would ultimately evolve into the three core foreign policy themes of peacebuilding, human security, and soft power that constitute the Axworthy Doctrine. The diversity of the political aspects of the paper was impressive. With respect to regional security matters the emphasis was on three objectives. The first of these was to try to develop confidence-building measures between the US and Cuba and bring Cuba back into the 'hemispheric family'. This was particularly important in a post-Cold War world because it was the remaining issue left in the hemisphere from that era. As Cuba and the US adjusted to the new era, '[t]he possibility for conflict should not be dismissed. Such conflict would strain both multilateral and bilateral relations in the hemisphere' (ibid., 18). The other two aspects involved a plan to continue to promote peace and security in Central America and a strategy with respect to arms control protocols, especially as they related to the drug trade.

There was also emphasis in using Canada's expanding bilateral relations (especially with Mexico and Brazil) and growing multilateral capabilities (in an era marked by greater Canadian capabilities due to interdependence and the 'new internationalism'), as well as a focus on development assistance, from large projects to helping the most poor. Finally, other important themes focused on horizontal issues such as the environment, human rights, and democratic development, as well as a more structured consultation and support for NGOs. Two other themes were mentioned: improving academic linkages and making a special effort to promote relations between Canadian and Latin American Aboriginal peoples. The underlying themes here concentrated on people-centred foreign policy foci as opposed to state-centred ones, which, of course, foreshadows Axworthy's human security agenda.

The authors further argue that Canada should continue the policy directions represented in the Latin America portion of *Foreign Policy for Canadians*. They state that although Canada has fostered better relations with Latin America and the Caribbean for over 20 years, 'since 1984 we have drawn closer to the US orbit, even though the potential for a greater role in world affairs has been afforded to us through our increased capabilities in multilateral affairs.' Axworthy and MacLaren thus conclude that 'the Liberal Party believes that the time has come to give Canada some significant role in hemispheric affairs as one means of redressing the balance in our own foreign policy as well as providing Canada with better balance in the politics of the Western Hemisphere' (ibid., 26). These ideas were reflected in the so-called 'Red Book' that formed the Liberal election platform in 1993 (Liberal Party of Canada, 1993).

An important influence on both MacLaren and Axworthy was the growing interest of business groups and NGOs in Latin America and the Caribbean. This would create some tension between the strategic requirements of diversifying Canada's trade policy by promoting trade liberalization, on the one hand, and the demands of Canadian NGOs for a role in these discussions and for guarantees with respect to labour, democratic principles, human rights, and environmental concerns, on the other. Both trade liberalization and the promotion of good governance are, of course, fundamental tenets of Canadian foreign policy. Finding a way that Canada could promote both at the same time was not the central problem, but finding a formula that could bring both elements to the negotiating table with Canada's trading partners in the region was quite another question. The growing influence and importance of NGOs and greater public interest in Latin America and the Caribbean in the 1980s had set the stage for a potentially powerful new force that would influence policy in a new way. There is early recognition of this tension in the document. But the fact that there was consensus between the authors on the direction of Canadian foreign policy in the western hemisphere was a reflection of a need to balance trade and political issues in foreign policy and especially in domestic politics. It was also agreed that there was a need for diversity in Canadian trade and foreign policy and that Latin America and the Caribbean comprised a region of priority for the expansion of these hopes, even though the results might not be immediate.

MULTILATERAL ACTIVITIES AND INITIATIVES

Perhaps the most important initial signal that Chrétien could have sent after becoming Prime Minister in 1993 was the establishment of a new cabinet position, Secretary of State for Latin America and

Africa. He appointed to the position Christine Stewart, a member of Parliament from Ontario who had founded and run an NGO in Central America before entering politics and who had been critic for international development while in opposition. Under the direction of the new Foreign Minister, André Ouellet, Stewart travelled to the region to increase Canada's profile. Both Ouellet and Roy MacLaren, then Minister of International Trade, began to visit Latin America to implement the ideas contained in the western hemisphere discussion paper and in the Red Book.

The Liberals had inherited the issue of NAFTA, which they had opposed, and this became their first challenge in the hemisphere. Soon after forming the government they faced the task of ratifying the agreement the Tories had signed. Only after the side agreements on labour and the environment were added did they agree, along with the Clinton administration, to ratify the agreement. From the new government's perspective NAFTA was not the global approach they desired, but by bringing another actor into the fold, it was better than the strictly bilateral FTA. Besides, the business community was already committed to NAFTA.

Given the trade and economic ties to which Canada was now committed with Mexico, the new government began a closer relationship. In the first few months of the Chrétien government, the PM, Ouellet, and MacLaren all travelled to Mexico and Ouellet ordered an internal review of Canada's relations with Mexico. In fact, as if to emphasize the difference between himself and former Prime Minister Mulroney, Chrétien's maiden trip abroad was to Mexico, not to the United States. The visit took a dramatic turn when, while preparing to attend the state dinner in honour of Chrétien, President Carlos Salinas de Gortari received the news that his party's presidential candidate for the 1994 election, Luis Donaldo Colosio, had been shot. The dinner was cancelled and both leaders and their wives personally bid farewell to several hundred guests. Chrétien was both shaken and moved by the experience. Subsequently, through both the political and economic crises that followed, he provided political and financial support to Mexico.

On the multilateral front, the most important event was the invitation by President Bill Clinton to the heads of government in the hemisphere to attend the Summit of the Americas in Miami in December 1994. This had been only the third time such an event had occurred (the first two were presidential summits in 1956 and 1967), but this was the first time that Canada and the island states of the Caribbean had also been invited (Cuba, of course, remained conspicuously uninvited). The summit was important to Canada for two reasons. First, it afforded Chrétien an opportunity to be exposed to his colleagues in the hemisphere and to be presented with an agenda that included the theme of democratic development and human rights. Second, it dealt with the issue of trade liberalization, an issue that had been gaining momentum in light of the establishment of NAFTA and the successful negotiations of the Uruguay Round of the GATT. Both of these themes were central to the Liberal policy paper published only three years earlier.

Of significance, too, was that the summit process occurred outside the formal structure of the OAS and allowed for government leaders to deal directly with hemispheric issues without the constraining legalistic structure of the OAS. The plan of action included strengthening democratic development, promoting economic integration and free trade, combatting poverty and discrimination, and seeking ways to promote sustainable development. Canada accepted the role of 'Responsible Co-ordinator', along with other countries, on strengthening democracy and human rights. The summit process also resulted in the agreement to create a Free Trade Area of the Americas (FTAA) by 2005. Both agenda items suited the new Liberal government's approach to the western hemisphere and Canada would enthusiastically support both.

By the time the second Summit of the Americas was held in Chile in April 1998, Chrétien was quite comfortable with hemispheric issues. He travelled to Chile with the Caribbean heads of government on the Canadian government plane, after they had all attended the meeting of the Caribbean Commonwealth countries (CARICOM) heads of government meeting. Chrétien had gained some notoriety because of his government's stand on the Helms-Burton Act (see Chapter 13). At the summit, the news of Chrétien's impending visit to Cuba was leaked and other leaders congratulated him on his stand and his visit, which was seen as an important step in normalizing Cuba's status in the inter-American system. The agenda of the Santiago summit had been refined and a number of important issues for Canada were now included, both on the governance side (including indigenous issues) and on the trade side. At the suggestion of Foreign Affairs Minister Lloyd Axworthy, who replaced Ouellet in the Foreign Affairs portfolio in January 1996, Chrétien also proposed the establishment of a

Foreign Minister's Dialogue Group on Drugs, which was accepted and included in the summit agenda. At the same time, Chrétien announced that Canada would be hosting the next Summit of the Americas, which promised to be the most important hemispheric meeting that Canada had ever held.

On the trade front, MacLaren not only lent support to the FTAA process but also promoted the launching of Chile's accession into NAFTA. He felt that expansion of NAFTA to those countries that were sufficiently ready to accept the rigours of this framework was important in order to diversify the membership. The launch of Chile's accession negotiations was announced shortly before the first Western Hemisphere Trade Ministerial in June 1995. Unfortunately, as discussions for Chile's accession proceeded, it became apparent that the United States Congress was not inclined to give the Clinton administration the support needed under fast-track authority. Without such authority, the American government was unable to negotiate and the initiative collapsed. Once it was clear that NAFTA accession for Chile was not possible, MacLaren then pursued a bilateral agreement, which would be 'NAFTA-compatible', in order to continue the momentum towards opening all trade possibilities.

But the bilateral agreement was also a signal to the US Congress that if they did not support hemispheric free trade, Canada would pursue greater access to markets in the region, even to the disadvantage of the United States. The Canada-Chile Free Trade Agreement was completed under International Trade Minister Art Eggleton in 1997, who also strongly believed in trade diversification in the western hemisphere and who began to explore the possibility of negotiating a co-operation agreement with MERCOSUR, the southern-rim common market comprised of Argentina, Uruguay, Paraguay, and Brazil. The new International Trade Minister, Sergio Marchi, took on this agenda and successfully negotiated a Trade and Investment Co-operation Arrangement in 1998, which, although modest, further supported the principle of diversification.

The FTAA offered Canada three potential advantages: market access, protection for investment, and a clear dispute settlement mechanism. But as negotiations for the FTAA proceeded, it became clear that there was a fundamental problem: the US Congress was reticent to give the Clinton administration fast-track authority for the FTAA negotiations. Although this authority was not immediately needed, most countries in the hemisphere were not prepared to proceed with substantial negotiations until they knew that Congress was going to support the FTAA. Added to this was less than enthusiastic support for the negotiations by countries such as Brazil, which wanted to maintain its prime position as the leader of MERCOSUR. Even with the relatively dim prospect for an agreement, the Canadian government made the FTAA a priority in its relations in the hemisphere, becoming one of the rotating chairs of the negotiations leading up to the Toronto FTAA Ministerial in November 1999.

But Canada's political priorities at the OAS and in the summit process were reflected in the desire to include a mechanism that would involve NGO consultation. The injection of governance, labour, and environment into the FTAA process further complicated the trade discussions, already troubled by more technical trade matters that would take time to resolve. Although this approach created further dismay among some member countries, Canada argued that consultation with civil society and the inclusion of these themes were very important for creating long-term support for the agreement. Some countries in the hemisphere were less than thrilled with what they perceived to be an intrusion into strictly business-related issues that they believed should be discussed and negotiated on the basis of trade criteria alone.

During the 1990s Canada became an active player in the hemisphere, particularly in multilateral affairs. Whether in the summit process, through the OAS, at the FTAA negotiating table, or through bilateral or plurilateral agreements, Canadian diplomats were acting under a new set of guidelines and a fresh mandate, one that involved balancing trade imperatives and governance values. No longer preoccupied with intruding into the sphere of influence of the United States (but always sensitive to the implications) or worrying about offending other partners in the hemisphere, Canada came into its own in this decade and slipped into the inter-American system with ease. But getting closer to the Americas has also brought conflict. In the mid-1990s Canada and the US clashed over the fundamental issue of extraterritoriality. The passage of the Helms-Burton Act had the effect of sharpening the decades-old differences between US and Canadian policies towards Cuba. Canada was also engaged in a bitter dispute with Brazil in the aerospace industry, following accusations made by Bombardier of Canada over unfair subsidies to Brazil's Embraer. Ironically, of course, the decade ended with the cooling of relations between Cuba and Canada after the Cuban government tried and jailed four prominent dissidents. This created a conflict that was later to be described by the Prime Minister as resulting in Canada giving Cuba the 'Northern Ice' treatment (see Chapter 13).

PUBLIC PRESSURE: THE NEED FOR FREE TRADE AND DEMOCRACY

Since the mid-1960s, Canadian NGOs have become increasingly active in Latin America and the Caribbean. The roots of this activism can be found in the missionary activities of Canadian churches and in the involvement of Canadian unions, particularly the Canadian Labour Congress (CLC), in the region. Beginning with the Dominican Republic intervention in 1965, continuing with the military coup in Chile in 1973, and culminating with the Central American crises of the 1980s, Canadian NGOs became more effective in pressuring the Canadian government to become involved in governance and human rights issues in Latin America and the Caribbean (see Stevenson, 2000: esp. ch. 7). For most of the 1970s and 1980s the pressure was directed at having the Canadian government criticize and oppose US policy in the region, and much of the effort concentrated on reacting to particular crises, such as the Chilean coup and the political turmoil in Nicaragua, El Salvador, and Guatemala.

Although some NGOs, frustrated with government policies, tried to make a linkage between Canadian commercial interests and the government's 'quiet diplomacy' approach, the fact was that for the most part investment and trade, and even interest by the private sector, were minimal. During the early 1970s, sensitivity to US interests and the desire not to get embroiled in regional problems outside traditional multilateral forums meant that Canada was not very engaged. By the 1980s, as pressure surged from the press and civil society, and as the government gained greater ability to act internationally with the waning of the Cold War structure, Canada began to participate with other Latin American countries in facing the various crises of the day. This meant that a new relationship was being forged among civil society, Parliament, government, and the press. This relationship arose as much from the loosening of the international system in an era of complex interdependence as from parliamentary reforms to allow public input into the foreign policy domain.

Organizations like the Inter-Church Committee for Human Rights in Latin America (ICCHRLA), the Canada-Caribbean-Central America

Policy Alternatives (CAPA), the Latin America Working Group (LAWG), the Jesuit Centre for Social Faith and Justice, plus a myriad of local and regional NGOs that took on single issues, bombarded the government with letters, presentations before parliamentary committees, and editorial opinions and also staged numerous demonstrations. The 1980s were a particularly dynamic time for these organizations. The Central American crisis not only provided heart-wrenching instances of human rights abuses and violations of democratic processes, but, perhaps more importantly, the Sandinista Revolution in Nicaragua also provided many Canadians with what they felt was a political, social, and economic model for other Latin American nations. At the centre of the crisis was not only the struggle against oppressive governments but also the preservation of the Nicaraguan Revolution. When the Sandinistas' loss of an OAS-supervised election in 1989 took the wind out of the sails of many NGOs in Canada, the next decade became a time to refocus.

By the early 1990s Canadian NGOs interested and active in Latin America and the Caribbean were well organized and experienced, but they lacked the major issue or issues that could put them regularly in the front pages of newspapers and in the meeting rooms with politicians. By this time, however, they had evolved an articulate and sophisticated vision for Canada's relations with the region that was far beyond the more reactive approach of single-issue lobbying of the past. With the Central American crisis out of the news, the end of the Cold War, and a new administration in the White House more interested in expanding trade relations than in promoting Cold War rhetoric, NGOs had to redefine their tasks for the new era. Several major themes emerged at this time: Canadian participation in the OAS and the inter-American system; Mexico and NAFTA; human rights issues, particularly in Peru and Colombia; and the new emerging multilateral hemispheric agenda.

In its submission to the 1994 foreign policy review, for example, CAPA's principal recommendation was that 'Canada should base its foreign policy on a human focused notion of security for all peoples, one based on human needs and the full complement of human rights—civil, political, social, cultural and environmental' (CAPA, 1994: 23). With this as the underlying theme, CAPA made a full set of recommendations that included greater use of the OAS to promote human rights and democratic development, Canada's ratification of the American Convention on Human Rights, the reintegration of Cuba into the political-economic affairs of the hemisphere, the establishment of a code of conduct for multinational corporations, and continuation of Canadian participation in regional UN peacekeeping operations. This submission called for a broad approach to Canadian foreign policy towards Latin America and the Caribbean, which would include looking at human security from all aspects, not just physical and state security. CAPA also expressed a deep concern over trading arrangements impinging on these security concerns and a desire for Canada actively to use the institutions of the inter-American system to further the underlying values of Canadian internationalism. Significantly, CAPA was making this statement to a new Liberal government that had already articulated a similar policy direction. By the late 1990s, NGOs had taken on the trade and governance agenda in the hemisphere. This is exemplified by two reports made by the Canadian Council for International Co-operation (CCIC), both of which demonstrate the broader set of items included in NGO activities (CCIC, 1998, 1999).

Canadian businesses have been interested in Latin America and the Caribbean since at least the 1960s. Some companies, especially banks, have had a presence in the region, but restrictive business practices, limits of foreign investment, and easier opportunities in Europe and the United States always limited the possibilities. The perception of Latin America changed when Canada began to negotiate NAFTA and Canadian businesses began to follow the reforms that the Mexican government implemented in the 1980s and 1990s. The private sector's participation in the negotiation of NAFTA brought them closer than ever to breaking through into the region. When discussions began to surface about an FTAA, this created a surge of interest by the private sector.

Three business organizations took the lead in this process: the Business Council on National Issues (BCNI), representing the major business interests; the Canadian Council for the Americas (CCA), representing businesses already present or in the process of establishing operations in Latin America; and the Alliance of Manufacturers and Exporters Canada, which represented a broader portion of the business spectrum in Canada. These organizations, along with others, pressed the government and assisted it in trade liberalization talks. For example, business representatives were present at parallel meetings each time trade ministers met to further the FTAA agenda, they contributed to public debate about the economic and political relations between Canada and the region, and they took every opportunity to extend their business and government networks in the region. Another important element was the two Team Canada trips to Latin America, one in 1995, the other in 1998. These trips helped both to make the necessary personal connections and to raise Canada's profile as a trading partner in each of the countries visited.

As Daudelin and Dosman (1998) have pointed out, these activities have not, as yet, significantly altered the share of Canadian exports that go to the region. In addition, these activities have not served to bring the FTAA closer to completion and, in more general terms, have not guaranteed greater trade liberalization. Nonetheless, Canadian businesses have become more engaged and more interested in Latin America and the Caribbean, to a degree that is unprecedented; and the social and governance agenda advocated by the NGOs has filtered into the discussions of the FTAA. It is significant that the FTAA includes a formal consultative process with business *and* with other elements of civil society. Although some in the private sector have been reluctant to accept this, others have assisted the government by explaining to their business counterparts in the region that these consultations are important for the successful completion of the FTAA negotiations.

If one accepts the premise that for Canada to continue to expand and deepen its relations with Latin America and the Caribbean there must be significant developments with respect to both governance issues and economic matters, it is perhaps in this respect that Canadian business activities in the hemisphere have been most fruitful. The immediate payoff in economic terms is less important than the medium- or longer-term benefits associated with creating relationships. Trade and investment have indeed increased in absolute terms. From an individual firm's point of view this means that more Canadian companies are involved in the region: Canada is a major investor in Chile and Peru, for example, and many sectors in the Canadian economy are increasingly becoming more active in the region, even if modestly. However, it is clear that business interest will wane, and may even evaporate, if trade liberalization and investment protection agendas do not advance significantly—particularly the establishment of transparent business practices, laws, and judicial procedures. Economic and political instability in the region will also greatly affect business interest and participation, which is one more reason why the governance and economic agendas are both important.

The dual pressures from both the NGO community and business are a significant agenda item for any Canadian government. Although there are conditions under which these two forces reinforce each other, there are also tensions. The task of government in attempting to balance sometimes conflicting demands is not easy. But it is clear that Canada needs the support of both business and NGOs in furthering the hemispheric agenda, and cases such as the WTO meeting in Seattle in 1999 indicate the perils of ignoring or excluding critical sectors of civil society. At the same time, Canada's prosperity depends on trade and open markets, and some balance has to be sought. What is certain is that the tension between these two sectors of Canadian society promotes healthy debates, both at home and abroad, that attempt to address some of the difficult problems inherent in a global economy and society.

THE AXWORTHY DOCTRINE AND THE WESTERN HEMISPHERE

After taking over as Foreign Minister in 1996, Lloyd Axworthy began to bring together the work that he had started while in opposition and the work done by his predecessor. His strategy was organized into three distinct but related policy frameworks that constitute what has come to be known as the Axworthy Doctrine: soft power, human security, and peacebuilding. At the heart of this doctrine is the belief that the international system has gone through a structural change that has allowed Canada to play a more significant role in world affairs, one that Canada should consciously and actively pursue. The first change involves Canada's ability to influence international affairs in a post-Cold War environment. In an era of complex interdependence it involves the ability of a middle power like Canada to be able to convince others, not through the use of force, but by the power of diplomacy, persuasion, and international public opinion. This does not mean that the use of power is not fundamentally important or necessary, as the case of Kosovo proved, but that it becomes less useful, frequent, necessary, and desirable.

The second change involves adding a new dimension to how we view international relations: instead of viewing these relations only from the perspective of states, the Axworthy Doctrine argues that we should *also* view them from the perspective of the individual. This is particularly so in an era of globalization when the security of the individual is much less protected than the security of the state. The human security agenda does not replace the state security agenda; it adds to it and provides a new strategy and a different dimension in the international system. Finally, the third change comes from the fact that conflict in the post-Cold War world occurs primarily within and not between states and that addressing conflict through peacekeeping alone does not get to the root of the matter. Rebuilding institutions, or preventing them from collapse, becomes the primary focus of a predominantly civilian task of peacebuilding.

In order to understand Axworthy's approach to the hemisphere it is important to view Canada's policies from the perspective of this doctrine rather than from a traditional geographic approach, because his approach is focused on thematic policy matters viewed from the perspective of soft power, human security, and peacebuilding. This position is well represented in two major speeches on hemispheric matters, one given to the OAS Conference of the Americas in Washington (DFAIT, 1998) and the other delivered at the Instituto Tecnológico Autónomo de México in Mexico City (DFAIT, 1999). Both speeches emphasize institution-building and how Canada is using its 'soft power' through the inter-American system, especially the OAS, to bring forward new agenda items for the new times. Some of the items he concentrated on were the reintegration of Cuba, the ratification of the Landmines Treaty, addressing the proliferation of small arms and the drug trade, the promotion of human rights, and peacebuilding—all, except landmines, themes present in the 1991 Liberal policy paper.

Two related topics were at the heart of much of Axworthy's preoccupation in the hemisphere: Cuba and the conflict with the United States over the Helms-Burton Act. As we have seen in the 1991 Liberal policy paper, the reintegration of Cuba was a major theme for the Liberals. In 1994 the Liberal government reinstated development aid to Cuba and began to forge closer relations with that country than those of the Mulroney government. Axworthy and many other Liberals believed that Canada could play a role in the conflict between the US and Cuba. But when the Helms-Burton Act was passed after the Cubans shot down two civilian aircraft flying over Cuban territory and piloted by Cuban-Americans, the conflict spilled over to other countries. Canada disagreed with US policy towards Cuba because of both the political and diplomatic isolation from the inter-American system it imposed on Cuba. In addition, the maintenance of the trade embargo, which Canada felt was counterproductive, created economic hardship for the island population. But it was the extraterritorial nature of the Helms-Burton legislation that was most objectionable to the Canadian government. The objection, however, was quite separate from and more fundamental than the Cuban issue itself, since the principle of extraterritoriality hit at the very heart of Liberal concerns over an independent foreign policy. For the United States to tell its citizens what to do in Cuba was one thing, but for it to tell Canadians what to do there was another. The unacceptable nature of this legislation was shared by the European Union and the OAS and both Axworthy and Eggleton worked hard to build a consensus against Helms-Burton as well as to implement countervailing legislation in Canada that would penalize any companies complying with the US law.

In the meantime, Axworthy dedicated himself to building strong ties with Mexico and met frequently with his Mexican counterpart to discuss and resolve bilateral and multilateral matters. The three principal agenda items were: building up the bilateral relationship, working more closely with Mexico on multilateral issues, and addressing the issue of the indigenous rebellion in Chiapas. On the first issue, Axworthy sought to deepen and diversify the relationship between the two countries and to support the democratic reforms that the Zedillo administration and the Mexican legislature were implementing. In 1996, for example, Canada and Mexico established a Declaration of Objectives and an Action Plan, which were part of the Join Ministerial Committee (JMC), a bilateral mechanism established in 1968. This mechanism allowed the two governments to expand the issues addressed in the bilateral relationships. In 1999 the theme of the JMC revolved around social policy and expanded beyond the traditional ministries that had previously been involved in the JMC. On the multilateral front, Canada and Mexico worked more closely in the inter-American system, the UN, the Asia-Pacific Economic Cooperation (APEC) ministerial meetings, and on themes such as landmines and control over small arms proliferation in the hemisphere.

Axworthy had emphasized the importance of indigenous issues to his foreign policy. He sent Blaine Favel, whom he had earlier appointed Counsellor on International Indigenous Issues, to Mexico to seek out economic opportunities between indigenous peoples of the two countries. In this context, the case of the Zapatista rebellion in Chiapas, which involved a very complex situation, was a delicate theme in the bilateral relationship. Axworthy sent two parliamentary delegations with indigenous representatives to Chiapas in 1998, including Favel, to report to him and Parliament on the situation in the Mexican state. He also offered Canadian support for the dialogue between the government and the rebels.

On the multilateral front, Axworthy sought the support of countries in the hemisphere to sign and ratify the Landmines Treaty. Ironically, all but Cuba and the United States fully supported the treaty. But this initiative gave Axworthy high profile in the hemisphere and demonstrated that his emphasis on soft power was more than rhetoric. Interestingly, his promotion of the human security agenda gained notoriety and support after the Landmines Treaty was signed and ratified. Axworthy also supported Mexico's initiative on the Convention Against the Illicit Manufacturing of and Trafficking in Firearms, Ammunition, Explosives and Other Related Material, and proposed taking the issue of small arms one step forward by establishing policies to reintegrate child soldiers and set up programs to buy back weapons.

Another issue intimately tied to the disarmament agenda was that of illicit drug trafficking. Axworthy's proposal for a Ministerial Dialogue Group on Drugs at the Santiago summit was followed by a discussion paper distributed throughout the hemisphere (Baranyi, 1998) and an experts conference in San José, Costa Rica, in March 1999 to initiate discussions in the hemisphere. Axworthy sent the new Secretary of State for Latin America and Africa, David Kilgour, and senior officials from the department to the region to explain the government's discussion paper. The discussion paper purposely linked the theme of human security to the problem of illicit drug trafficking and initiated a debate in the hemisphere focused on a people-centred approach to the issue.

These initiatives demonstrate Axworthy's ability to translate soft power, human security, and peacebuilding into the inter-American agenda and make an impact on the hemisphere. However, each of these issues poses enormous obstacles because they are rooted in deep and complex problems. Although successes like the signing and ratification of the Landmines Treaty are impressive, achieving full ratification by all the nations of the Americas—and even implementing the treaty in those countries that have already ratified it—will be a major challenge that will take years to achieve. On the issue of small arms and illicit trafficking of drugs, the challenges are even greater. But if Canada's contribution to these issues accomplishes nothing more than refocusing the tension between the United States and key countries in Latin America to a more constructive multilateral approach that looks at the impact on the security of individuals and the impact on their communities, then it would have been a positive contribution.

CONCLUSION

The dynamics of Canada's relations with the rest of the hemisphere are the result of at least three interrelated forces. First, there is the tension between demands made by the private sector for open and transparent business practices and the equally pressing demands by NGOs for good governance and the protection of human rights. The second has to do with the dynamics between Canada's ever-deepening economic relationship with the United States and its desire to seek balance by diversifying its trade partners and projecting its foreign policy principles and values to the rest of the hemisphere, but without in any way lessening its economic ties to the United States. The third derives from the complex structural changes occurring in the international system, which are creating a more interdependent world in which Canada has become a major player through the projection of 'soft power'.

Although government and civil society activities point to an important long-term deepening of the relations with the rest of the hemisphere, a crucial breakthrough will only occur once Latin American countries develop more open, more transparent, and more stable economies and commit themselves fully to commonly accepted democratic practices. A more active relationship with the rest of the hemisphere, therefore, has to satisfy the dual domestic demands of business and civil society. Although the hemispheric dynamics create some tensions between Canada's relations with the United States and its emerging linkages to countries in the Caribbean and Latin America, these tensions have been manageable and should continue to be so. However, it seems that no matter how much Canada seeks to exercise the Third Option, the fact of the matter is that the disproportionate influence of the United States persists. For this fundamental reason, if for no other, Canada must continue to forge close relationships in the hemisphere and to bring its unique contribution and character to the inter-American system.

NOTES

The author wishes to thank Michael K. Hawes and Michael Brock for comments on an earlier draft and Monica Flores for her research assistance.

1. The events are: the XIII Pan American Games held in Winnipeg (23 July–8 Aug. 1999); the Ninth Conference of Spouses of Heads of State and Government of the Americas (29 Sept–1 Oct. 1999); the FTAA ministerial meeting (3–4 Nov. 1999); the Fifth Americas Business Forum (1–3 Nov. 1999); General Assembly of the OAS in Windsor (4–6 June 2000); and the Summit of the Americas (Spring 2001).
2. For an excellent analysis of the limited trade benefits of Canada's relation with Latin America, see Daudelin and Dosman (1998: 211–38) and Daudelin and Molot (2000).

REFERENCES

Axworthy, Lloyd, and Roy MacLaren. 1991. 'Part of the Americas: A Liberal Policy for Canada in the Western Hemisphere' (Ottawa: Federal Liberal Caucus, 29 Nov.), mimeo.

Baranyi, Stephen. 1998. 'Drugs and Human Security in the Americas' (Ottawa: Department of Foreign Affairs and International Trade, Dec.).

Canada-Caribbean-Central America Policy Alternatives (CAPA). 1994. *A New Vision for the Americas: CAPA's Submission to the Foreign Policy Review*, Occasional paper. Toronto: CAPA.

Canadian Council for International Co-operation (CCIC). 1998. *The Hemispheric Partnership Initiative: A Project of the Americas Policy Group*. Ottawa: CCIC, Americas Policy.

———. 1999. *Linking Globalization to Human Development in the Americas,* Group Brief on the Free Trade Area of the Americas. Ottawa: CCIC, Americas Policy.

Daudelin, Jean, and Edgar J. Dosman, eds. 1994. *Beyond Mexico*. Ottawa: Carleton University Press and the Canadian Foundation for the Americas.

——— and ———. 1998. 'Canada and Hemispheric Governance: The New Challenges', in Fen Osler Hampson and Maureen Appel Molot, eds, *Canada Among Nations 1998: Leadership and Dialogue*. Toronto: Oxford University Press, 211–38.

——— and Maureen Appel Molot. 2000. 'Canada and the FTAA: The hemispheric bloc temptation', *Policy Options* 21, 2 (Mar.): 48–51.

Department of External Affairs. 1970. *Foreign Policy for Canadians*. Ottawa: Queen's Printer.

Department of Foreign Affairs and International Trade (DFAIT). 1998. Notes for an Address by the Honourable Lloyd Axworthy, Minister of Foreign Affairs, to the

Organization of American States Conference of the Americas, Washington, DC' (Ottawa, 6 Mar.).

———. 1999. Notes for an Address by the Honourable Lloyd Axworthy, Minister of Foreign Affairs, to the Instituto Tecnológico Autónomo de México, 'Canada's Human Security Agenda for the Hemisphere' (Ottawa, 11 Jan.).

Liberal Party of Canada. 1993. *Creating Opportunity: The Liberal Plan for Canada* (the 'Red Book'). Ottawa: Liberal Party of Canada.

Sharp, Mitchell. 1972. 'Canada-US Relations: Options for the Future', *International Perspectives*, Special Issue (Autumn).

Stevenson, Brian J.R. 2000. *Canada, Latin America and the New Internationalism: A Foreign Policy Analysis, 1968–1990*. Montreal and Kingston: McGill-Queen's University Press.

13

Our Dictatorship: Canada's Trilateral Relations with Castro's Cuba

YVON GRENIER

Over the past forty years, Cuba has developed a highly effective machinery of repression. The denial of basic civil and political rights is written into Cuban law. In the name of legality, armed security forces, aided by state-controlled mass organizations, silence dissent with heavy prison terms, threats of prosecution, harassment, or exile. Cuba uses these tools to restrict severely the exercise of fundamental human rights of expression, association, and assembly. The conditions in Cuba's prisons are inhuman, and political prisoners suffer additional degrading treatment and torture. In recent years, Cuba has added new repressive laws and continued prosecuting non-violent dissidents while shrugging off international appeals for reform and placating visiting dignitaries with occasional releases of political prisoners. (Human Rights Watch, 1999: 1)

CUBA WITHOUT CUBANS

The main thesis presented in this chapter is that the Chrétien government's foreign policy towards Cuba is immature, mistaken, and ultimately irresponsible. It is first and foremost immature because it is designed as an identity-soothing ceremonial, not as a serious blueprint for sustainable relations with that country. It is mistaken because we are going out of our way to associate ourselves with an end-of-the-road dictatorship. Finally, it is irresponsible because its only possible impact in Cuba, if any, is the bolstering of a police state.

Canada's 'bilateral' relationship with Cuba is implicitly trilateral in the sense that it has as much to do with the US as with Cuba. It is also a domestic issue because it probably has more to do with us than with the US. Thus, our policy towards Cuba has little to do with Cuban politics or Cubans, beyond the necessary and sufficient condition that Cuba is the United States' enemy and victim. More than any other country or issue, Cuba gives Canada the chance to indulge in cost-free anti-Americanism, a service that Cuba has rendered by simply stopping time. The Canadian left and many Canadian nationalists are mercifully prepared to justify, condone, or simply ignore how Cubans are ruled.

This policy of 'constructive engagement' towards Cuba has been, with its ups and downs, a fixture of Canada-Cuba relations since 1959, though never with as much gusto as under the current Liberal government (Gorman, 1991; Kirk and McKenna, 1997, 1998, 1999). We have paid more high-level political attention to Cuba, had more diplomatic and policy initiatives, and invested more resources in a one-sided rapprochement with Cuba than ever before, and more so than any other Western democracy. Canada's policy initiatives towards Cuba have been misguided and even sloppy, as though the real goal was to offer the spectacle of cosy relations with Cuba in and of itself, quite independent of the so-called objectives that officially justify the pursuit of this relationship. We officially 'support movement in that country in the direction of peaceful transition and eventual reintegration into the hemisphere' (Axworthy, 1998). Yet, we have no specific target, no timetable, no evaluation criteria, not to mention no specific 'demands' or 'preconditions' attached to our diplomatic and economic largesse (unlike the European Union, for instance). With this perspective, our policy of 'constructive engagement' (also called 'principled pragmatism') does not have to be constructive and can make do without much response from the 'engaged'. What matters is 'to maintain the dialogue', to 'build confidence' *per se*, a goal for which we are prepared to ask little beyond co-operation in the building of a diplomatic façade.

On two recent occasions Cuba embarrassed Canada and recklessly damaged our spectacular ties. First, when Fidel Castro—who is President, Chief of State, Head of Government, First Secretary of the Communist Party, and Commander in Chief of the armed forces—sent to jail the four dissidents whom Prime Minister Chrétien singled out for clemency during his visit to Havana in April 1998. In other words, Castro imprisoned not just any dissidents, as has happened countless times for four decades in Castro's Cuba, but the ones to whose fate our government attached its credibility. As Mark Entwistle, Canada's ambassador in Cuba from 1993 to 1997, said, Prime Minister Chrétien was very upset 'because he had gone out on a line as a politician' (Scoffield, 1999). The second time was when Fidel Castro called Canada 'enemy territory', among other undiplomatic terms, an inflammatory declaration that prompted Foreign Minister Axworthy to be present at the Pan-American Games medals ceremony in Winnipeg to congratulate Cuba's baseball team, thus eliciting some 'warm words' from the offending/offended dictator. What these two episodes remind us is that the rapprochement with Cuba is Canada's initiative and that, contrary to appearances and logic, Canada seems to want the partnership more than Cuba.

Canada's reaction to Castro's splendidly incautious acts—putting some of our co-operation initiatives and some top officials' visits to Havana 'on hold', and delaying the opening of a new Cuban consulate in Vancouver—suggests that our government is anxious to save face without changing the parameters of its flawed policy. As Canada's ambassador in Cuba, Keith Christie, affirmed in October 1999, 'relations between both countries are growing and will continue to improve' (Radio Havana Cuba, 1999).

REVISITING THE BASICS

A review of the scant literature on Canada-Cuba relations reveals a fascinating incongruity. On the one hand, the most vocal intellectual defenders of our rapprochement with Castro routinely downplay the question of how Cubans are governed. The authors of the only recent book on the subject, John Kirk and Peter McKenna, hardly mention it at all, methodically redirecting their fondness for the Caribbean dictator towards a nationalistic defence of ever closer relations with a US foe (Kirk and McKenna, 1997, 1998, 1999). This clever strategy befits the key Canadian disposition towards Cuba, which is to use it as a symbol against the US while remaining serenely unbothered by the life of real Cubans. In the 1990s, one could not come across as a Castro groupie and expect to be taken seriously by the movers and shakers in Ottawa. On the other hand, criticizing Castro harshly, which few do in Canada, immediately tags one as pro-American, or worse, as pro-Cuban American, as though the Castro regime ranked a distant third as a violator of human rights in Cuba. Consequently, the whole issue of how Cubans are governed is routinely expunged from the discussion on Canada-Cuba relations.

Yet, the way Cubans are ruled has everything to do with our policy there. In fact, Cuba is the only political regime in the world that we officially want to change in a dramatic fashion. Our policy in Cuba, Foreign Minister Axworthy routinely reminds us, is 'to encourage further commitment to human rights and assist in the economic and institutional development of the country'.[1] On that account, the importance of knowing what is to be changed is self-evident. So to put the problem clearly, let me start with four propositions about this four-decade-old government/regime.

Castro's Cuba

1. Cubans have been ruled by an authoritarian regime for the past 40 years, one that conjugates the fairly standard Communist paraphernalia with a Latino type of 'charismatic' or 'caudillistic' leadership. Cubans are systematically deprived of some of the most basic freedoms: speech, association, and movement. The Cuban government has refused to engage in anything like 'glasnost'. As Raul Castro stated less than a year before the Joint Declaration on Canada-Cuba Co-operation (more on this later), 'The glasnost which undermined the USSR and other socialist countries consisted of handing over the mass media, one by one, to the enemies of socialism' (Castro, 1996: 35). The dynamic brothers are not about to let that happen in their island. In sum, one looks in vain for solid indicators that this regime could significantly change as long as Fidel Castro is in power—that is, as long as he lives.

2. Signs of liberalization have been few and far between. Over the past decade, the regime has tested enclaves of economic liberalization (mostly from 1993 to 1995). All the evidence suggests that they remained 'tests' and 'enclaves', not first steps towards a fundamental change in the island's economic policy.[2] Over and over again (especially since 1996), Cuban officials have stated that these experiments were attempted reluctantly, out of necessity, that none of these experiments should be understood as a 'transition' to something other than Leninist socialism, and that what matters most and is at the centre of the economy, i.e., politics, is not affected by these experiments and should never stray from its time-honoured path.

3. According to human rights organizations, the situation of human rights in Cuba has deteriorated during the past several years—this corresponding, roughly, to the period of our government's rapprochement with Castro's Cuba. According to Human Rights Watch, 'in recent years, rather than modify its laws to conform with international human rights standards, Cuba has approved legislation further restricting fundamental rights. Only a restoration of religious freedoms [the Cuban state has not been officially 'atheist' since 1992] stands out as a notable exception to this trend' (Human Rights Watch, 1999: 2). Hundreds of political prisoners are in jail. Cuba's constitution and criminal code are tailored to give the highest political authorities all the leverage necessary to exert the most absolute and arbitrary power over its citizens. Human Rights Watch is particularly severe in its assessment of the criminal code (the section is called 'codifying repression'), which criminalizes non-violent dissent with highly malleable provisions against (the list here is incomplete) 'Enemy propaganda', 'Persons demonstrating criminal tendencies', 'Dangerousness', 'Anti-social conduct', 'Contempt for the authority of a public official', 'Defamation of institutions, mass organizations, heroes, and martyrs', 'Insulting the Nation's symbols', 'Clandestine printing' (the state is the only provider of typewriting machines, computers, and photocopy machines, and it strictly controls their use), 'Abuse of freedom of religion', 'Disobedience and resistance', 'Illegal exit', 'Illegal entry', 'Failure to comply with the duty to denounce', 'Insult, calumny, and defamation', and so on. All of these are subject to all possible interpretations in a context where, according to Human Rights Watch, 'due process is denied', 'courts lack independence and impartiality', trials are held behind closed doors 'violating

the right to a public trial' (this year, 60 dissidents were jailed as a preventive measure to keep them away from the closed trial of the four prominent opposition leaders mentioned by Prime Minister Chrétien during his April 1998 visit to Havana), and there is widespread use of 'arrests and pretrial detentions', 'confessions and witness tampering', 'restrictions on the right to a lawyer', and the failure to 'inform detainees of the charges against them'.

Appeal exists but it is 'worthless'. Human Rights Watch reports that 'in an extraordinary June 1998 statement, Cuban Justice Minister Roberto Díaz Sotolongo justified Cuba's restrictions on dissent by explaining that, just as Spain had instituted laws to protect the monarch from criticism, Cuba was justified in protecting Fidel Castro from criticism, since he served a similar function as Cuba's "king" ' (ibid.). Human Rights Watch also denounces the presence of labour camps in Cuba, as well as the overall treatment of prisoners (namely, torture). It reveals that 'prison authorities insisted that all detainees participate in politically oriented reeducation sessions, such as chanting "long live Fidel" or "Socialism or Death", or face punitive measures including beatings and solitary confinement' (ibid.).

4. The freedom that Cubans are known to enjoy more than their fellow Latin Americans is the freedom from want. The Cuban government has invested more in health and education than any other Latin American state. In health the achievements have apparently been significant. This effort has earned Cuba a great deal of legitimacy in Latin America and beyond. At the same time, it is clear that the ruinous economic model stubbornly maintained by the Cuban leadership for political reasons has cancelled out the potential benefits of these policies, especially after the cessation of the Soviet subsidy. Alarming reports on the overall health of Cubans are commonplace. On the 1998 UN Human Development Index, Cuba ranked 85th out of 174 countries, between Jamaica and Peru (UNDP, 1998: 128–9). In education, the greater accessibility to resources is offset by the systematic repression of freedom in the educational system, as in society in general. In sum, a pragmatic assessment of Cuba's trade-offs between liberty and standard of living leads to the conclusion that the absence of civil and political liberties is an exorbitant and unnecessary price to pay for what practically amounts to not much at all in terms of tangible benefits for the population.

The Use and Abuse of the US Embargo

According to all supporters of the Castro regime, much of what is wrong in Cuba results from the US embargo, imposed by Washington in the early 1960s and further tightened by the Torricelli law (1992) and the Helms-Burton Act (1996). During Prime Minister Chrétien's visit to Cuba in April 1998, the first by a Canadian Prime Minister in 22 years, President Castro compared the US embargo to the Nazi genocide—without so much as a twitch from the Prime Minister. (Chrétien was remarkably uncritical during his visit to Havana, in comparison to the Pope, the Governor of Illinois, and more than half of the delegates to the 1999 Ibero-American Summit.) Apparently, Chrétien wanted to go to Havana to be seen in Havana. Foreign Minister Axworthy can hardly talk about Cuba at all without criticizing the embargo, which in his view is the cause of most problems in Cuba, all the way from 'economic crisis' to 'prostitution'.[3] When criticized for the deteriorating human rights situation in Cuba, Foreign Minister Axworthy typically responds: 'What have the Americans accomplished?' (quoted in Kirk and McKenna, 1997: 173). These comments suggest one more benefit of lifting the US embargo: it would force our legislators to think about Cuba as a country inhabited by Cubans, not merely as a symbol in Canada-US relations.

Nobody can absolutely ascertain how different the situation might have been in Cuba if history had unfolded differently. Four brief comments on the economic and political significance of the embargo are worth making.

1. It is highly probable that without the embargo the political regime in Cuba would have been a dictatorship anyway because its fundamental configuration responds to a conception of authority and leadership that has much deeper roots than a mere ad hoc response to adversity. Anti-Americanism, caudillism, and authoritarianism were already dominant in the '26th of July Movement' at the time of the insurgency. The Communist model fixed on these predispositions left little room for institutional improvisation, emulating a fairly standard model that Russians or East Europeans would immediately recognize. Reading the human rights organizations' reports on Cuba year after year makes one realize how systematic and extensive oppression is in that country, how it affects citizens for the most benign offence, and how it targets groups for a wide variety of political, religious, and sexual reasons (persecution of

homosexuals in Cuba is well documented). It is hard to imagine how this regime could cope differently with freedom of the press, freedom of association, and freedom of movement if the embargo were lifted.[4]

2. The US embargo is certainly the most dramatic that Cuba could possibly experience from any single country. The US is a neighbour and a world giant with unparalleled sway in international institutions. Nevertheless, in the end, it remains the embargo of one single country, a country, incidentally, on which Cuba was dependent prior to 1959 and that was blamed for most of the political and economic woes of pre-Castro Cuba by the same observers (or same type of observers) who now lament the severing of economic ties with the imperial United States. Cuba can trade with Canada, Mexico, France, England, Germany, or any other country—any country, that is, except the US. Since the downfall of the Soviet Union, Cuba has concluded co-operation agreements with 142 countries and attracted foreign investment into key areas of the economy, including mining, petroleum, manufacturing, telecommunications, and tourism. Spain, Canada, Italy, and Mexico are the leading sources of investment. According to *Oxford Analytica*, (1999: 3) Cuba has also been

> engaged in renegotiating its debts with other countries, and since 1997 has begun to tap medium and long-term credit markets, raising 500 million dollars over the past two years. There are to date some 370 joint ventures with foreign companies in Cuba, and in 1995 the government introduced legislation to permit completely foreign-owned operations on Cuban soil. The EU is the source of more than 50 per cent of the foreign capital. Spanish companies are involved in 72 association agreements, with total investments in the island of about 200 million dollars.

The same source indicates that 'Havana claims that more than one-third of its 370 association agreements with foreign companies have been concluded since the Helms-Burton Act was passed.'

Legislation such as the Torricelli law (1992) or the Helms-Burton Act (1996) was largely a response to the embargo's failure to prevent Cuba from purchasing US goods through trading houses in third countries or the black market. (The US embargo is generally said to harm Cuba because it prevents the country from buying US goods and services, not because it closes its market to Cuban products.)

What is more, the US embargo is somewhat ameliorated by remittances from Cuban Americans, who in 1998 injected $800 million US into the Cuban economy—roughly twice the amount of the *total* two-way trade between Canada and Cuba during that year. And that was before the relaxation of rules for remittance transfers announced by President Clinton in 1999. Furthermore, the Helms-Burton Act, adopted a month after two civilian aircraft were shot down in international air space by Cuban MiGs in February 1996,[5] never had the dramatic impact denounced by Canada and other countries because President Clinton repeatedly (every six months) suspended the right of otherwise eligible claimants to file lawsuits against some of Cuba's foreign investors (clause three). As Sherritt International, the only Canadian company targeted by Helms-Burton, noted in its 1998 *Annual Report*, 'the Foreign Extraterritorial Measures Act (Canada) was amended as of January 1, 1997, to provide that any judgment given under the Helms-Burton Act shall not be recognized or enforceable in any manner in Canada' (Sherritt International, 1998: 24). The Helms-Burton Act did not prevent the Vancouver-based multinational from investing in Cuba in properties expropriated from American owners in 1959. As both Mark Entwistle, the Canadian ambassador to Cuba from 1993 to 1997, and Allan Ibbison, the president of Leisure Canada, another Canadian company with sizeable investment in Cuba and involved in the tourist industry, recently told a conference of people interested in doing business in Cuba, the embargo is 'essentially dead' and Helms-Burton 'has no teeth' (Scoffield, 1999).

The embargo is an obstacle, but not an insurmountable one, for US investors and companies who want to do business in Cuba. There are now many exceptions to the embargo allowing US companies to sell medical and agricultural supplies (provided that they go to non-governmental organizations for distribution). As *Washington Post* journalist John Lancaster recently pointed out, 'their salesmen regularly travel there under licenses granted by the Treasury Department', adding that 'the law also gives exceptions to the entertainment and communications fields, among other areas' (Lancaster, 1999). Cuba's limitations in purchasing goods and services derive primarily from its lack of hard currency and the overall insolvency of its economy.

3. By far the most tragic impact of Helms-Burton is the one methodically overlooked by the promoters of our 'constructive engagement' in Cuba: its political consequences in the island, with

the adoption of new repressive legislation. Eight months after the US Congress enacted Helms-Burton, the Cuban government responded with the Law Reaffirming Cuban Dignity and Sovereignty (Ley de Reafirmación de la Dignidad y Soberanía Cubanas), explicitly a response to Helms-Burton. According to Human Rights Watch, this law criminalized 'even the appearance of support for U.S. policies' (Human Rights Watch, 1999: 4–5). A follow-up on the 'Law for the Protection of the National Independence and the Cuban Economy' (Ley de Protección de la Independencia Nacional y la Economía de Cuba) was adopted in February 1999, only a few weeks after an important visit by Foreign Minister Axworthy to Havana. During that visit, new areas of 'co-operation' were announced between Canada and Cuba, and a new treaty on the 'transfer of offenders' was signed between the two countries.

4. There seems to be a consensus (even in the White House) that the US embargo has not worked, presumably because Fidel Castro is still firmly at the helm. Still, the debate on this issue is confusing. Most opponents of the embargo neglect to explain what precisely they oppose: the goal of forcing Castro to change his policies or step down (roughly the US position), or simply the means used by the US government to achieve this goal.[6] Officially, Canada and the European Union share the US goal, albeit with less fanfare. Of course, the result is the same in Havana but their policies towards Cuba are never denounced as a 'complete failure'. True, many critics of the embargo, including Foreign Minister Axworthy, do not display much enthusiasm or clarity in pursuing or affirming this goal, preferring oblique declarations about Cuba's political and economic transition from an unqualified present to a mysterious future. (Declarations by Axworthy against the fall 1999 military coup in Pakistan indicate that neither he nor his government is opposed to economic sanctions *per se*.) Thus, although Ottawa officially shares Washington's goal in regard to Cuba, the confusing signals coming from Axworthy prompted the *Globe and Mail* to devote an editorial to the issue, arguing among other things that 'Mr. Axworthy seems not even to understand his own policy' (*Globe and Mail*, 1998).

No doubt the lifting of the embargo would have a tremendous impact on Cuba, but the bulk of the shock would be political, not economic. President Castro would have to find another justification for his failures—or maybe not ('the US lifted its embargo but we still suffer the consequences of it'). In the end, those products that the

US, and only the US, produces and that Cuba wants would remain unaffordable for the Cuban government.

Cuba's fate lies in Cuba, not in Washington, Ottawa, or Brussels. In fact, the world can help Castro much more than it can harm him. But again, if the proposition is accepted that the world's policies towards Cuba do make a huge difference for the better, then why is it that the US embargo is said to have failed and not the absence of embargo by all other nations? Are there two Cubas: an authoritarian and bankrupt state victimized by the US, and a prosperous, democratizing one rescued by the rest of us?

CANADA-FIDEL RELATIONS

Since 1959, all Canadian governments have had more than cordial relations with Castro's Cuba, primarily because it was consistent with our tradition of having normal relations with 'constituted' and not overly monstrous governments. Before long, as the US and Cuba kept poisoning each other's well, Cuba provided an easy way for Canada to demonstrate its independence vis-à-vis the Yankees. In Canada, there is only one way to be independent: it is to be independent from the US. And the only unmistakable way to be independent from the US is to oppose the US.

My point here is not that Canada should have emulated US policy towards Cuba or that Canada craved to do so but refrained, choosing instead to hold its nose and score easy political points. Rather, I suggest that our decision to have cordial relations with the new Cuban regime, while being consistent with our diplomatic tradition, took on an extra dimension (Canada-US relations) that inflated its overall importance in our foreign policy. This is true for all the governments since Diefenbaker's. What has changed is the magnitude of this 'extra dimension' and how much it has affected (and distorted) our relations with Cuba. The governments of Diefenbaker, Pearson, and Mulroney shaped Canadian foreign policy towards Cuba with a mixture of opportunism and benign neglect. All of them sent enough positive signals to Cuba to distinguish clearly our policy from the one formulated in Washington. Even under the openly pro-US government of Brian Mulroney, the Assistant Deputy Minister for Latin America and the Caribbean (and subsequently Canadian ambassador to the UN), Louise Fréchette, visited Cuba in April 1990, reiterating Canada's policy of good relations and calling for enhanced co-operation. Four years later, Canada's Secretary of State for Latin America and Africa, Christine Stewart, publicly stated that it was her 'impression that Castro is still supported by a majority of Cubans' (Fagan, 1994). Nevertheless, none of these prime ministers went as far as the Trudeau or Chrétien administrations in making friendly gestures to Castro. Indeed, in the case of the current government, it has the warmest policy towards Cuba, with the fewest strings attached, of any Western democracy. To put it simply: with Diefenbaker, Pearson, and Mulroney we had relations with Cuba. With Trudeau and now Chrétien, we have a relationship with Castro.

Some observers suggest that commercial interests have determined Canada's Cuba policy. Indeed, our government has never spent so much time and energy facilitating Canadian investment in Cuba as it has in the past few years. The Canadian government, through the Industrial Co-operation Program, 'has contributed more than $6 million to 30 activities such as feasibility studies, training, and environmental and technology transfer' (CIDA, 1999). This policy is coherent with Prime Minister Chrétien's tendency to see foreign policy as trade by other means. The real story here is not the volume of trade with Cuba *per se*: our two-way trade with Cuba in one year represents about a third of our exports to the United States in one day. Rather, it is the fact that trade with Cuba has grown significantly over the past five years and increased more in percentage terms than our trade with any other Latin American or Caribbean country.

Canadian investors do take full advantage of the undemocratic environment offered by Cuba. For instance, Human Rights Watch mentions laws 'barring employees from forming unions or even from entering into independent, direct discussions of labor rights with their foreign employers' (Human Rights Watch, 1999: 18). But these investors are not naïve about the risk incurred. Canada and Cuba are still trying to negotiate a bilateral investment protection agreement that would presumably protect Canadian investments from unreasonable expropriation—this being an indicator, more than anything else, of the Canadian officials' belief in the existence of the rule of law in Cuba. The biggest Canadian investor in Cuba, Sherritt International, may have underestimated the risks of investing in Cuba, but it did not ignore them completely: 'the Corporation is entitled to the benefit of certain assurances received from the Government of Cuba and certain agencies of the Government of Cuba that protect it from adverse changes in law, although such changes remain beyond the control of the Corporation and the effect of any such changes cannot be accurately predicted' (Sherritt International, 1998). There are no guaranteed property rights in Cuba, and foreign investment is welcomed only as a necessary evil, as a way of importing capital without capitalism. Sherritt concedes that its 'experience to date in Cuba has been satisfactory', a rather modest adjective that still rings like an overstatement given that the ratio of capital assets and goodwill versus revenues in Cuba is by far the worst of all Sherritt's global investments. Sherritt's chairman, Ian W. Delaney, who unlike academics cannot afford to stray too far from reality when addressing his audience (shareholders, auditor), admits that his company is overstretched in Cuba, that it is examining 'a broad range of investment alternatives', and, implicitly, that its performance in Cuba explains the company's failure to 'meet management's internal targets' (ibid.). The idea that our companies will be better positioned than those of the US after the downfall of the Communist regime, merely because they were there before, is a monument to our political naïvety. Being there before by cutting deals with the dictator may well be a powerful magnet for hostility in the new regime.

In sum, our trade relations with Cuba, while strengthened over the past years, are still relatively marginal and remain negatively affected by the uncertainties that necessarily derive from dealing with an aging and temperamental president-for-life in a volatile political and economic environment. Trade opportunities are not and cannot be the overarching factor explaining Canada's infatuation with Cuba.

The Chrétien-Axworthy Policy

Soon after the Liberal government assumed office in October 1993, Canadian policy towards Cuba went from being moderately friendly to a level of engagement unprecedented in Canadian history. No other democratic government in the world is as close to the Castro regime as the current Canadian government. We have never before had so many high-ranking officials visit Cuba, something that the Castro regime, always striving to break out of its perceived isolation, openly relishes. Most prominently, Prime Minister Chrétien visited Cuba in April 1998 and Foreign Minister Lloyd Axworthy went there in January 1997 and again in 1999. In addition, there have been visits by cabinet members, the speakers and clerks from both houses of

Canada's Parliament, other high government officials and provincial premiers, and, of course, the many visits by Cuban officials to Canada. Only missing is a visit to Canada by Fidel Castro himself, which might very well happen in the year 2000 for the Organization of American States (OAS) meeting in Windsor and/or in 2001 for the Summit of the Americas in Quebec City. Canada never offered as much assistance to Cuba as it has done over the past several years, so much so that it is now one of the largest donor countries for Cuba. The Canadian government spends little in development aid in Latin America, and Cuba is not an exception. Still, statistics from the Canadian International Development Agency (CIDA) show a sharp increase in development aid to Cuba under the current Liberal government, going from $0.96 million in 1993–4 to $10.97 million in 1997–8. Significantly, this took place while the government was submitting its foreign aid budget to severe cuts.

The rapprochement with Cuba deepened after Lloyd Axworthy became Foreign Minister in 1996. Axworthy is identified with the 'left' of the Liberal caucus (red tory is probably a more accurate label). This may not mean much, considering his role in the reform of Unemployment Insurance, but it points at least to this: in harmony with the Canadian left, Axworthy has both interest in, and sympathy for, Cuba. As Kirk and McKenna point out, Axworthy 'has taken almost a personal interest in things Cuban' (Kirk and McKenna, 1999: 397).

An interview with Axworthy when he was Foreign Affairs critic for the Official Opposition indicates that for him the most pressing problem in Canadian foreign policy is its closeness to the United States. Axworthy identified this as 'a flaw that must be overcome if we are to play an effective role in world affairs. . . . it is for this reason that the priority of a Liberal foreign policy centres on how to develop a more independent role for Canada' (Axworthy, 1992–3: 7). In this same interview, the future minister asserted that Canada should de-emphasize its commercial relations with the US, courting instead the markets of the Caribbean region and Central America. Furthermore, the government should seek the participation and support of non-governmental organizations (NGOs), churches, universities, business organizations, and Aboriginal groups in the implementation of our foreign policy.

None of these statements contradicts the Liberal Party's public objectives to pursue a more 'independent foreign policy' (i.e., different from the US) and to 'democratize' foreign policy (platforms of 1993 and 1997). Nevertheless, this government has never felt bound by its electoral promises, and Lloyd Axworthy was the most suitable candidate to turn what could have been little more than another electoral manoeuvre into something more concrete, that is, into a real effort to distance ourselves from the Americans whenever it could be done with maximum publicity and minimal economic and political cost. If Cuba did not exist, the Liberals would have to invent it.

Interestingly, in this interview, Axworthy did not say in what particular cases Canada's policies mistakenly converged with those of the US: the convergence itself is the problem. Similarly, one can only guess for what purpose Canadians should trade more with Lilliputian economies and less with the closest neighbour and biggest market in the world, or how the input of unaccountable, if politically correct, interest groups would better the outcomes of our foreign policy. To side with the right people, not with the US, is not a means but an end in itself, one that requires few resources beyond a microphone and a roomful of journalists to broadcast the words and deeds of the minister. Incidentally, our defence and peacekeeping capabilities, as well as our foreign aid budget, seem inversely proportional to the frequency and immodesty of the Foreign Minister's utterances. Under Axworthy, the message is the medium.

A FRAMEWORK FOR CONSTRUCTIVE ENGAGEMENT

The Joint Declaration on Canada-Cuba Co-operation signed by both countries in January 1997 constitutes, according to Axworthy, 'an officially sanctioned framework for constructive engagement' with Cuba (Axworthy, 1998). The Declaration contains 14 points, the first six of which are quite far-reaching since they aim at reforming the core of the state machinery (the other points deal with issues such as sport, audiovisual co-operation, and so on). One immediately realizes that our government is interested in slogans and image-making rather than in serious initiatives when one considers the amount of funds allocated: $1.2 million (through CIDA) over three years. Given how mistaken the key points of the Declaration are, we (and especially the Cuban people) can only rejoice that they were never given the chance to be fully implemented. The key points of the Declaration (DFAIT, 1997) were:

1. co-operation in the area of the administration of justice and the judicial-legal system, including exchanges of judges and judicial training;
2. support exchanges between the House of Commons and the [Cuban] National Assembly, focusing on the operations of both institutions;
3. exchange of experiences between both countries relating to the Cuban intention to strengthen within the National Assembly of People's Power a Citizens' Complaints commission;
4. broadening and deepening co-operation on the issue of human rights, which will include the preparation of seminars on diverse matters of mutual interest, academic exchanges between officials, professionals, and experts, as well as sharing experiences and positions on the work of the specialized organizations of the United Nations;
5. supporting the activities of Canadian and Cuban non-governmental organizations within the framework of bilateral co-operation between both countries and in accordance with the laws and regulations of each country;
6. continuation of macroeconomic co-operation, with an initial focus in the areas of taxation and central banking, while studying joint areas in which Canada might continue to support the Cuban policy of economic reform.

Let us examine each of these points briefly (the human rights issue will be discussed separately).

Canada's proposal to help make the Cuban judicial system more efficient with new computers and Internet technology is tantamount to perfecting what Human Rights Watch calls 'Cuba's repressive machinery'. The problem with the administration of justice in Cuba is hardly technical in nature. As Human Rights Watch notes, 'Cuban courts continue to try and imprison human rights activists, independent journalists, economists, doctors, and others for the peaceful expression of their views, subjecting them to the Cuban prison system's extremely poor conditions' (Human Rights Watch, 1999: 1). Professor Stephen Toope, then Dean of McGill Law School, went on a CIDA mission to Cuba in June 1998 to give advice on the possible parameters of a program of legal and judicial reform in Cuba. Not surprisingly, Professor Toope 'came away convinced that there was very little room for engagement with Cuba right now; there was simply no openness to legal reform' in Cuba. In reply to a letter outlining my misgivings about our government policy, he responded: 'I agree that a fundamental overhaul of the legal system is needed, and that this cannot be accomplished through "technical assistance" with court registries, etc.' Particularly interesting is his assessment that 'the Minister had made promises during his visit before adequate scoping had been done.'[7] This is what happens when you rush to co-operate for the sake of showing the world that you are co-operating.

The other dimension of point one—exchanges of judges and judicial training—is deflated by the unwillingness of Cubans to discuss seriously the fundamentally unlawful and anti-democratic nature of their legal structure. As in other points of the Declaration, Cuba is willing to accept free technological resources but has no interest in the Canadian 'content', even if this does not mean much. Canada, on the other hand, pleads to maintain the dialogue, hopefully without losing face. So we are going nowhere, going 10 feet in their direction and imploring them to give an inch, all of which is in order to 'build confidence' and 'maintain the dialogue'.

Supporting exchanges between the House of Commons and the Cuban National Assembly, with a focus on the operations of both institutions, is absurd at best since the National Assembly in Cuba is not a legislative assembly in any meaningful (democratic) sense of the term. It meets four days a year to rubber-stamp the laws adopted by the Council of State under the dictatorial rule of President Castro and his single-party state. What exactly House of Commons Speaker Gilbert Parent had in mind when he publicly affirmed that our elected representatives have much to learn from Cuban 'parliamentarians' (among other irresponsible comments of his)[8] is anyone's guess. Parent visited Havana in March 1997, resulting in the establishment of a Parliamentary Co-operation Program financed by CIDA. The House of Commons also delivered computer hardware to the Cuban National Assembly. In sum, not much came from this project, apart from giving some badly needed credibility to a discredited Cuban institution and providing our House Speaker with an opportunity to embarrass himself.

A Citizens' Complaints Commission (Oficina de Atención a la Población) is presumably like an ombudsman's office where citizens can go to complain about their government. In Cuba, the idea is reminiscent of the famous practice of the *'cahiers de doléances'* of France's *ancien régime*, with the difference that the Bourbons never had the opportunity to use Rapid Response Brigades, Committees for the Defence of the Revolution ('the eyes and the ears of the revolution'), or a modern police state to handle complaints. Cuban citizens who complain too much do not go to a commission: they go to jail. Thus, it is not clear what Foreign Minister Axworthy meant when he publicly affirmed that such a commission could 'provide transparent due process for citizens' complaints', since in Castro's Cuba due process *does not exist*, not by accident or temporarily, but because of the very nature of the political system in place (Axworthy, 1997). Although the Commission has apparently been in place for quite some time, there is no evidence that it was ever 'used' (or could be) in any proper way. *National Post* journalist Isabel Vincent went to Havana in the fall of 1998 to learn more about the Commission and found that 'the commission's activities have never been mentioned in the official Cuban press', 'there is no sign on the commission's main office door', 'it is not listed in the Havana telephone book, and even those who live next door to it do not appear to know that it is there' (Vincent, 1998). Even the staff at the Canadian embassy in Havana did not seem aware of its location in town. When Vincent finally located the Commission office, the three officials refused to talk to her 'without government authorization'.

There is also no evidence that Canada's plan to 'strengthen' the Commission (or to consolidate into one single office the various legal institutions where citizens, in theory, can express grievances) ever went anywhere. This is probably good news, for it is clearly misguided and always will be as long as it fails to take into account the political environment in which this Commission (or anything similar) must operate.

NGOs are Axworthy's instrument of choice for 'democratizing' foreign policy. Thus the minister enhances his profile as the number-one patron of NGO projects abroad, assuring himself the loyalty of the NGO community and their many 'consultants', as well as their assistance in an organizational context where the Department of Foreign Affairs and International Trade (DFAIT) bureaucrats may not always like (and may even resist) the orientation chosen by its minister.[9] It is far from clear that the co-optation of non-accountable (if righteous) NGOs amounts to 'democratizing' foreign policy. What is quite evident, however, is that for all the commendable humanitarian work done by NGOs in Cuba, none of it should be misconstrued as a strategy for democratization. The main agency overseeing the work of Canadian NGOs in Cuba is the Cuba-Canada Interagency Project (CCIP), a coalition of 25 Cuban 'social organizations' and 20 Canadian NGOs, churches, and funding agencies, all striving to carry out grassroots projects without hurting the sensibility of Cuban officials while not completely losing their credibility as 'non-governmental' organizations. Founded in January 1995, CCIP is supported by the Canadian government and CIDA and led by Oxfam-Canada. Its main objective is the 'strengthening' of democratic participation 'at all levels of Cuban society' (Kirk and McKenna, 1997: 156).

The government of Cuba regards NGOs with a great deal of suspicion. After a few years of not knowing with what degree of hostility it should handle all these (mostly sympathetic) foreign NGOs willing to fill the void created by the end of the Soviet Union's subsidy, ideological purity and state control came back *en force*. In his 1996 report to the Central Committee of the Communist Party, Raul Castro stated: 'our concept of civil society is not the same as the one they refer to in the United States. Rather, it is our own Cuban socialist civil society, encompassing our strong mass organizations'—that is, state organizations (Castro, 1996: 18). Castro deplores that the Cuban state 'did not react in time' to all these 'creators of stratagems to spy on us, to find recruitment possibilities and to announce ideological platforms favoring the transition to capitalism'. For Raul Castro, the state must respond with renewed firmness, for 'adopting a neutral or confused position, in order to avoid a confrontation or elude a thorny topic, is a show of unacceptable weakness before one's adversary; it is tantamount to admitting that the adversary's position is the correct one' (ibid., 35). Yet, Canadian NGOs working in Cuba are quite explicitly favourable in their attitudes to the Castro regime. (After the passage of the Helms-Burton Act, Oxfam led a coalition of 28 Canadian groups encouraging Canadian vacationers to boycott Florida and visit Cuba instead.) In fact, they are arguably the only NGOs in Latin America that are friendly to and, in fact, largely controlled by the Cuban government. Cuba is also Latin America's only remaining dictatorship, which speaks volumes about the general and dominant passions in the small world of NGOs.[10] Too bad Castro did not make it to the World Trade Organization conference in Seattle in 1999, for it would have clarified the political debate to see thousands of 'anarchist' and 'progressive' organizations prostrate themselves before the totalitarian dictator.

Ultimately, Canadian NGOs and the Canadian government are the victims of their overarching desire not to democratize the Cuban government but to do business with it, within the confines of existing Cuban 'laws and regulations'.

Macroeconomic co-operation would be helpful if the Cuban economy were truly experiencing a transition towards a market-based economy. It is not. Co-operation here means essentially (again) the shipping of informatics and statistics equipment to various government agencies, plus providing some 'technical training' for public officials. Over 150 work-stations have been delivered and installed, and officials from the Central Bank of Cuba have received technical training from the Bank of Canada. Through CIDA, Revenue Canada, and Statistics Canada, we have also 'co-operated' in the area of taxation, an instrument used by the Cuban government to suffocate the nascent private micro-enterprises in Cuba (Ritter, 1999: 13). Emerging as a popular strategy for survival in the early 1990s, when the government was no longer able to supply food for more than (roughly) 10 days a month, these very small businesses were tolerated until 1996, when they became increasingly 'asphyxiated by hostile public policies' (ibid.). According to Ritter, here is how the tax works:

> First, the tax is levied on 90% of *gross* revenues [of private micro-enterprises], and not on *net* revenues after the deduction of legitimate input costs. Second, the state determines the minimum amount of total revenues for many activities, this serving then as the tax base. Third, the National Tax Office requires that the taxpayers pay any assessed tax shortfall if their monthly payments are less than the amount due, but does not compensate the taxpayer if an overpayment of taxes on the monthly instalments has occurred. Finally, the tax is regressive as it imposes a lump-sum tax at the beginning of each month. (Ibid., 15)

This 'asphyxiation' coincided roughly with our government's proposal to help the Cuban government fine-tune its taxation capability. CIDA is apparently enthusiastic about Canada's role in the rapid expansion of the new taxation system. New regional taxation offices are being opened, and Cubans use the Canadian system of 'voluntary declaration' (finally, some Canadian content) with a tremendous rate of success! Micro-enterprises amount to little as springboards for democratization and liberalization in the island. Yet, they are the beginning of enclaves for the quasi-autonomous organization of people under a totalitarian regime. Helping the government to crush them should not be an objective of Canadian foreign policy.

Human Rights or Co-operation?

The project of broadening and deepening Canada-Cuba co-operation in the area of human rights is officially the cornerstone of our 'constructive engagement' policy. The human rights issue is also at the centre of what is wrong with the Chrétien-Axworthy policy. The reason is plain and simple: our government wants co-operation with Cuba much more than it wants human rights in Cuba.

For a start, Cuba does not recognize that it has a human rights problem. For Fidel Castro, Cuba is a beacon of human rights and democracy, much more than Canada. At the past two Ibero-American summits, the Cuban delegation gladly signed the declaration upholding a 'commitment to democracy, the rule of law and political pluralism'. Thus we have one more area of 'co-operation' where Cuban officials agree to talk about human rights issues to Canadians who need this concession to legitimize their rapprochement with Cuba. In exchange, Canada agrees to lend its support and credibility to an exercise from which anything potentially embarrassing for Cuba has been methodically expurgated. Rather than having specific initiatives of co-operation that challenge the systematic repression of basic freedoms (speech, association, movement) and the absence of free elections and due process in Cuba, in the context of a dialogue involving one country that respects human rights (Canada) and another one that does not, we prefer to 'build confidence' by 'exchanging views' in CIDA-sponsored and closed-door seminars, to which only a handful of NGOs and academics are invited. Furthermore, these seminars (three have been held so far)[11] were not directly about issues of democracy and citizenship, but on 'children's rights' and 'women's rights', two important sets of issues, to be sure, but ones that could easily be handled in the abstract and without reference to the kind of political setting in which they appear. East European and Soviet government officials could lecture on these issues in their sleep. In fact, they used to lecture *us* on these topics, burying the thorny issue of democratic rights under canned condemnations of 'capitalism' and 'imperialism'—nowadays, neo-liberalism and globalization.[12] In April 2000, the Canada-Cuba seminar series was to continue in Canada. According to CIDA, this time the human rights topic would be pay equity.

In closing on this point, it is pertinent to recall that Ottawa claimed a small measure of progress in its Cuba policy when Ismael Sambra and 12 other political prisoners were released from jail and sent to Canada (Sambra in 1997, the others in 1998). Two comments need to be made in that respect. First, Sambra credits PEN Canada, not the Canadian government, for his release from jail. Second, according to Human Rights Watch, the other prisoners were, for the most part, reaching the end of their sentences (in fact, the Cuban government wanted to send more of its undesirable subjects to Canada, but Canadian officials had to refuse some candidates for security reasons). Forcing them into exile is a violation of their right to stay in their own country. While it is arguably better to be free here than in jail in Cuba, especially considering the conditions in Cuban jails, Castro's systematic policy of exiling opponents is ultimately part of the problem rather than of the solution. While it may be a good idea, for humanitarian reasons, to be at the receiving end of that dubious policy, we should not delude ourselves into thinking that we are facilitating a great human rights victory. The same comment applies to Canada's role in facilitating the emigration of Cuban Jews to Israel. While this was conceivably a welcome development for the Cubans involved, its significance is mixed at best for the situation of Jews in Cuba, and our Foreign Minister should have refrained from using the case as another opportunity to brag, this time about our constructive engagement with Cuba (Oziewicz, 1999).

CONCLUSION: OUR DEMOCRATIC DEFICIT

> There is no dividing line between domestic and foreign policy. (Axworthy, 1992–3: 14)

This discussion on Canada's foreign policy towards Cuba could now take us in two directions. First, it could naturally lead us to recommend policy alternatives to our government. Here my propositions would be: (1) to drop the 'constructive engagement' policy at once, replacing it with a basic and minimal relationship with the Cuban government; (2) to continue providing humanitarian aid while linking any additional development aid or co-operation programs (not to mention official visits and other diplomatic niceties) to significant improvements in the area of democratic rights; and (3) to adopt a government-endorsed code of ethics for Canadian companies investing in Cuba—exactly what Foreign Minister Axworthy is now recommending for Canadian companies in Sudan.

My fourth recommendation necessitates a detour. Our policy towards Cuba points to a major flaw in the policy of 'human security' promoted by the current Foreign Minister. As late as April 1999, Axworthy was still admitting that 'greater clarity on the meaning of the term is needed' (DFAIT, 1999a). To know more we have had to follow the minister and decipher his every utterance. Still, the concept remains elusive. In a DFAIT document entirely devoted to spelling out the nature and scope of his new 'doctrine', Axworthy states that human security encompasses 'seven dimensions of security': 'economic, food, health, environmental, personal, community and political' (ibid.). That is, one dimension out of seven is politics, with democratic rights being arguably only a part of that political variable. Doubtlessly, totalitarian and authoritarian regimes would rather be 'engaged' in human security than directly in democracy and human rights. This is without mentioning that increased vigilance on humanitarian problems in the abstract is nothing but 'pulpit diplomacy' and wishful thinking if it is not matched with adequate resources and cost-benefit assessments (Hampson and Oliver, 1998). All of this is to argue that my fourth recommendation would be to clearly separate the issues of national security, humanitarian concerns, and democratic rights. Conflating them in the hopelessly vague concept of human security introduces nothing but confusion, in addition to shifting the attention of the public from the problems at hand to the public revelations of the minister.

I have a fifth recommendation for our government, as well as for many of my fellow citizens who use Cuba as an outlet for identity problems: grow up! If we need to prize a Caribbean dictator to shore up our sense of identity as Canadians, we are in trouble. This is more than a recommendation, however: it is the other direction in which this analysis of Canada's foreign policy towards Cuba can take us. As a matter of fact, our infantile Cuba policy points to a broader issue for Canadians: our democratic deficit here at home. Nothing else can ultimately explain why Castro's Cuba has been for so long the fetish of choice among a great many well-informed Canadians, why so many academics who make a living out of criticizing governments and policies gladly condone the absence of such liberty for their Cuban colleagues, why Canadian unions wax eloquent about a regime that bans independent unions and freedom of association, why government officials, bureaucrats, and NGOs with fine educational backgrounds and experience in world affairs can put together irresponsible policies such as the one included in the Joint Declaration of January 1997, and why so many Canadian universities (more than 15 now) are rushing to develop exchange programs with (and send their students to) Cuban universities where freedom of thought and association are systematically repressed, as though Cuba was not dictatorial, just interestingly different. These are the kinds of questions we must seriously ask ourselves as Canadians, for they will be relevant long after Fidel Castro and his regime are gone.

NOTES

1. Official document of the Department of Foreign Affairs and International Trade, available on the Web. The other country we tried to 'fix' is South Africa. For Adam and Moodley, 'in reality Canada's intervention has made little difference to South African developments', but 'it has contributed to Canadian self-definition and international credibility' (Adam and Moodley, 1992: 1).
2. For an overview of the legal parameters of these enclaves, see DFAIT (1999b). Incidentally, this is also an interesting guide for Canadian biases towards Cuba. Independent Cuban 'journalists' (the Guide's quotation marks) are referred to as 'sometimes interesting, in spite of a strong anti-government bias', whereas the Cuban government's news agency (Prensa Latina) is plainly recommended without comment. It also presents CubaWeb as 'an American site with the same name as the official Cuban government service', one that is oriented to a 'post-Castro Cuba' but that 'nonetheless' includes a reasonably balanced collection of business news.
3. See some of his comments and the *Globe and Mail*'s editorial (1998) on the subject.
4. To give only one recent example with a Canadian resonance: a Cuban academic and member of the Communist Party (i.e., not a vocal critic of the government, let alone a dissident) lost his position at the University of Havana after he expressed pessimistic views about the Cuban economy in a public lecture. This economist, incidentally, was hired by the government-funded International Development Research Centre (IDRC) in Canada, which funds exchange programs with Cuban universities and which normally does not worry overly about disregard for academic freedom in Cuba. This time, however, the IDRC president, Maureen O'Neil, had to protest, for as she pointed out, 'We have a responsibility to go in and defend *our* researchers if they fall into trouble' (in Knox, 1999; my emphasis). Presumably, this responsibility could remain dormant

before and cheerful co-operation could continue unabated when only ordinary Cubans fell into trouble.

5. Here we have three factors and a riddle: (1) Cuban-Americans flew countless times in the same area and for years before the Cuban air force was ordered to intervene; (2) the infamous Helms-Burton Act, which instantly pitted the US against the rest of the world, was not likely to be adopted by Congress until that tragedy took place; (3) Fidel Castro understands very well the dynamic of US politics. The riddle is: Was the timing of President Castro's bold decision a pure coincidence?

6. According to a Web document of the US State Department: 'The fundamental goal of United States policy toward Cuba is to promote a peaceful transition to a stable, democratic form of government and respect for human rights. Our policy has two fundamental components: maintaining pressure on the Cuban Government for change through the embargo and the Libertad Act while providing humanitarian assistance to the Cuban people, and working to aid the development of civil society in the country.' See http://www.state.gov/www/regions/wha/cuba/country_info.html

7. Letter from Professor Toope, 19 Oct. 1999, quoted with permission. His report to CIDA is considered confidential.

8. He also likened the Cuban one-party state to Frank McKenna's government in New Brunswick (the Liberal leader won all 58 seats of the legislature in 1987), and mocked Cuba's 'so-called political prisoners'.

9. Michael Pearson, a former senior policy adviser to Foreign Minister André Ouellet (1993–6) and Lloyd Axworthy (1996–7), points out in a recent article that when Ouellet proposed a rapprochement with Cuba, 'senior management in the department was not enthusiastic' (Pearson, 1999: 10).

10. It is not an accident that, among the many ingredients that entered into the making of the 'constructive engagement' policy towards Cuba, John Kirk and Peter McKenna mention (first!) 'appeasing the NGO community' (Kirk and McKenna, 1997: 175).

11. A seminar on children's rights was held in May 1997 in Havana, followed by another on the same subject in December 1998 at the University of Victoria. A seminar on women's rights was held in June 1997 in Ottawa, headed by MP Jean Augustine. The second seminar on women's rights, scheduled for late spring 1999 in Havana, was put on hold.

12. A top official from CIDA assured me that before the May 1997 seminar on children's rights held in Cuba that the Canadian delegation was informed that, indeed, they were going there to learn from the Cuban model.

REFERENCES

Adam, Heribert, and Kogila Moodley. 1992. *Democratizing South Africa: Challenges for Canadian Policy*. Ottawa: Canadian Institute for Peace and Security, Occasional Paper No. 9, June.

Axworthy, Lloyd. 1992–3. 'Canadian Foreign Policy: A Liberal Party Perspective', *Canadian Foreign Policy* 1, 1 (Winter): 7–16.

————. 1997. Interviewed by Margaret Warner, PBS network, 23 Jan.: http://www.pbs.org/newshour/bb/latin_america/january97/canada_1-23.html

————.1998. 'Why Canada is involved so closely with Cuba', *Globe and Mail*, 18 Mar., A23.

Castro Ruz, Raul. 1996. 'Maintaining Revolutionary Purity', excerpts from a report presented to the Central Committee of the Communist Party of Cuba, 23 Mar., reproduced in *Cuba: Political Pilgrims and Cultural Wars*. Washington: The Free Cuba Center of Freedom House.

CIDA. 1999. 'Canadian Co-operation with Cuba', CIDA Web site: http://www.acdicida.gc.ca/cida_ind . . . 40716e852567e500400ad3

Department of Foreign Affairs and International Trade (DFAIT). 1997. 'Joint Declaration of the Ministers of Foreign Affairs of Canada and Cuba', 22 Jan.: www.dfait-maeci.gc.ca/english/foreignp/jd_w_cba.htm

————. 1999a. 'Human Security: Safety for People in a Changing World': http://www.dfait-maeci.gc.ca/foreignp/HumanSecurity/secur-e.ht

————. 1999b. 'Guide for Canadian Businesses': http://www.infoexport.gc.ca/docs/cuba-e.ht

Fagan, Drew. 1994. 'Cuba Policy Sparks Debate at the Summit of the Americas', *Globe and Mail*, 12 Dec., A11.

Globe and Mail. 1998. 'Canada's Cuban confusion', 11 Mar., A14.

Gorman, Richard V. 1991. 'Canada-Cuban Relations: A Brief Overview', in H. Michael Erisman and John M. Kirk, eds, *Cuban Foreign Policy Confronts a New International Order*. Boulder, Colo.: Lynne Rienner, 203–6.

Hampson, Fen O., and Dean F. Oliver. 1998. 'Pulpit Diplomacy: A Critical Assessment of the Axworthy Doctrine', *International Journal* 53, 3 (Summer): 225–50.

Human Rights Watch. 1999. *Cuba's Repressive Machinery: Human Rights Forty Years After the Revolution*. New York: Human Rights Watch.

Kirk, John M., and Peter McKenna. 1997. *Canada-Cuba Relations: The Other Good Neighbor Policy*. Gainesville: University Press of Florida.

————. 1998. 'Canadian-Cuban Relations: "Principled Pragmatism" in Action?', in *Cuba Today: The Events Taking Place in Cuba and the Ensuing Issues for Canadian Policy*. Ottawa: FOCAL, Background papers, 37–47.

————. 1999. 'Canadian-Cuban Relations: A Model for the New Millennium?', *Global Development Studies* 1, 3–4 (Winter-Spring): 385–409.

Knox, Paul. 1999. 'Cuba Muzzles Reformer with Ties to Canada', *Globe and Mail*, 10 July, A1, A4.

Lancaster, John. 1999. 'State Dept. Web Site Errs on Travel to Cuba', *Washington Post*, 12 Nov., A04.

Oxford Analytica. 1999. 'Cuba: Global Reintegration', 24 Nov.

Oziewicz, Estanislav. 1999. 'Canada Aids Cuban Exodus', *Globe and Mail*, 11 Oct., A1, A4.

Pearson, Michael. 1999. 'Reflections on Implementing Canadian Foreign Policy', *Canadian Foreign Policy* 6, 2 (Winter): 1–18.

Radio Havana Cuba. 1999. 'Relations between Canada and Cuba are excellent and continue to grow', Havana, 27 Oct.: http://www.radiohc.org/english.html

Ritter, Archibald. 1999. 'Is Cuba's Economic Reform Process Paralysed?', *World Economic Affairs* (Winter): 13–22.

Scoffield, Heather. 1999. 'Grits' Approach to Cuba's Human Rights Wrong: ex-envoy', *Globe and Mail*, 15 July, A4.

Sherritt International Corporation. 1998. *Annual Report*: http://www.sedar.com/dynamic_pages/issuerprofiles_e/i00002460.htm

United Nations Development Program (UNDP). 1998. *Human Development Report*. New York: Oxford University Press.

US State Department. 1999. 'Cuba: Country Information': http://www.state.gov/www/regions/wha/cuba/country_info.html

Vincent, Isabel. 1998. 'Havana's House of Ill Repute', *National Post*, 7 Nov., B6.

14

Canada's Participation in the NATO-led Intervention in Kosovo

The North Atlantic Treaty Organization's decision to use force in Kosovo marks a significant departure from the original defensive purpose of the alliance. Canada's decision to participate in the NATO-led intervention is both a departure from, and consistent with, Canadian foreign policy practice. This chapter will explore why Canada joined the NATO bombing campaign, entailing the use of force against a sovereign country, without the sanction of the United Nations. The primary motivation for Canada's participation in the bombing campaign was humanitarian; however, traditional state interests were also at play, as were Canada's historic links with Europe.

The combination of motivating factors for Canada's (and NATO's) intervention in Kosovo means that it does not serve as a valid precedent for the doctrine of humanitarian intervention under international law. NATO's intervention was not in response to a direct or immediate security threat, thereby pushing forward NATO's evolution from a purely defensive alliance towards a policing and peace enforcement role in Europe. What is striking about the NATO intervention is the convergence of core values shared by Canada's key allies, including Britain and the United States. Canada's human security agenda has led to significant policy differences with the United States over such issues as landmines and the role of nuclear weapons in NATO. The decision to intervene in Kosovo represented a coming together of policy priorities in promoting humanitarian values.

The first section of this chapter outlines the evolution in the Canadian government's thinking about the primacy of individual rights over absolute notions of state sovereignty in situations of severe human rights abuses. The willingness to intervene under UN auspices for humanitarian reasons can be traced to the Mulroney government. Under the Chrétien government there was a further shift, reflected in the gradual acceptance of the need for a more robust military role than can be provided through traditional UN peacekeeping, with an explicit role for NATO. There was therefore already a considerable evolution in thinking and practice before Kosovo, which was consistent with the decision to intervene militarily to resolve the Kosovo crisis.

Next I set out the background to the Kosovo conflict and outline the steps taken by NATO, considering Canada's support for NATO's role in Kosovo that culminated with the commencement of bombing on 24 March 1999. During the same period, the government undertook a variety of measures to further a diplomatic solution to the crisis.

In the following section, an explanation is given as to why Canada ultimately accepted the use of force in Kosovo without UN authorization. This decision is the point at which there is a clear departure from traditional Canadian foreign policy practice. The final section addresses the problems associated with the bombing campaign and their implications for Canadian foreign policy.

THE EVOLUTION OF CANADIAN FOREIGN POLICY DOCTRINE AND PRACTICE, 1990–1999

In the early 1990s, in the aftermath of the Cold War, the Mulroney and Chrétien governments respectively redefined the conceptual underpinnings of Canadian foreign policy. The decision to intervene in Kosovo represents the logical conclusion of Canadian foreign policy practice in humanitarian crises. Yet, despite the primacy of humanitarian values, the NATO-led intervention in Kosovo is a unique case, stemming from its location in Europe and the history of that region. Although the human security concept is associated with the foreign policy of the Chrétien government and with Foreign Minister Lloyd Axworthy in particular, the dramatically changed international context that gave rise to the concept was enthusiastically addressed by the Mulroney government in its second mandate. The concept of human security, in acknowledging the dramatic changes in the international political context, embraces a broader definition of security that places individual or human security above state security. The most significant changes are seen to be the evolving international norm about the primacy of individual human rights, the declining utility of military force to resolve international disputes, and the proliferation of non-traditional international actors, such as international non-governmental organizations.

The recognition that human rights are a legitimate concern of the international community has strengthened since the end of World War II. By the 1980s, international momentum in favour of a human rights agenda was reflected in the concerted international effort to end apartheid in South Africa and to promote respect for human rights and democratization in Africa, Latin America, Asia, and Eastern Europe.[1] With the end of the Cold War, state sovereignty has been further eroded. State boundaries have become more permeable because of the effects of globalization and of transnational forces such as the international trade in drugs. Furthermore, certain pressing global concerns, such as environmental degradation, are not amenable to resolution within the traditional confines of national boundaries and require international co-operation. Threats to international peace and security arise not just from inter-state conflict, but from internal conflict as well. The pressure for international action comes from a TV/Internet-connected public, who see humanitarian catastrophes arising out of civil war as legitimate grounds for intervention.

The perception that internal conflicts constitute a threat to international peace and security has given rise to growing demands on the UN to expand significantly the mandate of peacekeeping and to embrace peacemaking, peacebuilding, and peace enforcement.

Former Prime Minister Brian Mulroney and his Secretary of State for External Affairs, Barbara McDougall, were quick to embrace both the shifting foundations of the sovereignty principle and the need to act on them. The emphasis on human security, at the expense of state sovereignty, when human rights are threatened or abused has been evident in foreign policy statements since the early 1990s.

On 29 September 1991, Mulroney observed that 're-thinking the limits of national sovereignty in a world where problems respect no borders' is appropriate in light of new threats to international stability and order (cited in Cooper, 1997: 183). In an address on 17 May 1993, McDougall remarked: 'we have to reconsider the UN's traditional definition of state sovereignty. I believe that states can no longer argue sovereignty as a licence for internal repression, when the absolutes of that sovereignty shield conflicts that eventually could become international in scope' (DEAITC, 1993b: 5). These statements reveal a fundamental shift in the traditional Canadian foreign policy approach to the sanctity of the sovereignty principle. For example, as late as the mid-1980s, External Affairs resisted certain measures taken against apartheid South Africa because of concerns about sovereignty (Redekop, 1985). The articulation of the human security approach brought the Mulroney government's shift in views about sovereignty forward into the Chrétien era.

The consistency in thought about the place of sovereignty is revealed in the address to Parliament by the new Minister of Foreign Affairs, André Ouellet, on 15 March 1994:

> It is my profound belief that the concept of intervention as a right and a duty represents a turning point in the history of humankind. The world has only recently understood and accepted this concept which, to some, constitutes interfering in a country's domestic politics but to many others is a sign of hope. . . . We cannot remain indifferent to the fact that throughout the world, millions of human beings—millions—are being denied their most basic rights. (DFAIT, 1994b: 13)

Ouellet was clearly suggesting that sovereignty considerations are eclipsed by the higher value of protecting individual human rights.

The foreign policy review launched by the newly elected Chrétien government in 1994 also revealed continuity in terms of its acceptance of a broader understanding of security, as demonstrated in the report of the Special Joint Committee Reviewing Canadian Foreign

Policy, *Canada's Foreign Policy: Principles and Priorities for the Future* (November 1994). In assessing the relevant external circumstances in which Canada must conduct its foreign policy, the report noted the new types of security threats in the post-Cold War context. Such security threats might include ethnic conflict, environmental degradation, nuclear proliferation (not new, but more salient), and globalization. Emphasis was placed on the need to address non-military security threats and the importance of co-operating to promote common security goals. In the foreign policy White Paper, *Canada in the World* (1995), the term 'human security' was used in the context of the need to embrace a broader concept of security (Canada, 1995: 25). A complex range of security threats was identified: mass migration, epidemics, overpopulation, underdevelopment, global warming, and humanitarian tragedies. The paper argued that 'All of this demands a broadening of the focus of security policy from its narrow orientation of managing state-to-state relationships, to one that recognizes the importance of the individual and society for our shared security' (ibid.).

The human security concept was articulated more clearly once Lloyd Axworthy became Minister of Foreign Affairs in January 1996. While not negating the requisites of state security (as his critics have suggested), Axworthy gave clear priority to the security needs of individuals: 'At a minimum, human security requires that basic needs are met, but it also acknowledges that sustained economic development, human rights and fundamental freedoms, the rule of law, good governance, sustainable development and social equity are as important to global peace as arms control and disarmament' (Axworthy, 1998a: 184).

A number of major foreign policy initiatives, informed by the concept of human security, have been launched or carried forward under Axworthy's direction. These include the Ottawa initiative that led to the signing in December 1997 of the Convention on the Prohibition of Anti-personnel Mines (begun under André Ouellet), the peacebuilding initiative to assist war-torn societies to rebuild after civil war has come to an end, a major role in the establishment of the International Criminal Court, a sustained campaign to promote the rights of the child, and efforts to prevent the proliferation of small arms.

Canadian foreign policy practice has demonstrated a strong, if sometimes wavering, commitment to humanitarian intervention. Canada's participation in UN-led operations in Somalia and the former Yugoslavia, while technically not entailing an infringement on state sovereignty, nevertheless was motivated primarily by humanitarian concerns. Canada was at the forefront of UN humanitarian missions in the former Yugoslavia and Somalia, committing, in March 1992, 1,200 peacekeepers to the United Nations Protection Force (UNPROFOR) in Croatia, and, in April, 750 troops to the United Nations Operation in Somalia (UNOSOM 1). Both of these missions reflect the fact that the Mulroney government was clearly an enthusiastic supporter of humanitarian intervention under the auspices of the United Nations.

The election of the Chrétien government in 1993 corresponded with both an international and domestic waning of enthusiasm for the humanitarian missions the Mulroney government had so optimistically embraced. The disastrous conduct of the Canadian Airborne Division in Somalia, coupled with the serious risk to peacekeepers' lives associated with the Bosnia mission and the questioning of the utility of peacekeepers in situations such as Bosnia, underscored this change in attitudes. The growing complexity and scope of UN mandates led to a similar waning of support at the international level. The evidence for this was found in the tragic failure to respond to the genocide in Rwanda in 1994.

The Chrétien government was reluctant to continue with the Mulroney government's commitment of Canadian forces in the former Yugoslavia. The new Foreign Minister, André Ouellet, urged withdrawal after Canada was excluded from the Bosnia Contact Group, formed in April 1994 to bring a solution to the Bosnian conflict. After subjecting the question of Canada's continued participation to parliamentary debate, the Chrétien government extended the forces' mandate for six-month intervals, beginning on 10 March 1994, then 22 September 1994, and again in February 1995.

The intractable nature of the conflict in Bosnia led to divisions among its allies, including Canada, as to how best to proceed. Some countries, especially the US, came to support the use of force to resolve the conflict, necessarily entailing NATO involvement, because organizations, such as the Organization for Security and Co-operation in Europe (OSCE) and the Western European Union (WEU), lacked the requisite military clout. Canada, on the other hand, strongly endorsed the use of UN peacekeepers and the primacy and authority of the UN as the legitimate organization that should respond to the Bosnian civil war.

The acceptance in theory of the need to respect human rights over state sovereignty did not automatically translate into a willingness to intervene militarily on humanitarian grounds. Canada was initially opposed to a NATO role in Bosnia, preferring to provide humanitarian assistance under the UN and to maintain a strict arms embargo, in contrast to the US preference for a 'lift and strike' position. Furthermore, the government was strongly opposed to the use of force by NATO to resolve the conflict:

> We have also energetically supported peacekeeping efforts and have constantly upheld the idea of NATO participation in a comprehensive peace plan under the auspices of the UN. At the same time, we oppose and will continue to oppose proposals for military action that do not favour resolution of the conflict and do endanger the lives of peacekeepers. (DFAIT, 1993: 3)

Canada's resistance reflected its concern about the safety of peacekeepers. The government continued to maintain that humanitarian aid could be delivered in a war zone without allowing a more robust military role for UN peacekeepers.

At the NATO summit in January 1994, Canada (along with Greece) opposed NATO-led air strikes to protect UNPROFOR. Canada was prepared to accept NATO air strikes only if UN peacekeepers were under direct attack and if authorized by the UN Secretary-General (as planned in June 1993). However, if the purpose was to protect UNPROFOR in circumstances where no direct threat was imminent, such a strike would have to be discussed at the NATO Council, where consensus would be required (DFAIT, 1994a: 6).

In April 1994, the Chrétien government reluctantly came to support NATO-led air strikes in spite of the fact that these subsequently led to Canadian peacekeepers being taken hostage by the Serbs. The lack of a Canadian say on Bosnia, however, continued to rankle. The pressure by the US to launch air strikes, which had no forces of its own on the ground, proved difficult to resist, even though it meant that Canadian peacekeepers would be put at risk. As Cooper notes:

> Notwithstanding repeated assurances that Canada would have a veto over this important decision [whether to launch air strikes], the Chrétien government discovered that when push came to shove the safety of Canadian peacekeeping personnel on the ground came second to what was deemed

to be in the interests of the big powers in the Western Alliance. (Cooper, 1997: 195)

In May 1995, in his address to the NATO Council, Ouellet endorsed the use of force to counter violations of resolutions passed by the UN (DFAIT, 1995b: 2). This was seen to be necessary to restore the credibility of UNPROFOR, whose activities were being undermined by Serb forces. Subsequently, the government decided to withdraw Canadian peacekeepers from the former Yugoslavia. In August 1995, Canada ordered the withdrawal of 1,200 peacekeepers from Croatia. On 5 October 1995, in anticipation of the imminent Dayton settlement, Canada announced the immediate withdrawal of its remaining 1,300 ground forces from the former Yugoslavia as a whole.

Had there not been such strong inter-party and public support for a peacekeeping role in the former Yugoslavia, the Chrétien government would very likely have withdrawn its peacekeepers sooner. Developments in Bosnia, including the failure of UNPROFOR to preserve safe havens in areas such as Srebrenica, confirmed the government's doubts about how positive a role peacekeepers could play in the circumstances in which they had to operate. The government's subsequent actions suggest that it had come to accept that a more robust military role under NATO command was appropriate in situations, such as Bosnia, where severe human rights abuses had been perpetrated literally under the UN peacekeepers' noses. A shift can therefore be discerned in Canadian policy towards an acceptance that the use of force may be necessary and appropriate to stop and prevent humanitarian disasters. This shift in thinking coincided with the spectacular and tragic failure of UNPROFOR to protect so-called safe areas in Bosnia.

As a result of this reassessment, on 6 December 1995 the government announced it was committing 1,000 logistical and combat forces to Bosnia to participate in the NATO-led Implementation Force (IFOR). A year later, on 4 December 1996, Foreign Minister Lloyd Axworthy announced that Canada would contribute 1,200 troops to the SFOR follow-on force. Canada would assume more front-line responsibilities and a larger area of operations. Axworthy stressed the need for peacebuilding activities (DFAIT, 1996). These decisions were made easier for the Chrétien government by the remarkable degree of inter-party consensus for a continued role for Canada in the former Yugoslavia, a consensus that was to appear again over the Kosovo issue.

CANADA'S ROLE BEFORE AND DURING THE NATO BOMBING CAMPAIGN

When the Kosovo issue resurfaced on the international agenda in early 1998, a precedent for a dominant NATO role had already been set in Bosnia. The experience of Bosnia had demonstrated that humanitarian peacekeeping missions under UN auspices, if not backed up by sufficient force, can fail, and even be counterproductive to resolving conflict. It is noteworthy that, in contrast to Bosnia, where peacekeepers were inserted in the middle of a civil war with shaky ceasefires and no political settlement, there was no consideration of sending in peacekeepers in Kosovo until *after* a political settlement had been reached. Canada's experience in Bosnia meant that it was not such an illogical leap to accept a primary role for NATO in Kosovo, although preferably this would be under UN auspices.

In the year leading up to the commencement of NATO bombing on 24 March 1999, the Canadian government was supportive of a NATO role in Kosovo, including, if need be, the use of force. At the same time, the government sought to promote a political solution to the conflict by supporting the efforts of the UN and the OSCE and through diplomatic efforts on the part of Axworthy and other high-level Canadian government officials. By the spring of 1998, a consensus clearly had emerged among NATO allies that diplomacy, third-party mediation, and sanctions would not be sufficient to induce Yugoslavia leader Slobodan Milosovic to negotiate in good faith; a credible threat of the use of force was a necessary further inducement. This conclusion was based on past experience with Milosovic, who, it was felt, had come to the negotiating table at Dayton only after NATO had used force in Bosnia. Unfortunately, this was not an accurate inference. As events would show, Milosovic was not easily swayed by the threat and subsequent use of force in Kosovo.

Before we consider Canada's role in NATO, a brief overview of the background events leading up to the bombing campaign is required.[2] Although one can trace the historical context of the crisis in Kosovo back almost one thousand years, the conflict's more recent origins are to be found in Milosevic's infamous speech given in April 1987, at Kosovo Polje, shortly before he became leader of the Serbian

Communist Party. Milosevic's speech, given at the site of the Battle of Kosovo Polje in 1389, inflamed Serbian nationalism with the now well-known words: 'No one will ever beat you again.' On 3 February 1989 the Serbian National Assembly passed constitutional amendments revoking the status of autonomous province that had been granted to Kosovo in 1974. Shortly after becoming President of the Republic of Serbia in May 1989, Milosevic made another inflammatory speech on 28 June 1989, on the occasion of the 600th anniversary of the Battle of Kosovo Polje. A year later, on 5 July 1990, the Serbian Assembly suspended the Kosovo Assembly after it issued a proclamation declaring Kosovo an independent republic within the Yugoslav Federation. Delegates of the dissolved Kosovo Assembly responded by electing, on 7 September 1990, a clandestine government and legislature.

Developments from 1991 on were caught up by the breakup of the Yugoslav Federation, with the declarations of independence by Slovenia, Croatia, Macedonia, and Bosnia and Herzegovina. The outbreak of the vicious war in Croatia and then in Bosnia had the effect of distracting the attention of the international community away from the growing crisis and repression in Kosovo. The failure to address the Kosovo issue in the December 1995 Dayton Peace Agreement left the moderate leadership in Kosovo increasingly marginalized and paved the way for a greater willingness on the part of the Kosovar population to accept more radical tactics. With small arms readily available from neighbouring Albania, it was not long before the Kosovo Liberation Army (KLA) became active. In June 1996 the KLA committed its first terrorist act, killing six Serb policemen. Attempts by the international community, including Canada, to promote dialogue between Milosevic and the moderate Kosovar leader, Dr Ibrahim Rugova, proved futile. By 1998 the situation in Kosovo was deteriorating rapidly.

As the fighting between the KLA and Serbian security forces escalated in February and March 1998, a variety of international actors became directly involved in seeking to defuse the situation. These included the OSCE, which had been engaged in the Kosovo issue since 1992; the Contact Group, which had been formed to resolve the Bosnian conflict and whose members consisted of the US, Britain, France, Germany, Italy, and Russia; the United Nations Security Council; the International Criminal Tribunal for the Former Yugoslavia (ICTY); and NATO.

During the summer of 1998, the international community watched as the KLA launched a major offensive, seizing 40 per cent of Kosovo before it was pushed back by Serb security forces and the Yugoslav army. The tactic of the Serbs was to destroy entire villages rather then targeting KLA strongholds. This greatly exacerbated the humanitarian situation, producing growing numbers of displaced persons and refugees. In response to the looming humanitarian catastrophe, the United Nations Security Council (UNSC) adopted Resolution 1199 on 23 September 1998. From this point on, strenuous efforts were made on several fronts to stem the escalating violence and work towards a political settlement. US special envoy Richard Holbrooke negoti- ated an agreement between the former Republic of Yugoslavia (FRY) and the OSCE on 16 October 1998, allowing for a Kosovo Verification Mission (KVM) to verify observance of a ceasefire, the withdrawal of troops, and compliance with UNSC Resolution 1199. Meanwhile, from mid-October to December 1998, US special envoy Chris Hill sought to work out a political settlement for Kosovo.

In January 1999, the humanitarian situation took another sharp turn for the worse when ethnic Albanians were massacred in two separate incidents. On 29 January, NATO issued an ultimatum to both Milosevic and the KLA that they agree to a Western-mediated political settlement or face NATO air strikes. Talks began in Rambouillet, France, on 6 February and ended on 23 February. The talks resumed again on 15 March, but Milosevic refused to sign the Rambouillet accord. Amid evidence of a buildup of Serbian security forces and Yugoslav forces, NATO commenced its bombing campaign on 24 March.

NATO members began to consider a possible role for NATO early in 1998 as the security situation in Kosovo deteriorated further, with potentially destabilizing implications for neighbouring countries. At the NATO Council meeting of foreign ministers on 28 May 1998, NATO set out two major objectives with respect to Kosovo: (1) to achieve a peaceful resolution to the crisis by contributing to the response of the international community; and (2) to promote stability and secu- rity in the neighbouring countries of Albania and Macedonia (NATO, 1999a: 2).

NATO had two main concerns with respect to Kosovo: the grow- ing number of refugees and internally displaced persons as a result of increased repression beginning in February 1998; and the threat to peace and stability in neighbouring countries, in particular, Albania and the former Yugoslav Republic of Macedonia. In response to this concern, the NATO Council meeting of defence ministers decided on 11 June 1998 to conduct an air exercise over Albania and Macedonia, 'with the aim of demonstrating NATO's capability to project power rapidly into the region' (NATO, 1998b).

In support of NATO's decision, Canada moved six CF-18s and 130 Canadian Forces members to Aviano, Italy. Canada participated in two NATO air exercises in support of the effort to show NATO's resolve to promote stability in the region (DFAIT, 1998b: 1). At the same NATO meeting of defence ministers, authorization was given to military authorities to pursue other 'effective and readily available' options towards meeting the following goals: (1) halting the campaign of violence and repression in Kosovo; (2) supporting international efforts to obtain a ceasefire; (3) helping to create conditions for serious negotiations towards a political settlement; and (4) preventing spillover of violence into neighbouring countries.

The emphasis on effective and readily available options tilted the balance strongly in favour of air operations. This was confirmed a few months later, on 24 September 1998, when NATO issued an activation warning for both a limited air option and a phased air campaign in Kosovo. While this measure did not constitute authorization to use force, it allowed NATO air commanders to identify the assets required for any air operations and was also intended to serve as a political signal to Milosevic of NATO's willingness to use force (Solana, 1998a).

On 13 October 1998, NATO issued activation orders authorizing air strikes in the event Milosevic failed to comply with diplomatic efforts to secure a ceasefire, in accordance with UNSC Resolution 1199, to withdraw Serb forces from Kosovo, and to work towards improving the humanitarian situation. In addition, the threat of air strikes forced Milosevic to reach an agreement with the OSCE on the Kosovo Verification Mission (KVM) allowing observers to monitor the situation on the ground on 16 October. The threat of force also led Milosevic to reach an agreement with NATO on 24 October on an unarmed aerial surveillance mission over Kosovo. The ground and air verification missions were endorsed by UNSC Resolution 1203 on 24 October.

Canada's support of NATO's threat to use force was clear and unwavering. In anticipation of the activation orders, Canada committed on 12 October the use for air strikes, if necessary, of the six

CF-18s already based in Aviano. By this time, Canada had 180 military personnel in Aviano. Canada also lent its support to the special military task force set up by NATO to assist with the emergency evacuation of members of the KVM, should the need arise. The extraction force was deployed in Macedonia, under the overall direction of the Supreme Allied Commander Europe (SACEUR). On 17 December, Canada sent 62 people to Macedonia to take part in the NATO extraction force.

By January 1999, activities on the part of both the KLA and Serb security forces had caused the agreements reached with both the OSCE and NATO to unravel. In the aftermath of the massacre of Kosovar Albanians in mid-January, NATO issued a statement on 17 January calling on Milosevic to comply with the conditions set out in the agreements (NATO, 1999b). The statement confirmed that, although the earlier threat of air strikes had been called off, the activation orders for air operations were still in effect. Significantly, the statement called 'on both sides to cease hostilities immediately and to begin negotiations towards a lasting political solution which provides greater autonomy for Kosovo and which preserves the territorial integrity of the FRY' (ibid., 2).

In what was a final major diplomatic effort, the Contact Group set in motion attempts to arrive at a political settlement to the conflict. NATO indicated its support for this initiative by calling on both sides to agree to the proposals set forth by the Contact Group for completing an interim political settlement within an established time frame. In a statement by the Secretary-General of NATO, Javier Solana, reference was made to the failure of the FRY to comply with the agreements reached with the OSCE and NATO and indicated that 'NATO stands ready to act and rules out no option to ensure full respect by both sides of the demands of the international community' (NATO, 1999c: 1). Javier Solana alluded to a 'critical turning point' that had been reached in the Kosovo crisis and warned of the need to carry through with the use of force when all other means had failed. On 30 January, NATO announced that it was prepared to 'compel compliance', and delegated to the NATO Secretary-General the authority to call for air strikes on FRY territory (NATO, 1999d).

On 23 March 1999, in the aftermath of the failure of the Rambouillet negotiations for a political settlement, Javier Solana directed SACEUR, General Wesley Clark, to initiate air strikes. In his statement, Solana cited Milosevic's failure to comply with three demands of the international community: (1) failure to accept the political settlement reached at Rambouillet; (2) failure to meet the terms of the 25 October agreement with NATO in withdrawing the Serb army and special police forces; and (3) the use of excessive and disproportionate force in Kosovo (NATO, 1999f). In a separate statement, NATO indicated that its military objectives were to halt violent attacks being committed by Yugoslav armed forces and the special police and to 'disrupt their ability to conduct future attacks against the population of Kosovo' (NATO, 1999g).

During the preparations for the air campaign, NATO military planners envisaged a three-phased campaign of air strikes. In light of the rapid intensification of the Serb offensive on the ground, NATO very quickly moved to phase two, representing an intensification of the air campaign, when on 27 March the Secretary-General authorized SACEUR to broaden the range of air operations. In response to the broadening of the air campaign, Canada, on 30 March, contributed an additional six CF-18s for a total of 12 CF-18s based in Aviano. The total number of military personnel reached approximately 250. On 19 April, Canada contributed yet another six 6 CF-18s. A few days later NATO moved into the third phase of its air campaign, as decided upon at the Washington summit held from 23 to 25 April. Overall, compared to its European counterparts, Canada made a significant contribution to the bombing campaign, contributing about 10 per cent of total sorties.[3] As European countries were painfully aware, the US made by far the biggest contribution, at 70 per cent.

The Canadian government clearly determined that it was appropriate for NATO to play the robust role it did and for Canada to be an active participant. In assessing whether Canada worked strenuously enough to bring about a diplomatic solution to the Kosovo crisis, one naturally has to keep in mind that there were a multitude of players, and Canada was not among the most important. Canada is not a member of the Contact Group, a sore point for the government when it was formed to address the Bosnia situation. This fact makes Canada's contribution to the NATO campaign all the more noteworthy.

On the other hand, Canada is a member of other organizations involved with Kosovo, including the UN, the OSCE, and the G-8, and government ministers, in particular Axworthy, engaged in traditional diplomacy. Canada first became involved in Kosovo in 1992 through the OSCE (then still the CSCE) when it took part in two separate mis-

sions to Kosovo—a fact-finding mission in May and a conflict pre-
vention mission from October to December.[4] The conflagration in
Bosnia caused the Kosovo issue to fade away, but when it flared up
again in 1998 Canada again supported OSCE initiatives. In August
1998 Canada participated in the Kosovo Diplomatic Observers
Mission (KDOM), and on 20 November 1998 Canada committed 60
civilians and 20 military personnel to the OSCE Kosovo Verification
Mission (KVM). The OSCE was hampered by the fact that its activities
in verifying compliance with the ceasefire and UN resolutions
depended on the goodwill of Milosevic and his military and security
personnel, which proved elusive. This reality necessitated the creation of the NATO Extraction Force, in which Canada participated.
Once it was decided to commence the bombing campaign, the OSCE
could no longer play a useful role in Kosovo, and the KVM, including 65 Canadians, withdrew from Kosovo on 20 March 1999.

Axworthy devoted a tremendous amount of personal energy to
seeking a diplomatic solution to the crisis. In April 1996, after the
conclusion of the Dayton Peace Agreement the previous December,
Axworthy went to Belgrade to speak to the government of the FRY
and to serve notice that the development of Canada's relations with
the FRY would depend on the human rights situation in Kosovo and
Yugoslavia as a whole. After the situation in Kosovo deteriorated in
1998, Axworthy used the occasion of a visit to Bosnia and Macedonia
to speak to the moderate leader of the shadow government in
Kosovo, Dr Rugova. In October, Axworthy sent an envoy to speak
to FRY authorities in an effort to push forward the negotiations to
secure Milosevic's compliance with UNSC Resolution 1199 and to
reach agreement for ground and air verification with the OSCE and
NATO. The FRY ambassador to Canada was called in on numerous
occasions, as the government registered its displeasure over human
rights abuses in Kosovo. This occurred in March 1998, after the intensification of the Serb offensive against the KLA, in August 1998, after
the Serb forces had pushed the KLA into retreat, and again in January
1999, after the massacre of civilians in Racak, Kosovo. In November
1998 the FRY ambassador was called in so that Canada could express
its concern about the failure of the Yugoslav government to co-operate with the ICTY. Axworthy wrote to Yugoslav Foreign Minister
Zivadin Jovanovic on this matter (DFAIT, 1998c: 1). A very clear signal was being sent to Belgrade that Canada took the human rights
abuses in Kosovo very seriously.

Other steps short of the use of force were also taken by Canada and other countries. On 9 March 1998, in response to the Serb offensive of February and March, Axworthy announced a number of economic sanctions. These included the suspension of Export Development Corporation (EDC) credits, the suspension of discussion on landing rights in Canada for Yugoslav Airlines, and suspension of discussions on any bilateral agreements. These sanctions were reinforced by UNSC Resolution 1160, which reimposed an arms embargo that had been imposed on the FRY in November 1992 (UNSC Resolution 787). Further sanctions were announced on 10 June 1998, following a G-8 foreign ministers meeting in London. Axworthy announced a ban on investments in the Republic of Serbia and a freeze on the assets in Canada of the FRY and Serbian governments. Further sanctions were imposed after the bombing began. On 30 April 1999 Canada added the FRY to the Area Control List prohibiting oil exports.

Canada's efforts to support diplomacy and a peaceful resolution to the conflict are most clearly evident in the UN Security Council's engagement on the issue. On 7 August 1998, Axworthy condemned the escalating violence in Kosovo. With a group of Canadian diplomats he approached members of the UNSC and urged them to address the situation. Whether this had any concrete impact on the Security Council is hard to say, but the Secretary-General did issue a 'Presidential Statement' on 24 August calling for a ceasefire. A month later, on 23 September, the UNSC adopted Resolution 1199, calling for an immediate cessation of hostilities, the maintenance of a ceasefire, and for the FRY to 'implement immediately the measures towards achieving a political solution to the situation in Kosovo as contained in the Contact Group statement of 12 June 1998' (UN, 1999a). Significantly, the resolution was placed under Chapter VII of the UN Charter, stating that the situation in Kosovo constitutes a threat to international peace and security, and describing the situation in Kosovo as an impending humanitarian catastrophe. While NATO interpreted this as a green light to issue its activation warning the following day, there was no explicit sanction in Resolution 1199 for the threat or use of force.

On 1 October, Axworthy met with UN Secretary-General Kofi Annan, calling on the UNSC to act further on the situation in Kosovo. Again, whether this had any definite impact on the UNSC is difficult to judge, but on 24 October the Security Council passed Resolution

1203 demanding the FRY's implementation of the agreements with US negotiator Richard Holbrooke and the OSCE on verification of compliance with Resolution 1199. The Security Council also called on both the FRY and the KLA to co-operate with international efforts to improve the humanitarian situation. A day later, NATO signed an agreement with the FRY, adding its weight to the efforts to secure compliance.

After the adoption of Resolution 1207 on 17 November on the failure of the FRY to comply with the International Criminal Tribunal, no further Security Council resolutions concerning Kosovo were passed until after the bombing campaign had begun. The momentum for addressing the humanitarian situation and working towards a political settlement thus moved away from the UN, to NATO and the Contact Group (whose members, with the exception of Russia, are the dominant players in NATO). Nevertheless, Canada continued its efforts to sustain the engagement of the UNSC. As Canada is not a member of the Contact Group, it was not directly involved in the negotiations at Rambouillet. This disadvantage was offset somewhat, however, by the fact that Canada became a non-permanent member of the Security Council on 1 January 1999. Excluded from the Contact Group, Canada had a strong interest to promote the role of the UNSC.

When Canada assumed the Security Council presidency in February, it worked hard to induce the Council to take action and to play a supportive role during the Rambouillet talks. By then, however, NATO had already indicated its resolve to launch air strikes if a political settlement was not reached and if the humanitarian situation did not improve. Although a presidential statement was issued on 19 January, condemning the massacre at Racak and the FRY's refusal to allow in the ICTY, and another one was issued on 29 January, welcoming the proposals to negotiate a political settlement at Rambouillet, no UNSC endorsement was forthcoming. On 23 February, in its capacity as president of the Security Council, Canada made a statement supporting the Rambouillet talks. On 1 March Axworthy made a last-ditch effort to find ways to involve the UN on the Kosovo issue, in other words, to win UNSC endorsement of the use of force, which by then was imminent.

A shift is discernible in Canada's diplomatic efforts away from supporting initiatives towards a political settlement. Canada wanted the UNSC to go along with punishment of the FRY if it failed to co-operate in good faith in the Rambouillet talks. Given Milosevic's objections to the settlement, the KLA was free to sign the Rambouillet agreement safe in the knowledge that the FRY would not go along. Canada's support for the Rambouillet process, in a context of the threat of military punishment if an agreement was not reached, has questionable legal authority and moved beyond the realm of traditional diplomacy. The threat of NATO air strikes in the fall of 1998 was directed primarily at bringing a stop to the violence, alleviating human suffering, and securing a withdrawal of Serb forces. By the winter of 1999, those elements were still in question, but with the further condition that Milosevic go along with the Rambouillet process. By the time the air strikes began, there was the added rationale of the FRY's refusal to sign a specific agreement, a troubling development.

The Canadian government was thus committed to a peaceful settlement to the Kosovo crisis but was prepared to resort to force if necessary. However, a distinction needs to be made between punishing Milosevic for failing to sign the agreement reached at Rambouillet and for the human rights abuses committed by his forces. NATO justified punishing Milosevic's failure to sign the accords on the grounds that a political settlement was inextricably linked to improvement in the human rights situation. In reality, the distinction was blurred, and the bombing came to be justified primarily on humanitarian grounds.

SIGNIFICANCE OF THE INTERVENTION FOR CANADA AND THE UN

In order to understand why Canada ultimately decided to participate in the NATO bombing campaign without UN authorization, it is important to reiterate the distinction between supporting the use of force with UN authorization and supporting such force without UN authorization. As has been demonstrated, Canada came to accept the utility of force in situations such as Bosnia, where ceasefires were not being respected, where humanitarian efforts of peacekeepers were being hampered, and where peacekeepers were inserted before a political settlement had been reached. The evidence suggests that Canada was committed to the use of force by NATO if necessary, and worked strenuously to secure UNSC authorization for the use of force by NATO. Canada's clear preference was for UN authorization, but when it became clear that UN authorization would not be forthcoming, it was prepared to bypass the UNSC. The explanation for why this was so can be found in the factors motivating Canada to participate in the NATO bombing campaign.

Neither UN Resolution 1199 nor Resolution 1203 explicitly endorsed the use of force, although they acknowledged the humanitarian crisis in Kosovo as a threat to international peace and security. As already elaborated, Canada made numerous efforts throughout 1998 and into 1999 to get the Security Council to endorse the use of force. When Axworthy, joined by a team of Canadian diplomats, urged in August 1998 that the UNSC become 'fully engaged on the Kosovo issue', he stressed that the Kosovo crisis could spiral out of control unless the UNSC demonstrated the will to act (DFAIT, 1998a).

By October 1998, as evidenced by Canada's support for the NATO threat of air strikes, Canada was prepared to back the use of force without UN authorization. On 12 October 1998, Axworthy stated:

> The Yugoslav government has failed to comply with the terms of United Nations Security Council Resolution 1199. The United Nations Secretary-General has appealed to the international community to undertake urgent steps to prevent a humanitarian disaster in Kosovo. Regrettably, despite our repeated efforts, it has proven impossible at this time for the Security Council to agree on further action. Canada, like others, still hopes for a diplomatic solution, but believes that NATO's decision today can contribute to ending the conflict and avoiding an even greater human tragedy. (DFAIT, 1998c)

Yet, even as Canada confirmed its readiness to participate in NATO air operations if necessary, the government still attempted to win UNSC endorsement. In an address to the OSCE on 22 October 1998, Axworthy urged that the recently reached Kosovo agreement with the OSCE should receive Security Council endorsement. Furthermore, he called for 'an unambiguous Council mandate', which can reasonably be inferred to mean authorization for the use of force (DFAIT, 1998b: 1). Such a clear mandate was not forthcoming. The ensuing Resolution 1203 only called for compliance with Resolution 1199 and the agreements on verification, but failed to endorse the use of force should attempts to resolve the situation fail.

Canada's insistence that the UNSC play a central role reflects its belief that the UN remains the legitimate international organization for addressing humanitarian disasters. The government was concerned that the UN would be marginalized by other organizations competing to stake out a dominant role on the issue, including NATO, but also the OSCE and the European Union. Axworthy's address to the OSCE revealed that Canada was especially concerned that the Contact Group not be the dominant actor: 'Self-appointed contact groups have little legitimacy, are often counterproductive in the search for answers, and undermine the role of duly constituted institutions in advancing peace and security. In particular, we cannot allow the Security Council to be sidelined' (DFAIT, 1998d: 2).

Once the Contact Group took the initiative from January to March 1999, Canada took advantage of its newly gained seat on the UNSC to continue to press for an active UN role in Kosovo. The divisions within the Security Council, in particular, Russia's strong opposition to armed intervention against its traditional Serbian ally, made endorsement of the use of force impossible. Canada ultimately demonstrated strong support for the use of force, even without a UN mandate.

The acceptance by the Canadian government of the need to use force created a serious dilemma. Canada has always been a staunch supporter of the UN, and participating in the bombing campaign without UN endorsement pushed Canada beyond what until then had been the acceptable parameters of Canadian foreign policy behaviour. The government expressed concern about the impact of the Security Council's failure to act on the UN's legitimacy. There was clear frustration with the tendency of some Council members to uphold traditional notions of state sovereignty. In an address to the UN General Assembly on 25 September 1998, Axworthy had noted: 'To remain credible, the Council must re-examine the traditional interpretation of its mandate. The Council needs to broaden its horizons in addressing emerging threats which impact on our security' (DFAIT, 1998b: 5).

In the absence of UN endorsement, the government was prepared to push the parameters of acceptable foreign policy behaviour because of the plight of the ethnic Albanians in Kosovo: 'We cannot stand by while an entire population is displaced, people are killed, villages are burned and looted, and a population is denied its basic rights because it does not belong to the "right" ethnic group' (DFAIT, 1999b: 3). Humanitarian considerations were the primary factors motivating the Canadian government, as is demonstrated in numerous statements made by Axworthy. In short, Canada's willingness to act without UN authorization reflects the government's belief that a new international norm has emerged on the need to give primacy to individual over state rights in situations of egregious human rights abuses: 'human security is no longer simply a theoretical construct—it is becoming a new norm of international behaviour, where the security of the person is at the centre of our attention and care' (DFAIT, 1999d: 2).

Contrary to what might be expected, Canada was not unduly concerned about NATO alliance solidarity and credibility, although this was a major concern for other members, especially the US and Britain.[5] Nor was this a case of Canada being compelled to participate in an American-dominated alliance. For Canada, as for other NATO members, the precedent of Bosnia was a key motivating factor. As already suggested, the experience of Bosnia influenced the importance and acceptance of NATO's role in Kosovo. However, the Bosnia example went beyond merely influencing the mode of action. The reality of the human rights atrocities committed by Bosnian Serb forces, with support from Belgrade, was one that no one was prepared to see repeated again in Kosovo. A key factor motivating the Canadian government was evidence that Serb forces were preparing for a massive spring offensive (DFAIT, 1999g: 3). The experience of Bosnia had revived memories of World War II, and no one had expected to witness a repeat of those horrors, if on a smaller scale, again in Europe. At the close of the twentieth century no one was prepared to allow Kosovo to descend into another Bosnia. As it was, such a number of refugees and internally displaced persons had not been witnessed in Europe since the war.

This is not to suggest that NATO's actions were primarily motivated by humanitarian concerns. For many members mixed motives were involved. Even for Canada, where the humanitarian concern was sufficiently compelling that it overrode the country's traditional reluctance to sidestep the UN, other interests were involved. These included Canada's historical ties to Europe, based on two world wars and the many Canadians of European descent. Security concerns were also apparent, especially the danger of regional instability and the potential of drawing NATO allies into the conflict. Canada's willingness to revert to historic practice is also reflected in the decision, after the bombing campaign ended, to place Canadian troops under British command in Kosovo.

The fact that there was broad support across the political spectrum, even within the traditionally pacifist NDP, also made it politically easier for Canada to participate without UN authorization. Special House of Commons debates revealed near-universal support for the government's actions in Kosovo, although NDP MP Svend Robinson later changed his mind. Support was also evident in the special appearances made by Axworthy and Defence Minister Art Eggelton before the Standing Committee on Foreign Affairs and International Trade. A high point was the address to Parliament on 29 April by Vaclav Havel, who reiterated the primacy of human values. The Canadian public made an impressive show of generosity towards suffering Kosovar Albanians. With the notable exception of Canadians of Serb (and Greek) extraction with friends or relatives in the former Yugoslavia, there was overwhelming support for the government's humanitarian initiatives. The role of the media in conveying images of exhausted and anguished refugees clearly was influential in shaping public opinion.

The primacy of humanitarian factors motivating the Canadian government is also evident in the generous government support for international humanitarian relief efforts. By April 1999, Canada had committed nearly $14 million towards assisting the Kosovar Albanians, distributing its resources to such humanitarian agencies as the International Red Cross, Care Canada, the World Food Program, the UN High Commissioner for Refugees, and UNICEF. In April, the government announced that another $30 million was to be allocated for humanitarian and economic assistance. Canada also welcomed 5,000 refugees from Kosovo, who arrived in May 1999.

Still, as the bombing campaign dragged on, Canada continued to work hard to keep the UN engaged. Resolution 239, passed on 14 May, formalized the UN's role in addressing the humanitarian consequences of the war, as well as supporting the principles for a political solution adopted by the G-8. Significantly for Canada, the locus for working out a ceasefire and political settlement shifted to the G-8, which allowed Canada a formal, institutionalized role to play, in contrast to Canada's exclusion from the Contact Group. Canada was therefore directly involved in efforts to devise a draft resolution that would then be passed by the Security Council. Thus, the UN, having been sidelined at the start of the bombing campaign, could now sanction the role of KFOR and assume responsibility for civilian administration in Kosovo. On 10 June 1999, the Security Council adopted Resolution 1244, which granted the Council control over civilian administration and sanctioned NATO's security role through KFOR.

IMPLICATIONS FOR CANADIAN FOREIGN POLICY

Canada's participation in the NATO bombing campaign both vindicates and challenges the human security agenda. According to Axworthy, 'the pursuit of human security is a natural and logical projection of both our values and our interests. Consequently, from a human security perspective, the crisis in Kosovo—and its resolution—mark a defining moment' (DFAIT, 1999c: 5). Whether or not Kosovo sets a clear precedent for the doctrine of humanitarian intervention under international law, the government's actions clearly demonstrate support for this doctrine.

Axworthy has been strongly criticized for the emphasis he has placed on 'soft' power, the ability to achieve preferred outcomes through persuasion rather then coercion, in pursuing the human security agenda. It is true, and the Ottawa initiative demonstrates, that Canada is particularly well-suited to promote the human security agenda through soft-power techniques, including working with 'like-minded' countries. However, it is precisely when hard-power capabilities are required to promote humanitarian values that human security in practice confronts its weakest link. Kosovo demonstrates that the government has not completely rejected the utility of hard-power capabilities, contrary to the minister's earlier statement about the declining utility of force in international affairs. Yet, one should not be too sanguine about the utility of force in solving intractable conflict, given the attenuated nature of the bombing campaign and its counterproductive results. It was not until the real threat that NATO was prepared to use ground troops that Milosevic finally backed down on 3 June 1999, agreeing to withdraw Serb forces from Kosovo. In the meantime, the bombing may have exacerbated the refugee situation. The extension of the bombing campaign led to inappropriate targets being hit (including the Chinese embassy) and exposed NATO members to charges of violation of the laws of war on proportionality and even to violation of existing environmental laws. Kosovo, like Bosnia, has become a permanent ward of the international community, with the strong likelihood that the removal of NATO forces would lead to a resurgence of violence. The decision to

resort to force sits uncomfortably with some of the strongest supporters of the Axworthy Doctrine, such as in the NGO community.

It is also true that the persistent erosion of resources available to
the Canadian military ultimately undermines Canada's ability to practise what it preaches. As Robin Hay put it, 'Human security has to be
developed as a necessary complement of our hard-power obligations
and as a realistic response to a world in which Western societies are
reluctant to commit their sons and daughters to military adventures
abroad' (Hay, 1999: 227). Kosovo demonstrates that the issue, for
Canada at least, is not so much the willingness to risk Canadian lives
but the need for resources to fulfil military commitments. While there
is a certain measure of public tolerance for loss of life in humanitarian missions in Europe, this tolerance is likely much lower for other
parts of the world where Canada's historic ties are weaker. Given the
lack of military capabilities, it is questionable how consistent Canada
is likely to be (or can be) in upholding the doctrine of humanitarian
intervention anywhere in the world. In that sense, Hay makes the
point that a workable framework for the human security agenda
needs to be devised if Canada is to maintain international credibility
and influence.

For key alliance members, in particular the US, unwillingness to
risk lives adversely affected what NATO could do. For that reason,
Kosovo serves as an imperfect model for future humanitarian operations. It was clear, at least to the military leaders, that aerial bombing is not likely to help the people on the ground. Indeed, it has been
widely observed that the bombing precipitated the marked escalation of Serbian ethnic cleansing of Albanians, which resulted in the
massive flow of refugees to neighbouring countries. The possibility
of a ground invasion was not seriously discussed by political leaders
until it was clear that the bombing campaign was causing more harm
then good and was certainly not forcing Milosevic's acquiescence to
NATO's goals. The preservation of NATO solidarity was one of the sin-
gular accomplishments of the war. The situation now unfolding in
Kosovo is also unsatisfactory, as human rights abuses once committed against the Albanian majority have now been replaced by human
rights abuses committed against the Serb minority.

The ability of NATO to act with singularity of purpose is in marked
contrast to ongoing divisions within the Security Council. This situation raises a central dilemma bedevilling the Canadian government:

how to maintain the credibility of the UN while responding effectively to humanitarian emergencies. Canadian efforts in the UNSC show that Canada has not abandoned the UN, but, clearly, there is frustration at the difficulty of achieving consensus within the Security Council. As Axworthy noted during the bombing campaign: 'We worked hard to engage the Council, to ensure that it fully assumed its responsibility for advancing peace and security. Unfortunately, certain members of the Council could not reconcile yesterday's assumptions about sovereignty with today's imperatives of human emergency' (DFAIT, 1999c: 3). Canada has used its time on the Security Council to push its human security agenda. However, the frustration is real. In September 1999, Defence Minister Eggleton declared that Canada would be prepared to bypass the UN, if necessary, in situations of humanitarian emergencies (Koring, 1999).

As noted above, however, it is highly unlikely that Canada and NATO will intervene militarily on the scale of Kosovo outside Europe. The example of Chechnya reveals that NATO is not willing to intervene militarily everywhere. Although the primary impetus behind the intervention in Kosovo was humanitarian, historic and state security interests propelled that decision. However, the decision to bypass the UNSC cannot be taken lightly, and has serious implications for the preservation of international order. It gives licence to other countries, such as China and Russia, to ignore the UNSC in the future within their own spheres of influence.

NATO has assumed the role of international policeman, at least in Europe. The fact that NATO acted without explicit UN authorization calls into doubt how consistently the doctrine of humanitarian intervention can be applied globally. The willingness to antagonize Russia will also have long-term negative security implications for NATO members, including Canada. Human security and state security need not be contradictory goals, but they may well prove to be in the long term, unless the deterioration in relations with Russia can be reversed.

NOTES

1. The dramatic transformation in South Africa and the domestic and international pressures for political reform in other parts of Africa are especially noteworthy.
2. For background to the events, see Weller (1999), Austin (1998), and the DFAIT Web site: www.dfait-maeci.gc.ca

3. Figure provided by Christopher A. Shapardanov, Adviser (Russia/PJC), Political Affairs Division, NATO, in guest lecture to Canadian Foreign Policy class, University of Windsor, 24 Nov. 1999.
4. A chronology of Canada's involvement in Kosovo, upon which the following paragraphs are based, can be found at the DFAIT Web site.
5. Information in this paragraph was confirmed in confidential interviews with DFAIT officials, April and November 1999.

REFERENCES

Austin, Robert C. 1998. 'Albania and Kosovo: Roots of Instability', *Canadian Foreign Policy* 6, 1 (Fall): 61–72.

Axworthy, Lloyd. 1997. 'Canada and Human Security: The Need for Leadership', *International Journal* 52, 2: 183–96.

Bercuson, David, and Barry Cooper. 1999. ' "Soft Power" Won't Get Job Done', *Windsor Star*, 2 Feb., A9.

Canada, Government of. 1995. *Canada in the World*. Ottawa.

Canadian Centre for Foreign Policy Development. 1999. 'Report from the Roundtable on Canada, NATO and the United Nations: Lessons Learned From the Kosovo Crisis', 1 Oct.

Cooper, Andrew Fenton. 1997. *Canadian Foreign Policy: Old Habits and New Directions*. Scarborough, Ont.: Prentice-Hall.

Dalder, Ivo H. 1997. 'Fear and Loathing in the Former Yugoslavia', in Michael Brown, ed., *The International Dimensions of Internal Conflict*. Cambridge, Mass.: MIT Press.

Department of External Affairs and International Trade Canada (DEAITC). 1993a. 'Address by the Honourable Barbara McDougall to a Seminar on Canada's Agenda for International Peace and Security', 93/7, Ottawa, 8 Feb.

———. 1993b. 'Address by Barbara McDougall to the Americas Society: Co-operative Security in the 1990s—From Moscow to Sarajevo', 93/36, New York, 17 May.

Department of Foreign Affairs and International Trade (DFAIT). 1993. 'Address by André Ouellet to the Ministerial Meeting of the North Atlantic Council', 93/63, Brussels, 2 Dec.

———. 1994a. 'Address by André Ouellet at the Parliamentary Debate on Peacekeeping', 94/2, 25 Jan.

———. 1994b. 'Address by André Ouellet to the Parliamentary Debate on Canada's Foreign Policy Review', 94/11, Ottawa, 15 Mar.

———. 1994c. 'Address by the Honourable André Ouellet to the 49th General Assembly of the United Nations', 94/55, New York, 29 Sept.

———. 1995a. 'Address by André Ouellet to the Standing Committee on Foreign Affairs and International Trade', 95/16, Ottawa, 14 Mar.

———. 1995b. 'Address by André Ouellet to the NATO Council: The Situation in the Former Yugoslavia', 95/34, Noordwijk, Netherlands, 30 May.

———. 1996. Press Release, No. 233, 4 Dec.

———. 1998a. Press Release: 'Axworthy Condemns Latest Violence in Kosovo and Calls for United Nations Action', No. 185, 7 Aug.

———. 1998b. 'Address by Lloyd Axworthy to the 53rd Session of the United Nations General Assembly', 98/59, New York, 25 Sept.

———. 1998c. Press Release: 'Canada to Participate in NATO Military Enforcement Action in Kosovo', No. 242, 12 Oct.

———. 1998d. 'Address by Lloyd Axworthy to the Permanent Council of the Organization for Security and Co-operation in Europe', 98/70, Vienna, 22 Oct.

———. 1998e. Press Release: 'Axworthy Deeply Concerned Over the Federal Republic of Yugoslavia's Refusal to Cooperate with the International Criminal Tribunal for the Former Yugoslavia', No. 257, 5 Nov.

———. 1999a. 'Address by Lloyd Axworthy to the United Nations Security Council: The Protection of Civilians in Armed Conflict', New York, 12 Feb.

———. 1999b. Press Release: 'Canada Prepares for NATO Action in the Federal Republic of Yugoslavia', No. 62, 20 Mar.

———. 1999c. 'Speech by Lloyd Axworthy on the Conflict in Kosovo', 99/23, Ottawa, 24 Mar.

———. 1999d. 'Address by Lloyd Axworthy to the Woodrow Wilson School of Public and International Relations: Kosovo and the Human Security Agenda', 99/28, Princeton, NJ, 7 Apr.

———. 1999e. 'Address by Lloyd Axworthy to the G-8 Foreign Ministers' Meeting', 99/40, Cologne, 9 June.

———. 1999f. 'Crisis in Kosovo—Chronology of Events in Kosovo', prepared by the South European Division, July 1999: www.dfait-maeci.gc.ca/foreignp/kosovo/text/chrono-e.asp

———. 1999g. 'Canada and Kosovo': www.dfait-maeci.ca/foreignp/kosovo/text/back3-e.asp

Hampson, Fen Osler, and Dean F. Oliver. 1998. 'Pulpit Diplomacy: A Critical Assessment of the Axworthy Doctrine', *International Journal* 53, 3: 379–406.

Hay, Robin Jeffrey. 1999. 'Present at the Creation? Human Security and Canadian Foreign Policy in the Twenty-first Century', in Fen Osler Hampson, Martin Rudner, and Michael Hart, eds, *Canada Among Nations 1999: A Big League Player?* Toronto: Oxford University Press, 215–32.

Keating, Tom, and Nicholas Gammer. 1993. 'The "new look" in Canada's Foreign Policy', *International Journal* 48, 4 (Autumn): 720-48.

Koring, Paul. 1999. 'Will fight for just cause, Eggleton says', *Globe and Mail*, 2 Oct., A21.

NATO. 1998a. 'Statement on Kosovo', Press Release M-NAC-D-1(98)77, 11 June.

———. 1998b. 'Statement on Kosovo', Press Release M-NAC-2(98)143, 8 Dec.

———. 1999a. 'NATO and Kosovo: Historical Overview—NATO's Role in Relation to the Conflict in Kosovo': www.nato.int/kosovo/history.htm

———. 1999b. 'Statement', Press Release (99)003, 17 Jan.

———. 1999c. 'Statement to the Press', Press Release (99)11, 28 Jan.

———. 1999d. 'Statement by the North Atlantic Council on Kosovo', Press Release (99)12, 30 Jan.

———. 1999e. 'Statement by the North Atlantic Council on the Situation in Kosovo', Press Release (1999)038, 22 Mar.

———. 1999f. 'Press Statement', Press Release (1999)040, 23 Mar.

————. 1999g. 'Political and Military Objectives of NATO Action with Regard to the Crisis in Kosovo', Press Release (1999)043, 23 Mar.

————. 1999h. 'Statement: on the initiation of a broader range of Air Operations in the Federal Republic of Yugoslavia', Press Release (1999)044, 27 Mar.

————. 1999i. 'The Situation in and Around Kosovo', Press Release M-NAC-1(99)51, 12 Apr.

Nossal, Kim. 1998. 'Foreign Policy for Wimps', *Ottawa Citizen*, 23 Apr., A19.

Redekop, Clarence. 1985. 'Constructive Dis-engagement', *Behind the Headlines*, CIIA.

Solana, Javier, NATO Secretary-General. 1998a. 'Statement to the Press', Vilamoura, 24 Sept.

————. 1998b. 'Statement to the Press, following the ACTWARN Decision', Vilamoura, 24 Sept.

United Nations. 1999a. 'Kosovo: Security Council Resolutions': www.un.org/Depts/dhl/da/kosovo/koso_scl.htm

————. 1999b. 'Kosovo: Security Council President's Statements': www.un.org/Depts/dhl/da/kosovo/koso_sc2.htm

Weller, Marc. 1999. 'The Rambouillet Conference on Kosovo', *International Affairs* 75, 2 (Apr.): 211.

15

Canada at the UN: A Human Security Council?

PAUL KNOX

Imagine a large family, wealthy enough to populate its domestic landscape with servants (for they are required in the analogy that follows). The parents are certain they know what's best, and they are not ashamed to use their money, wills, and connections to enforce it. They hand out prizes and penalties in equal portions, managing somehow to be at once respectful and patronizing. The children chafe under their tutelage, baffled by a domestic regime that seems only loosely tied to reality. The servants, well paid and generally indulged, observe the daily proceedings with a mixture of affection and exasperation. But no matter what folly the family descends into, they remain committed to it.

Now imagine that no one in this family grows older. The parents remain middle-aged, the children juvenile, the help in a state of suspended subservience. As a result the power relationships among them are frozen, unlike those in a normal unit. They are condemned to a living Sartrian hell, except that their pain is greater, for they can see the rest of the world changing. Everyone else ages—grows up, if you will. The world becomes hotter, or colder. It is swept by new fashions and passions, racked by conflict, transformed by invention and discovery. The members of our family, largely oblivious to anything but their own oppressive personal circumstances, respond slowly and poorly. The parents know any change in the structure of power is likely to leave them with less of it. The children cannot look forward to a time when they will be free of this nightmare, able to face the world on their own terms. And all take out their frustrations on the servants.

This is one way of looking at the United Nations as it endures its fifty-fifth year. It is not the only way and the UN is not, as some would have it, a paralysed or useless organization. As a global bureaucracy, the UN, its subsidiary programs, and its affiliated agencies perform a vast range of bread-and-butter functions essential to human interaction. As an emergency-measures organization it is capable of heroic work. But as a family of nations it is fractious, frustrated, and dysfunctional. It cannot evolve as a natural organism or keep pace with rapid change. Moreover, it is undermined by continuing challenges to its legitimacy and attempts to circumscribe its activities.

Its defects are most evident at the Security Council, where Canada is currently serving a two-year term ending 31 December 2000. The Security Council is the UN's most powerful organ, and therefore the one most likely to be on view during serious global crises. It is charged under the Charter with preserving international peace and security, and is authorized to order the use of force to do so. Canada has successfully sought election to the Council six times—roughly every 10 years since 1946. This is consistent with its strong commitment to multilateralism, which leads it to seek the highest possible degree of involvement in the UN and its agencies.

Canada's current term is unlike those it has held in the past in several respects. It is the first since the breakup of the Soviet Union ended the era of superpower rivalry known as the Cold War. It is being served at a time of great uncertainty about the principles governing relations among the world's peoples and the role the UN should play in regulating them. Moreover, the current Canadian Foreign Affairs Minister, Lloyd Axworthy, has embarked on a crusade to make the protection of 'human security' a guiding principle in Canada's relationship to the rest of the world.

By the halfway point in its two-year term, Canada's representatives at the UN had made a significant impact on some issues, using both traditional and innovative types of diplomacy. The events of 1999, however, highlighted both the need to reform the Security Council's structure and function and the fact that such reform seems as remote as ever. When the United States and its allies, including Canada, decided to apply military force in support of threatened ethnic Albanians in the Serbian province of Kosovo, NATO and not the UN was the political and military mechanism that was used. However, Canada would have preferred that the NATO-led operation had the UN's blessing (see Chapter 14). Canada did succeed in pushing the UN towards more aggressive action against Angola's rebel movement. It was instrumental in winning a strong mandate for the UN's peace-keeping mission to Sierra Leone. But on several questions where its voice was heard loudly, it was as one of the global household's perpetual adolescents—railing against graceless authoritarian elders, a power structure that never changes and arbitrary rules that make no sense outside the family home. It remained clear that there were strict limits to the UN's usefulness as a mechanism for pursuing Canada's global interests.

HUMAN SECURITY AND THE COUNCIL CAMPAIGN

As election day at the UN General Assembly neared in the autumn of 1998, Mexican ambassador Manuel Tello offered a bleak assessment of the prospects for changing the Security Council's structure and function. 'Any country that thinks it will have leverage to take initiatives that will transform in any way the Security Council,' he said, 'in my opinion they are dreaming.' He wished Canada well, but noted Mexico's view that the advantages of temporary Council membership are outweighed by the disadvantage of being forced to take stands on issues irrelevant to its national interest. But at the Dutch mission to the UN, a political counsellor stated a more optimistic view: 'If you're really serious about wanting to contribute to international order, then the Security Council is the place to be' (Knox, 1998).

Lloyd Axworthy was certainly serious. His shift to the Foreign Affairs portfolio in 1996 followed several dramatic and well-publicized global-security disasters, including the failure of peace enforcement in Somalia (1992–3) and Bosnia (1992–5) and the genocidal massacre of an estimated 800,000 people in Rwanda in 1994. The Canadian Forces were stretched almost to the breaking point by a dramatic increase in the number of UN peace missions authorized. Yet it was evident that multilateral peacemaking as practised during the Cold War was inadequate in situations where large numbers of civilians were at imminent risk of slaughter. Meanwhile, non-traditional security threats such as terrorism, drug trafficking, infectious disease, and organized crime demanded a response. Increasingly, it seemed a gross cop-out to invoke the principle of non-interference in the affairs of sovereign nations as a justification for inaction in the face of such challenges.

Soon after taking over at Foreign Affairs in 1996, Axworthy began espousing the notion of human security, which his department defines as 'safety for people from both violent and non-violent threats' and 'an alternative way of seeing the world, taking people as its point of reference, rather than focusing exclusively on the security of territory or governments' (DFAIT, 1999: 5). To many, focusing foreign policy efforts on human well-being rather than relations among states appeared natural in an age of economic integration, the rapid expansion of electronic communications, and the development of international law. The human security approach also includes policy implementation by non-traditional means, such as working alliances with non-governmental organizations. In his previous post at Human Resources Development, Axworthy had been struck by the power of global networks of activists, in particular at the 1995 Copenhagen summit on social development (Knox and Sallot, 1999). At Foreign Affairs, he actively supported a government-activist alliance that led to the 1997 adoption of a global treaty to ban anti-personnel landmines.

The human security concept may be attractive to Canadians who have strong connections to the rest of the world through family or non-government activities. It is also likely to appeal to policy-makers seeking maximum impact at minimum cost, since it offers the prospect of 'security' without the level of military engagement usually implied by the term. And it seems to mesh well with the traditional concerns of the UN's 'soft' side—the development, environmental, and human rights work that accounts for most of the organization's spending and activity. Canada has sought to insert the term into UN proceedings, including through a group of countries known as the 'human security network'.[1]

But on the 'hard' side, where peacemaking and *realpolitik* intersect, the notion of human security meets resistance. While the expansion of global norms in such areas as human rights and the environment is the UN system's stock in trade, so is the principle of respect for non-interference in members' affairs. Moreover, the structure of the Security Council makes it an inherently cautious and conservative organ. The price of winning agreement on the formation of the UN in 1945 was the veto power given to the Council's five permanent members—the United States, Russia, China, France, and the United Kingdom, collectively known as the P-5. In theory the 10 elected members, who serve staggered two-year terms, represent the rest of the UN's 188 members, and in practice a formal veto is now cast only rarely. But its threat is often brandished, at times in the pursuit of the narrow national interest of one of the P-5. In addition, the Council at the beginning of 1999 was still suffering from the effects of the over-extension of the early 1990s. It was reluctant to approve new and potentially costly peace missions.

Canada and other middle powers pushed for years for reform of the Security Council's structure, without much success. Canada argued against increasing the number of permanent, veto-holding members, but said the Council could be expanded to include more elected, non-permanent members. It also called for the Council to open up its activities, especially to members directly affected by its decisions—not only the parties to conflicts but also those countries most likely to be major contributors to peace missions (Fowler, 1996). To avoid the grandstanding and paralysis that characterized its proceedings at the height of the Cold War, the Council developed the practice of conducting substantive discussions in informal closed-door sessions, holding open formal meetings only to take recorded votes after the issues had been thrashed out (Meisler, 1995: 249–50). Only occasionally would it hold open meetings on acute conflicts or broad global themes. The Council had also shown little desire to embrace a Canada-supported initiative that predated the human security approach but could be said to be consistent with it. This was the proposal for a rapid-reaction combat capability, later scaled down to a rapidly deployable headquarters unit, designed to enable the UN to respond more quickly to looming security threats.

Nevertheless, Canada pushed hard for the Council seat. It was rewarded on 9 October 1998, when the General Assembly rejected Greece and chose Canada and the Netherlands for the two seats accorded to the group of nations known as Western Europe and Others. It was the culmination of four years of work for Canadian ambassador Robert Fowler, who says his passion for the 'great *souk*', as he calls the UN, dates from the time he served there as a junior foreign service officer in the 1970s.

A YEAR IN THE LIFE

The task of serving as Security Council president rotates monthly by alphabetical order, and new members are inserted into the lineup on 1 January. As it happened, Canada's turn came up in February, so there was no easing into the term for the staff at Canada's permanent mission to the UN. Anticipating victory, Canada had been planning February's agenda for some time. On a mid-December trip to New York, Axworthy fleshed out the details with mission staff during a morning meeting. Festering civil wars in Angola, Sierra Leone, Sudan, and the Democratic Republic of the Congo figured in the discussions, and all proved to be recurring topics during the year. But Canadian planning centred on getting the UN to pay increased attention to a concept central to the human security agenda: the protection of civilians caught up in armed conflict. The centrepiece was to be an open meeting on the subject during Canada's presidency. Besides focusing attention on the subject matter, Canada hoped the session would demonstrate the value of open Council meetings that push members to state positions on topical questions.

Before assuming the presidency, Fowler was forced to turn his hand to more urgent matters. On 2 January, the second of two UN-chartered planes was shot down in Angola over territory held by the União Nacional para a Independencia Total de Angola (UNITA), the rebel movement led by Jonas Savimbi that is the target of broad UN sanctions. Twenty-three lives were lost; strong evidence later emerged that Savimbi's forces attacked the aircraft. It was the latest tragedy in an on-again, off-again war that dated from Angolan independence in 1975. Three UN missions and UN-sponsored elections had failed to produce a lasting peace, and on 17 January, UN Secretary-General Kofi Annan reported that the latest ceasefire had broken down and recommended terminating the latest UN mission. The Council agreed, but Fowler, who had taken over the chairmanship of its Angola sanctions committee, pledged to work to tighten the anti-UNITA embargo.

A second sanctions matter occupied much of the Council's time during January. This concerned Iraq, which was refusing to allow UN weapons inspectors to return after US and British air strikes the previous month. There was growing pressure, particularly from France and Russia, to ease sanctions on Iraq, but the United States and Britain refused to do so until UN inspectors certified it free of chemical, biological, and nuclear weapons and delivery systems. UNSCOM, the controversial inspection commission, had clearly outlived its usefulness; the problem was how to reconstitute it. At Canada's suggestion, three panels were set up to consider available evidence on weapons systems, Iraq's humanitarian needs, and issues arising from the 1991 Persian Gulf War. The panels reported in March, and in December the Security Council passed a resolution setting up a successor to UNSCOM. But it was hard to see this as a success. France, Russia, and China abstained in the formal vote, and by mid-April 2000, the new agency, UNMOVIC, had not been accepted by Iraq. Richard Butler, the Australian diplomat who headed UNSCOM for four years, noted acidly in September that the Council 'has been unable to reach a decision that would restore, even in a modified way, the implementation of its own law.' And he accused Canada of working to 'lower the standard of Iraqi compliance', possibly because at one point Canada suggested the Council formally recognize that total verification of disarmament was unattainable (Butler, 1999: 9–10; Efstathiou, 1999).

Canada began its month as Council president with Fowler sidelined by appendicitis and Michel Duval, the deputy permanent representative, in the chair. As expected, security brush fires in Africa occupied much of the Council's time. Several sessions dealt with the Angola debacle and an ongoing peace mission in the Central African Republic. On 10 February, the Council demanded that hostilities cease along the border between Ethiopia and Eritrea (UNDPI, 2000: 16). Canada also had an opportunity to move the UN closer towards intervention in Sierra Leone, where a vicious civil war was raging, the hallmark of which was the chopping off of civilians' hands and arms as an intimidation tactic by anti-government rebels. Canadian NGOs and individuals with a connection to the tiny West African nation lobbied Axworthy heavily to become involved, and Canada was able to schedule a briefing by UN officials late in the month.

On 12 February, Axworthy took his place in the president's chair for the open meeting on civilians in armed conflict. Behind him was the giant allegorical painting by Norway's Per Krogh, depicting the ascent of humanity from primitive labour and strife to a contented state of fruitful industry and contemplation. The world described by Axworthy had more in common with the dark tones and grim expressions in the lower half of the work:

> The victimization of civilians in war is as old as time, but never more so than in our century. . . . More than ever, non-combatants—especially the vulnerable—are the principal targets, the instruments and overwhelmingly, the victims of modern armed conflict. The number of casualties from armed conflict has almost doubled since the 1980s to about one million a year, and of those, 80 per cent are civilians. (Axworthy, 1999: 1)

The session's primary goal was to underscore the need to bring the UN's approach to peacekeeping, peacemaking, and peace enforcement in line with the post-Cold War evolution of conflict. Surprisingly, protecting civilians has not traditionally been a key part of the mandate of missions under UN peacekeeping command. They have been geared to policing formal ceasefires or keeping apart warring armed factions. Defusing threats to civilians or taking care of their needs was regarded either as unwarranted interference in the internal affairs of a member state, more properly the job of humanitarian agencies, or as a slippery slope leading to unending involvement. This, of course, produced well-publicized fiascos such as the failure of UN troops to prevent massacres of civilians in Bosnia and Rwanda.

As the Chinese and Russian representatives listened impassively, Axworthy listed four challenges: (1) preventing conflict in the first place; (2) ensuring respect for international humanitarian and human rights law; (3) pursuing war criminals and other gross violators of humanitarian law; and (4) targeting arms traffickers. He urged the Security Council to put civilian protection at the core of its international missions. 'This', he said, 'would enable the council to act rapidly when civilians are threatened, and to propose ways to give peacekeepers the authority, guidance and resources they need to defend civilians.' He suggested measures to limit the ability of mass media to incite hatred, and called for a fine-tuning of sanctions regimes to maximize the impact on warriors and minimize the harm to non-combatants (ibid., 3–4).

It will be several years before the full effect of this Canadian thrust is measurable. But the 12 February meeting did adopt a statement noting that large-scale suffering was not only a consequence of conflict, but could in itself constitute a threat to international peace and security. For the first time, the Council explicitly 'expressed its willingness to respond, in accordance with the Charter of the United Nations, to situations in which civilians, as such, have been targeted or humanitarian assistance to civilians has been deliberately obstructed.' It also instructed UN Secretary-General Kofi Annan to compile a report on protecting civilians in combat, and this was presented to the Council on 16 September (Annan, 1999). Its recommendations included (1) considering armed response in the face of massive abuses; (2) sending preventive missions to tense regions; (3) imposing arms embargoes; (4) making greater use of targeted sanctions; (5) underscoring the importance of unimpeded civilian access to humanitarian assistance; (6) monitoring conditions in refugee camps; and (7) authorizing UN missions to shut down so-called 'hate media' during fighting. Canada planned to take up the issue again in April 2000, when it was again due to hold the Council presidency.

February ended with a reminder of the extent to which a rogue uncle's self-interest can block collective action in the UN family. On 25 February, China vetoed the extension of UNPREDEP, the UN force deployed in Macedonia to help prevent the explosion there of the kind of ethnic conflict that rocked the other components of the former Yugoslavia during the 1990s. Chinese ambassador Qin Huasun argued that UNPREDEP had fulfilled its mission and was no longer needed, but that was not Annan's judgement, nor was it the desire of 13 out of 15 council members (Russia abstained). Most UN observers believed the veto was actually cast in retaliation against Macedonia's decision to establish diplomatic relations with Taiwan, which China considers a renegade province. The use of the veto was described as 'unfortunate and inappropriate' by Fowler. 'These accusations are totally groundless', Qin replied (UNDPI, 2000; Penketh, 1999).

A month later, Canada was forced to recognize that the UN was incapable of passing a much more serious test. There was strong evidence that the government of Yugoslavia under President Slobodan Milosevic had begun a campaign of intimidation and forced expulsion aimed at cleansing the province of Kosovo of its ethnic Albanian majority. Milosevic had signed the Dayton Accord that ended years of ethnic slaughter in Bosnia and Herzegovina, but in general he constituted a serious threat to stability in the Balkan region. NATO made plans for a bombing campaign designed to force Milosevic to halt the planned aggression. It was a perfect example of the kind of issue addressed by Axworthy's human security agenda. It was a conflict internal to a UN member state. Most of those targeted were civilians (although Milosevic argued that Yugoslavia had a right to combat attacks by the autonomist Kosovo Liberation Army). The ethnic Albanians appeared likely to pour out of Kosovo into Albania and Macedonia. Both of these countries, however, lacked the infrastructure to care for them and Macedonia, in particular, feared a large refugee population would constitute a threat to its own security and, by extension, to the region.

On the facts, then, Kosovo was a prime candidate for Security Council-mandated UN intervention along the lines favoured by Canada. There was not a hope of that happening. Russia, Milosevic's backer in the Balkan wars, was sure to veto any resolution supporting NATO action. China, following Canada in alphabetical order, was Council president, and among the P-5 it was always the least likely to favour intervention of any kind. 'We looked very carefully at whether it would be better to try to get Council approval', Fowler said later. 'We were virtually certain it would have been vetoed, and then we had the option of doing it anyway. Needless to say the veto powers didn't like that much, didn't like the option of doing it over vetoes' (Author interview, 1999). So for the first time since World War II, the Western alliance undertook military action without explicit Security Council approval. Canadian pilots participated in a three-month bombardment that eventually led Milosevic to abandon his campaign.

The irony of Canada seeing the UN sidelined in a crucial test of commitment to human security concerns, just three months after taking up a Security Council seat it had campaigned four years to get, was not lost on Fowler. Kosovo, he argued, was a useful reminder that the UN has always been least relevant when East-West issues—such as those over which the Cold War was conducted—are at stake. 'The fact that at the fault line between East and West the veto is still relevant and the Security Council is not relevant is absolutely unsurprising to me', he said. 'The only thing [that] is surprising is why we would think anything else.' The UN was eventually given a role in Kosovo—that of postwar reconstruction. It was an underfunded and thankless task, and one that many found poorly conceived since it involved setting up a government in a province that was still nominally part of a sovereign country (Garton Ash, 2000).

With bombs falling on Belgrade, the Security Council turned to other matters. As chair of the Angola sanctions committee, Fowler visited several southern African countries in May to gather facts about the civil war and the role played by diamond sales, arms trafficking, and money-laundering in the UNITA insurgency. All were supposedly targeted by a UN sanctions regime that had been in place for several years. Savimbi, backed by the United States and apartheid South Africa in the 1980s, had few friends among world leaders. But Kenya, the previous committee chair, had done little to raise awareness of the situation. Revenue from diamonds smuggled out of UNITA-held territory allowed Savimbi to purchase quantities of sophisticated weapons and fuel from international brokers, prolonging a conflict that had claimed an estimated one million lives and uprooted one-sixth of Angola's population of 12 million. It was clear that even targeted sanctions were of little use unless aggressively enforced.

Following to some extent the model adopted in January on Iraq, Fowler appointed a specialist panel to research and advise the Security Council. His contacts on the May trip included officials of the Anglo-South African conglomerate De Beers Consolidated, which controls about 70 per cent of the world diamond trade. In October, De Beers said it would no longer buy any diamonds believed to be of Angolan origin—an announcement counted as a victory by Fowler. In January 2000, following a second trip to Africa, Fowler appeared before the Council to show excerpts from videotaped interviews with UNITA defectors now serving in the Angolan army. They told of huge transport aircraft landing at UNITA-controlled airstrips with shipments of armoured vehicles, weapons, and fuel. They also stated that the order to shoot down aircraft over UNITA territory, including UN-chartered planes, came directly from Savimbi. Fowler promised more details with the release of the panel's report (Knox, 2000). The show was designed for maximum impact at the UN, whose personnel are increasingly subject to attack in the field. Meanwhile, the Angolan army scored important combat victories against UNITA, capturing the key towns of Andulo and Bailundo in October. It was not clear to what degree this was attributable to UN sanctions in general or to Fowler's aggressive publicizing in particular. The panel's report, released in March, took the unusual step of naming the sitting presidents of two countries (Burkina Faso and Togo) as Savimbi's collaborators. But the Security Council put off a decision on whether to take reprisals against them.

In the second half of the year, the UN faced new and quite different security challenges in East Timor and Sierra Leone. The first was partly of its own making. A UN-sponsored referendum on the Indonesian-occupied territory's future produced a clear vote in favour of independence. In response, pro-Indonesian militias acting in concert with government troops went on a rampage of burning, looting, and attacks on civilians, in which at least 200 were killed and an estimated half-million were driven from their homes. Many thought the UN should have foreseen the potential for trouble; had it done so it might have postponed the vote or refused to rely on Indonesia's agreement to provide security. In any case, the violence made it clear that a full military-civilian mission would be needed to supervise the transition to independence. Canada and others successfully argued that the force needed the authority to use whatever force was necessary under Chapter VII of the UN Charter. But the initial force was made up of troops from willing and interested countries and was funded by voluntary contributions. It was more than four months before a UN force, paid for out of peacekeeping assessment, took charge of East Timor.

Sierra Leone, like Kosovo, was a textbook case for advocates of human security. Its barely functioning state had an elected president, Ahmed Tejan Kabbah, but large sections of the country were under the control of Revolutionary United Front (RUF) rebels under Foday Sankoh, allied with Liberia in another battle over lucrative diamond fields. Non-combatants had suffered horrendous casualties, with an estimated 50,000 killed over an eight-year period. Both the RUF and a Nigerian-led regional intervention force were accused of committing atrocities. With UN help, a ceasefire was signed on 7 July. In October, the Security Council authorized one of the largest UN peace forces since World War II—a 6,000-member mission that was to work together with the Nigerian-led force and, most believed, eventually supplant it. Canada argued successfully that the mission needed not only a Chapter VII mandate to halt ceasefire violations and protect its own members, but also instructions 'to afford protection to civilians under imminent threat of physical violence'. The UN protection force in Bosnia was authorized only to 'deter' attacks on civilians (Knox, 1999b). There seems little doubt that the year-long focus on protection of civilians in combat made it easier to do this. But the issue was not simply one of the wording of the mandate. As part of the ceasefire agreement, Sankoh and other rebel leaders were welcomed into the cabinet, despite being in command of forces that committed unspeakable acts. Four months after the force was authorized, UN troops were encountering serious difficulty in disarming rebel forces (Lynch, 2000).

Pressure by Canada and other members for the Security Council to shine a spotlight on its activities translated into a marked increase in the number of open meetings. The pace accelerated throughout the year. In January 2000, newly arrived US ambassador Richard Holbrooke raised eyebrows on both sides of the Atlantic by declaring a 'month of Africa' and scheduling no less than five open Council meetings. Their topics ranged from the devastating effects of AIDS to strife in the Democratic Republic of the Congo. But the public displays failed to hide continuing problems with the Council's structure and procedure. Annan continued a long-standing practice of meeting privately with the P-5 to sound them out on key issues. The reasoning behind this was that it made little sense for the UN's top bureaucrat to embark on policy initiatives that were certain to be vetoed. But Fowler argued that Annan's methods slighted the 183 other UN member states and their representatives on the Council— the 10 non-permanent members.

Allowing his frustration to boil over, Fowler publicly criticized Annan over meetings on Iraq and Sierra Leone and a session on East Timor that preceded the visit to the UN of Indonesian Foreign Minister Ali Alatas. 'I've said to the secretary-general', Fowler said, 'that who he decides to have over for cognac after dinner is none of my business, but summoning the five to his boardroom to ask "What will I say to Ali Alatas this afternoon about a peacekeeping operation in East Timor?", when the 10 people who were elected to take those decisions are excluded, and only five people who have never been elected are included, it strikes me that something is wrong with the machinery' (Trickey, 1999). Axworthy declined to repeat the criticism of Annan, but made it clear he thought Canada had had little success in prying open the doors of the Security Council: 'We wanted to make it more transparent, more democratic, more open, and I think the trends have been going the other way' (Knox, 1999a).

Fowler was also one of the most vocal critics at the UN of the United States' failure to pay its dues on time, in full, and without conditions. Like others, he made much of the paradox of the world's richest nation being the UN's biggest and tardiest debtor. But there was a practical side to Canada's outrage over US arrears, which amounted to well over US$1 billion. Most of the money owed was for peacekeeping assessments. As a major troop contributor, Canada was among those countries owed millions of dollars for past service. Underlying Canadian frustration with this situation was the debate at home over the optimum size, strength, and budget of the Canadian Forces. Canada pledged troops to the multinational forces in Kosovo and East Timor, but when a Canadian Hercules C-130 transport had to turn back twice on its way to the region because of mechanical difficulties, doubts about whether Canada could follow through on its UN commitments were renewed (Sallot, 1999).

In any case, the Canadian outbursts had little effect. Throughout the autumn the P-5 held private meetings on the Iraq weapons inspection impasse. Other Security Council members relied on infrequent briefings from Britain to keep abreast of the sessions. Moreover, it became clear that whatever inroads the Council might make on the sovereignty and internal affairs of relatively small and weak nations, the P-5 were untouchable in this regard. Russia blocked any Security Council discussion of its bloody campaign to crush the breakaway movement in the state of Chechnya. (So much for the 200,000 civilians threatened by armed conflict there.) In doing so it had harsh words for Canada, which had been trying to get the issue on the Council's agenda (Knox, 1999c). Meanwhile, the ongoing debate on the Council's structure in a working group of the General Assembly was getting nowhere. 'We are, in fact, not much farther along on these questions than when we initiated our discussions six years ago', Fowler told the assembly in December. 'Are we, perhaps, trying to fit a square peg in a round hole?' (Fowler, 1999: 2).

CONCLUSION

The United Nations is neither a world government nor a global policeman, nor is it a cure-all for international ills. It is a structured forum for conducting business among the world's leaders, who increasingly are the formally elected representatives of its peoples. It is a huge mutual aid society that enables massive amounts of relief to be delivered to victims of natural disaster and economic upheaval. It is a global civics operation, codifying rights and obligations accepted by the bulk of humanity. And it is a last resort for relieving war-induced suffering that no individual country or bloc has a compelling reason to address. These functions are essential to any civilized country's national interest, and so is a strong and effective presence at the UN.

Canada, in particular, has a vital interest in orderly international affairs, as a supplier of raw materials, manufactured goods, and intellectual resources to a rapidly changing world. Canadians are moved also by the plight of threatened and downtrodden people, and many have specific ties with countries or regions that lead them to demand action to resolve specific security crises. For all these reasons the Chrétien government wishes to be an important player in areas where the UN can make a difference. Specifically, Canada and other 'friends of human security' are gambling that enough UN members in enough crisis situations will see no alternative to UN mandates that claim a role in internal policing and institution-building in countries where human security is threatened. In this way, they hope to build a series of precedents that will be difficult to overturn.

It is important, however, to have realistic expectations. For the foreseeable future, the scope for UN action in problems of global security will remain limited, chiefly because of the growing distance between its organizing principles as laid out in the Charter and the realities of geopolitics. The Security Council—the ossified nuclear unit of the UN's extended family—does not accurately reflect the distribution of population, wealth, contributions to the UN, or ability to project military force in today's world. As long as this remains true, not only will it lack credibility in many of the most acute security crises, but key members and coalitions will have structural incentives to paralyse or undermine it. It seems absurd to think that in 50 years—when China, India, Pakistan, Nigeria, and Indonesia are projected to account for more than four billion people—the Security Council will still look the same. But there seems little prospect of real reform before Canada makes its next bid for a seat. The events of 1999 amply demonstrated the difficulties, and the aptness of Fowler's East-West fault-line metaphor. The Council was sidelined during the NATO-Yugoslavia conflict, the biggest security crisis of the year. It was barred from considering the Russian campaign in Chechnya. It was humiliated by China's veto on Macedonia, and a year of wrangling could not solve the Iraq weapons inspection impasse.

Nevertheless, there were several positive steps. It is not clear whether open Security Council meetings will lead to stronger decisions, but they offer some hope of demystifying the arcana of UN procedure and exposing to public view those who advocate inaction in the face of massive injustice. Fowler's drive to expose Angola sanctions-busters may come too late to affect the outcome of the war, but it may save some lives and will certainly constitute a benchmark against which future sanctions enforcement can be measured. In the same way, while Sierra Leone may not be the ideal place to put a civilian-protection mandate to the test, it will be difficult henceforth to argue that the UN should send peacekeeping troops into an ugly conflict zone with orders to stand by as innocent non-combatants are massacred. Amazingly, that is a breakthrough.

Whether Canada's experience at the UN vindicates the human security approach to foreign policy is another matter. As it stands, the concept of human security appears to assert a right to intervene selectively in selected crises, championing some causes while refusing to support others, on unilaterally defined criteria. In theory at least, it slights the right of states—including those with electoral mandates—to act autonomously to deal with internal conflicts among their peoples. Some commentators are now arguing for a return to the concept of 'protectorates' or 'mandates' in the case of so-called failed states, with all the overtones of neo-imperialism the terms imply (Rieff, 1999). This is really the logical consequence of the imposition of the human security agenda by force, as Kosovo demonstrated that Canada was prepared to do.

This could easily spark a backlash at the UN, turning it back into the largely irrelevant forum it was during the Cold War. Depending on how aggressively the agenda is pursued, it could also have serious consequences for bilateral relations between Canada and other countries. The UN Charter begins with the words 'We, the peoples . . .' But the members, the ones that vote, are still nations, represented by governments. The United Nations is not—not yet, anyway—the United Peoples, much less the United Individuals, or the United Humans with Rights. In 1999, for all the talk of centring foreign policy on people, strategic calculation and classic principles of geopolitics still underpinned the conduct of international affairs, rather as boring old MS-DOS lurks underneath Microsoft's flashier and allegedly revolutionary Windows computer operating system.

Canada's participation in the UN has been dynamic. The desire in Ottawa to help design a world in which conflicts are solved by lawyers and peacemakers instead of warriors is genuine. But by joining in the bombing of Yugoslavia, Canada showed that when the chips are down it remains prepared to resort to the quite traditional application of force in justification of its human security goals—at least as long as they are shared by its allies. Seeing this, its NATO partners expect a clear commitment to military preparedness. Yet Ottawa's assessment of the implications of the human security doctrine for the Canadian Forces is unclear. The theory suggests a renewed emphasis on humanitarian intervention and peace enforcement. In practice, as applied in Yugoslavia, it points to combat readiness.

As for the world's weaker nations, they may be happy that Canada is working to revitalize UN efforts to relieve suffering and channel effective aid to beleaguered peoples. But they may be forgiven if they recall the bombing of Belgrade and pray that the needle of human security's moral compass never points at them.

NOTE

1. As of February 2000, the group included Canada, Austria, Chile, Greece, Ireland, Mali, the Netherlands, Norway, Slovenia, Switzerland, and Thailand, with South Africa as an observer.

REFERENCES

Annan, Kofi A. 1999. *Protecting Civilians in Armed Conflict: Towards a Climate of Compliance.* S/1999/957. New York: United Nations Office for the Co-ordination of Humanitarian Affairs.

Author interview. 1999. Telephone interview with Robert Fowler, 21 Dec.

Axworthy, Lloyd. 1999. 'Address by Lloyd Axworthy to the United Nations Security Council: The Protection of Civilians in Armed Conflict', New York: Permanent Mission of Canada to the United Nations, 12 Feb.

Butler, Richard. 1999. 'Bewitched, Bothered, and Bewildered: Repairing the Security Council', *Foreign Affairs* 78, 5 (Sept.-Oct.): 9–12.

Department of Foreign Affairs and International Trade (DFAIT). 1999. *Human Security: Safety for People in a Changing World.* Ottawa, Apr.

Efstathiou, Jim. 1999. 'Diplomacy fails to mend UN council divide on Iraq', *Dow Jones International News*, 7 May. Available on-line through Dow Jones Interactive.

Fowler, Robert. 1996. 'Statement . . . before the 51st session of the General Assembly', New York: Permanent Mission of Canada to the United Nations, 30 Oct.

———. 1999. 'Statement . . . to the 54th session of the United Nations General Assembly', New York: Permanent Mission of Canada to the United Nations, 16 Dec.

Garton Ash, Timothy. 2000. 'Losing the peace in Kosovo', *Globe and Mail*, 8 Feb., A17.

Knox, Paul. 1998. 'Canada's quest for UN's top prize', *Globe and Mail*, 25 Sept., A1.

———. 1999a. 'Canada tempers its criticism of UN', *Globe and Mail*, 1 Oct., A7.

———. 1999b. 'UN heeds Canada's appeal, boosts peacekeepers' powers', *Globe and Mail*, 23 Oct., A14.

———. 1999c. 'Chechnya focus of Turkish summit', *Globe and Mail*, 18 Nov., A11.

———. 2000. 'Rebels explain mystery of downed UN planes', *Globe and Mail*, 19 Jan., A13.

——— and Jeff Sallot. 1999. 'Axworthy's maxim: "All politics are local"', *Globe and Mail*, 1 Jan., A1.

Lynch, Colum. 2000. 'UN troops disarmed in Sierra Leone; U.S. worried about peace-keeping ability', *Washington Post*, 7 Feb., A1.

Meisler, Stanley. 1995. *United Nations: The First Fifty Years*. New York: Atlantic Monthly Press.

Penketh, Anne. 1999. 'China vetoes continued UN force in Macedonia over Taiwan links', *Agence France-Presse*, 25 Feb. Available on-line through Dow Jones Interactive.

Rieff, David. 1999. 'A New Age of Liberal Imperialism?', *World Policy Journal* 16, 2, (Summer): 1–10.

Sallot, Jeff. 1999. 'Hercules is a workhorse for the skies', *Globe and Mail*, 11 Oct., A6.

Trickey, Mike. 1999. 'Canada excluded by two-tier UN, Fowler charges', *National Post*, 29 Sept., A1.

United Nations Department of Public Information (UNDPI). 2000. Press Release: Security Council 1999 Round-up, SC/6784, 18 Jan.

16

The WTO in the Aftermyth of the Battles in Seattle

JOHN M. CURTIS AND ROBERT WOLFE

If a forest falls, would the WTO hear?

—Greenpeace fortune cookie, Seattle, December 1999

Participants in the world trading system stumbled onto the Seattle battlefield. Everybody knew that official preparations for the launch of a new round of multilateral trade negotiations at the third ministerial meeting of the World Trade Organization (WTO) in December 1999 had gone badly. The United States and the European Union (EU), the two giants of the trading system, differed both on the comprehensiveness of the agenda as well as on specific issues—including the classic issue of agriculture. Developing countries made no secret of their unhappiness with their role in the trading system and the lack of the promised benefits from the Uruguay Round. The American hosts by turns tried to manipulate the agenda to their own advantage and genially hoped for the best, while allowing logistical difficulties to multiply. Traditional interest groups favouring more open markets, such as North American grain farmers and multinational service industries, did little to support the WTO process. All the while, the unofficial preparations were superb. Non-governmental or 'civil society' organizations concerned about the further extension of what they saw as global governance in the exclusive interests of big business used the Internet to prepare massive protests during the meeting. The phrase 'battle in Seattle', an insider's joke for months beforehand, was seized by the world's press to describe the spectacular confrontation between the small number of violent anti-globalization forces and the riot police. The phrase applies equally well to the shambles inside the meeting room.

If borders appear to be vanishing, as suggested by the title of this volume, multilateral institutions of global governance are more vital. Yet, paradoxically, they are more feared. The drama in the streets of Seattle aroused an unprecedented degree of public interest in an international economic event, yet the real work of the WTO remains as obscure as it was before. We agree with the lead in *The Economist* after the meeting: the losers in Seattle were the world's poor (*The Economist*, 1999).[1] The broken windows and tear gas were easily cleared from the Seattle battlefield; repairing the damage to the trading system will take longer. It will also require a renewed attempt to balance the needs for development, civil society engagement, and systemic governance while maintaining and expanding an open rules-based trading system. It will require attention to old issues and learning about the new problems of policy adaptation to a rapidly evolving world economy.

The effort to avoid stumbling onto another battlefield while repairing the damage begins with a diagnosis of what went wrong. Accounts of what it all means are already assuming the character of myth, the stories we tell each other about who we are. In the aftermyth[2] of the battles wild claims as well as sobering analyses are being made about the meaning of Seattle, the changed nature of global governance, and the supposedly tarnished role of the WTO. We use the plural because we argue in this chapter that five battles took place in Seattle; in our discussion of each one we try to show that all contributed to the outcome:

1. The most transitory, yet consequential battle, that between the contending forces of US domestic politics, was expressed in comments by President Clinton made with an eye on the November 2000 elections.
2. The most intractable battle of all, one between small and large members of the WTO, or insiders and outsiders, was an institutional fight within the meeting itself.
3. The new and painfully visible dispute with civil society groups, who often deny or cast doubt on the legitimacy of the enterprise, took place in the streets.
4. The equally venerable North-South dispute, present since the 1950s but exacerbated in an organization with 136 members,[3] focused on implementation of existing agreements.
5. Finally, as in the Kennedy, Tokyo, and Uruguay Rounds, the traditional transatlantic dispute over the role of the market was expressed as a fight about agriculture.

Whether or not borders are vanishing or should vanish is an element in all these fights, but inconsistently so. The last three fights were based on differing views of the trading system, exacerbated by the second, the organization's continuing institutional weakness, and the first, which illustrated a growing US problem in providing multilateral leadership. We think that the widespread perception that borders might be vanishing is the wrong way to think about the WTO and about Canadian strategy. We argue that the authority of the Canadian state has not been and should not be transferred to the WTO, or to the US Congress, the most likely options if borders actually did vanish. Other authors in this volume ask if the Canada-US border is less significant; we ask about the implications of such a development for Canadian multilateral relations. The fact that the WTO ministerial was in Seattle should serve as a reminder not only that the United States is the largest WTO member, but also that the WTO is that country's most important trade agreement. Many people who were present claim that the Americans did not advocate a systemic interest in Seattle. As with the ballistic missile defence issue discussed by Jockel in this volume, if Americans think in narrow domestic or regional terms, should we as Canadians throw our lot with them or pursue our interests multilaterally? Those Canadian protesters in Seattle who wanted to stop the WTO, it follows, were asking the wrong question. The WTO did not start globalization, nor would its demise end the process. The right question is whether the WTO helps to mediate the effects of globalization, not least for a relatively small, open country living next to the world's dominant economy.

THE CONTEXT

Members of the WTO had planned at least since the successful Singapore ministerial meeting in December 1996 that their third ministerial meeting in 1999 would launch a new round of multilateral negotiations. This expectation had many dimensions. It arose largely in the institutional dynamic of the WTO, notably the decision at the end of the Uruguay Round that new negotiations in both agriculture and services were mandated to start in January 2000; the expectation was fed also—insufficiently as it turned out—by economic change and the politics of globalization. As events unfolded, these influences did not operate in the same way or in the same time frame.

The WTO is a process, not a destination. The Uruguay Round (1986–94), a major achievement in postwar international economic relations that concluded with the creation of the WTO, was not the end of history for the trading system. It left many things to one side, among them, importantly, the items now included on the so-called built-in agenda. Tensions are emerging both because of flaws in the structure and because of the rapid pace of global change. The WTO Agreement is not a 'negative list' that covers everything not explicitly excluded. It is instead a 'positive list', since it applies only to those tradeable items covered by the rules and mentioned explicitly in the 'schedules' of market access commitments submitted by members. The WTO must keep adding to this positive list as the world economy changes and expands. Things not on this list, such as the rapidly evolving domain of electronic commerce, are effectively outside the system. Two separate things go on in the WTO: first, contractually agreed trade liberalization, seen as important and good in its own right; and second, policy reconciliation. The need for the second is sometimes occasioned by the first, but it is more often needed because of change in the global marketplace, not policy change. The WTO adds new issues to its negotiating agenda as quickly as they are observed, both to avoid conflict and to ensure that obstructions to trade do not become obstructions to growth for individual countries and for the world economy.

In retrospect, it may have been a mistake to engage in this effort in the absence of consensus on what a new round might contain and when mistrust of globalization and its agents is high, never mind the fact that the results of the Uruguay Round had not been fully implemented. Many people could see only a bureaucratic agenda devoid of deeper substance. A sense of urgency since preparations began in early 1997 came from the need to avoid a protectionist response to the financial crisis in Asia, rising transatlantic trade conflict (e.g., over beef hormones and bananas), declining growth in world trade, in part due to the Asian crisis, and falling commodity prices. The urgency also came from the inherent logic of the WTO as a 'single undertaking'. Further negotiations on many issues were mandated by the Final Act of the Uruguay Round, but the only way to avoid acrimony and to make real progress on this built-in agenda was to bundle all the issues into a comprehensive or broad-based round.

Members naturally want shorter rounds, especially political leaders and those business interests whose background support for ongoing liberalization is essential. After Seattle, many now clearly want a less cumbersome process, but anything less than a full round will be difficult because of the 'single undertaking'. At the end of the Uruguay Round, all of the agreements, including all of the revised agreements from the Tokyo Round, were included in the WTO Agreement, which countries could accept or reject only in its entirety. This principle may make easy issues take longer, but it may also force an earlier resolution to tough issues, and it avoids the fragmentation of the trading system observed after the Tokyo Round. The single undertaking only works as a forcing mechanism, however, because of the implicit corollary: nothing is agreed until everybody agrees. That is why understanding all the battles in Seattle is so important.

AMERICAN BATTLE

The first of the battles in Seattle should be understood as the traditional US domestic struggle about its role in the world, or the battle in Washington. The actors in this fight include environmentalists and other representatives of civil society who have been growing increasingly worried about trade liberalization and globalization for most of this decade. Another actor is the union movement, whose help is essential to Vice-President Al Gore's campaign for the Democratic presidential nomination. When leaders are preoccupied by domestic politics, special interests like the steel industry are adept at making their voices heard. The US formulated both specific demands and areas 'off limits' for discussion in the WTO, but appeared to have no overall strategy. The consequences of this US ambiguity and in some cases disarray were obvious in the streets of Seattle, and are most salient within US domestic politics rather than in the WTO, but the consequences were also obvious inside the hall, where they were more serious. President Clinton's visit to Seattle was a campaign stop that in itself disrupted the meeting. His speech to the ministerial, a domestically oriented effort, was a source of conflict exacerbated by his subsequent ill-judged remarks to reporters about using trade sanctions to enforce labour rights. While that idea appeals to American unionists, it enrages politicians from developing countries, who take a different view of the social implications of global trade. Foreign leaders may not vote in US elections, but union leaders do not vote in the WTO. The inability of Washington to define general objectives for the meeting, part of a general sense of drift with respect to multilateral economic co-operation, resulted in weak leadership from the American hosts.

The battle in Washington (co-ordination within the G-1, some call it)[4] is always a vital factor in multilateral politics, but it also affects consideration of how Canada should focus its trade efforts bilaterally, regionally, or in the WTO. Do we try to create vehicles for collective leadership, accept that multilateralism will go slowly for now while finding other ways to work with more distant trading partners, or pursue our economic interests directly with the US? Overall, Canada is doing very well in the US market, but the current American temptation to retreat within a territorially defined perimeter (e.g., on terrorism, immigration, and the social consequences of trade) could pose difficulties. Worse, if Congress perceives the WTO to be fatally damaged (even if by US-inflicted wounds) the political effort needed to complete the WTO accession of China might not be sustainable. Canada needs the US market, but it is hard to believe that many of our businesses have as much potential for rapid growth there as in the recent past, which means that like the Americans themselves, we need to consider how best to expand our trade with developing and transition countries, the most likely source of significant growth for the world and North American economies. If we are not to let the Americans negotiate with the world on our behalf, we have to ensure a vibrant WTO.

THE BATTLE INSIDE THE WTO

The conclusion of the WTO ministerial without a declaration launching a new round of multilateral trade negotiations cannot be described as a success, but it was neither a catastrophe for the WTO nor a triumph for its civil society opponents. It was not a 'debacle in Seattle'. Ministers and other delegates attacked neither globalization nor the legitimacy of the WTO, but the tensions between insiders and those members who feel themselves to be outsiders were serious.

One reason that Seattle was not a debacle is that these setbacks in the trade negotiations arena are common, notably during the Uruguay Round. The early steps towards new negotiations were taken at the General Agreement on Tariffs and Trade (GATT) ministerial of 1982, but that meeting ended in failure. The Uruguay Round was finally launched in 1986 after four years of trying, but only with an eleventh-hour fudge in Punta del Este on agriculture and a compromise with Brazil and India under which discussion of trade in services was split from the main negotiations. The Montreal ministerial review meeting in 1988 collapsed, as did the Brussels ministerial of 1990, both because of farming. Trade negotiations are always complex, fractious, and time-consuming. Everyone hoped that the creation of a new institutional structure in the WTO would make the process easier. Clearly, that task also remains incomplete.

Weak leadership from the US hosts, from the Quad (EU, US, Japan, Canada), and from the secretariat contributed to a sense that after a zombie-like preparatory process, members came to Seattle prepared for failure. The reasons for the failure were substantive as much as external and conjunctural. The WTO's problems before and during the Seattle ministerial were in part due to inadequate collective leadership—reflected, for example, in a poor draft declaration forwarded by Geneva ambassadors for ministerial consideration in Seattle—and insufficient transparency.[5] Some participants also attributed some of the difficulties in Seattle to the inexperience of the senior leadership of the WTO and lingering resentments from the rancorous process by which the new Director General was selected. It was obvious that Mike Moore and his weak deputies, who had been appointed on a regional basis, had difficulties managing the process, but many countries, perhaps including the host, were not well prepared. The WTO is the site—not the source—of co-operation among its members, and the Director General is their servant, not their leader. In the absence of leadership the WTO responded, as did the GATT, with a series of small ad hoc informal meetings, largely involving the most influential members. The many countries excluded from such meetings complained that they did not know what was going on, and resented being presented with deals they did not even see being negotiated. This lack of transparency was more acute for the public. When the important tables are invisible, demonstrators in the street can be excused for claiming that the WTO is nothing but a bunch of faceless, unaccountable bureaucrats.

Demonstrators in the streets of Seattle and representatives of developing countries inside the meeting hall had at least one thing in common—they wanted a seat at The Table. International organizations have plenty of tables, but it is a mistake to assume that the WTO has one real Table where everything is decided; 136 countries cannot effectively debate contentious issues. The WTO provides the forum for negotiations among its members concerning their multilateral trade relations and the institutional framework for the implementation of the results of such negotiations. It is, in other words, a permanent conversation among the members that takes place in a bewildering variety of formal and informal settings. The WTO governing body, holder of all decision-making authority, is the *ministerial conference*, composed of representatives of all members. Its biennial meetings were meant to give the WTO the kind of regular political guidance that the GATT lacked. The first two ministerial conferences, in Singapore (1996) and Geneva (1998), did force the pace of WTO work, but it is now obvious that the ministerial conference cannot provide leadership and co-ordination to the vast and diffuse WTO process. Rather than ending the WTO practice of holding biennial ministerials, these weaknesses might be better addressed with more public political engagement through the creation of a WTO consultative committee, much like the old Interim Committee of the International Monetary Fund (IMF), an old idea whose time has surely come again (Wolfe, 1996; Wolfe and Curtis, 1998).

If such a committee of ministers had been created when the WTO began, many of the logistical and structural difficulties of the past year might have been avoided. It would not be the one real Table replacing the ever shifting mass of tables where the WTO conversation takes place, but: (1) it is likely that the new Director General would have been chosen from the members of the commitee, allowing a faster and less acrimonious process; (2) ministers charged with the co-ordination of the trading system would have been engaged long before Seattle in the process of shaping a draft declaration for a new round; (3) a public 'table' could have been created in Seattle where all countries and the public could see decisions being taken—everyone would have known who was in the room; smaller countries would have known who to approach for information; and (4) most important, an experienced group of ministers might have been available in Seattle for exercising the collective leadership needed to bring a fractious process to any sort of conclusion.

Institutional structures cannot replace politics. Small groups of powerful ministers will meet to discuss important issues in private, whether or not a WTO consultative committee exists. But creation of a focal point for co-ordination and consensus-building cannot fail to improve the functioning of the WTO, and should help to create a more comprehensible public face for the organization.

FROM TEAMSTERS TO TURTLES: THE BATTLE IN THE STREETS

The mass theatre piece called 'The Battle in Seattle' dominated the world's TV screens for several days because the WTO has become a handy lightning rod for globaphobia, in part because many people think it is infected with globaphilia, the love of globalization. The real story is that the WTO exists to manage conflict between states and to promote prosperity; both goals require rules that balance legitimate policy and open markets. Both goals also require democratic participation, but that is easier to say than do. Images of people dressed as turtles made for colourful TV, and thousands of organized unionists helped provide bulk for the demonstrations, but civil society had little direct impact on the meetings, other than to make life difficult for delegates, thereby reducing the time available for discussion. The indirect effect of the protests on the climate of opinion and thereby on the positions adopted by ministers is harder to assess.

In the more heated claims made after Seattle, civil society groups thought the earth had moved, that the WTO would never be the same again. We are dubious: the protests were disruptive but in no sense creative. The problems the WTO is meant to address have not been transformed by the protests. The claim that democratically elected governments do not represent the will of their citizens seems foolish to us. Even if it were true, by the same logic the claim to representation by civil society groups would be incomparably weaker because they are even less demonstrably representative. But that does not mean that democracy is necessarily served when government officials talk only to each other. Democratic values of participation and debate are also important, and they depend on transparency and engagement with non-state actors.

The involvement of non-governmental organizations (NGOs) in the trade policy process, in Canada and increasingly internationally, is one of the most significant developments in trade policy in the last decade. While it has clearly become a central element of, and contributed to, the unprecedented degree of consultation, transparency, and openness that now obtains, whether the protestors in the streets of Seattle would agree or not, the nature and scope of such involvement are also highly sensitive because the process of domestic policy formulation, including trade policy, differs widely from country to country; no one set of institutional arrangements can be said to be right or appropriate for all.

The factors affecting increasing public involvement can be described by a number of stylized facts. First, while the NGOs in Seattle were superbly organized to disrupt the process, they were not well placed to advance an alternative. The WTO is an inter-state instrument of governance; the negotiators of trade agreements remain state officials. At the same time, the policy process has been opened up to a wider range of so-called stakeholders in many countries. Business representatives have been consulted by governments on trade policy matters regularly or on an ad hoc basis since the 1950s. Over time, other voices increasingly demanded to be heard: neither NGOs nor the media were content to leave trade policy exclusively in the hands of politicians and their expert advisers in the bureaucracy. By the 1990s, the consultation process had come to include large firms, small and medium-size enterprises, trade associations, social advocacy groups, labour unions, consumer groups, and environmental activists. The changing trade policy agenda—what might be called the 'in-reach' or the 'border-in' character of today's trade policy—has created and will continue to create strains both within and among trading partners by engendering tension over domestic norms and the social institutions or regulatory policies that embody them. In consequence, public discussion is increasingly directed to addressing issues of fairness and justice. What many see as the success of more open markets and better international trade rules, others in our societies see as an irreversible march down a road they do not understand and over which they have little control. And technology has transformed the debate. While governments have never had a monopoly on information, they did have great advantages. Now the Internet facilitates the sharing of both substantive analysis and tactical information among like-minded non-governmental groups all over the world.

In the aftermyth of Seattle, the implications of these stylized facts for the future are not clear. Canada's preparations for the new round involved an unprecedented degree of public engagement. In addition to meeting frequently with provincial governments and issuing a call for public and industry comments, the Minister for International Trade asked the House of Commons Standing Committee on Foreign Affairs and International Trade for advice on the proposed negotiations. In June 1999, the Committee released a 300-page report in response. *Canada and the Future of the World Trade Organization: Advancing a Millennium Agenda in the Public Interest* (House of Commons Standing Committee, 1999) contains 45 detailed recommendations about active Canadian participation in the next negotiating round based on the largest public consultations the Committee has ever held on trade. Traditional interests and industry associations, especially in agriculture, were well represented in the Committee's hearings across Canada, as were academics. What was new was the high representation from 85 'civil society organizations' and 64 individuals.

The WTO itself made extraordinary amounts of information available on its Web site and held special symposia with NGOs. The ministerial was preceded by a symposium open to 'accredited' non-governmental organizations. The list included 672 organizations, from Acción Ecológica based in Ecuador through Greenpeace to the Zimbabwe Women's Resource Centre and Network. Half the groups were American, and close to 10 per cent were Canadian. The list seems surprising in light of the loud claims about how opening the WTO to NGOs will make it a more democratic institution. Aside from the over-representation of North Americans, a point acerbically noted by politicians from developing countries, the list of accredited groups based in Canada was dominated by traditional business associations, such as the Business Council on National Issues, and agricultural lobbies, for example, the Canadian Cattlemen's Association. Only a handful, such as the Canadian Environmental Law Association, were what some call citizen advocacy groups.

NGOs are now included, and the process is more open, yet still there was battle in the streets of Seattle. Many of the accredited groups accepted the legitimacy of the WTO, working only to modify it to suit their purposes. Many participants in the street battle, in contrast, opposed the existence of the organization and of any international economic arrangements or organizations. On the one hand, many civil society organizations think they achieved a greater triumph even than their supposed (but disputed) role in the failure of the Multilateral Agreement on Investment (MAI) negotiations, which took place under the auspices of the Organization for Economic Co-operation and Development (OECD) between 1995 and 1998. But correlation is not causation: NGOs may be disappointed when they discover that a round has been delayed for reasons that had little to do with them.

On the other hand, the general public seems to believe that the protesters were right. Despite valiant efforts to tell the trade story and poll results that suggest strong public support for trade negotiations, most people paid no attention until the riots, and then were disinclined to believe governments. It is surely right to say that Seattle was in part the Woodstock of the 1990s, but to leave it there would trivialize an important political event. The challenge is to determine the political significance of Seattle rather than accept the claims of participants at face value. We find the Seattle protests very worrying, but not for reasons the activists would set out. We think that the source of the protest had little to do with what actually happens at the WTO (except in the case of protectionist trade unionists) and a lot to do with a growing perception within the Atlantic area at least that all our large organizations cannot be trusted, especially governments, and that consequential decisions affecting our lives are taken by people for whom we did not vote. It is vital that citizens be able to see and understand what their governments are doing in the WTO, but nothing the WTO can do will restore citizens' trust of their own governments. That process must begin at home.

NORTH-SOUTH MISUNDERSTANDINGS

The fourth battle in Seattle was a traditional North-South conflict, with a twist. With the creation of the WTO in 1995, developing countries are now inside the system demanding that it be made to work as promised. An essential aspect of any new round must be the full integration of all states into the trading system on a fair and equitable basis. Developing countries, including the transition economies, want to assume more of the benefits and obligations of full participation in the system. If they do not feel part of the process, and many felt excluded in Seattle, they can block it. If an eventual round does not consider issues of importance to them, it cannot succeed.

Developing countries think they did not get as much as they had hoped, or as economists promised, in the Uruguay Round. At Seattle, Canada's Trade Minister, Pierre Pettigrew, chaired a special working party on implementation. Certain themes emerged again and again. Developing countries want to ensure the full implementation by OECD countries of their Uruguay Round commitments; having open markets at home is not much use if they are excluded from the much larger markets of OECD countries, as is the case still for agricultural products, textiles, and other labour-intensive sectors. And open markets are of little help if products cannot be shipped, if distribution is weak, or if marketing is unprofessional. Many countries need help in implementing their own commitments. It would be a pity if instead of help all they get is continued 'special and differential treatment' under the rules or provisions for 'flexible' implementation. Developing countries, especially the poorest, need help administering complex modern trade rules; they need technical inspection and customs services; and they need the full governance infrastructure of a modern economy. Finally, developing countries often lack sufficient bureaucratic resources to participate in drafting standards in the International Organization for Standardization (ISO), the Food and Agriculture Organization's Codex Alimentarius, or even in the WTO itself.

In the end, developing countries never got the chance to walk out in Seattle, as they did on previous occasions, but they might have. The working party on implementation made significant progress on such issues as technical assistance, but the market access and institutional issues might well have led to breakdown. And the social dimension of trade remains contentious. Developing countries insist that any new issues on the agenda should be directly and clearly trade-related, but OECD countries fear that markets in developing countries still lack transparency, or are marked by practices with respect to labour and the environment that would not be tolerated in a developed country and should not be tolerated internationally. The WTO cannot address all of these issues on its own. Other international organizations help countries with governance, economic regulation, competition policy, the legal system, education, social policy, and the environment, although they do it in different ways with different objectives. The institutional agenda discussed above also includes improving the coherence of global economic governance though better co-ordination of the major economic and social organizations.

TRANSATLANTIC BATTLES

Despite all of the above difficulties, ministers in Seattle might well have been able to launch a new round had there been agreement among the largest participants in the trading system, the US and the EU. But their relations remained confrontational. The elaboration of the trading system has been slowed by transatlantic battles since Churchill and Roosevelt met at Quebec in 1941 to draft the Atlantic Charter for postwar reconstruction. The Atlantic countries agree about many things now, but there was considerable conflict in Seattle, symbolized as in the past by agriculture. Farm trade is simply the oldest form of trade in goods, and the slowest to be liberalized in the GATT era. Members of the WTO bound themselves under Article 20 of the agriculture agreement to begin new negotiations by the end of 1999. If anybody would prefer to duck the issue this time, the peace clause, Article 13 of the agreement, creates an incentive: it restrains the use of things like countervail against agricultural subsidies, but only until 2003, four years after the new negotiations were set to begin. The Uruguay Round was a ceasefire in the farm war of the 1980s; it established a framework but nothing more. The war began with skirmishes in the dispute settlement system, but soon subsidies skyrocketed. The relative calm observed since the conclusion of the Uruguay Round has been helped initially by favourable market conditions. Skirmishes are starting again, notably over the role of science-based evidence in food safety and over continuing frustration, especially in the US and in members of the Cairns Group,[6] with the slow pace of reform of the EU's Common Agricultural Policy (CAP). The EU and US still differ about whether the goal in agriculture negotiations should be stable markets or an end to export subsidies. That is, should governments manage the process of structural adjustment, or should the market be largely unfettered? (The two sides answer this question in a different way in the domain of competition policy, where the Americans see pressure for new negotiations as a veiled attack on antidumping rules.) Failure to launch a round could mean that when the peace clause expires, the farm war will start again. (Paradoxically, the EU Commission might hope for eventual movement in the WTO negotiations as a means to move member countries towards reform of the CAP prior to the proposed enlargement of the union to the east.)

Contemporary 'trade' agreements are now more about strengthening markets than about liberalizing trade. Services, the newest form of trade, was not a contentious issue in Seattle. The new services negotiations to begin in 2000, whether or not eventually part of a new round, will continue the process of redefining what we mean by 'trade policy'. Trade always takes place between firms, not countries, but in the past it was possible to conceptualize international trade as flows of physical things between distinct territories. Trade policy, therefore, could be seen as measures that directly influenced the flow of identifiable things across a physical border. No longer. It is clear that the advanced economies are dominated by services and that trade in services, including the importantly economic activities of affiliates established in foreign countries, is growing faster than any other form of international exchange, but the General Agreement on Trade in Services (GATS) is still only a partial structure. Further liberalization matters both to producers of services and to firms, including more traditional businesses, whose business depends on using advanced business and other commercial services. Failure to keep working on the framework for regulating this expanding domain could both hurt growth and be a source of conflict among governments. Services liberalization is a slow and tedious process, not least because of its close connection to investment and competition policy. It requires extensive conversation among governments just to understand what a given service is and what makes it tradeable.

Discussion of other new issues, the most important being electronic commerce, was put on hold by failure in Seattle. Technology creates the possibility for new digital entities that cross borders. These entities matter for Canadians who want to be able to learn about, to order, and even in some cases take delivery of the best the world has to offer, quickly, at low prices. And it matters for our firms who want to be found by and to sell to consumers in other places, while remaining confident of being paid promptly. Free trade in electronic commerce is certainly desirable, but stable and open markets will require some form of regulation. Members of the WTO must first understand what these new entities are before they can discuss how to assimilate them to the norms and principles of the trading system. In this domain, what might national treatment mean? What aspects of the national legal or regulatory framework are hostile to electronic commerce? What essential regulations or social practices, such as a right to privacy, are undermined by such trade? How important is it if the multiple components of an electronic transaction are governed by different national rules and practices? New WTO rules will emerge as countries grapple with these issues. They must be designed to accommodate the variety of democratic objectives expressed through governments while facilitating the ability of firms, including new firms in small countries, to get on with things.

CONCLUSION: CANADA AND THE WTO IN THE AFTERMYTH OF SEATTLE

The 1985–95 decade was an extraordinary period of trade policy activism both regionally—e.g., the North American Free Trade Agreement (NAFTA) and the Single European Act (SEA), as well as the ASEAN Free Trade Agreement (AFTA), Asia-Pacific Economic Co-operation (APEC), and the beginnings of the Free Trade Area of the Americas (FTAA) process—and multilaterally, with the creation of the WTO. The Atlantic area has since been in a period of consolidation. The major public concern is social and environmental policy, while business thinks it has already achieved most of its liberalization objectives. In the language of bargaining, it is one thing to move to the contract curve, but negotiating on the curve can be difficult. Put differently, it is easier to negotiate when everyone thinks they have something to gain and harder to negotiate when participants think that gains for others necessarily involve losses for oneself. Is there a possibility of further joint gains in the trading system? Or was the Seattle ministerial the last gasp of the Uruguay Round, a sign that the agenda for trade liberalization has run its course?

It is important to recognize that the Uruguay Round is indeed now over. The fact that the Final Act wisely or unwisely mandated new negotiations on various issues—the so-called built-in agenda—will be insufficient in itself to provide the basis for a new round of negotiations. New negotiations on agriculture and services will begin during 2000 in fulfilment of Uruguay Round commitments, but little can be expected from such talks absent the framework of a round. The situation in agriculture is unstable, however, with the possibility of rising surpluses. Subsidies remain high, if down from the worst levels, and developing countries are still suffering because of the excesses of the advanced economies. Meanwhile, the world economy keeps changing in ways that the rules established as recently as 1994 in the Uruguay Round did not envisage, so new negotiations on services and e-commerce are essential. The WTO also faces the risk of unmanageable disputes in areas where the Seattle preparatory process had been trying to build a new consensus, such as the use of the 'non-violation nullification and impairment' provisions of the trade-related intellectual property rights (TRIPs) agreement. A spate of new disputes would add to pressures for a new round.

We argue that each of the five battles in Seattle contributed to the failure of the ministerial. If this diagnosis is correct, efforts to generate new momentum in the trading system must address the source of the difficulty in each area.

The American Battle

Difficulties in this pre-election period make it unlikely that the US can play much of a leadership role until after the next President takes office in 2001. Some people wonder whether the failure in Seattle will affect the accession of China to the WTO or encourage the United States in particular to place renewed emphasis on regional arrangements like NAFTA, the FTAA, or APEC, or on strengthened bilateral arrangements. We think that the temptation exists, but it should be resisted. Canada should ensure that regional agreements contribute to multilateralism, but we should not be diverted by them. The WTO serves as Canada's basic trade agreement with all our trading partners, ensuring that Canadian firms face one coherent set of rules governing trade. Since firms in other countries face the same rules, decisions about investment in Canada are less distorted by trade barriers elsewhere. No other forum is sufficiently comprehensive in membership or sectoral coverage. We benefit from our proximity to the US market, but geography alone does not determine our access to the US market, and many obstacles we now face are ones we share with other countries. Since so many of our exports to the US end up in things they export to the rest of the world, open markets for them mean open markets for us. What we do not want is for the US to turn its back on the WTO, to negotiate a series of deals that do not include us, or to be so distracted by debates over multiplying regional deals that the WTO suffers. Ensuring a strong multilateral trading system serves our broad economic and foreign policy interests.

The Battle at Home

The creation of the WTO as a formal international organization in 1995 was a major achievement of the Uruguay Round, but clearly more work is needed to strengthen its bureaucracy, enhance the role of ministers, and ensure that the public understands what is going on.

The Battles with Civil Society

The fact that the WTO process stalled at the same time as protestors battled police in the streets is an interesting coincidence, but the causal link as argued above may not be particularly significant. The battles in the streets and the ones inside the meeting room were not directly connected. The greatest danger after Seattle is believing the myths by over-reacting to the apparent civil society challenge to the WTO. That does not mean that the WTO is now as democratic as it should or could be, but it does mean that we should resist the trend to seeing the WTO as a master agreement that can regulate all domains of life. Why do so many Canadians think that the WTO either should be stopped or that it should incorporate environment and labour standards? The first reason is that since difficulties in this area are seen as effects of globalization, and the WTO is seen as responsible for globalization, it is important to make the WTO accountable for the forces it has unleashed. Globalization is a consequence of technological change, especially in transportation and communications, along with increasing engagement by developing countries in the world economy. The trading system has facilitated the process, and it can be a force for moderating the pace of change, but it cannot be accountable for such forces. The second reason for wanting to incorporate social concerns, or for stopping the WTO, is a belief that the WTO is a world trade court whose supposed capacity to 'enforce' its own agreements can be used to coerce compliance with agreements that lack such power. This broadly shared belief is misguided. The WTO can rule only on whether states are in compliance with their agreed, mutual obligations under the covered agreements. States tend to comply with the rules more often than not because they wish to remain members in good standing of the system. Such an instrument cannot be effective with respect to agreements not per-ceived to be part of its associated mutual obligations. And getting rid of the agreements will not change the underlying need for states to have some means of understanding their interactions with each other in a complex global economy.

The trading system can and must balance social and economic objectives, but sometimes this will require deference to action taken in other formal and informal organizations or within states. The WTO will be best placed to make a contribution if the aim is accommo-dating the trading system to other international regimes, rather than by asking the WTO do all the heavy lifting on its own.

The North-South Battle

The conflict with developing countries is by far the most important challenge facing the WTO, and it occupied the bulk of Pierre Pettigrew's attention in the weeks after Seattle. Ensuring that the WTO plays a supportive role in development may well be the key to unblocking the system. Developing countries must see the benefits of participating in the multilateral system; the public in OECD coun-tries must similarly see that the best way to address our own envi-ronmental, labour, and human rights concerns is by the full integration of everyone rather than by the balkanization of the system.

The Battle of the Atlantic

EU-US issues continue to receive a great deal of attention, as indeed they should given the size and volume of trade accounted for by both entities. A compromise on traditional aspects of agricultural trade was close in Seattle and should be easy to incorporate in an eventual new round. The same can be said of most of the new issues. The US approach to Seattle was parochial, but Canada, too, was inward-looking and defensive; even the EU showed more vision. The Japanese were expected to be invisible, and delivered, but 'Where is Canada?' was a frequent question in the weeks before the meeting. Pettigrew did well in the event, gaining a lot of attention for his skil-ful chairmanship of the working group on implementation. At Seattle, Canada was a leader on institutional adaptation and a laggard on contributions to the proposed Quad package of offers for the poor-est countries. The Canadian position was ambiguous on agriculture, as it has been for years, and on other older areas where the issue is reconciling states and markets. The larger difficulty among the advanced economies will be the role of science, for example in food safety. But the real problems in the WTO are elsewhere.

The international trade system remains intact following Seattle; nevertheless, a shadow is cast by the failed ministerial meeting that will take creative efforts by all participants in, and observers of, the system to work through. New approaches to old ways and old ideas will be required—by international economic organizations in working more effectively together, by governments large and small, and between governments and their societies on whom they ultimately depend—to keep the system itself and the WTO at its centre vibrant, relevant, trusted, and capable of helping to manage our common economic and social well-being.

NOTES

The views expressed do not necessarily represent the views or the policy of the government of Canada.

1. This paper is based on an extensive reading of press accounts in Canada and other countries, especially in the *Financial Times* and *Inside US Trade*, as well as confidential interviews with officials. As we base our judgements on information that is widely available, it seemed simpler not to try to cite all the sources.
2. We borrow our title (by way of Randle Wilson) from 'The aftermyth of war', a 1960s satire of inflated British wartime memories. See Bennett, Cook, Miller, and Moore (1987).
3. There were 136 members as of December 1999.
4. This is a reference to the G-7(8) group of major industrial countries (plus Russia) that meets annually to discuss global economics and other issues.
5. Furthermore, this ministerial conference literally ran out of time. Normally, these conferences are planned to last five days. This time, the hosts devoted the Monday to planned consultations with NGOs. The long-planned (if not by the hosts) protests then disrupted the Tuesday schedule, and President Clinton's visit to Seattle disrupted Wednesday, so that the real work was limited to just two days.
6. The Cairns Group of 18 agricultural exporting countries was formed in 1986 to influence agricultural negotiations within the GATT. Following the conclusion of the Uruguay Round, the Group has continued to push for fair trade in agricultural exports, a cause that unites the Group across language, cultural, and geographic boundaries. Members are: Argentina, Australia, Bolivia, Brazil, Canada, Chile, Colombia, Costa Rica, Fiji, Guatemala, Indonesia, Malaysia, New Zealand, Paraguay, Philippines, South Africa, Thailand, and Uruguay.

REFERENCES

Bennett, Alan, Peter Cook, Jonathan Miller, and Dudley Moore. 1987. *The Complete Beyond the Fringe.* London: Methuen.

The Economist. 1999. 18 Dec.

House of Commons Standing Committee on Foreign Affairs and International Trade. 1999. *Canada and the Future of the World Trade Organization: Achieving a Millennium Agenda in the Public Interest.* Ottawa: Public Works and Government Services Canada.

Wolfe, Robert. 1996. 'Global Trade as a Single Undertaking: The Role of Ministers in the WTO', *International Journal* 51, 4: 690–709.

———— and John M. Curtis. 1998. 'Providing Leadership for the Trade Regime', in Fen Osler Hampson and Maureen Appel Molot, eds, *Canada Among Nations 1998: Leadership and Dialogue.* Toronto: Oxford University Press.

The *Canada Among Nation* Series

Canada Among Nations 1998: Leadership and Dialogue, edited by Fen Osler Hampson and Maureen Appel Molot
0-19-541406-3

Canada Among Nations 1999: A Big League Player?, edited by Fen Osler Hampson, Michael Hart, and Martin Rudner
0-19-541458-6

Canada Among Nations 2000: Vanishing Borders, edited by Maureen Appel Molot and Fen Osler Hampson
0-19-541540-X